MEMOIRS

OF THE

Lower Ohio Valley

PERSONAL AND GENEALOGICAL

WITH PORTRAITS

VOLUME II

Southern Historical Press, Inc.
Greenville, South Carolina

Originally Published 1905

All rights reserved. No part of this publication may be
reproduced, stored in a retrieval system or transmitted
in any form or by any means without the
prior permission of the publisher.

SOUTHERN HISTORICAL PRESS, INC.
PO BOX 1267
Greenville, SC   29601

ISBN #978-1-63914-078-7

Printed in the United States of America

MEMOIRS

OF THE

LOWER OHIO VALLEY

PERSONAL AND GENEALOGICAL

WITH PORTRAITS

VOLUME II

ALVIN PETERSON HOVEY (deceased), soldier, lawyer, statesman and ex-governor of the State of Indiana, was born near Mount Vernon, Posey county, Ind., Sept. 6, 1821, and died at Indianapolis, while serving as governor, Nov. 23, 1891. His parents both died while he was still in his boyhood and he began life for himself as a brick mason. While working at this occupation he spent his evenings and leisure hours in reading law under the tutorage of John Pitcher, of Mount Vernon, and in 1843 was admitted to the bar. He soon won for himself a name among the leading lawyers of Southern Indiana, served as prosecuting attorney with signal ability and in 1850 became the judge of the circuit court of the First judicial district. When the time came to select delegates to the constitutional convention of 1852, he was chosen to represent his county and although one of the youngest members of that body he was one of the most intelligent and active, and the organic law of the state today bears the impress of his high emprise and strong personality. At the age of thirty-two he was appointed to a place on the supreme bench of Indiana, being the youngest man in the history of that tribunal to sit as one of its justices. In 1856 President Pierce appointed him district attorney for Indiana, where he fully sustained the high character of the office until removed by President Buchanan because of his attitude in supporting Stephen

A. Douglas when a split occurred in the Democratic party. When the Civil war broke out he at once began the organization of a company, which became a part of the First regiment of the Indiana legion, of which he was commissioned colonel. When the Twenty-fourth Indiana infantry was mustered in he was given the command of the regiment and joined Fremont's army in Missouri. For gallant conduct at Shiloh he won the rank and insignia of a brigadier-general. At Champion Hills he again distinguished himself and won the rank of major-general. General Grant in his Memoirs makes special mention of General Hovey's conduct in this engagement. In 1864 he was appointed to raise ten thousand new troops and it was ordered that none of them should be men of families. The result was that a large number of boys enlisted under the call and they became known as "Hovey's Babies." But when they were fully initiated they proved to be good soldiers and on the great "March to the sea" rendered a good account of themselves. Late in 1864 General Hovey was appointed military commander for Indiana and while serving in that capacity played an important part in the prosecution and conviction of the leaders of the Knights of the Golden Circle, a treasonable organization. After the war was over General Hovey was appointed minister to Peru by President Andrew Johnson and served in that position from 1865 to 1870, when he returned to Mount Vernon and resumed the practice of law. Two years later he declined the nomination for governor, declaring his intentions at that time to never re-enter politics. He did remain in private life until 1886, when his party unanimously tendered him the nomination for congressman from the First district. He accepted and although the district was nearly fifteen hundred Democratic in 1884 he was elected by a majority of over thirteen hundred. In 1888 the Indiana Republican state convention nominated him without opposition for the office of governor and at the election in November he was victorious, defeating Col. C. C. Matson by a plurality of twenty-two hundred. The same year he was elected president of the service pension association of the United States, at the national Grand Army encampment at St. Louis, which was a fitting recognition of his labors in Congress in behalf of his old comrades in arms. In January, 1891, he received the support of the Republican members of the general assembly for the office of United States senator, but was defeated by Daniel Voorhees, the legislature being Democratic. Such, in brief, is a report of the stewardship of one of Indiana's most illustrious citizens. As a public official he was always conscientious and fearless in the discharge of his duty; as a soldier he was always to be found at his post; as a legislator his voice and vote were always on the side of right and justice, and as a man he was universally loved for his purity of character, his sympathetic nature and his generous charity. His remains rest in the Mount Vernon cemetery, in sight of the house in which he was born, where they were tenderly laid to rest by the Grand Army of the Republic, some of those participating in the last sad rites having fought under him during the war. Governor Hovey was twice married, first to Mary James, by whom he had two children: Esther, now the wife of Maj. G. V. Menzies of Mount Vernon, and Charles James, also of that city. His second wife was a daughter of Caleb B. Smith, a prominent citizen of Indiana and secretary of the interior under Lincoln.

GUSTAVUS V. MENZIES, a prominent attorney of Mount Vernon, Ind., and one of the Democratic leaders of the Hoosier state, was born in Boone county, Ky., Dec. 24, 1844. He is a son of Dr. Samuel G. and Sally (Winston) Menzies, both natives of Kentucky, where the name of Menzies has been prominent in the annals of the state for fully a century. In his day Doctor Menzies was an eminent physician. When the Civil war broke out he enlisted as surgeon of the First Kentucky regiment and served in that capacity during the war. His duties as an army surgeon brought on disease, from which he never recovered, and from which he finally died on Dec. 21, 1882. Gustavus V. received his early schooling in the Cincinnati high school. Although but little over sixteen years of age when the war began in 1861 he enlisted in the First Kentucky, of which his father was surgeon, and served in the ranks until the succeeding September, when he was appointed midshipman in the naval academy at Annapolis and graduated from that institution with the class of 1864. After completing the course he served in various positions with the European, West Indian and South American squadrons; was flag lieutenant on the staffs of Admirals Dahlgren and Turner, and was with Poor a short time in Cuban waters, during the insurrection there in 1869. In the school year of 1870-71 he was an instructor in the naval academy and while thus engaged he began the study of law. In 1871 he located at Mount Vernon, where he has ever since been engaged in the practice of his profession. Mr. Menzies is well fitted, both by nature and education for a lawyer. He has an analytical mind, an even temper, a sound judgment, is a close student and an indomitable worker. These qualifications soon manifested themselves after he came to Mount Vernon and the result was he rapidly forged his way to the front. Few lawyers in Southern Indiana enjoy a more lucrative practice or have a higher standing at the bar. For many years he has been prominent in the Democratic councils of the state and active as a public speaker during campaigns. He is at home on the hustings, is a forcible and convincing speaker and is always in demand from the beginning to the close of the contest. The political reputation and labors of Mr. Menzies have not been confined by state boundaries. For more than a quarter of a century he has been an active participant in national politics. In 1876 he was the Democratic elector for the First congressional district of Indiana and cast his vote for Tilden and Hendricks. In 1878 he was elected state senator from the counties of Posey and Gibson and served in the sessions of 1879 and 1881. In the session of 1881 he was a member of the senate committee on the revision of the laws of Indiana and acted with the Hon. David Turpie, James S. Frazer and John H. Stotsenberg, the board of revision appointed by Governor Porter for the codification and revision of the laws. In 1895 he was appointed by the United States supreme court, on the recommendation of Governor Matthews of Indiana, one of the commissioners to determine and establish the boundary between Indiana and Kentucky at Green River island near Evansville, Ind. The boundary line as established by the commission was affirmed by the court, and a dispute of long standing between two states finally settled. He has been a member of the board of regents of the Indiana State Soldiers and Sailors Monument since 1895. He was a district delegate to the national convention of 1884 and in the last three national conventions he has represented the State of Indiana as a delegate at large. At Kansas City, in 1900, he was chairman of the delegation. He was one of the Indiana leaders in the movement to secure the nomination of Judge Alton B. Parker and was prominently mentioned for the vice-presidency at the St. Louis convention of 1904. Mr. Menzies is a member of the State Bar Association and the United States Supreme Court and the Supreme Court of Indiana, Harrow Post of the

Grand Army of the Republic, at Mount Vernon, the Indiana Loyal Legion, and he is as popular in fraternal circles as he is in politics or the bar association. He was married on November 11, 1869, to Miss Esther Hovey, only daughter of Gen. Alvin P. Hovey, who was elected governor of Indiana in 1888, and died while in office. Mr. and Mrs. Menzies have three children: Mary is the wife of Walter A. Seymour, of New York City; Juliette is the wife of Lloyd B. Fitzhugh, of Galveston, Tex.; Winston was the captain of Company B, One Hundred and Sixty-first Indiana infantry, commanded by Col., afterward Gov., W. T. Durbin, during the Spanish-American war, and now lives at Mount Vernon. He married Miss Erma Wasem of Mount Vernon.

WALTER A. TOWLES.

THE TOWLES FAMILY, of Henderson, Ky., and their connections who settled in the Lower Ohio Valley, are descendants of one of the oldest families in America. The record extends back to Henry Towles, who came from Liverpool, England, and settled in Accomac county, Va., about the middle of the seventeenth century. He married Ann Stokely and to this union there were born two sons, Stokely and Henry. Stokely settled in Middlesex county, and Henry, who was born in 1670, settled in 1711, in Lancaster county, at the junction of the Rappahannock and Corotoman rivers, the place still being known as Towles' Point, and now in the possession of his descendants. He married Hannah Therrott, and died in 1734, leaving one son and four daughters, viz.: Stokely, Judith, Ann, Elizabeth and Jane. Stokely was born in 1711, and died in 1755. After the death of his parents he continued to live at Towles' Point, and married Catherine, daughter of Thomas Martin, of Corotoman, Lancaster county. The children of Stokely and Catherine Towles were: Henry, Thomas, Stokely and three daughters, Mrs. Dick, Mrs. Reevely and Mrs. Payne. Henry, the eldest son, was born in 1738 and became closely connected with the history of Virginia during the Revolution; a member of the house of delegates in 1783; a member of the Virginia convention in 1788; county lieutenant in 1794; and clerk of Lancaster county until his death in 1799. Stokely, the second son, went to Goochland county, where he was a major in the militia during the Revolution. After the war he removed to Spottsylvania. His wife was Elizabeth, the third child of William Downman. Thomas, the third son, was born at Towles' Point, Feb. 21, 1750, and died at Millbrook, Spottsylvania county, May 22, 1800. At the commencement of the Revolution he was quartermaster to the Caroline county battalion of militia, and later in life held the rank of colonel. In 1783 he represented Spottsylvania county in the house of delegates. He married Mary, daughter of John Morris and Mary (Chew) Smith, of Richahock, King and Queen county. The children born to this marriage were Elizabeth, Mary Smith, John, Thomas, Therit, Oliver, Ann, Larkin and Frances. Elizabeth first married William Brock, son of Joseph Brock, and after his death Capt. Phil. Slaughter. They were the parents of Rev. Philip Slaughter, a distinguished minister of the Episcopal church, and author of numerous works on church history and genealogy. Mary Smith married Anthony Thornton and settled in Bourbon county, Ky. One of their sons, Anthony, afterward went to Shelby county, Ill., where he became a distinguished lawyer, represented the county in the legislature, and served on the bench in the highest court of the state. John settled in Louisiana and became a sugar planter. He was twice married: first to Susan Turnbull, and second to Ann Alexandria Conrad, of Virginia. Thomas was born at Millbrook, Va., June 1, 1784. In the spring of 1806 he removed to Henderson, Ky. Before leaving Virginia he was granted license to practice law in the courts of that state. His certificate is dated Dec. 5, 1805, and is signed by Peter Lyons, Spencer Roane, and Francis Brooke, all prominent men in their day. After settling in Kentucky he practiced in the counties of Henderson, Christian, Logan, and Ohio, and was contemporary with John J. Crittenden, Christopher Tompkins, George M. Bibb, and other eminent lawyers, when the court was presided over by Judge Henry Broadnax. He was appointed one of the justices of the Territory of Illinois, which was approved by the United States senate, and he took the oath of office before Ninian Edwards, governor of the territory, March 2, 1816. From 1821 to 1824 he represented Henderson county in the state legislature, and was magistrate for twenty consecutive years. In politics he was an uncompromising Whig, and Old Court man and was for many years prominent in all the affairs of the county. In fact a complete biography of Judge Towles would be a fairly good history of Henderson county in his time, as he was a successful lawyer with a large practice.

In religion he was an earnest churchman. Bishop B. B. Smith in his account of the Kentucky church, says his greatest troubles were over when he gained the support of several men as Thomas Towles of Henderson. In 1809 he was married to Ann Taylor Hopkins, daughter of Gen. Samuel Hopkins, of Revolutionary fame, and by this marriage had one son, Thomas Towles, Jr., who became widely known throughout the state, both for his legal lore and his spontaneous wit. His toast to water was: "It is valuable for navigation and for its mixable qualities." He served several terms in the Kentucky legislature. After the death of his first wife, Judge Towles, on April 23, 1816, was married to Elizabeth, daughter of Walter and Amelia (Johnston) Alves, and granddaughter of James Hogg, who was sent by the Transylvania Company to Philadelphia, an "embassy" to the Continental Congress, in January, 1776, to solicit the privilege of forming the fourteenth colony to gain independence. (American Archives, Vol. IV., and Filson club publications by George Ranck, page 224.) Her parents came to Kentucky in 1813 from Chapel Hill, Orange county, N. C., and were the representatives and descendants of two of the original members (James Hogg and William Johnston) of the Transylvania or Richard Henderson Land Company. To this marriage several children were born, only three of whom—Walter Alves, John James, and Bettie—lived to maturity. Judge Towles finally retired from the practice of law and became a successful planter. He died Dec. 12, 1850, and his second wife on June 28, 1852. Walter A. Towles was born Feb. 7, 1825. On Feb. 12, 1854, he married Susan Daniel Anderson, who was born Feb. 26, 1834. To this marriage there were born the following children: John Anderson, Lucy Marshall, Elizabeth Alves, Sue Starling, Walter A., Jr., Lillia, Mary Lucy, William and Therit. He has been commissioner for Atkinson Park, for the city of Henderson since 1894. John James, the second son, was born Jan. 22, 1827, and on March 13, 1851, married Louisa Alves. Their children were Minna, Florence, Louisa, John J. and Stokely. Bettie married William T. Barret, May 9, 1850, and their issue was William, Thomas, Strathan and Betty. Henry, son of Col. Thomas Towles, of Virginia, was born June 24, 1786; came to Bourbon county, Ky., and died near Ruddle's Mills in 1854. He joined Capt. William Garrard's company of mounted men, in Maj. James V. Ball's squadron, and was at the siege of Fort Meigs in the war of 1812. He married Sally Bedford and left one son, Larkin S., who married Mildred Gass, of Paris, Ky., removed to Missouri and died there. Frances, the youngest child, came to Henderson, married John H. Sublette, a native of Richmond, Va., and bore him the following children: Mary S., Ann, Fanny, Hannah More, John W., and Conrad Speece.

EDWARD W. WOOD, junior member of the firm of Turpin & Wood, rehandlers of tobacco for export, Owensboro, Ky., was born in that city, Aug. 7, 1853. His father, Dr. A. C. Wood, was born in New Hampshire, his ancestors coming from the Isle of Wight. After graduating from medical colleges at Cincinnati and New York, he located in Shelby county, Ky., and began the practice of his profession. Subsequently he came to Owensboro, where he died Jan. 2, 1905. He was an elder in the First Presbyterian church, took an interest in political affairs as a Republican, and belonged to the Masonic fraternity. The mother of E. W. Wood was Miss Mary Frances White, a native of Virginia, who came with her parents to Kentucky while she was still a little girl. She is a descendant of the French Huguenots, is still living, and is a member of the Presbyterian church. E. W. Wood is the only child of his parents. He grew to manhood in Owensboro, received the degree of Bachelor of Arts from the University of Michigan in 1873, and two years later the degree of Master of Arts. Soon after completing his education he engaged in the tobacco business, and since 1877 has been associated with the firm of Turpin & Wood as the junior partner. This firm makes a specialty of rehandling tobacco for export, and is one of the best known concerns in the Lower Ohio Valley. Mr. Wood is also connected with other business institutions of Owensboro. For a number of years prior to 1901 he was interested in the affairs of the First National bank, and in 1901 was elected to the presidency, which tells how he is regarded by those who know him best, and who are associated with him in business ventures. On Dec. 6, 1893, he was united in marriage to Miss Elizabeth Harbison, a daughter of Samuel Harbison, of Shelby county. Mr. and Mrs. Wood are both members of the First Presbyterian church.

MARTIN YEWELL, mayor of Owensboro, Ky., was born in Daviess county, of that state, Dec. 22, 1853, and is a son of Harrison and Sarah (Lewis) Yewell, both natives of Nelson county, Ky. The grandfather, Martin Yewell, was a son of James Yewell, whose father was one of three brothers who came from England at a very early date and settled in Virginia. Martin Yewell was a native of Virginia, but came in his early manhood to Kentucky, settling in Nelson county, where he was engaged in agricultural pursuits and milling operations all his life. Harrison Yewell was also a farmer and miller. He located in Daviess county in 1840, and there followed these occupations until his death in 1885. During his life he was one of the well known and influential citizens of the county. His wife died in 1895. Both were members of the Baptist church and consistent practitioners of the tenets of their religious faith. They had the following children: Joseph and John, who both died in the Confederate service during the Civil war, the former at Tunnel Hill, Ga., and the latter at Bardstown, Ky. Thomas and Martha died in infancy; Linda is now living at Owensboro as the widow of H. M. Haskins; Nannie married William Mobbelly and is now deceased; Vardeman lives in Missouri; Martin is the subject of this sketch; Mary Belle is the wife of E. Rice, of Louisville; Sarah Todd is at home, and Robert Lee is a farmer in McLean county, Ky. Martin Yewell received a good common school education, studied law under Judge Yost, of Greenville, Ky., and was admitted to the bar on April 20, 1880. He first began practice at Uniontown, where he was elected city attorney, but in 1881 came to Owensboro, where he has ever since practiced his profession until elected mayor in 1901. In August, 1882, he was elected county attorney of Daviess county and held the office for two terms of four years each. Mr. Yewell, until 1896, was an adherent of the Democratic party; since that time he has affiliated with the Republicans. He was elected mayor in November, 1901, and his term expires in December, 1905. On Jan. 7, 1885, he was married to Miss Mamie B., daughter of George and Volinda Taylor, and they have two children: Taylor, aged seventeen, and Martine, aged fifteen. Mr. and Mrs. Yewell are both members of the Baptist church.

LUCIUS P. LITTLE, of Owensboro, Ky., one of the leading lawyers of the Daviess county bar, was born in that county, Feb. 15, 1838. His great-grandfather, George Little, was a native of Scotland. After his marriage in that country he came with his wife to South Carolina before the Revolutionary war. In that contest he served in the American army, was wounded and disabled, and after the war settled at Fort Vienna, Ky., where he passed the remainder of his days. When he came to Kentucky he was accompanied by his son, Jonas, who afterward married Betsy Douglas and followed the vocation of a farmer in the vicinity of Fort Vienna until his death in 1850. His wife died during the Civil war. The second son of this marriage was Douglas Little, the father of Lucius P. In his early life he was a farmer and a manufacturer of wagons and plows. He was always active in politics, held the office of constable, was then justice of the peace for eight years, and county judge for twelve years, three terms of four years each. He married Martha Wright, a native of Charlotte county, Va., who came to Kentucky in 1820. Lucius P. Little was educated in the common schools of Calhoun and in his early manhood entered the office of the clerk of the circuit court, as a deputy, in which position he remained for three years. During this time he studied law and after leaving the office attended the law department of the Cumberland university, of Lebanon, Tenn., graduating in 1857. Soon afterward he was admitted to the bar at Calhoun and practiced there until 1860, when he was made deputy United States marshal and took the census of his county. The next year he spent in Louisville and was then in California until the fall of 1862, when he returned to Calhoun and acted as recruiting officer for Adam Johnson's regiment, John H. Morgan's command, of the Confederate army. While engaged in this work he was arrested and taken to Bowling Green, where he was tried for the offense of recruiting inside the Federal lines. Under an order of General Burbridge the penalty of this offense was death, but through the mediation of friends Judge Little was released under bond and did not take any further steps in active support of the Confederacy. Shortly after this he went to Texas on legal business and remained there until the fall of 1864, when he resumed his practice at Calhoun. In 1868 he removed to Owensboro, where he has ever since lived, and where he has been an active participant in many of the political events of the county and city. In 1874 he was a candidate for the office of circuit judge, but was defeated. Six years later he was nominated by the Democratic party for the office and this time was elected. During his first term he won friends, both with the members of the bar and the general public, by his straightforward course on the bench and his clean cut, impartial decisions. In 1886 he was re-elected for another term of six years. Upon retiring from the bench in 1893 he resumed the practice of his profession and has been retained in many important actions. He prefers civil cases and in such matters he is regarded as an authority. Judge Little has also done something in the literary line. From 1876 to 1879 he was the chief editorial writer on the

Owensboro Examiner; between 1884 and 1887 he wrote "Ben Hardin, His Times and Contemporaries," and he has delivered numerous lectures on literary subjects. He has always taken an active part in political affairs and as a political speaker he has few equals. He is a prominent member of the Masonic fraternity, and is a Past Eminent Commander of the Knights Templars. Judge Little has been married three times. His first wife was Lizzie E. Freeman, of Woodford county, Ky., to whom he was married on April 16, 1868. Her death occurred in March, 1873, and on Oct. 5, 1875, he was married to Louise A. Holloway. She died on March 4, 1887, and on Jan. 15, 1889, he was united in marriage to Miss Fannie Beach, of Maryland. To these marriages there were born the following children: L. Freeman, Lizzie E., Laura S., William, Martha B., Francis W., Catherine D., and Stanhope. Judge Little is a member of the Methodist Episcopal church and has been on the board of trustees for years. He is also a member of several literary clubs. In all these organizations, as well as in the community at large, he is universally respected for his many sterling qualities.

JOSIAH HALE, M.D., a retired physician of Owensboro, Ky., was born in Ohio county, of that state, Jan. 25, 1829. His parents, Caleb and Sally (Huff) Hale, were both natives of Virginia, but came in their childhood to Kentucky with their parents. Caleb Hale's father was Armstrong Hale, who was born in London, England, but came to America, settling first in Virginia and in 1800 in Ohio county. He was a farmer all his life. Caleb Hale was a farmer and also a cabinet maker. In political opinion he was a Whig and took an active interest in all public questions. At one time he was sheriff of Ohio county, where he passed his whole life. Doctor Hale received a common school education and studied medicine under Doctor Haines, beginning in 1852. In 1856 he was graduated from the University of Louisville, with the degree of M.D., and began practice at Fordsville in his native county. Later he removed to Hartford and practiced there until 1863, when he took a post-graduate course in New York and located in Owensboro.

In 1872 he again attended post-graduate lectures in New York, and in 1881 was delegate to the International Medical Congress, which met at London, in August of that year. During his professional career Doctor Hale was regarded as one of the most progressive and successful physicians in his section of the state. He still retains his membership in the American Medical, the Kentucky State and the Tri-State Medical societies, the last named being composed of the States of Indiana, Illinois and Kentucky, and belongs to the Owensboro Medical society. He was a member of the state board of medical examiners as long as the board was in existence and his retirement from active practice caused regret among his many patrons. While actively engaged in professional work he was honored with the vice-presidency of the Kentucky State Medical society. Doctor Hale is an honored member of the Free and Accepted Masons. Before the war he was a Whig, during the war he was a Republican, then affiliated with the Democratic party until 1896, when he rejoined the Republicans. He owns a fine farm, property in the city of Owensboro, and is one of the substantial citizens of Daviess county. He has been twice married. His first wife, to whom he was married in 1852, was Nancy J. Willis, of Ohio county. She died in 1862 and in 1873 he was married to Emily McHenry, daughter of Judge John H. McHenry, of Hartford. Doctor Hale has had three children, only one of whom is now living. Bettie and Emma both died in infancy and Mary is now the wife of J. A. Dean.

HON. AUGUSTUS OWSLEY STANLEY, of Henderson, Ky., member of Congress from the Second district of Kentucky, was born at Shelbyville, in that state, May 21, 1867. He is a son of Rev. William Stanley, a minister of the Christian church, now located at Nicholasville, Ky. During the war William Stanley served as judge advocate-general on the staff of Gen. Joseph E. Johnston, of the Confederate army. His father was Joseph Stanley, a native of Virginia, who came to Kentucky in the twenties and settled in Nelson county, where he followed agricultural pursuits all his life. On the maternal side Augustus O. Stanley's mother was Amanda Owsley, daughter of Hon. Nudicat Owsley, of Shelby county, once a member of the legislature, and a brother of Hon. William Owsley, at one time governor of the commonwealth of Kentucky and afterward justice of the state supreme court. She, too, is still living. Augustus O. Stanley grew to manhood in the heart of the "Blue Grass State," having been reared in Shelby, Woodford, Boyle and Mercer counties. In 1889 he graduated from Centre college, at Danville, Ky., and for the next year held the chair of belles-lettres in Christian college at Hustonville. Then for two years he was principal of an academy near Springfield. During all this time he devoted such time as he could spare from his school work to the study of law, and in 1894 he was admitted to the bar. There is one fact connected with the college life of Mr. Stanley that is worthy of especial notice. While at Centre college he was chosen to represent the institution in the state oratorical contest, and also had a similar honor conferred on him by the Kentucky State college, being the only man that ever represented two colleges in the contests. Upon being admitted to the bar he began practice at Flemingsburg, Ky., and continued there until March, 1898, when he came to Henderson, landing in the city on March 17th—St. Patrick's Day—a total stranger, for Flemingsburg is four hundred miles from Henderson. His progress, both in a professional and political way, since coming to Henderson, has been little short of phenomenal. In 1900 he was made an elector on the Democratic presidential ticket; in 1902 he was nominated and elected to Congress from the Second district; in 1904 he was unanimously renominated for another term by acclamation; and on all occasions in the house of representatives he has faithfully cared for the interests of his constituents. In his professional life he is a member of the law firm of Dorsey and Stanley, one of the strongest in Western Kentucky, his partner being John L. Dorsey, ex-judge of the Henderson circuit court. Mr. Stanley has few equals as a public speaker, either before a jury or on the political hustings. Ever since he became a voter he has made it a point to take a part in every political campaign and has repeatedly canvassed the state at his own expense. His popularity with his party comes from his ability as a public speaker and his well known devotion to Democratic principles. In the house he is a member of the committee on mines and mining, and is always an advocate of every measure to secure a nine-foot channel in the Ohio river from Pittsburg to Cairo. This question he looks upon as one of the most important touching the country's public utilities. He is, therefore, always an attendant at every meeting to agitate the subject and frequently appears before the committee on rivers and harbors to urge legislation favorable to that end. In fraternal circles Mr. Stanley is a member of the Knights of Pythias, the Ancient Order of United Workmen, the Buffaloes, and the Benevolent and Protective Order of Elks. On April 29, 1903, he was united in marriage to Miss Susan, daughter of William Soaper, a prominent tobacco factor of Henderson. To this marriage there has been born one son, Augustus Owsley, Jr., who was born July 1, 1904.

HON. JOHN L. DORSEY, senior member of the law firm of Dorsey & Stanley, Henderson, Ky., is one of the leading lawyers of the Henderson county bar and an ex-judge of the circuit court. He was born at Corydon, Henderson county, Dec. 17, 1853, and has lived in the county all his life. His father, Dr. John N. Dorsey, was born in Jefferson county, Ky., Dec. 30, 1811, and died Sept. 23, 1888. He was the son of Noah Dorsey, who came to Kentucky from Maryland. Doctor Dorsey married Patsy Atchison, a native of Shelby county, Ky. She died Aug. 16, 1873, aged fifty-one years. Her parents were Virginians who were among the pioneers of Shelby county. Judge Dorsey was reared at Corydon, received his collegiate education at Bethel college, Russellville, Ky., read law in the office of Malcolm Yeaman, of Henderson, and was admitted to the bar in 1876. By his earnestness, his native ability, and his sheer force of will he soon won a high position at the Henderson county bar, and it is no disparagement to the other lawyers of Henderson to say that few are his equals and none his superior in a thorough knowledge of the law. In 1879 and 1880 he represented the county in the legislature, and in 1897 he was elected judge of the Fifth judicial circuit for a term of six years. Except the time employed in the discharge of his official duties in these positions his entire time since his admission has been taken up with the practice of his profession. At the expiration of his term on the bench he retired voluntarily to resume his practice, which has more attractions for him than holding office. He is a member of the State Bar association and is well known in legal circles all over Kentucky. His partner, A. O. Stanley, is the present Congressman from the second district of Kentucky, and both members of the firm are prominent in the councils of the Democratic party. Judge Dorsey was married on Dec. 10, 1885, to Miss Nannie, daughter of Robert Dixon, of Henderson, and they have four children: Alice Young, John L., Jr., Nancy Dixon, and Robert Milton.

JAMES EWING RANKIN, well known in the commercial life of Henderson, Ky., was born in the city of Paducah, in that state, March 17, 1847. Until his sixteenth year he attended the schools of his native city. Then the disturbances incident to the Civil war and the occupancy of Paducah by the Federal troops broke up the school and so affected his mother's estate that he was compelled to enter business. His first employment was with the wholesale grocery house of J. M. Moore & Co., after which he was with Ashbrook Ryan & Co. and still later with L. S. Trimble & Co. From the last named firm he went to the banking house of Watts, Given & Co., where he remained until the house suspended on account of the failure of the parent firm of Watts, Crane & Co., of New York. He then went to Evansville, Ind., where he became associated with R. K. Dunkerson, and later became the head of the wharfboat and forwarding firm of J. E. Rankin & Co. and the boat-store of Rankin, Hurt & Co. In 1876 he acquired an interest in the business of John H. Barret & Co., exporters of tobacco, with headquarters at Henderson and branches at Owensboro and Uniontown, which interest he still retains. In 1885 he organized the Henderson Cotton Mills and has been president of the company ever since its incorporation. He is also president of the Coquillard Wagon Works, which owes its corporate existence to his energy and ability as an organizer. Mr. Rankin was instrumental in securing to Henderson the union passenger station and the elevated roadway over the streets of Henderson, which enables the railroad trains to run at a high rate of speed without danger to pedestrians and traffic. He was interested in the several turnpike roads radiating from Henderson and aided in negotiating the sale of same to the county, thus freeing the travel from toll. He was also the president of the Pythian Building association, the builders and owners of the late Pythian office building and Park theatre, the finest office building in the city and the best appointed theatre in the state. Mr. Rankin inherits to a great extent his business ability and tact from his father, Adam Rankin, who was a member of the wholesale dry goods firm of Leight, Barret & Rankin, afterwards Bull, Rankin & Leight, of Louisville. Adam Rankin married Sophy Hayes Smith, daughter of Richard Ewing and Catherine (Hayes) Smith, the former of Louisville and the latter of Rochester, N. Y. He afterwards moved to Paducah where he was cashier of the Branch bank of Louisville until his death in 1857. His father was Dr. Adam Rankin, an eminent physician of Henderson who married Elizabeth Speed, of Louisville, an aunt of James Speed, President Lincoln's attorney-general. James E. Rankin was married on Dec. 5, 1871, to Miss Sue Rankin Barret, daughter of John H. Barret, of Henderson. They have two children living: Miss Susan Daniel, and James Ewing, Jr., the latter now being the junior partner of John H. Barret & Co.

JAMES R. BARRET, president of the Ohio Valley Bank and Trust Company, of Henderson, Ky., is a native of that city, where he was born Dec. 16, 1841. He is the second son of the late John Henry Barret, who was for many years at the head of the well known tobacco firm of John H. Barret & Co. James R. was educated at Sayre's academy, of Frankfort, Ky., from which institution he graduated at the age of nineteen and soon afterward entered upon his business career in his native city, where he has ever since continued to reside. The bank and trust company, of which he is the official head, erected in 1904 a fine five-story office and store building, on the corner of Main and Second streets, of fire proof construction, at a cost of $60,000. It is regarded as the finest building of its kind in the city. In addition to his interests in this concern Mr. Barret is the largest stockholder in and was one of the organizers of the Henderson cotton mills; is interested in the Henderson National bank; the Coquillard Wagon Works; is the heaviest taxpayer in the county, and has the reputation of being the wealthiest man in Henderson. Yet not a dollar of his wealth has been acquired except by the application of correct business methods, coupled with his rare tact and persistent industry. He also has extensive farming interests in Henderson and adjacent counties. Mr. Barret is a man with broad ideas regarding charity and religion. He is a deacon in the First Presbyterian church of Henderson, and is a liberal contributor to its good works. On May 15, 1862, he was married to Miss Lucy F. Stites, who died June 6, 1902, leaving two children: Henry P., a tobacco merchant of Henderson, and Susan R., wife of Dr. S. G. Gant, professor of surgery in the post-graduate institute of New York City.

JOHN H. BARRET (deceased), late a prominent citizen of Henderson, Ky., and head of the well known tobacco firm of John H. Barret & Co., was born in Louisa county, Va., Feb. 4, 1818, and died at Henderson, Feb. 4, 1890, on his seventy-second birthday. His parents, Peter Straghan and Matilda (Winston) Barret, were both natives of Louisa county, and both his grandfathers were born, lived their entire lives, and were buried in Virginia. John H. Barret received his education in the common schools. He was reared on the farm, where his father required him to plow furrow by furrow with others more physically able than himself, but even in boyhood he displayed that tenacity of purpose, which in later years contributed in so large a measure to his success, and kept up with the best of his father's plowmen. Another line of employment was driving oxen— a pastime well calculated to make a boy forget his Sunday school vocabulary. In 1833 his brother, Alexander B., came to Henderson and engaged in the general merchandise and tobacco stemming business. Two years later John H., then seventeen years of age, left the parental roof and in December, 1835, joined his brother in Kentucky. He accepted a position in his brother's stemmery and in a little while his diligence and quick perception enabled him to master many of the details of the trade, with the result that he became a valuable assistant to his brother. In December, 1839, he was married to Miss Susan D. Rankin, a lady noted for her even temper, affectionate disposition, good sense, active benevolence and earnest piety. Soon after his marriage he formed a partnership with his brother-in-law, James E. Rankin, under the firm name of Rankin & Barret, in the dry goods business, and this association continued until 1851, when the partnership was dissolved by mutual consent. About this time Mrs. Barret died, leaving three children: John H., Jr., James R., and Susan. (Sketches of the two sons appear elsewhere. The daughter married James E. Rankin, whose sketch is also included in this work.) In 1861 Mr. Barret returned to the tobacco stemming business, this time as a partner with his brother, the partnership being dissolved by the death of the latter in 1861. Alexander B. Barret left an estate valued at from three to four millions of dollars, consisting of all sorts of property and investments. By the terms of his will his two brothers, John H. and William T., were made his executors and the entire estate left to their hands without asking them to give security for the performance of the trust. Seven years were allowed by the will for the settlement of the estate, yet, at the end of five years the entire business of the estate was settled, the books balanced, the legacies all paid, and all this without any semblance of ill feeling or dissatisfaction. The settling of this vast estate in so short a time, and in such a manner as to cause no discontent among the heirs, stands as an imperishable monument to the fidelity, the rare judgment, the sound business ability, and the high integrity of the executors. After the death of Alexander Barret the stemming business was continued by the subject of this sketch. As his sons arrived at the age of manhood each was given an interest in the concern, and upon the marriage of his daughter to James E. Rankin, he, too, became one of the firm. Aside from his large and constantly growing tobacco interests Mr. Barret was associated with other great enterprises. During the building of the Evansville, Henderson & Nashville railroad he was one of the board of directors, and was one of the moving spirits of the undertaking. When the city of Henderson voted three hundred thousand dollars of her bonds to assist in building the road the city council unanimously directed those bonds to be placed in the custody of Mr. Barret, without the formality of asking him for security. The first locomotive—known as the "Pony"—was purchased of the Baldwin Locomotive Works, by Mr. Barret, and paid for out of his own private means. He continued to act as one of the directors of the company until the road passed into the hands of the Louisville & Nashville system. Other institutions in Henderson owe their existence in a great measure to his enterprising spirit. He was one of the chief promoters of the First National bank, which was organized in November, 1865, and began business on the following New Year; was one of the originators and largest stockholders of the second telegraph line between Henderson and Evansville, Ind.; was active in promoting the establishment of the Henderson woolen mills, one of the largest and best equipped concerns of its kind in the West; and gave to Henderson the largest cotton mill in the state and one of the largest in the country outside of New England. Although he has passed over to the silent majority these great industrial establishments stand as mute witnesses to his progressive spirit. In addition to all these investments, which required a certain amount of time and attention, he was the owner of nearly two thousand acres of land in Henderson county, most of which was cultivated under his direction and personal supervision. He was also the owner of lands in other parts of Kentucky, and in Delta county, Texas, aggregating nearly five thousand acres. Truly he was "a man of affairs." But the great business of Mr. Barret was primarily that of stemming and exporting tobacco. As his trade in this line expanded he established stemmeries at Uniontown and Owensboro, and became a large holder of tobacco in European warehouses. Since his death this gigantic business has been conducted by his sons, and the character and credit he established have been fully maintained by his successors. Politically Mr. Barret was a

Whig in his earlier manhood, but after the dissolution of that party he became a Democrat. Although not a professed Christian he was a man of the highest moral character, with broad ideas as to charity, and was a liberal supporter of all religious denominations. He was an honored member of the Masonic fraternity, in which he was known and respected for his generous deeds. In 1852 he married a second wife in the person of Miss Mary Augusta Haddock, of Smithland, Ky. She was a woman of many Christian virtues who was for many years a fitting helpmate for her worthy husband. To this marriage there were born four children, all of whom died in infancy or early childhood. The only public office Mr. Barret ever held was that of city councilman from his ward. He was elected to this over his protest, but having once put his hand to the plow he did not look back, and the city of Henderson will remember his official acts as those of a man actuated by the highest impulses, with an eye single for the public weal. Here, as in his private affairs, his course was marked by a strict devotion to duty, his only guides being his conscience and his unswerving honesty.

JOHN HENRY BARRET, eldest son and namesake of the late John H. Barret (see sketch), and now the head of the great tobacco stemming interests of John H. Barret & Co., was born in the city of Henderson, Ky., Oct. 3, 1840, and has resided there all his life. When he was twenty years of age he became associated with his father in the tobacco stemming business, which had been founded by Alexander B. Barret in the early thirties. Alexander B. Barret died in 1861, and from that time until 1890 the business was conducted by his brother, the elder John H. Barret, and his two sons and his son-in-law, James E. Rankin. The firm during that time became widely known as John H. Barret and Co., and since the death of Mr. Barret, in 1890, the name of the firm has remained unchanged, the subject of this sketch becoming the senior member, and the "Co." being formed by his brother, James R., and his brother-in-law, Mr. Rankin, already mentioned. Mr. Barret was married on Sept. 15, 1863, to Miss Henrietta S. Offutt, of Shelby county, Ky. She died June 27, 1895, leaving two daughters. Mary is the wife of Dr. James W. Heddens, an eminent physician of St. Joseph, Mo., and Augusta is at home with her father. For nearly three quarters of a century the Barret family have been closely identified with the growth and development of the city of Henderson, and to their enterprise is due some of the most important industrial establishments of that thriving city. Its banks, factories, railroads, mercantile concerns, and its great tobacco mart have all felt the touch of the Barret hand, while its educational, charitable and religious institutions have received their generous support. John H. Barret is connected with several of the leading concerns of the city and is one of the charitable men of the place, giving liberally of his means to worthy causes. He has for years been one of the deacons of the First Presbyterian church.

RICHARD HENDERSON SOAPER, one of the leading business men of Henderson, Ky., was born in that county, Feb. 7, 1836, and is the eldest son of William and Susan Fannie (Henderson) Soaper, who were married Nov. 2, 1830. The father was born in Loudoun county, Va., April 28, 1795. In 1820 he came to Henderson, where for a number of years he followed the saddlery business in a modest way, frequently traveling through the country. Subsequently he formed a partnership with Judge Thomas Towles for the purchase and stemming of tobacco. After a successful business for several years this partnership was dissolved by mutual consent. William Soaper died Jan. 3, 1881. During his life he was noted for his strict business integrity and his unostentatious charity. For many years he was a prominent member of the Masonic fraternity, and was honored by being elected Worshipful Master of his Lodge; High Priest of his Chapter; and Eminent Commander of his Knights Templars Commandery. Had he shown a disposition to push himself forward he might have been Grand Master of Kentucky Masonry. Susan Fannie Henderson was born, May 9, 1813, upon what is known as "The Bluff" a few miles below the city of Henderson, her parents being Richard and Annie (Alves) Henderson, both natives of North Carolina, where they were married in 1807. Her father was the nephew of that Richard Henderson who was president of the Henderson Grant Company, and for whom the county and city of Henderson were named. When twenty-two years of age Mrs. Soaper became a member of the Episcopal church, and during all her subsequent years was a consistent practitioner of the tenets of her religious faith. Richard H. Soaper was named for his maternal grandfather. He was educated in the best private schools in Henderson, at Shelby college, Shelbyville, Ky., and during the years 1854-55 was a student at Kenyon college, Gambier, O. Upon leaving college he was given a position in his father's business establishment and a few years later was admitted to a partnership. This partnership continued until his father's death in 1881. Besides the parent house at Henderson a branch was established at Uniontown in 1868, having a capacity of five hundred hogsheads annually. In addition to this large tobacco interest Mr. Soaper is the owner of nearly 2,000 acres of the best river bottom land in the county, well adapted to raising both corn and tobacco. He is also one of the organizers of the Henderson National bank, which was founded in 1865 and opened its doors for business on the first of January, 1866. Ever since the bank was instituted he has been one of the board of directors, and since Dec. 14, 1897, has held the office of president. The bank has a capital stock of $200,000 and from the start he has been the largest stockholder. When his father died Richard H. was made executor of the will, which included a large and varied estate, to be divided among ten legatees. The difficulty of such an undertaking can be readily seen, yet Mr. Soaper settled this estate without litigation or without a murmur from any one of the devisees. This attests his ability and integrity as a business man and bears witness to the thorough methods that have characterized his whole business career. He has traveled extensively in his own country and Canada and in 1865 spent the summer in Europe, partly on business and partly for sight-seeing. He was reared a Whig, but since the dissolution of that party he has never been closely allied with any political organization.

HENRY DIXON, sheriff of Henderson county, Ky., with offices in the city of Henderson, was born at Corydon, in that county, March 30, 1860. He is a son of the late John E. and Mary C. (Sugg) Dixon, the former for many years a well known farmer near Corydon, and the latter now living in Henderson. Henry Dixon was reared at Corydon and at the age of eighteen graduated from the Corydon high school. He then attended the Vanderbilt university, Nashville, Tenn., for two years—1878-79—after which he engaged in farming, operating a saw mill, and running a threshing machine, during the threshing season. Part of the time he held the office of constable. In 1896 he was elected tax collector of the Corydon district and served until 1902. In the meantime he was elected sheriff of the county, taking charge of the office on the first day of January, 1902, for the term which expires Jan. 1, 1906. In addition to his official duties he owns and operates a saw mill and a shingle mill in the south part of the county. In politics Mr. Dixon is a Democrat of the Andrew Jackson school—one of the kind that can always be relied on to stand up for his political opinions and the interests of his party. He is a member of the Modern Woodmen of the World, the Ancient Order of United Workmen, the Benevolent and Protective Order of Elks, and the Baptist church. On March 30, 1886, Mr. Dixon was united in marriage to Miss Mary E. Green, and they have three daughters: India M., Nannie L., and Augusta Irene.

HON. J. H POWELL, mayor of Henderson, Ky., is a native of that city and a descendant of one of the most illustrious families of the Blue Grass State. He is a son of Lazarus Powell, who occupied with distinction the gubernatorial chair of Kentucky, and also represented the state in the United States senate with signal ability. After receiving a liberal education J. H. Powell took up the study of law and, in a short time after his admission, won a distinguished place among the leading lawyers of his section of the state by his earnest efforts in behalf of his clients, his careful preparation of the cases entrusted to him, and his eloquence as an advocate. For eighteen years he occupied the office of district attorney, and during that time established a reputation as an able, fearless, and conscientious public official. Mr. Powell is a man of varied attainments. As a public speaker he is justly entitled to a place among the leading orators of the day. The demand for his services in this line led him, some years ago, to enter the lecture field, where he met with popular favor, and only discontinued the vocation on account of failing health. His well known progressiveness and public spirit marked him out as a suitable candidate for the mayoralty and he was elected to the office by his fellow townsmen. As the chief municipal executive his course has been at once conservative and positive. His highest aim has been to subserve the city's interests, and to this end he has carefully avoided everything that would involve the city in needless indebtedness or expensive litigation, yet he has always stood up for those measures that he felt confident would redound to the interests of Henderson and her people. Were he eligible for re-election it is safe to say that he would succeed himself by an overwhelming majority. Mr. Powell has five sons and a daughter. Each of the sons has made a name for himself in his chosen calling. Robert A. is the representative at Henderson, of the St. Bernard Coal and Coke Company, the largest concern of its kind in the state; Laz. W. is the county clerk of Henderson county; Henry J. is the state agent for the Equitable Life Insurance Company of New York; J. Stephen is associated with his father in the practice of law, and is regarded as one of the most promising young attorneys at the Henderson bar, and William is associated with his brother in writing insurance for the Equitable.

SINGLETON H. KIMMEL, city engineer of Henderson, Ky., was born in that city, Sept. 19, 1869, his parents being Maj. Manning M. and Sibella (Lambert) Kimmel, the former a native of Missouri and the latter of Henderson. The paternal grandfather, whose name was Singleton H., was a native of Pennsylvania, but went to Missouri in an early day, where he practiced law, engaged in mercantile pursuits, and conducted a newspaper. Maj. M. M. Kimmel was graduated from West Point, served four years in the regular army with the rank of lieutenant, went South at the beginning of the war, joined the Confederate service, rose to the rank of major and was chief of staff of General Van Dorn. After the war he went to Mexico, where he was for some time interested in railroad construction, and after that came to Kentucky. For a number of years he was superintendent of the St. Bernard Coal Company and opened up many of the coal mines of the state. He relinquished this position in 1884, came to Henderson at that time and engaged in the coal business. He took an active interest in public affairs and served on the Henderson school board and as a member of the city council, and has held the office of county magistrate. He now lives retired, is the owner of considerable real estate in the city, much of which is productive and yields him a comfortable income. He is a prominent member of the Masonic fraternity, is a Democrat in politics, and with his family belongs to the Presbyterian church. His wife is the daughter of Joel Lambert, who was one of the pioneers of Henderson county, a farmer and minister of the Cumberland Presbyterian church, and for several terms sheriff of the county. Major Kimmel and his wife are the parents of the following children: Singleton H., the subject of this sketch; J. Lambert, teller in the Ohio Valley bank, a prominent Mason, member of the Grand Lodge of the state; Fannie, a graduate of the Louisville kindergarten college, now a teacher in Henderson; Polly, a teacher in Miss Bunch's private school for girls, at Henderson; H. Edward, a graduate of the United States naval academy, in the class of February, 1904, and now an officer on the battleship, Kentucky; Sibella, a graduate of Miss Bunch's school, and with the youngest son, Manning M., Jr., lives at home. Singleton H. Kimmel was educated at the private school of Prof. J. Tevis Cobb, and afterward took a course in civil engineering, graduating in 1888. For two years he was engaged on various pieces of engineering and in February, 1890, was elected city engineer, being at that time but little over twenty years of age. This office he has held ever since, the longest time it was ever held continuously by one man. This tells the story of his efficiency better than words. He is a member of the Knights of Pythias and the Presbyterian church, in both of which he stands well because of his genial disposition and his intrinsic merits. In his professional line he is one of the best qualified civil engineers in Western Kentucky and the work entrusted to his care is always promptly and faithfully executed.

RICHARD P. FARNSWORTH, the leading contractor and builder of Henderson, Ky., and also a manufacturer of brick, was born at Hopkinsville, Ky., March 21, 1863. His father, O. J. Farnsworth, was a native of Bakersfield, Vt., but both his parents dying while he was still in his boyhood, he left his native state, went to New York City, where he learned the trade of bricklayer, after which he went to Tennessee. He worked in that state until the breaking out of the Civil war, when he entered the Union army and served through the war, after which he went to Hopkins county and engaged in contracting. There he formed the acquaintance of and afterward married Annie E. Watwood, a native of Clarksville, Tenn., and a daughter of George W. Watwood. He continued in the contracting business at Madisonville with unvarying success, until his death in 1901. During his life he was recognized as one of the foremost contractors of his section of the state, and Richard has inherited many of his leading characteristics, which have contributed in no small degree to his own successful career. Richard P. Farnsworth is the third of six children born to his parents, all of whom are living and doing well. The mother is now living at Earlington, in Hopkins county. After receiving a good common school education Richard went to work with his father and learned the bricklayer's trade. He laid the first brick that was ever laid in a brick house at Earlington, although but a boy at the time. At the age of twenty-three years he commenced contracting for himself at Greenville, Ky., and remained there until 1889, when he came to Henderson, where he engaged in the drug business. After two years in this line he sold out his drug store and again became a contractor. Since then he has steadily worked his way upward in his business until he occupies a position in the front rank of the builders of the Lower Ohio Valley. In 1903 he did the brick and stone work on the new $25,000 library building at Henderson; in 1904 he did similar work on the Ohio Valley bank, the first fire-proof building in Henderson, the opera house, and numerous other structures of less importance. His business extends to all the surrounding counties, and nineteen of the twenty-five houses in the village of Sebree were built by him. His brick manufactory has a capacity of over 4,000,000 a year, most of which are used in carrying out his own contracts. He employs about sixty men in his various lines of business and is one of the active, progressive men of Henderson. On Feb. 9, 1886, Mr. Farnsworth was united in marriage to Miss Ada, daughter of Armstrong and Julia Sisk, of Hopkins county, where her father is one of the well-to-do farmers. To this marriage there have been born the following children: Olin John, Harold Pratt, Ada Louise, Richard Armstrong, and George Shepard. All are living and are students in school. Mr. Farnsworth and his wife are members of the Cumberland Presbyterian church. In politics he is a Republican and takes an interest in all questions touching public policy, particularly those of a local nature. For eight years he served as a member of the city council, and in 1903 was elected mayor pro tem. He is a member of the Independent Order of Odd Fellows and is a Royal Arch Mason, in both of which societies he is deservedly popular because of his genial disposition, his liberal views, his intrinsic moral worth, and his liberal charity.

THE KLEYMEYER & KLUTE BRICK AND TILE WORKS, one of the substantial business concerns of the city of Henderson, Ky., was founded in 1865 by Henry Kleymeyer, who conducted the business in a small way for three years, when he formed a partnership with Frederick Klute and increased the capacity of the plant.

Since then the output has annually increased until now the trade extends over a radius of 150 miles from Henderson. Tile making was added to the brick manufacture and in both lines the Kleymeyer & Klute company stand at the head. The drain tile, which has a range of from two and a half to ten inches in diameter is of the best quality, owing to the fine character of the clays used in its construction and the improved machinery employed in its manufacture. During the year 1903 the company shipped 200 carloads of tiling and 6,000,000 brick more than 500,000 of the latter going outside the state. The brick made by this company are of a high grade building brick which have become favorites wherever introduced. From fifty to sixty men are constantly employed during the brickmaking season, and the company has 150 acres of land devoted to raising feed for the stock used at the plant. The company was incorporated in 1900, under the above name, with Henry Kleymeyer as president; F. C. Klute as secretary and treasurer; and F. Klute as superintendent. From the humble beginning, nearly forty years ago, this concern has worked its way to the front until it is regarded as one of Henderson's leading industries. Its success is due to the thorough knowledge of the business possessed by its proprietors, and to the fair dealing which has distinguished all their transactions.

Henry Kleymeyer, the founder of this company was born in Germany, Jan. 29, 1841. When he was seventeen years of age he came to the United States and located at Evansville, Ind., where he learned the business of making brick. In 1865 he removed to Henderson and started a brick-yard there, which has since developed into the magnificent plant of the company of which he is the official head. Although he takes an interest in all matters affecting the public welfare he is independent in his political affiliations, and acknowledges the claims of no party to his suffrage. In 1870 he was married to Miss Louise Bruenig, a native of Germany, who came with her parents to America when she was about one year old. The family settled near Evansville, where her father was for many years a well known farmer. Mr. and Mrs. Kleymeyer have had the following children: Two who died in infancy; Carl, who died at the age of two years; Louise, now the wife of Rev. T. C. Tebour, one of the field workers of the Kentucky Sunday School association; Henry C., who lives in Evansville, Ind.; Mary, wife of T. Andes and lives in Henderson; Carrie, now Mrs. John Andes, residing in Evansville; and Minnie and Alfred at home. All the children received good practical education to fit them for the duties of every day life. Mr.

and Mrs. Kleymeyer are both members of the Evangelical Lutheran church.

Frederick Klute, who since 1868 has been identified with the growth and development of the brick and tile industry of Henderson, was born in Westphalia, Germany, Nov. 3, 1843, his parents being Frederick and Mary (Forstmeyer) Klute. In 1856 he came with his parents to the United States on a sailing vessel, and after a tedious voyage of nine weeks landed in New Orleans. The family remained in that city one winter and then came north to Knox county, Ind., where the father bought a farm and both he and his wife there passed the remainder of their lives. The children still own the old home. In 1863 Frederick went to Evansville, where he learned the trade of brickmaker, and two years later located in Henderson. In 1868 he formed the partnership with Henry Kleymeyer, which has since become the Kleymeyer & Klute Brick and Tile Works. Mr. Klute was married on March 16, 1871, to Miss Caroline, daughter of Charles and Louise (Kruger) Brunine, who came from Germany when she was in her girlhood and located on a farm not far from the city of Evansville. The children of Mr. and Mrs. Klute are: Louise, wife of Herman Unverzaght, a butcher of Henderson; Frederick C., secretary and treasurer of the brick and tile works; Frederick and Caroline are twins, the latter is the wife of Jacob Zimbro, Jr., who is a dealer in harness and vehicles at Henderson; Henry, Carl, and Walter and Edward, who are twins. All the boys received good business training and give promise of becoming successful men in the affairs of life. Mr. Klute and his family belong to the Evangelical Lutheran church, of which he is one of the charter members and takes an active interest in promoting its good works. He and all his sons who are old enough to vote are advocates of Democratic principles and are affiliated with that party. Fred C. is a member of the Independent Order of Odd Fellows and the Knights of Honor. He married Miss Ann Neucks of Evansville, and has a family of three children.

LAZ W. POWELL, clerk of the county court, Henderson, Ky., was born in that city, Jan. 19, 1865, and is a son of J. H. and Mary A. Powell. His father is the present mayor of Henderson. Laz W. received a good common school education and at the age of fifteen years started in life as an employe in the woolen mills. After three years in this occupation he went to the Henderson Mining and Manufacturing Company as a clerk. Four years later he became bookkeeper for George S. Norris in the hardware store, and remained there until 1891, when he was elected constable of district No. 5. This office he filled in a creditable manner for one year, when he was appointed deputy clerk under Judge Hart. He held the position of deputy clerk for ten years, or until 1902, and was then elected clerk. Mr. Powell is a well known figure in the fraternal circles of Henderson, being a popular member of the Independent Order of Odd Fellows, the Knights of Pythias, the Ancient Order of United Workmen, the Benevolent and Protective Order of Elks, the Knights and Ladies of Honor, and the Modern Woodmen of the World. Mr. Powell was married in 1886 to Miss Kittie W., daughter of Randolph and Ellen F. Walbridge. Mrs. Powell is a native of Union county, but came with her parents to Henderson county, where her father followed farming until his death. Mr. and Mrs. Powell have six children, viz.: Lucy M., Mary A., Frances W., Robert A., James Henry, and Katherine W. Both parents are members of the Episcopal church. Mr. Powell is one of the sturdy Democrats of Henderson. To his activity and his unswerving support of Democratic principles he owes, in some degree, his nomination and election to the office of county clerk. But behind all mere political considerations stand his intrinsic merits, his superb qualifications that have come through his long experience in the office, and his uniform courteous treatment of those who have business to transact with him as a public official.

HERMAN MARSTALL, principal owner and general manager of The Marstall Furniture Company, of Henderson, Ky., was born in the northern part of Germany, May 22, 1855. His parents, Henry and Rosa Marstall, came to the United States in May, 1869, and located at Evansville, Ind., where his father followed the trade of cabinet maker until his old age. The last years of his life were spent with his family in Henderson, where he died in August, 1896. The mother is still living and makes her home with the subject of this sketch. Both parents were devout members of the Catholic church, and reared a family of four sons and two daughters in that faith. Herman Marstall learned the cabinet makers' trade in his youth, and afterward learned every detail of wood-working and furniture construction. His introduction to a furniture factory was in 1869, when he started in as a shaving-boy. From then on he worked his way up by his energy and close attention to his business until 1881, when he was selected from among fifty men for the position of superintendent of the Reitz & Schmits furniture factory in Evansville, which position he held until 1893, when he came to Henderson and leased the plant of the Henderson Furniture Manufacturing Company for four years. He started on a small capital, but by honest workmanship and a knowledge of what lines of furniture were most in demand, he soon came to be known to the furniture world. The factory was purchased at the expiration of the lease, new machinery being added which increased the capacity of the plant. The products of the Marstall Furniture Company are sold all over the United States, Mexico and Cuba; they make a specialty of oak and walnut wardrobes, ranging in price from six to thirty-five dollars, and do an annual business of over $110,000. Mr. Marstall was married in November, 1878, to Miss Elizabeth, daughter of George and Elizabeth Feldhaus, of Evansville, Ind. Their children are G. Edward and Joseph J., who are with the furniture company, and Mary, Frank and Leona, all in school with the exception of the last named, who is but three years of age. While Mr. Marstall is nominally a Democrat in his political belief he votes for principle rather than party name. He is a fine example of a self-made man, who enjoys the confidence and respect of his associates.

HOY C. BOAZ, osteopathic physician, of Henderson, Ky., was born in Simpson county of that state, March 4, 1868, his parents being Z. H. T. and Sarah Boaz, the former a native of Tennessee and the latter of Kentucky. The father was left an orphan in his boyhood, came to Kentucky in early life and finally, by his thrift and industry, became the largest landholder in Simpson county. He was a Democrat politically, was a prominent member of the Masonic fraternity, and both himself and wife belonged to the Baptist church. He died in 1889 and his widow is still living at Franklin, the county seat of Simpson county. They had five children, viz.: Sally, widow of Dr. C. L. Barton; John H., a farmer at home; V. T., a physician in Kansas; Elizabeth, deceased, and the subject of this sketch. After acquiring a common school education Dr. Boaz attended Ogden college, Bowling Green, Ky., graduating in 1887. He then learned the trade of machinist and entered the employ of C. Aultman & Co., of Canton, O., with whom he remained until 1899, part of the time as a traveling salesman in the United States and Canada. After severing his connection with this concern he took up the study of osteopathy and in 1900 was graduated from the Southern school of osteopathy at Franklin, Ky. He then located at Henderson, where he has built up a lucrative business. Dr. Boaz is a Democrat in his political affiliations; is a member of the Knights of Pythias, the Benevolent and Protective Order of Elks, the Improved Order of Red Men, and both he and his wife belong to the Presbyterian church. He was married on Oct. 15, 1890, to Miss Sena Bogan, daughter of Ira and Sarah Bogan, of Simpson county. Her father is a farmer, a prominent citizen, and judge of the county court. Dr. Boaz and his wife have one son, Raymond, now seven years old.

ROBERT C. McFARLAND, one of the leading druggists of Henderson, Ky., was born in that county, near Hebbardsville, June 16, 1847. He is a son of Dr. Robert M. and Catherine (Boswell) McFarland, the former a native of North Carolina and the latter of Henderson county. The paternal grandfather, Joseph McFarland, was a native of North Carolina, but of Scotch descent. He came to Kentucky in 1806, settling first at Grissom's Landing in Daviess county, where he bought and cleared six hundred acres of land. In 1815 he came to Henderson county, bought land near the city and there passed the remainder of his life. Dr. R. M. McFarland studied medicine in Philadelphia, and was one of the pioneer doctors of Henderson county. He was also interested in agricultural pursuits and before the war owned a number of slaves. He was successful in both his farming and professional life and had a large circle of friends to mourn his death, which occurred in 1869. His wife survived until 1897. Both were members of the Cumberland Presbyterian church. Dr. McFarland in his day was a Whig in his political opinions, took an active part in campaigns as a public speaker, but was never an office seeker. He was a stanch Union man on the questions that led to the Civil war and an opponent of secession. He and his wife had seven children, four of whom are now living, viz.: Robert C.; Mattie, Mrs. H. T. Priest, living near

Hebbardsville; Thomas M., lives on the old homestead, as does Mary G., the eldest of the family. Robert C. McFarland received a good common school education in a Hebbardsville private school and then attended college for one year at Albion, N. Y. After completing his schooling he lived on the farm until 1885, farming and dealing in live stock, and then came to Henderson, where he engaged in the livery business. This vocation he followed with success for twelve years, when he sold out and associated himself with his son in the drug store, which had been started in 1893. Mr. McFarland still owns three fine farms in the county. He is a Republican in his political views and in early life was somewhat active. He belongs to the Knights of Pythias, and with his entire family to the Cumberland Presbyterian church. In 1869 he was married to Elizabeth Schaeffer, a native of Henderson county, and they have three children: Robert M. is a graduate of the Philadelphia school of pharmacy and associated with his father in business; Annie Belle is the wife of W. H. Lewis, a farmer of Henderson county, and Catherine W. is the wife of Robert L. Zubrod, a druggist of Louisville.

MILES COOKSEY DUNN, M.D., specialist in diseases of the eye, ear, nose and throat, of Henderson, Ky., was born in that county, Aug. 21, 1864. He is a son of George O. and Martha S. (Cooksey) Dunn, both natives of Virginia, who came with their parents to Kentucky in their childhood. The paternal grandfather, David Dunn, came in the year 1829 and settled near Henderson, where he cleared a farm and in subsequent years became an influential citizen. George O. Dunn was a farmer all his life. Politically he was a Democrat and both himself and wife belonged to the Baptist church. He died in 1887 and she in 1895. They had seven children, of whom the doctor and Mrs. Crawley are the only ones living. Dr. Dunn attended the common schools in his boyhood, afterward was at normal school, read medicine with Dr. Robert Stuart of Zion, entered the medical department of the University of Louisville in 1889, and graduated in 1892. Soon after leaving college he located at Zion and practiced there until 1900. He then went to New York and took a post graduate course, having taken a similar course some time before, and in 1901 located in Henderson, where he has built up a successful practice in his specialties. He is a member of the American and State Medical associations, and a member and ex-president of the County Medical society. At the present time he is a member of the city school board and takes an interest in every thing calculated to promote the material interests of Henderson. In politics Dr. Dunn is a Democrat, but is not an active politician, preferring the more congenial work of his profession. He is a member of the Knights of Pythias and the Benevolent and Protective Order of Elks. His prominence in his profession has been achieved by his own untiring energy and determination. As a young man he clerked in a dry goods and grocery store, and for some time he was in the drug business in Zion, Ky. But the great aim of his life has been to succeed as a physician. In 1888 he was married to Miss Mary, daughter of Dr. Robert and Sue E. (Read) Stuart, and a native of Henderson county. Her mother is dead and her father now lives at Spiceland, Ind. Her grandfather, great-grandfather, and great-great-grandfather were all Presbyterian ministers and she belongs to that denomination. Her grandfather, David Todd Stuart, founded the Stuart female college, at Shelbyville, Ky.

JOHN T. BETHEL, M.D., a well known physician and surgeon of Henderson, Ky., was born near Ranger's Landing, in Henderson county, his parents being Peter and Ann (Wilson) Bethel, both natives of Virginia. His paternal grandparents came from Virginia in 1802 and settled in Henderson county. The grandfather bought three hundred acres of land on Green river, for two dollars an acre, cleared a farm and lived the life of a typical pioneer. He built a two story log house, the lumber in which was sawed with a whip saw, and his wife spun the yarn, wove the cloth, and made all the clothes worn by the family. It was on this farm that Peter Bethel grew to manhood and lived all his life. When his father died he inherited the place and died on the old homestead in 1892 at the age of ninety years. In his early years he was an active Whig, but after the dissolution of that party he affiliated with the Democrats. He was looked upon as one of the progressive farmers of his neighborhood and was an influential citizen. Both he and his wife were members of the Methodist Episcopal Church South. Doctor Bethel was born on this old homestead, the third child in a family of twelve, and he, one sister and a half brother are now living in this county. He was educated in the public schools and the Corydon high school. In 1862 he commenced the study of medicine, and after reading two years under Doctors Powell and Dorsey, of Corydon, began practice in March, 1864, at Pooltown, Webster county, Ky. He remained there until 1893, when he removed to Henderson, where he has built up a lucrative business. His practice is of a general character and few physicians enjoy to a greater extent the confidence of their patients. He owns a nice residence and office in the city and until recently owned farm property in the county. Doctor Bethel is a member of the Free and Accepted Masons, is a Democrat in his political opinions, and with his family belongs to the Methodist Church South. He has been twice married. In 1865 he was married to Miss Fannie Thurman of Ohio, and by this marriage has two children: Laura Adel is now Mrs. W. E. Royster, and John T., Jr., lives in Pudacah, Ky. The mother of these children died in 1882, and the following year Doctor Bethel was united in marriage to Belle Sullenger, a native of Hartford, Ky. Two children have been born to this union: Effie and Lila, both at home with the parents. All the children are well educated and Mrs. Royster is proficient in music.

WILLIAM HENRY OVERBY, attorney at law, and a prominent Republican of Henderson, Ky., was born in Henderson county, Nov. 8, 1859. He is a son of William H. and Mary Jane (Hicks) Overby, the former a native of Virginia and the latter of Henderson county. The father came to Kentucky in 1836 and bought a farm near Zion. He was a hatter by trade and followed that occupation for a short time after coming to the state, after which he gave attention to his farming interests until his death. The last years of his life were spent in the city of Henderson, where he died on April 23, 1895. His widow is still living in Henderson. Both were members of the Baptist church and during his life he was by no means a partisan in politics, but at all times an independent voter. The Overby family is of English extraction, the first of the family in America settling in Virginia. Alexander Overby, the grandfather of the subject of this sketch, came to Kentucky late in life and passed the remainder of his days near Henderson. William Henry Overby is the fourth child in a family of nine children, four of whom are still living. He received his primary education in the common schools and then took the high school course in the Henderson high school. Then, after teaching for a year, he entered the Hopkins grammar school, at New Haven Conn., where he prepared for Yale university, and took the classical course in that institution. He completed his education in 1885, returned to Kentucky, and for the next two years was principal of the Union academy, at Morganfield. He was then elected principal of the high school at Henderson and taught there for two years, when he was appointed deputy collector of United States internal revenue. After eight months in this position he was appointed postmaster at Henderson and served four years in that capacity. In 1898 he was again appointed deputy collector of internal revenue and held that office until July, 1904. Mr. Overby studied law while still a young man and in 1894 was admitted to the bar. Since that time he has devoted the greater part of his time to the practice of his profession. For several years he has been active in political matters and stands high in the councils of the Republican party. In 1895 he was nominated for state senator and in 1904 he was the Republican candidate for Congress from the Second district. In 1887 he was married, at Franklin, Ky., to Miss Fannie B. Moore, a native of Todd county. Three of the children born to this marriage are living, viz.: Harry Moore, Yeaman Moore and William Henry, Jr., the first two dying in infancy. Mr. and Mrs. Overby are both attendants of the Methodist Episcopal church, and take a commendable interest in its good works.

N. POWELL TAYLOR, attorney at law, Henderson, Ky., and county attorney for Henderson county, was born on a farm in that county, Jan. 2, 1864. He is a son of William H. and Mary (Powell) Taylor, the former a native of Tallahassee, Fla., and the latter of Henderson county. John S. Taylor, the grandfather, was a native of Virginia, but went to Florida soon after his marriage, lived there until some time in the forties, when he came to Henderson county, there bought a farm and passed the remainder of his life. One of his brothers, B. Waller Taylor, was one of the first United States senators from the State of Indiana. Upon the death of John S. Taylor his son, William H., took charge of the farm and still conducts it, being regarded as one of the successful farmers of his neighborhood. His wife, the mother of the subject of this sketch, died in 1900. She was a devoted member of the Baptist church, to which her husband still belongs. They had two children: J. Stokes, a farmer of Henderson county, and N. Powell. After obtaining a high school education in Henderson, N. Powell Taylor entered the law office of Judge J. L. Dorsey of that city and read under him from 1886 to 1889, when he was admitted to the bar. He commenced practice at Henderson and has won for himself an honorable position at the bar by his industry and native ability. Like his father before him he is a Democrat and takes an active part in shaping the affairs of his party. In 1895 he was elected to the state senate, where he made an enviable record, and in 1897 was elected county attorney. To this latter office he was re-elected in 1901 and again in 1904. These repeated re-elections to an important position attest his fidelity and popularity better than any complimentary language that could be used in writing a sketch of his career. Mr. Taylor was married in 1897 to Miss Alice, daughter of George and Alice Augusta (Thompson) Partridge. Her father is a wholesale oil merchant. To this marriage there has been born one son, N. Powell, Jr., now in his third year. Mr. Taylor is a member of the Ancient Order of United Workmen, the Benevolent and Protective Order of Elks, the Improved Order of Red Men, and both he and his wife belong to the Presbyterian church.

WILLIAM W. W. WILSON, M.D., a promising young physician of Henderson, Ky., was born at Mount Sterling, in that state, Dec. 27, 1878. He is a son of Henry C. and Frances (Barnett) Wilson, the father a native of Mount Sterling and the mother of Virginia. The grandfather, George R. Wilson, was a Virginian, who came to Kentucky in pioneer days and for many years operated a distillery, accumulating considerable property. Doctor Wilson's father is a farmer and stockman, now living at Roachdale, Ind., retired from the active cares of business. He is a Democrat in his political faith and a member of the Independent Order of Odd Fellows. Three children were born to Henry C. Wilson and his wife, all of whom are living. George is in the Klondike, Charles is a contractor and builder at Ladoga, Ind., and the subject of this sketch. Doctor Wilson received his primary education in the common schools of Barnard, Ind., after which he graduated from Wabash college, at Crawfordsville, in the class of 1897. He then spent a year at Yale university and in 1899 entered the Kentucky school of Medicine and graduated as valedictorian of his class in 1902. During the summers of 1901 and 1902 he studied in Europe, notably in England, Ireland and Germany, holding a position at the time under his uncle, Harry Walters, as inspector of cavalry horses for the Boer war. He also took instruction in the celebrated medical schools of Glasgow and Edinburgh. Upon receiving his degree he engaged in hospital work in the United States marine hospitals, and was thus employed until Jan. 1, 1904, when he located at Henderson, where he has done well in establishing himself in practice and has demonstrated his success in the treatment of disease. Politically Doctor Wilson is a Democrat, but he is not an active politician. In fraternal circles he is well known, being a member of the Free and Accepted Masons, the Knights of Pythias, and the Improved Order of Red Men. On Oct. 14, 1903, he led to the altar Miss Lulu Mullins, a native of Covington, Ky., and a highly accomplished young lady, having graduated in 1902 from the Bartholomew-Clifton school of Cincinnati.

HENRY P. BARRET, tobacco exporter, of Henderson, Ky., was born in that city Sept. 2, 1865, his parents being James R. and Lucy F. (Stites) Barret (see sketch of James R. Barret). He was educated at the Central university, Danville, Ky., where he attended from 1880 to 1883. He then worked for the well known tobacco firm of John H. Barret & Co. for five years, and in 1888 embarked in business for himself as an exporter of tobacco. He first established himself at Roberts' Station, but went from there to Owensboro, where he continued in business for several years. He then opened large rehandling establishments at Wickliffe and Providence, and it is said he now handles as much tobacco as any other individual buyer in the world, if not more. Mr. Barret's success in his line is due to the fact that he keeps in close touch with his business, studies the market conditions, and is always to be relied on to carry out his agreements. He owns 2,500 acres of fine land and is reputed to be one of the wealthiest men in the county. Mr. Barret is a prominent Mason, being a thirty-second degree member of the Scottish Rite and a Knight Templar. On Oct. 20, 1904, he was elected Grand Junior Warden of the Grand Lodge of Kentucky. In 1901 he was united in marriage to Miss Marian Worsham, a native of California and a daughter of A. J. Worsham, now of Henderson.

WALTER BRASHEAR, a contractor and builder, of Henderson, Ky., was born in that city April 28, 1867. He is a son of Barack and Sarah Brashear, both native Kentuckians, and a great-grandson of that Capt. Richard Brashear who was with Gen. George Rogers Clarke in the conquest of the Northwest, and who served with distinction in the Revolutionary war. At the close of the war he received a captain's allotment of seven sections of land in Clark county, Ind., which can be seen in the "Original book of surveys" in the clerk's office at Jeffersonville. He married Lucy Phelps, it being the first marriage in Louisville. She survived him, being ninety-one years of age at death. Captain Brashear came to Kentucky in the days of Daniel Boone and located near Shepherdsville, where he owned a large tract of land. There his son Richard, the grandfather of Walter, was born and reared, and there passed his whole life, being a prominent farmer and an influential citizen. Barack Brashear became a contractor and builder on reaching manhood, and was for some time located in Louisville. About 1840 he came to Henderson, where he carried on the same business until his death in 1887. He was an enthusiastic Odd Fellow and was one of the charter members of Henderson lodge. He was politically a Democrat. His wife died in 1875. During her life she was a devoted member of the Baptist church. They had eight children, only three of whom are now living. Robert is a wholesale paper dealer in St. Louis, Mo.; Ella is the wife of S. W. Gibson, of Corydon, Ky.; and Walter is the subject of this sketch. He received a common school education, learned the business of his father, and at the age of twenty years commenced contracting for himself. Today he is one of the best known contractors in the Lower Ohio Valley. He has built several court houses in Kentucky; done a large amount of government work at Jeffersonville, Ind., and has erected buildings of various kinds in Kentucky, Indiana, Tennessee, and Alabama. Mr. Brashear is a Democrat in his political views, served as a member of the city council in 1896-97, and though always willing to do what he can to further the interests of his party, he can scarcely be called a politician. He is a member of the Knights of Pythias, and with his wife belongs to the Baptist church. He was married in 1892 to

Maude, daughter of Monroe and Jennie Johnson, of Henderson, and has had three children. Jennie died in infancy; Walter, Jr., is five years of age, and Sarah is still in her first year.

CHARLES G. HENSON, one of the oldest and best known residents of Henderson, Ky., was born in the city of Evansville, Ind., Aug. 4, 1830. His parents were both born in England. His paternal grandfather came to this country in 1816 and located first at Georgetown, D. C. Two years later the father of Mr. Henson came to Evansville, Ind., where he was married in 1820. He and his wife celebrated their golden wedding there in 1870. Two years later he died and she followed him in 1882. During his life his father was a contractor and builder. In early life he was a Whig and was later a Republican. Both parents were members of the Cumberland Presbyterian church, in which the father was an elder for fifty years. They had a large family, only three of whom are now living. Charles G. Henson received a common school education and after leaving school learned the carpenters' trade, which occupation he followed in Evansville until 1853, when he came to Henderson, where he continued to work at it until 1860. He then became interested in photography and followed that business until 1878, since which time he has been engaged in the real estate business. He now lives practically retired from active affairs, looking after the rentals of his houses, of which he owns several, both in Henderson and Evansville. Mr. Henson is seventy-four years old and is hale and hearty for one of his age. He laconically attributes his good health to the fact that he "never aspired to office." He has been a great student of music, especially vocal music, and was for over thirty years the musical director of the Presbyterian church. During most of that time his first wife, who was also proficient in music, was a member of the choir. Mr. Henson has been twice married. His first wife was Miss Frances A. Tileston, of Evansville, to whom he was married in 1853. His second marriage was in 1890 to Martha L., daughter of J. M. and Nancy L. (Calvert) Higgins, of Caldwell county. Nancy Calvert was a granddaughter of Spencer Calvert, who served in the Revolutionary war, came to Kentucky in the time of Daniel Boone, returned to Maryland, where he married, and then came back to Kentucky and there passed the rest of his life. His father, who was also named Spencer, was a relative of Lord Baltimore, and came with him to the United States. J. M. Higgins was born Dec. 15, 1822, and died Jan. 28, 1899. He was a very successful and prominent citizen of Princeton, though he suffered financially by the war. Three children born to Mr. Henson died in infancy.

HARRISON WILSON (deceased), who in his day was a well known citizen of Henderson county, Ky., was born in Union county of that state and died near Henderson in 1869. He was a son of Ambrose Wilson, whose father came from Illinois to Kentucky at an early date, and there the family for several generations were tillers of the soil. Harrison Wilson grew to manhood in Union county. In 1859 he was married to Miss Phoebe E. Taylor, of Henderson, a daughter of Brooking and Ann (Gale) Taylor, both of whom were natives of Virginia. Brooking Taylor and his wife came to Kentucky in pioneer times, settling first in Franklin county, and in 1848 came to Henderson, where they passed the remainder of their lives. Harrison Wilson was a man who pursued "the even tenor of his way" under all circumstances, doing his duty as he saw it without regard to the consequences. In his political affiliations he was a Democrat of the Jacksonian school, firm in his convictions concerning questions of public policy, and yet of such a temperament that he readily commanded the respect and friendship of his political opponents. He and his wife were both members of the Baptist church and were consistent practitioners of the tenets of their religious faith in their daily conduct. They had a family of five children: Sophronia is deceased; William A. is a banker at Kansas City, Mo.; Sally E., Mary G., and Phoebe T. still live at home. The daughters were all well educated and Mary has taught school. The three sisters have a cozy home in the city of Henderson where they live in the enjoyment of each other's companionship and the respect and friendship of their neighbors and acquaintances.

CHARLES L. KING, farmer, merchant and banker, of Corydon, Ky., was born in the county where he now resides, March 12, 1838. His parents, James H. and Caroline (Brinkley) King, both natives of Virginia, were married in that state and came to Kentucky about 1824, locating first in Union but two years later coming to Henderson county. The father bought a tract of wild land about five miles southeast of Corydon, cleared a farm and built a whipsaw mill and an old fashioned buhr grist mill. In 1856 he sold out there and removed to Hickman county, where he followed the milling business until his death in 1864. His wife died the previous year. He was a stanch Union man and opposed to secession but died before he saw the Union arms victorious in the Civil war. He and his wife were both members of the Christian church and were widely known for their deeds of Christian charity. They had a family of ten children, viz.: George W., now a resident of Sebree; John M., died at the age of twenty-two years; Mary J., wife of J. L. Luttrell of Hickman; James, deceased; Charles L., the subject of this sketch; Martha, who married a man named Buckman and now deceased; Alexander, residing at Sturgis, in Union county; Edward, a resident of Corydon; Sarah, now dead, was the wife of C. E. Harness, manager of the Anchor roller mills at Corydon; Harbart A., associated with Charles L. in business at Corydon. He attended Princeton college and married Miss Annie Dorsey. Charles L. King was associated with his father in business from the time he left school until 1863. He then engaged in the mercantile business at Hickman, for about a year, when he removed to Mount Vernon, Ind., and conducted a store there until after the war, when he went to Cairo, Ill. In 1866 he returned to Hickman and remained there until the following year, when he came to Corydon. At that time he had the only store in the place and in 1876 he erected the largest building for mercantile purposes in the town. In 1878 he and his brother formed a partnership under the firm name of C. L. & H. A. King, which still exists. In 1894 the Corydon deposit bank was organized with a capital of $25,000 and C. L. King was elected president, which office he has held ever since. In addition to his banking and mercantile interests Mr. King is the owner of a thousand acres of fine land, and is one of the progressive farmers of his section of the state. His farm is especially noted for its fine, full-blooded Hereford cattle, of which he makes a specialty in the way of stock raising. While Mr. King is entitled to be called a public spirited citizen, and one who takes an interest in public affairs generally, he belongs to no political party, preferring the exercise of his suffrage according to his own convictions. He was married in 1864 to Mrs. Sarah Sheffer, *nee* Powell, a daughter of Harrison A. Powell, and to this union there were born the following children: Annie Lee, now the wife of Ben. T. Davis, a lawyer of Hickman; Ada, wife of V. G. Conway, a farmer of Hickman county; Maud, widow of Dr. W. B. Cook and now lives with her father; Harbart L., a graduate of Central university, of Danville, Ky., with the degree of LL.B., was admitted to the bar Sept. 5, 1904, and has begun practice at Corydon. The mother of these children died on March 28, 1902. During her life she was a devoted member of the Christian church, and her widowed husband still holds his membership in that denomination.

ELIJAH SELLERS, a well known farmer, living four miles from Henderson, Ky., and one of the heaviest taxpayers in the county, was born in Henderson county, Oct. 15, 1824, his parents being Isham and Lydia (Barr) Sellers, both natives of North Carolina. Soon after his marriage Isham Sellers came with his wife on horseback to the wilds of Kentucky, carrying their household effects on pack horses, and began life in true pioneer fashion. The clapboards that formed the roof of their log cabin were fastened on with wooden pegs, as nails in that day were a luxury hardly to be thought of for such purposes. There this couple lived until their deaths, rearing a large family of children. He was a member of the old Baptist church and his wife was a Methodist. Elijah Sellers received such an education as the public schools of that day afforded and at the age of twenty-one bought 154 acres of wild land on credit and commenced life for himself by building a log cabin in the wilderness. He cleared a farm and in 1849 was married to Minerva Osborn, daughter of Randolph Osborn, one of the pioneer settlers of Henderson county. To this marriage there were born ten children, viz.: Orrie Belle, now Mrs. Andrew Thornberry of Webster county, Ky.; Frances, now dead, was the wife of A. D. Milton; Jane, now Mrs. Jack Milton; Isham J., a farmer of Henderson county; Annie, widow of Joseph Hargiss; Robert Lee and Randolph, both farmers in Henderson county; Addie, wife of William Mitchison, a farmer of Henderson county; Elijah, Jr., and Rufus, both occupying farms near the old homestead. At one time Mr. Sellers owned 2,500 acres of land. After giving each of his ten children a good farm he has about 800 acres left. Since 1879 he has lived in his present location, where he has one of the finest brick farm-houses in the county. While he has conducted a general farming business he has given a great deal of attention to tobacco, which has been one of his principal crops. After the death of his first wife he was married to Mrs. Mary Poor, *nee* Norris. She too passed away and he was married to his third and present wife, Mrs. Mary A. Vogle, whose maiden name was Rockencamp. His first wife was a member of the Methodist church; his present wife is a Lutheran; and he belongs to the Episcopal church. In his political opinions Mr. Sellers has always been a Democrat, though he has never been a seeker after office nor an active politician. He is a member of the Free and Accepted Masons and in earlier years was a regular attendant at the lodge meetings. Besides his farming interests he is a stockholder in the Planters' bank.

ROBERT T. HICKMAN, farmer and hardware dealer, of Henderson, Ky., is of Scotch descent, the first of the family to come to America, settling in Virginia. In 1809 James Hickman, the great-grandfather of Robert, came from Winchester, Va., with his family of seven sons and one daughter, and passed the remainder of his life in Shelby county, Ky., in the immediate vicinity of Shelbyville. Joseph Hickman, one of the seven sons and the grandfather of Robert, married Elizabeth Tolbert, daughter of one of the pioneers of that section, who came from Maryland. In 1832 they went to Shelby county, Ill., and there both died some years later. One of their sons was James W. Hickman, the father of the subject of this sketch. He was born in Shelby county, Ky., Aug. 8, 1813, there grew to manhood and learned the blacksmiths' trade, which he followed for over forty years. More than half of that period he had a shop in Shelbyville. In 1866 he came to Henderson county, where he rented and managed a farm, though he continued to work at his trade. In early life he was an ardent Whig, but after the downfall of that party he became a Democrat. He is still living with his son Robert, hale and hearty, at the age of ninety-two years. While living at Shelbyville he frequently went to Louisville, and remembers when that city was but little more than a village. He married Lucy G. Eubank, who was born in Clark county, Ky., March 21, 1821, and died March 20, 1891, lacking one day of having reached her three score and ten years. For many years they both belonged to the Methodist Episcopal church together, and he still retains his membership in that denomination. They had five children: Harriet E., Mary Alice, Claude Thomas, Robert T. and Harry Buckner. Harriet married J. B. Marshall, and both she and her husband are dead; Mary died at the age of sixteen years; Claude is a dentist in Henderson, and

Harry died in infancy. Robert T. Hickman was born at Shelbyville, Ky., Nov. 16, 1854. He received a common school education and at the age of twenty-two years went to Vanderburg county, Ind., where he rented a farm and conducted it successfully for two years. He then employed teams and was engaged in railroad construction for a time, after which he went on the road as a sewing machine salesman, and was later employed in the same capacity with the Dayton Hedge Fence Company. In 1886 he located on his present farm, where he has continued to live ever since. Mr. Hickman is one of the most scientific and progressive farmers in Western Kentucky. In addition to his own farm he rents quite extensively and carries on a general farming business, though he makes a specialty of apples. In this line his orchard products are the equal of any in the country. His house and barn are said to be the best equipped and most modern of any in the county. A gasoline eng'ne supplies water to every room in the house and for watering stock in the barn. Of the three automobiles in the county he is the owner of one, and is the only farmer in the county to own one of these modern vehicles. On Nov. 1, 1904, in connection with J. H. and H. P. Alves, he organized the Alves & Hickman Hardware Company, which does a general hardware and agricultural implement business. He makes his daily trips from his country home to his place of business in Henderson in his automobile. Mr. Hickman is a Democrat in his political views, is a member of the Tribe of Ben Hur, and of the Presbyterian church. He has never married.

THOMAS B. BOOK (deceased), a native of Henderson county, Ky., was born Aug. 5, 1858, and died Feb. 28, 1899. He was a son of James R. and Bennette Book, who were pioneers of Kentucky, his father being one of the foremost farmers of his neighborhood in his day. Thomas was reared on the farm and received his education in the public schools. When he was but eighteen years of age he went to Henderson, where he engaged in business for a short time, but soon tired of city life and returned to the farm. In 1880 he bought a tract of 60 acres on Frog Island, in Henderson county, and commenced farming on his own account. Shortly afterward he sold his place to a good advantage and bought a large farm near the city of Henderson. This farm he sold in 1894 and bought 98 acres, to which he soon after added 43 acres more, and it is upon this farm that his widow now lives. Mr. Book was married on Oct. 25, 1881, to Miss Julia Lockett, a daughter of Thomas J., and Martha J.

Lockett, old and honored residents of Kentucky. The father of Thomas J. Lockett was Capt. Francis Lockett, of Virginia, who settled in Kentucky in an early day. Mr. and Mrs. Book had two children. Annie, born March 3, 1885, is now the wife of J. N. Sites of Henderson. Their marriage occurred June 2, 1904. Lockett R., born Dec. 7, 1891, lives on the farm with his mother. Both parents were members of the Baptist church, to which Mrs. Book still belongs and is a regular attendant. He was a Democrat in his political affiliations, though he never was an aspirant for public office. Since his death his widow manages the farm and has one of the coziest country homes in Henderson county.

STRACHAN BARRET, manager of the Henderson, Ky., plants of the Imperial Tobacco Company, of Kentucky (incorporated), was born near that city, July 8, 1856. He is a son of William T. and Bettie (Towles) Barret, the former a native of Louisa county, Va., and the latter of Henderson county, Ky. (For the early history of the Barret and Towles families see the sketches of John H. Barret, deceased, and Walter A. Towles.) William T. Barret came to Kentucky in 1840. For several years he was engaged in the tobacco trade, after which he followed the vocations of pork packer and wholesale grocer, and was also the owner of a large farm in the county. His brother, Alexander B., died in 1861, leaving an estate of over three millions of dollars, and he was named as one of the executors, his brother, John H., being the other. In the settlement of this large estate he displayed good judgment and a high order of ability, as no lawsuits nor ill will among the legatees resulted. Politically he was a Democrat of the Jackson school; was a prominent member of the Free and Accepted Masons; and both he and his wife belonged to the Episcopal church. He died in 1897, and his widow now makes her home with her son Strachan. They had four children: Thomas T., Strachan, Bettie T., and Alexander B. Thomas is a farmer in Henderson county, president of the society of equity and a member of the Democratic committee; Strachan is the subject of this sketch; Bettie married Fred L. Eldridge, now vice-president of the Knickerbocker Trust Company of New York; Alexander is one of the Johnston, Barret Wholesale Dry Goods Company, of Los Angeles, Cal. After leaving school Strachan Barret became interested in the tobacco trade, with which he has ever since been connected. The company he now represents had five establishments in operation during the year 1904. The plants at Henderson handle most of the tobacco in the city, the annual product running from five million to six million pounds, all export goods. Mr. Barret is a director in the Planters' State bank, of Henderson, and owns a fine farm of nearly three hundred acres, upon which he resides, and which receives a portion of his time and attention. He is especially interested in raising Oxford Down sheep and fine cattle. The farm is the one settled by his grandfather Towles in an early day. In his political affiliations he has followed in the footsteps of his worthy sire and allied himself with the Democratic party. So, in choosing his religious associations, he has adopted the faith of his parents and belongs to the Episcopal church, of which his wife is also a member. Mr. Barret was married, Dec. 3, 1884, to Miss Maggie Rudy, daughter of John and Margaret Rudy, old residents of Henderson county, where her grandfather, John Rudy, was one of the pioneers. Mr. and Mrs. Barret have four children: Strachan, now a student at the Kentucky military institute, where he holds the rank of lieutenant; Thomas T.; John R.; and Heyward R.

ELIJAH SELLERS, Jr., one of the enterprising and successful young men of Henderson county, Ky., was born in that county, April 10, 1875. He is a son of Elijah Sellers, a sketch of whom appears elsewhere in this work. During his boyhood he attended the public schools, where he received his primary education. In 1888-89 he went to the West Kentucky college, in 1891 he entered the Louisville school of pharmacy and graduated the following year. Upon leaving school he embarked in the drug business at Sturgis, in Union county, where he remained for five years, after which he was for three years in Corydon and two years in Henderson. In 1902 his father gave him one hundred and fifty acres of land from the old homestead and since then he has been engaged in farming and stock raising. He carries on a general farming business, but inclines to the buying and feeding of stock as a specialty. In this line of work he has displayed good judgment and has been quite successful. In his political views Mr. Sellers is a Democrat and takes a laudable interest in all questions of public policy, particularly those of a local nature. On Dec. 10, 1902, Mr. Sellers was united in marriage to Miss Maude, daughter of Walter and Rena Lockett. Her father is one of the substantial farmers of Henderson county. Mr. and Mrs. Sellers are both members of the Second Presbyterian church of Henderson.

ABBOTT VEATCH, inspector of steamboat hulls, Evansville, Ind., was born on a farm in Posey county, of that state, July 4, 1861, his parents being Virgil S. and Margaret (Oatman) Veatch. The paternal grandfather, Thomas Stone Veatch, was an old settler in that portion of Indiana known as "The Pocket." On the maternal side quite a number of the family were river-men, though the grandfather of Mr. Veatch, Jesse Oatman, was a well-to-do farmer of Posey county. Virgil S. Veatch is a printer by trade, and when Abbott was about seven years of age the family removed to Evansville, where both parents are still living, and where the father follows his occupation. Abbott grew to manhood in Evansville, which city has always been his home, since his parents came there. Perhaps he inherited a love for the river from his mother's people. At any rate, when he was twelve years of age he became a dishwasher on one of the Ohio and Mississippi river steamers, and since then he has filled various positions in the steamboat navigation of those streams. His long experience gave him the essential qualifications for the position he now holds. Steamboat captains have faith in his ability to make inspections and the general public have faith in his honesty to know that his duties will be faithfully, fearlessly and impartially performed and the safety of the traveling public be thereby greatly enhanced.

JOHN P. WALKER, of Evansville, Ind., county treasurer of Vanderburg county, was born at Richview, Washington county, Ill., July 21, 1866. He is a son of William H. and Mary A. (Phillips) Walker, both natives of Washington county, Ill., the father born Jan. 8, 1827, and the mother on July 15, 1826. They were married on Feb. 15, 1848, and are still living, having celebrated their golden wedding in 1898. During the war the father was a captain and later a major in an Illinois regiment. In 1871 the family removed to Evansville, in 1888 the parents went to Kansas and now live in Pasadena, Cal., where the father is a retired Baptist minister. John P. is the eighth in a family of nine children, seven of whom are still living. James R. is a physician at Pine Ridge, S. D.; Sarah L. is now Mrs. Summers of Oklahoma City, O. T.; Rhoda is the wife of P. E. Sherrill of Bennettstown, Ky.; Emma is Mrs. Richardson of Oklahoma City; Laura married F. M. Saunders and lives at Los Angeles; Simeon O. lives at Buena Park, Cal. Those deceased are Mary, who died as the wife of a Mr. Allman of Evansville, and Anna, who died when only six years of age. John P. Walker was but five years old when his parents came to Evansville. After attending the public schools he learned the printers' trade in the office of the *Evansville Courier;* was for a time mailing clerk in the Evansville post office; went to Kansas City about 1887 and was there employed for two years in the accounting department of the Fort Scott & Memphis railroad; returned to Evansville in 1890 and entered the accounting department of the Mackey system of railroads, including nearly all the lines centering at Evansville, as well as some others. Mr. Walker continued in this position until Mr. Mackey lost control, after which he was with the Peoria, Decatur & Eastern, and Louisville, Evansville & St. Louis roads until 1897, at which time he was chief clerk in the auditor's office of the latter road. In March of that year he met with a railroad accident that necessitated the amputation of both legs. This would have caused many a man to become downhearted, but the cheerful disposition of Mr. Walker was now worth a great deal to him in helping him to keep up his spirits. He entered politics, and in the fall of 1898 was elected coroner of Vanderburg county. At the close of his first term he was re-elected, serving four years in all, and in 1902 was elected treasurer of the county on the Republican ticket by a majority of over 2,000. It is possible that some people voted for Mr. Walker because of his misfortune, but a large majority of his supporters gave him their suffrages because they knew he was both capable and honest. His skill as an accountant makes him competent to meet any problem in bookkeeping that may arise, and the taxpayers of the county know that the records will be kept straight under his supervision. Mr. Walker is a Royal Arch Mason, a Knight of Pythias and a member of the Benevolent and Protective Order of Elks. On Oct. 4, 1888, he was united in marriage to Miss Mary E. Burch, of Evansville, and they have three children living, viz.: Margaret B., Sherrill P., and Helen F.

SIDNEY W. DOUGLAS, the pioneer photographer of Evansville, Ind., and one of the leading artists in that line of work in Southern Indiana, was born in Clinton county, N. Y., March 25, 1840. In 1873 he located at Evansville, where he established himself in the business. His studio soon came to be popular, the result of his years of study and experience. It is the little details that make a great photographer, and in these Mr. Douglas is well fortified.

GUILD C. FOSTER, clerk of the circuit and superior courts of Vanderburg county, Ind., was born in the city of Evansville, Sept. 11, 1870. His father, James H. Foster, is an old and honored resident of the city and now holds the position of treasurer of the Evansville Gas and Electric Light Company. He is a native of Pike county, Ind., but came to Evansville in childhood with his parents, Matthew W. Foster and wife. James H. Foster married Henrietta Riggs, a native of Sullivan county, Ind., but like her husband, came to Evansville in childhood. Guild is the second of three children, all boys. Riggs, the eldest son, died in his youth, and Matthew W., the youngest, is now employed in the Evansville city engineer's office. Guild C. Foster is a splendid example of the younger generation of men who have made their own way in the world. After attending the city schools until he finished the grammar school course and the high school for two years he decided to map out his own career. At the age of sixteen he went into the offices of the Evansville & Terre Haute railroad company as a clerk. After nearly two years there he went to California, where for two years he was connected with the Southern Pacific railroad as a clerk in the offices at Los Angeles, San Francisco and San Diego. In 1890 he came back to Evansville, remained there a short time, and then went to Chicago for a year and a half as a clerk for the Wabash route. During the next two years he was with the Louisville, Evansville & St. Louis (now the Southern) railway, being employed in the offices at St. Louis, Louisville, and Princeton, Ind. In the fall of 1894 he returned to Evansville to stay. He became deputy clerk of the superior court in 1895, and when, about a year later, Charles Sihler was appointed to the vacancy in the county clerk's office, caused by the death of Charles Boepple, Mr. Foster took the clerkship of the circuit court, made vacant by Mr. Sihler's promotion. In this position he soon demonstrated his ability and became one of the most popular men who ever held it. The result of his long clerical experience and the many personal friendships he formed was his nomination for the office of circuit clerk, on April 7, 1904, by the Republicans of Vanderburg county, and on November 8th was elected by a large majority. In fraternal circles Mr. Foster is one of the best known men in Evansville. He is a member of Evansville Chapter, Royal Arch Masons, the Benevolent and Protective Order of Elks, the Modern Woodmen of America, the Fraternal Order of Eagles, the Ancient Order of United Workmen, and the Royal Arcanum. On Jan. 24, 1896, he was married to Miss Emma Heberer, of one of Evansville's leading families, and to this union there have been born two children, Henrietta, aged seven, and Edward, aged four.

CHRISTIAN W. KRATZ, of Evansville, Ind., sheriff of Vanderburg county, was born within two miles of that city, July 2, 1855, his parents being John and Louise (Buechtele) Kratz, both natives of Germany. The father was a son of John and Elizabeth Kratz, was born in 1830 and came with his parents to this country when he was but four years of age. After a residence of four years in Pittsburg the family came to Vanderburg county and located on the quarter section of land in German township, on which Meyer's station, on the Illinois Central railroad, is now situated. Some years later they removed to Centre township, where both the grandparents passed the remainder of their lives. Louise Buechtele was born in Würtemberg, July 3, 1831. When she was ten years old she came with her parents to the United States and settled in Armstrong township of Vanderburg county, where her father, Peter Buechtele, died at the age of sixty-one. John Kratz learned the trade of blacksmith and followed that occupation in Centre township the greater part of his life. On Aug. 10, 1854, he and Louise Buechtele were married, and Christian is the oldest child in a family of eight, three of whom are dead and the others all live in Vanderburg county. Elizabeth is the wife of William A. Elmendorf; Christine is the wife of William Aleon; Charles is the partner of the subject in the dairy business, under the firm name of C. W. & C. Kratz, and Martha is the wife of Henry Heiwinkel. Louise died at the age of twenty years. John R. learned the blacksmith trade and died on April 18, 1902, and Peter died in infancy. The mother of these children died on Dec. 19, 1875, and the father on Feb. 24, 1891. The settlement that grew up about the blacksmith shop of John Kratz, north of the city of Evansville, took the name of Kratzville, which it still retains, an honor to one of the early settlers in that part of the county. Christian W. Kratz received a common school education, after which he learned the blacksmith trade with his father. Upon reaching manhood he and his brother John succeeded their father in the business and conducted the shop for something like twenty years. Mr. Kratz became interested in politics early in life. When he became a voter he cast in his lot with the Republican party and soon became a recognized leader among the voters of the township, because of his wide acquaintance, his general good fellowship, and the central location of his shop, which made a gathering point for the neighborhood. He was elected trustee of the township in 1888 and two years later was re-elected, holding the office altogether for a period of seven years and four months. In 1893 he formed the partnership with his brother Charles in the dairy business, which still exists. They own one of the best appointed dairies in the county. About a year after retiring from the trustee's office Mr. Kratz received the nomination of his party for the office of representative to the state legislature. He was elected by a majority of 1,345, and the journal of the house for the session of 1897 shows that he did his duty by his constituents. In 1902 his name, with several others, was submitted to a public primary for the shrievalty of Vanderburg county. The vote which he received on that occasion tells the story of his popularity better than words. His majority for sheriff at the November election was 1,718, and on April 7, 1904, he was re-nominated without opposition. Mr. Kratz is a Royal Arch Mason, an Odd Fellow, a member of the Benevolent and Protective Order of Elks, the Ancient Order of United Workmen, the Knights of Honor, the Frontiersmen, the Buffaloes, the Eagles and the Tribe of Ben Hur. He was married on Nov. 3, 1880, to Miss Minnie Schemet, of an old family of the county, and they have two children living: Cora May and Clara Anna. Two children, Irene and Edwin, died in childhood.

CHARLES SIHLER, of Evansville, Ind., clerk of the circuit court of Vanderburg county and ex-officio clerk of the superior court, was born in that city, Aug. 30, 1869, and has lived there all his life. His parents, Louis and Charlotte (Sixt) Sihler, were both natives of Germany, both came to America the same year, 1853, became acquainted in Evansville and were married there on Feb. 22, 1860. Charles Sihler was the sixth child in a family of ten, himself and four sisters being the only survivors. The sisters are Mrs. Edward Stickleman and Misses Henrietta, Margaret and Clara Sihler, all living in Evansville. The father was twice elected recorder of Vanderburg county and died while in that office, Jan. 8, 1890. His wife survived him but a short time and entered her final rest on March 25th of the same year. Charles was educated in the Evansville public schools until he was about fourteen years of age, when he started in to learn the jewelry trade. While working at this business his father fell ill and Charles left the jeweler's bench to attend to the duties of the recorder's office. He continued as his father's deputy for nearly four years, or until the latter's death as already mentioned. An uncle of Charles, Otto Durre, was appointed to serve until the next election, Charles not being of age at the time of his father's death. He attained his majority, however, in the following August, and was nominated by the Republicans to serve the remainder of the term, the election occurring in November, 1890. This proved to be a Democratic year and young Sihler was defeated with the rest of his party ticket, only one man, the candidate for auditor, being elected. Upon retiring from the recorder's office in January, 1891, he entered the treasurer's office as a deputy and remained there for thirteen months, becoming deputy clerk on Feb. 22, 1892, and remaining in this place until Aug. 22, 1896, when he was appointed clerk to fill a vacancy. Mr. Sihler has since then been twice elected to the office, in 1896 and 1900, each time for four years. As a county official few men in Indiana are better qualified by nature, training or experience than Mr. Sihler. For twenty years he has been in the court-house, in that time he has come in contact with every county office and understands the manner in which the office should be conducted. He is one of the most efficient and popular county officers in Evansville and has a host of friends for whom he has at some time or another done some favor that makes them remember him. Mr. Sihler is a Mason, an Odd Fellow, a Knight of Pythias, an Elk and a Knight of Honor, and is a popular member in all those orders. He was married on April 17, 1895, to Miss Maria Haas, in

Evansville and they have two children, Louis F., aged eight, and Charlotte K., aged five.

HON. CHARLES G. COVERT, mayor of Evansville, Ind., was born at Washington, Daviess county, of that state, Sept. 4, 1864. He is a son of Jacob and Maria Catharine (Gooldy) Covert, both natives of the Hoosier State, the former of Wells and the latter of Lawrence county. Jacob Covert is a newspaper man by profession and now holds a responsible position in the government printing office at Washington, D. C., where he and his wife now reside. He was born in Wells county on Aug. 13, 1837, and is said to have been the first white male child born in the county. He was married on Sept. 26, 1859, and Charles G. is the second child of a family of two sons and two daughters. Harriet is now the wife of Grant L. Austin of Washington City; Martha is Mrs. Charles P. Beard of Evansville; William H. is married and lives in Cleveland, O. When Charles G. was about five years of age his parents removed to Evansville and there he was reared and educated. His father founded the Evansville *Tribune*, which he continued to publish for a number of years. In the office of this paper the son learned the printers' trade, after graduating from the high school at the age of sixteen, and afterward "held cases" in the office of the Evansville *Journal* for several years. He left this office to become the city editor of the *Tribune* in 1887 and remained connected with the paper until December, 1894, the last five years of the time being managing editor. His resignation was brought about by his election to the shrievalty of Vanderburg county in November preceding. In 1896 he was re-elected sheriff and served two full terms, being but twenty-nine years of age when he first entered upon the duties of the office, the youngest man ever elected to the position. His majority on his second election was nearly 2,000 votes, while President McKinley carried the county at the same election by only 926. In 1899 he was the Republican nominee for the mayoralty, but was defeated by the small margin of fifty-two votes. In the spring of 1901 he was again chosen as the Republican standard bearer in the municipal campaign, and this time was elected by a majority of eighty-eight, the office in the meantime having been made a four year office by legislative enactment. Mayor Covert is a member of the Masonic fraternity, the Knights of Pythias, the Benevolent and Protective Order of Elks, the Improved Order of Red Men, the Ancient Order of United Workmen, the Royal Arcanum, the Knights of the Ancient Essenic Order, the Buffaloes and the Foresters. He is a director in the White Oak Handle Factory and the Evansville Electric Plow Company. On Oct. 26, 1887, Mr. Covert was united in marriage to Miss Grace L. Tucker , and they have one daughter living, Jeannette, aged nine years.

EMIL G. HEEGER, president of the board of water works trustees of the city of Evansville, Ind., was born in that city, May 10, 1862. His father, Andrew Heeger, was a native of Germany who came to the United States in early man hood and located at Evansville, where he was for many years a prominent musician, being a member of the well known and popular Warren's band. Here he married Doretta Kollenberg. Two of their eight children died in infancy and the other six, with the mother, are still living. Jon C. is a member of the Evansville detective force; Frederick is a member of the celebrated Third regiment band of Kansas City, Mo.; George holds a responsible position with the Goodwin Clothing Manufacturing Company of Evansville; Emma conducts a dressmaking establishment in the same city, and Eleanora is a teacher of German in the Evans ville public schools. Emil G. Heeger attended both the English and German schools of his native city, after which he took a complete course in a commercial college there, graduating at the age of sixteen years. He then spent four years and a half in the Heilman and the Kratz machine works of Evansville, learning the trade of machinist, at which he worked as a journeyman in the different machine shops of the city. Turning his attention to the vocation of stationary engineer he soon became proficient in that line, owing to his thorough knowledge of machinery, and for five years he was first engineer at the Fulton avenue brewery. In 1890 he accepted a similar position with George Brose, at the Sunnyside flour mills, where he is still employed as chief engineer. In 1901 he was appointed by Mayor Covert to a place on the board of water - works trustees, of which he is now the senior member and president, having been elected to that office in July, 1904, upon the resignation of Alexander Gilchrist. Mr. Heeger is a member of the Free and Accepted Masons, the Benevolent and Protective Order of Elks, the Woodmen of the World, and the Evansville branch of the National Association of Stationary Engineers, of which he has been secretary for the last twelve years. Through his efforts the national convention of the association met in Evansville in 1903. At that time he was elected to the office of national conductor in the order and was chairman of the committee on reception, arrangements, etc. In connection with his sub - committees the arrangements for the entertainment of the delegates were so perfect that those who attended the convention expressed themselves as having been better taken care of in Evansville than had the delegates to any previous convention. They all recognized the guiding hand of Mr. Heeger in the work and as a token of their appreciation presented him with a fine silver service, suitably engraved — something that had never before occurred in the history of the organization. He is also president of the Indiana association of engineers. Mr. Heeger was married on Feb. 25, 1885, to Miss Elizabeth Kramer, and they have three living children: Edward is an electrician, Frederick and Helen are students in school. Mr. Heeger is an unwavering Republican in his political views and is always ready to do his part to win a victory for his party, yet in his political work, as in his private and official life, he never stoops to underhand methods, but makes a clean, open fight on the principles involved. Consequently his personal friend ships are not limited by party lines, many Democrats in the city recognizing him as a worthy, honest and manly man.

G. NETTER WORTHINGTON, president of the board of public safety, Evansville, Ind., was born in Spencer county, that state, July 30, 1862. He is the son of Henry H. and Laura (Ray) Worthington. His father is still living and is now in his eighty - second year. His mother died Nov. 2, 1904. Mr. Worthington was the third of five sons, the two eldest of whom died in infancy. Of his brothers living Charles V. is a newspaper artist, but at the head of the advertising department of the Keith - O'Brien Company, department store, Salt Lake City, Utah, and George W. is a clerk in the Evansville postoffice. Mr. Worthington learned the printers 'trade in Sedalia, Mo. Taking up his residence in Evansville, for the second time, in 1879, he completed his education in the public schools and then became a typesetter on the old Evansville Argus, now defunct. Later he was employed as a compositor in the newsroom of the Evansville *Courier,* but after about a year with that paper he went into the composing room of the Evansville *Journal,* and a few months later became a reporter for the paper, a morning publication, and for about three years was the only city news gatherer it had. He then became city editor of the paper, continuing until 1892, when an afternoon edition was started and was known as *The News.* Mr. Worthington was its first city editor, remaining in the position for a year, when he returned to the morning publication as the night editor, and held that position until the two papers were consolidated in 1900 under the name of the *Journal-News.* Mr. Worthington then became city editor of the "hyphenated" daily and is still filling the duties of that position. This paper is the only afternoon daily in Evansville. The local department under the trained hand of Mr. Worthington is bright and replete with well and carefully prepared news. Politically Mr. Worthington is a Republican and has shared in the work that has brought party success in Southern Indiana. The extent of his office holding has been brief. One term, a few years ago, he was secretary of the board of public safety, and in 1900 was one of three men selected by Mayor Covert to compose the board of which Mr. Worthington was elected president in 1902. In this position he has displayed rare tact and ability in handling delicate questions in connection with police affairs of the city, and has fully demonstrated the wisdom of his selection. He is a Mason, belonging to three branches of the order—the Blue Lodge, the Royal Arch Chapter and the Commandery of Knights Templars. He is also a Knight of Pythias. On the last day of January, 1884, Mr. Worthington was united in marriage to Miss Harriet McReynolds, only daughter of a former prominent steamboat owner and captain, Joseph McReynolds, now deceased. Two children blessed this union, a son, Roy, now nineteen years old, and a daughter, Jessie Marie, who died in 1903 at the age of eleven years. Mr. Worthington holds membership in the Methodist church.

JOHN F. HARTH, of the firm of Harth Bros., Harth Bros. Grain Company, and the Harth-Ames Company, of Caseyville and Paducah, Ky., was born in Dekoven, Ky., Nov. 4, 1859. He is the son of Leopold and Annie (Kieful) Harth, the former a native of Germany and the latter of France. Both came to America in an early day and settled in Union county, Ky. The father of John F. first followed the occupation of butcher in Union county, and afterwards that of merchant at Dekoven, Ky. He was a Union man, a Democrat and a communicant in the Catholic church. This family had six children, all living. The father died in 1868, and his widow still survives, being a resident of Caseyville, Ky. John F. Harth was reared and educated in Dekoven and Caseyville, Ky. Beginning as a clerk, he has spent his life in the mercantile business. For twenty years he has done a thriving general store business in Caseyville, utilizing the two floors of a brick building whose dimensions are seventy-five by eighty feet, and three warehouses. The firms of which Mr. Harth is a member also buy and sell grain, owning their own boats and barges and an extensive livery business. They own and cultivate four farms located in Union and Christian counties. The Curlew coal mine they lease to the Bell Union Coal and Coke Company. The names of the brothers associated with him in this extensive business are Joseph and Leopold. While Mr. Harth has always taken an active part in politics, he has never sought an office. He is a Democrat and a Knight of Honor. He married Miss Jennie Gregory. She is the daughter of John W. and Virginia (Henry) Gregory, both of whom spent their lives in Union county. Mr. Harth and wife have four children, named John Gregory, Lucile, Joseph and Charles P.

PROF. JAMES F. ENSLE, of Evansville, Ind., superintendent of the public schools of Vanderburg county, was born on Slim Island, in the Ohio river, March 17, 1872. This island is Kentucky soil but his parents were really residents of Vanderburg county, being at that time on the island temporarily to look after the planting of a large crop of corn there. The father, Young E. Ensle, and his wife were both natives of Vanderburg county, where he followed the occupation of farmer for many years. Aside from three years, between the ages of six and nine years, when the family lived in Henderson, Ky., the entire life of Professor Ensle has been passed in that county, where he now owns a farm, upon which he resides, a short distance from the city. He was educated in the Evansville schools, graduating from the high school in 1892. For the next five years he taught in the country schools, one year in Posey and four years in the county of Vanderburg. The school year of

1895-96 he spent at the State university and in 1897 he was elected superintendent of the Vanderburg schools, being at that time only twenty-five years old, the youngest man to ever be selected for the position. At the end of his two year term he was re-elected for four years, the tenure of office having been changed by the legislature, and in 1903 he was again elected for four years. As a student in school Professor Ensle imbibed modern ideas regarding education and those ideas he has brought into play in his management of the schools under his charge. The result is that the public schools of Vanderburg county will compare favorably with those in other parts of the state, while the progress is still going on toward a higher standard. The teachers under his supervision have a high regard for his character and ability and their relations are most cordial, one of the essential pre-requisites to good work in the school room. Professor Ensle is a prominent Knight of Pythias and a member of the County Superintendents' Association of Indiana, as well as the Southern Indiana Teachers' Association. He was married in September, 1899, to Miss Ella Clippinger, of Vanderburg county, and to this union there have been born three children: Charles, Mary and Ruth. Charles died in infancy and the others are still living.

GEORGE D. HEILMAN, one of the best known and most popular young attorneys of Evansville, Ind., was born in that city, May 15, 1873, and is a son of Daniel Heilman, a stockholder in and superintendent of the Heilman Machine Works. He attended the Evansville schools, leaving the high school at the age of sixteen years to learn the trade of machinist in his father's factory. In all, he spent about six years in the works, meantime taking a complete course in the Evansville Commercial college. Upon the death of his uncle, William Heilman, who left a large estate, George D. Heilman was selected by the widow as her private secretary and to aid in the settlement of the estate. The position was one of great responsibility, yet he filled it for several years to the entire satisfaction of his aunt, his counsel frequently proving a great advantage in the solution of delicate problems in connection with the estate. While in this position, he was thrown in contact with litigation of various sorts which aroused in him a desire to become an attorney. Accordingly, he resigned his place as secretary and entered the law department of the Indiana State university, from which he graduated in 1900. He immediately entered upon the practice of law in his native city, becoming associated with Andrew J. Clark, an association which still continues to the mutual satisfaction of both parties. Mr. Heilman's practice extends all over Southern Indiana and into Illinois and Kentucky, although he has been engaged in the active work of his profession for only about four years. In politics, he is one of the active and enthusiastic Republicans of his section of the state. In fact, his political acquaintance and labors extend all over Indiana and into Illinois. While a student at the State university, he organized a Republican club among the students and was elected its first president. In 1898 he was vice-president of the American Republican college league, which embraced Indiana and Illinois. He has served as county manager of the Lincoln League, has been vice-president of the same organization for the First congressional district, and is now serving his second term as secretary of the State league. He was also elected assistant clerk of the Indiana house of representatives in 1903 and again in 1905. Mr. Heilman is a member of the Evansville Bar association. He is a Master of his Masonic lodge; a Royal Arch Mason; also a Knight Templar, being a member of La Vallette Commandery No. 15, and belongs to the Delta Tau Delta and Phi Delta Phi college fraternities. In his fraternal societies and secret orders, he is popular because of his genial disposition and general good nature. In his practice, he commands the respect of both bench and bar by his dignified manner and great earnestness as well as his ability. In his political work, he is recognized as a fair fighter and one who keeps fully informed on the political questions of the day. Mr. Heilman is a young man, yet with the best years of his life before him. With a sound physical constitution, a bright mind and a laudable ambition, there is no doubt greater honors await him in the future.

PROF. FRANK W. COOLEY, M.S., superintendent of the public schools of Evansville, Ind., and a member of the Indiana State board of education, was born on a farm in Green county, Wis., Nov. 21, 1857, his parents being William B. and Mary A. (Bussey) Cooley, the former a native of Vermont and the latter of Fayette county, Ind. His father, who was a first cousin to Judge Thomas M. Cooley, the celebrated legal author, died in 1875 and his mother in 1899. Professor Cooley graduated from a high school in Green county at the age of eighteen; entered Lawrence university at Appleton, Wis., and graduated with the degrees of B.S. and M.S. in 1881; was superintendent of the schools at Stevens Point, Wis., from that time until 1890; then superintendent of the Janesville, Wis., schools for three years; president of the State Teachers' association of Wisconsin for one year; took charge of the schools at Calumet, Mich., in 1893 and remained there until he came to Evansville at the beginning of the school year in 1902; was president of the Upper Peninsula Teachers' association of Michigan in 1900, and vice-president of the National Education Department of Superintendents during the years 1901-02. While at Calumet he supervised the erection and equipment of a manual training school and since coming to Evansville he has introduced manual training in the public schools of that city. Although something of an innovation in that city it was a success from the start and has added to the already well established reputation of Professor Cooley as an educator. He has introduced other important changes in the city's school system, among which are departmental teaching in certain grades and the exemption from quarterly examinations of those pupils who show good deportment, good work and regular attendance, which has improved the attendance and character of the recitations. He has been twice re-elected since coming to the city and one of the Evansville papers said recently of his work: "Evansville schools seem to be taking on new life, and to be moving forward in accordance with the new industrial life which has taken possession of the city. The outlook is encouraging." During the twenty-three years of Professor Cooley's experience as a superintendent he has been employed in but fou. different cities—a reputation of which any man might justly feel proud. In Evansville he has about two hundred and fifty teachers under his supervision, yet his ability as an organizer is such that all work in harmony, without jealousy, friction, or any of those bickerings that so often mar the relations and destroy the effectiveness of organized bodies of workers in a common cause. The Evansville schools are well provided with buildings, etc., the office building having recently been erected at a cost of ten thousand dollars. By virtue of his office Professor Cooley is a member of the State board of education, so that his influence as an educator is felt beyond the confines of the city where he is regularly employed. He is also a member of the Indiana State Teachers' association, is a Royal Arch Mason and Knight Templar, and a Knight of Pythias. He was married at Stevens Point, Wis., Nov. 27, 1881, to Adelaide Rugg, a native of Green county of that state, and they have the following children: Beaumont B., aged nineteen; Russell R., aged fourteen; Albert F., aged eleven; and Will B., aged nine.

JULIUS A. ESSLINGER, of Evansville, Ind., deputy clerk of the Vanderburg circuit court, was born in that city, March 31, 1865, and is a son of Capt. Isidor Esslinger, a sketch of whom appears elsewhere in this work. Julius attended both the German and English schools of his native city and can read, speak and write both the English and German languages with fluency. After completing the course in the city schools he graduated from the Evansville commercial college at the age of seventeen years and for thirteen years, prior to 1896, he was employed as bookkeeper at the Evansville union stock yards, where he discharged his duties with signal ability and fidelity. Ever since attaining his majority he has taken an interest in political affairs as a Republican and in 1896 he was appointed deputy clerk of the circuit court. He assumed the position on the first day of September of that year and for the past eight years has been a familiar figure in the office, where he is recognized by officials and the general public as one of the most efficient deputies in the Vanderburg county court house. Mr. Esslinger is a member of the Knights of Pythias, the Fraternal Order of Eagles and the Benevolent and Protective Order of Elks, in all of which he is a popular fellow and a welcome attendant at the lodge meetings.

THE OLD STATE NATIONAL BANK, of Evansville, Ind., which commenced business under its present name on Dec. 23, 1904, is the successor of the Old National bank, one of the oldest and best known financial institutions in the state. It began business in 1834 when a charter was granted to the State Bank of Indiana. For the first three years the bank was located at the corner of Main and Water streets, but in 1837 it was removed to the site now occupied by the present bank. The State Bank of Indiana was succeeded in 1855 by the branch of the Bank of the State of Indiana, and the business was conducted under this name until 1865, when it was reorganized as the Evansville National bank, under the national banking act, and chartered for twenty years. Upon the expiration of the charter the bank was again reorganized and rechartered as the Old National bank, which occupied the same quarters at Nos. 20-22 Main street. The Old National had a capital and surplus of $700,000, and the new bank started off with a capital of $500,000 and a surplus of $100,000. For many years the bank has been recognized as one of the substantial concerns of the city of Evansville, and as the new institution is in the hands of the same men who made the old bank a success, it is safe to predict for it the same prosperity and conservatism that marked the career of its predecessor. The officers of the new bank are R. K. Dunkerson, president; Henry Reis, vice-president and cashier; the directors are, in addition to the two officers above named, Alexander Gilchrist, Allen Gray, Henry Wimberg, Sidney L. Ichenhauser, James L. Orr, William H. McCurdy, William M. Akin and Marcus S. Sonntag.

GEORGE A. CUNNINGHAM, a successful lawyer of Evansville, Ind., was born on a farm in a log house, just south of Enon church in Gibson county in that state, April 4, 1855. His parents, Joseph and Mary J. (Arbuthnot) Cunningham, moved a few years later to what afterwards became and still is known as the Cunningham residence, just south of King's Station on the Evansville & Terre Haute railroad, where the subject of this sketch lived until he was grown. His early life was spent on the farm, attending school alternately at the old Gourley and Ayers school houses, where he acquired the rudiments of his education. Later he attended the graded school at Fort Branch a number of terms, walking during one term a distance of about four and a half miles morning and evening. After teaching school one year he entered the Sophomore class (classical) at Asbury (now DePauw) university, where he spent one year, completing the Sophomore year in addition to "doubling" in one or two studies. Being unable to continue his college course he resumed teaching, which he followed until he came to Evansville. In the spring of 1876 he taught at Lynnville in Warrick county and in the fall of that year was made principal of the public schools at Haubstadt, on the conclusion of which in the spring of 1877 he removed to Evansville and began regularly the study of law in the office of the Hon. Thomas E. Garvin, one of the Nestors of the profession. Mr. Cunningham was admitted to the bar in 1878 and continued his association with Mr. Garvin for many years, Mr. Thos. E. Garvin, Jr., now deceased, being afterward admitted to membership in the firm. For a considerable number of years Mr. Cunningham has been alone in the practice and has perhaps as large and valuable a clientage as any lawyer in Southern Indiana. He is a member of the American and Indiana Bar associations and has a deservedly high standing as a lawyer, not only at home but throughout the state. For many years he was the regular attorney, as well as more recently a director, in the First National bank, and on the expiration of its charter in 1902 was one of the organizers, and is now attorney for, as well as director in the City National bank, generally considered to be Evansville's strongest financial institution. In fraternal circles Mr. Cunningham is a familiar figure not only in Evansville but throughout the state. In college he was a member of the Phi Kappa Psi fraternity and still maintains a close affiliation with the members of that order. He is also one of the older members of the Knights of Pythias, a member of the Benevolent and Protective Order of Elks and a Mason, having recently taken the degrees of Knight Templar and Knight of Malta. Notwithstanding his extensive business Mr. Cunningham has found time to mingle actively in politics and for twenty-five years has been an active party worker in the Republican party, believing that all good citizens should, instead of criticizing, take part in and help to elevate politics. For a number of years, in fact practically the entire period Mr. Hemenway has been in congress, Mr. Cunningham has been a member of the state committee from the first district and is now vice-chairman of the committee. In 1904 he was placed on the ticket as one of the two electors at large from Indiana, and received over five thousand more votes than any other elector, due largely to the fact that his name was first on the ticket. He has never been charged with being an office seeker, but on the contrary has declined on one or two occasions to be a candidate when the opportunity for success seemed favorable. He is at this time a candidate for the nomination for Congress to succeed the Honorable James A. Hemenway, recently elected United States senator for Indiana, and has a large following of friends and admirers who will push his candidacy with great vigor. Mr. Cunningham was married on Nov. 10, 1881, to Miss

Susan Shaw Garvin, daughter of his former law preceptor and partner. She died July 24, 1904, leaving three children: Mrs. Ralph A. Lemcke of Indianapolis, Marie G. and George A. Cunningham, Jr., who live with their father in Evansville.

COL. JOHN RHEINLANDER, secretary and treasurer of the People's Savings bank, Evansville, Ind., is a native of Germany, having been born at Heiligenstadt, Prussian Saxony, April 26, 1828. In 1844 he came with his parents, Godfried Rheinlander and wife, to America. The family lived for about a year in Cincinnati and then came to Evansville. In the spring of 1846 the son, who was at that time living in Covington, Ky., enlisted in the Second Kentucky regiment for service in the Mexican war. He fought with General Taylor at Monterey, where he was severely wounded in the left leg, and was afterward at Buena Vista. After a year's service in Mexico he was discharged and joined his family in Evansville, where he engaged in the manufacture of cigars. In a few years he built up a good business and at the beginning of the Civil war he had a large patronage as a wholesale manufacturer. But the military instinct was too strong in Colonel Rheinlander to permit him to pursue a peaceful vocation when a war was in progress. He therefore left his factory and raised a company, of which he was commissioned captain, and which was mustered into the service as Company B, Twenty-fifth Indiana infantry. On the first day's fight at Fort Donelson he and Captain Saltzman were sent forward as skirmishers, where they protected the main body of the regiment from the Confederate rifle pits and silenced some of the enemy's artillery that was brought to bear on the flank. On the third day Captain Rheinlander's company was the first to scale the walls of the fort, but having no flag the Second Iowa was the first organization to hoist its banner over the fallen stronghold. At Shiloh his company was constantly on the skirmish line and afforded some five or six hundred of General Prentiss' men an opportunity to escape. He fought at Corinth, where he won the rank of major, and was soon afterward promoted to lieutenant-colonel. At Hatchie River he was shot in the right knee, which for a time prevented him from participating in the active service of his command. Upon his recovery he took part in the Atlanta campaign until his disabilities became so great that he could not mount his horse, when he resigned, his resignation being accepted Aug. 18, 1864. He returned to Evansville, resumed the cigar manufacturing business, and during the years 1866-67 served as treasurer of Vanderburg county. He was one of the active organizers of the People's Savings bank, and has been one of the directors almost from the beginning. The bank was organized under a state law and opened its doors for business on Thursday morning, May 5, 1870. At that time the officers were J. M. Shackelford, president; John D. Roach, secretary and treasurer. The trustees were J. M. Shackelford, Eccles G. Van Riper, Dr. M. Muhlhausen, John Laval, James Steele, Fred Lunkenheimer, Christian Hedderich and James W. Lauer. The bank is one of five organized under the same act, the other four being located at Lafayette, La Porte, South Bend and Terre Haute. Of these five banks the People's is the second largest in the amount of business transacted, the one at South Bend leading by about $100,000. The first day's deposits in the People's bank amounted to three dollars, two dollars of which was deposited by one man and one by another. From that modest beginning it has grown until on June 30, 1904, the deposits amounted to $2,605,132.80, the number of depositors reaching eight thousand, and the increase in deposits in the preceding two years amounting to $500,000. Since the beginning accounts have been opened with 32,371 different depositors from various parts of the country, and the bank has paid in dividends a total of $953,668.79. The last dividend of four per cent was declared June 30, 1904. The assets of the bank amount to $2,866,145.92, and it has a surplus of $250,000. From $300,000 to $400,000 is kept constantly on hand to satisfy the ordinary demands of banking business, and the affairs of the institution have always been conducted in a conservative manner, with a view to thoroughly safeguard the interests of the depositors. During three periods of financial depression the bank has stood like the Rock of Gibraltar, and the result has been a large increase in its volume of business, because of the confidence established in its management in times when other financial institutions were in distress. The present organization of the bank is as follows: Dr. M. Muhlhausen, president; Col. John Rheinlander, secretary and treasurer; Frank Schwegman, cashier; Henry V. Bennighof and James T. Walker, vice-presidents. The directors, together with their period of service, are as follows: Dr. M. Muhlhausen, from the beginning; Col. John Rheinlander, from 1870; H. V. Bennighof, from 1871; James T. Walker, from 1893; Frank Schwegman, from March, 1899; Dr. Edwin Walker, from May, 1899; Charles F. Hartmetz, from December, 1901. Dr. Muhlhausen has been president since May 31, 1884, and Colonel Rheinlander has occupied his present position since May 14, 1888. Colonel Rheinlander is a member of the Free and Accepted Masons and the Ancient Order of United Workmen. He has been married three times. In 1849 he was married to Miss Maria Darling, and to this union were born four children: Eva, Alice, Florence and John W. The mother of these children died in 1862 and three years later Miss Margaret Barg, of Cincinnati, became the wife of Colonel Rheinlander. To this marriage was born one son, Alexander. The second wife died in 1872 and some years later he was married to Miss Christine Hedderich, by whom he has two children. One son, Albert, is an assistant in the bank.

ALFRED BUTSCH, junior member of the law firm of Posey & Butsch, Evansville, Ind., is one of the best known and most promising of the younger attorneys of that city. He was born there, April 3, 1874, of German parentage, his father, Philip Butsch, being a prominent Evansville contractor and builder. Mr. Butsch learned to speak the German tongue from his parents, afterward learning to read and write the language in school. He also attended the English schools, graduating from Evansville high school when he was eighteen years of age. Upon leaving school he became associated with his father in the building business and in time became a first class carpenter. After six years in this business he decided to study law and in 1894 he entered the office of Posey & Chappell, one of the leading law firms of the city, where he prosecuted his studies until 1898, when he was admitted to the bar. He at once began practice in the office where he had been a student. In September, 1901, Mr. Chappell retired from the firm and Mr. Butsch took his place, the firm name being changed to Posey & Butsch. The partnership thus formed still continues and is one of the strongest law firms in Southern Indiana, where Colonel Posey has been a prominent figure in legal circles for years. Their practice extends to all the State and Federal courts and they have a large and growing clientage. Besides his law business Mr. Butsch is interested in a number of other enterprises, particularly mining property in the vicinity of Evansville. Mr. Butsch is also the foremost of building block manufacturers in this city, having been the first to introduce and manufacture cement building blocks in this locality, and is now doing a large and prosperous business in that line. He is a member of the Evansville Bar association, and one of the active Republicans of Vanderburg county. On Oct. 10, 1901, Mr. Butsch led to the altar Miss Emma Stoermer, of Evansville, and to this union there have been born two sons, Alfred, Jr., and one who at this writing is unnamed.

DR. CHARLES E. PITTMAN, a leading dentist of Evansville, Ind., and president of the Business Men's Association, was born in Posey county, Ind., Feb. 17, 1854, his parents being Robert E. and Parthenia Ann (Ross) Pittman. Dr. Pittman's father, who was an expert machinist, met with an accidental death in 1857, and soon after the close of the Civil war the widowed mother came to Evansville, where she passed the remainder of her life, entering her final rest on July 14, 1898. Charles E. Pittman grew to manhood in Evansville, where he attended the public schools until he was nineteen years of age, after which he was employed for several years as a clerk in a shoe store and subsequently in a clothing house. In 1876 he took up the study of dentistry under the late Dr. Isaiah Haas, of Evansville, with whom he pursued his studies for three years. Dr. Pittman immediately began the practice of dentistry in Evansville, where he has continued for a quarter of a century, and it is perhaps no disparagement to the other dentists to say that he is the leader of the profession in that city. He is a member and ex-president of the State Dental association and was for two years a member of the State board of dental examiners. His skill as a dental operator is known from one end of the state to the other. He is a prominent member of the Knights of Pythias and is the first professional man to be honored by an election to the presidency of the Evansville Business Men's Association, to which he was elected in June, 1904. Dr. Pittman was married on Nov. 16, 1881, to Miss Anna Knowles of Clinton, Ind., who is popular in the social life of Evansville.

BENJAMIN BOSSE, secretary and treasurer and general manager of the Globe Furniture Company, of Evansville, Ind., was born on a farm in Scott township, Vanderburg county, Nov. 1, 1874. His parents, Henry and Caroline (Schlensker) Bosse, were both natives of Germany. Henry Bosse became in subsequent years one of the leading farmers of Scott township, and was also prominent in local political affairs. He is now deceased, and his widow resides in the city of Evansville. They had twelve children, viz.: William, Louisa, Mary, Frederick, John, Henry, Louis, Benjamin, George, Ella, August and Amelia. Eight of the children are still living; Louisa, Mary, Frederick and August being dead. Benjamin lived on his father's farm until he was fourteen years of age, attending the parochial schools during the winter seasons, where he obtained his primary education. When he was fourteen he came to Evansville and found employment in a grocery business at ten dollars a month and his board. Here he worked for some time, saving his money until he had enough to enable him to take a course in the business college, from which he graduated at the age of seventeen. He then was employed for two years with a wholesale grocery house and at the age of nineteen embarked in the retail grocery business for himself. After six years in this business he sold out to become one of the organizers of the Globe Furniture Company, of which he was elected secretary and treasurer. That was in 1899, in which capacity he has continued to serve up to the present time. Besides the interest in this company, Mr. Bosse is vice-president and treasurer of the Evansville Cooperage Company, which was organized in 1903; director in the Karges Wagon Company, which he helped organize in the same year; a director in the Evansville Hoop and Stave Company; president of the Bosse Furniture Company and is stockholder in several other manufacturing enterprises. He is the president of the West Side bank. This bank commenced business Jan. 1,

1903, and Mr. Bosse has been president of it ever since its organization. He has won the confidence of the business men and especially of the furniture manufacturing industry; having served for the past four years as president of their association, and previously as secretary and treasurer. He is also a member of the Evansville Business Men's association, the Evansville Manufacturers' association, and vice-president of the Traffic bureau of this city. Mr. Bosse is one the active members of the German Evangelical Lutheran church. On Sept. 2, 1896, he was united in marriage to Miss Anna Riechmann, daughter of the late Frederick Riechmann.

HON. FREDERICK WASHINGTON COOK, president of the F. W. Cook Brewing Company, of Evansville, Ind., and a prominent citizen of that city, was born at Washington, D. C., Feb. 1, 1832. His parents shortly afterward removed to Port Deposit, Md., then to Cincinnati, and in 1836 located at Evansville. There Mr. Cook received his education, afterward attending the Anderson collegiate institute at New Albany. About a year after the family came to Evansville Mr. Cook's stepfather, Jacob Rice, in connection with Fred Kroener, bought a site in Lamasco, near the terminus of the Wabash & Erie canal, and erected the "Old Brewery"—the first in Southern Indiana. Mr. Cook began his business career as a clerk in the dry goods store of L. W. Heberd, on Main street, but after being there two years his brother died, he was taken home by his parents and soon afterward started in to learn the brewing business. In 1853 he, in conjunction with Louis Rice, a brother of his stepfather, built the "City Brewery" on the site occupied by the F. W. Cook Brewing Company at the present time, though the place was then a cornfield. Their capital consisted of $330.00. Mr. Rice took charge of the brewing department, while Mr. Cook looked after the business management. Four years later Mr. Rice sold his interest to his brother Jacob for $3,500 and a new beer cellar was at once put in, the company soon afterward beginning the manufacture of lager beer. An extensive malt house was also added to the plant. Jacob Rice died on May 3, 1872, as the result of an accident some weeks before, and the mother of Mr. Cook died on Nov. 6, 1878, when he became sole heir to the property. The business was continued under the old name of Cook & Rice until 1885, when it was incorporated under the laws of Indiana, as the F. W. Cook Brewing Company, with F. W. Cook as president. On Dec. 3, 1891, the brew house and offices were destroyed by fire, but were immediately rebuilt and in March, 1893, the company boasted of one of the most complete brew houses in the United States. The brewery now has a capacity of 300,000 barrels annually and is known all over the country as one of the first class breweries of the United States. Mr. Cook has been for years a prominent member of the National Brewers' association, which is said to be the wealthiest co-operative body in the world. While Mr. Cook has been identified with the growth of the brewing business in Evansville he has also been closely connected with several other great enterprises, such as the Evansville, Newburg & Rockport railway, of which he is president; the F. W. Cook Investment Company, which owns as part of its property Cook's Park, one of the finest resorts about Evansville. He is president of this company, is a director in the Citizens National bank, the Ohio Valley Trust Company, the Evansville Trust and Savings Company, as well as other important corporations. Besides his large and growing business interests Mr. Cook has found time to devote to the public welfare. In April, 1856, he was elected councilman for the Fifth ward and in 1863 was elected to represent the Eighth ward, from which he was re-elected the succeeding year, but resigned to accept a seat in the Indiana legislature, to which he had been elected in the fall of 1864. In both the municipal and state legislatures he evinced a grasp of public questions that fully demonstrated the wisdom of his selection. He afterward represented the Fourth ward in the city council. Mr. Cook is the architect of his own fortune. Yet as he built up his own fortune he has not been unmindful of others, and has been a potent factor in the upbuilding of the city's most praiseworthy institutions. His pleasant face and sympathetic nature are known all over the city where he has passed nearly his entire life of more than threescore and ten years, and where thousands of people have benefited by his public spirit, charity and benevolence. Mr. Cook was married in 1856 to Miss Louise Hild, of Louisville, Ky. She died in February, 1877, and in November, 1879, he was united in marriage to Miss Jennie Himeline, of Kelley's Island, Ohio, who died in January, 1885.

ALBERT F. KARGES, who has for several years been prominently identified with the furniture manufacturing interests of Evansville, Ind., was born on a farm in German township, Vanderburg county, ten miles from that city, Nov. 3, 1861. His parents, Ferdinand and Rosa Karges, were both natives of Germany, who came in early life to the United States and were married in Vanderburg county. Ferdinand Karges was a cabinet maker, and when Albert was about two years of age, he went to Evansville, where he embarked in the manufacture of furniture, first as a member of the firm of Miller & Karges, and later as a member of the Evansville furniture company, which was organized in 1869. This corporation was the pioneer furniture manufacturing concern of Evansville. Some years later he sold his interest in the business and spent his closing years on a farm. He died at the age of fifty-six, his wife having died some years before at the age of thirty-two. Albert F. Karges was educated in the public schools and at the Evansville commercial college, from which he graduated at the age of seventeen years. For the next six years he was bookkeeper for the wholesale notion house of William Hughes. Then for a few months he was engaged in the lumber business, and in February, 1886, he formed a partnership with Henry Stoltz, under the firm name of Stoltz & Karges, for the manufacture of furniture. He continued in this connection for three years, when he bought out Mr. Stoltz's interest and incorporated the concern as the Karges Furniture Company, with Frederick Bockstege as president, and Mr. Karges as secretary and treasurer. Since that time the company has had a very successful career, and is today probably the largest furniture manufacturing establishment in the city, its specialty being high grade bed room suites. Mr. Karges was one of the organizers of the Globe Furniture Company, of which he is president. He is also president of the Karges Wagon Company; vice-president and director of the Evansville Mirror and Beveling Company, and a director in the Bockstege Furniture Company, the Jourdan & Loesch Furniture Company, the Evansville Metallic Bed Company, the Ohio Valley Seed Company, the Bosse Furniture Company and the City National bank. In numerous ways Mr. Karges deserves to be classed with the most progressive men of the city.

He is a member of the Business Men's association, a director in the Young Men's Christian association, and an elder in the Cumberland Presbyterian church. On Dec. 8, 1885, he was united in marriage to Miss Elizabeth Hauck, of Evansville, and to this union there have been born four children, three of whom are living. They are Albert F., Jr., Edwin F., and Esther C. One son, Arthur W., died in the fifth year of his age.

JOHN JOURDAN, secretary and treasurer of the Bockstege Furniture Company, of Evansville, Ind., was born in that city, Sept. 27, 1858, and is the eldest son of John and Eva (Heilman) Jourdan. The father was born and reared in France and upon coming to America settled first at New Orleans, but later made his way to Evansville, where he is still living at the age of seventy-five years. The mother, who is also still living, aged sixty-eight, is a native of Germany, and a member of the well known Heilman family of Evansville. They had a family of six children, two sons and four daughters, all of whom are yet living. John Jourdan was educated in the parochial schools of Evansville, in which he studied German and Latin. He mastered the English language by self-study, his only text book being the dictionary. Later he attended the Evansville Commercial college for one term. At the age of twelve years he began his business career as a cash boy in the dry-goods and notion house of Foster Bros. After a short season with this firm he went to a wholesale millinery store as errand boy, and remained with that concern for twenty-two years, rising by successive promotions to the position of head salesman, which he ably filled for several years before severing his connection with the house. In 1895 he engaged in the retail furniture business as the senior partner in the Jourdan & Loesch Furniture Company, which company still exists. In 1900 he was one of the incorporators of the Bockstege Furniture Company, and has been its secretary and treasurer ever since the organization. This company makes a specialty of fine oak and mahogany tables, and is one of the leading industries of the city. Mr. Jourdan is also a director in the Karges Furniture Company, and has interests in one of Evansville's leading banking institutions. He is a member of the

Business Men's association and one of the trustees of the First Avenue Presbyterian church. On Sept. 27, 1882, Mr. Jourdan was married to Miss Carrie J. Thuman of Evansville, and to this union there have been born nine children, four sons and five daughters, viz.: Elsie, Eva, Sophia, Ruby, John, Jr., Florence, Arthur, Ralph and Russell.

EDWARD BOETTICHER, president of the Boetticher-Kellogg Company, of Evansville, Ind., wholesale dealers in hardware, was born on a farm in Monroe county, O., Jan. 7, 1837. When he was about nine years of age the family removed to Cincinnati, where he grew to manhood and received his education. At the age of fifteen years he entered the well known hardware house of Tyler, Davidson & Co., where he served a five years' apprenticeship, at the end of which time he had acquired some knowledge of the wholesale hardware business. In 1857 he came to Evansville, which city has ever since been his home. He took a position in the wholesale hardware concern of Charles S. Wells, where he remained until the death of Mr. Wells in 1863. The following year the firm of Wells, Kellogg & Co. succeeded to the business and Mr. Boetticher acquired an interest in the new firm. Three years later his interest had grown to such proportions that the name of the house was changed to that of Boetticher, Kellogg & Co. The business was continued under this name until 1897, when it was incorporated as the Boetticher-Kellogg Company, with a capital stock of $100,000, all of which is held by the Boetticher and Kellogg families. Mr. Boetticher was made president when the house was incorporated and has held the position ever since. The death of Charles H. Kellogg occurred on Dec. 8, 1903, which ended their association as fellow clerks and partners that had existed for forty-five years, and his son, O. H. Kellogg, succeeded to the position of secretary and treasurer. Three sons of Edward Boetticher, viz.: William H., Oscar and Carl F., are connected with the company and hold responsible positions in its management. The house is the largest wholesale hardware concern in the city of Evansville, and the third largest in the state. It is a member of the National Hardware Association of America. Mr. Boetticher is connected with several other important enterprises in the city, being vice-president of the Evansville Trust and Savings Company, and a director of the Central Trust and Savings Company. He is a Republican in politics, but has never been an aspirant for office, though he has served as a member of the city council and is now president of the board of sinking fund commissioners of Evansville. He is a member of the Masonic fraternity and of St. John's German Evangelical church. He was married Nov. 27, 1859, to Miss Amelia S. Beste of Cincinnati, and they have three sons, already mentioned.

MAJ. ALBERT C. ROSENCRANZ, president of the Vulcan Plow Company, of Evansville, Ind., was born in Baerwalde, near the city of Berlin, Prussia, Oct. 26, 1842. His father, C. F. Rosencranz, was a watchmaker by trade and a man of some prominence in the affairs of his native village. In the revolution of 1848 he took up arms against the king and was compelled to leave the country. Accordingly in 1850 he came with his family to America, settling first near Evansville, and a year later removing to the city, where he resumed work at his trade. In 1867 he returned to Europe and died there twenty years later, his wife, whose maiden name was Dorothea Nohse, having died in 1884. Albert Rosencranz received his education in private schools, devoting part of the time while attending school to learning the watchmaker's trade under his father's instructions. When the Civil war commenced he left the shop of his father, where he was employed, assisted in organizing Company A, First regiment, Indiana Legion, and was made orderly sergeant. In July, 1862, he recruited Company F, Fourth Indiana cavalry, and was commissioned first lieutenant. His first service in the field was as body guard to Gen. Ebenezer Dumont, after which he was in a number of battles, among them being the engagement at Chickamauga. He was promoted to captain in 1863, and in March, 1864, his regiment was ordered to join Sherman for the march to the sea. Near Buzzard Roost, while making a reconnaissance, he was slightly wounded and captured. He was kept a prisoner at Macon and Savannah, Ga., Charleston and Columbia, S. C., and Charlotte, N. C., until March 1, 1865, when he was paroled, and on May 3, following, was exchanged. Soon after his release from prison he was made major, his commission dating from May 1, 1865. As soon as he was exchanged he rejoined his regiment and was mustered out on June 29. Upon his return home he succeeded his father in business, in which line he continued until 1868. In that year he married Miss Mary, daughter of William Heilman, and soon after his marriage accepted a responsible position in the office of the Heilman Machine Works. Confinement to office work impaired his health and in 1873 he went to Missouri, where he engaged in stock raising. He was successful in this business until 1876, when the death of his two children led him to sell out his interests there and return to Evansville. On the first of the following January he took charge of the Heilman-Urie Plow Company, and when Mr. Urie retired in 1878 Maj. Rosencranz assumed the entire management of the concern. By his executive ability he has since that time quadrupled the capacity of the works to meet the constantly growing demand, and has added the manufacture of chilled plows to their steel goods. Upon the death of Mr. Heilman in 1890 the works were incorporated under the name of the Heilman Plow Company, with Major Rosencranz as president. This office he has continually held since that time, though the name of the concern was changed to the Vulcan Plow Company in 1898. In addition to his large business interests in the plow company he is a member of the board of trustees of Oak Hill cemetery, and for several years has been president of the board. He is also a member and ex-president of the Business Men's association, and a member and director of the Manufacturers' association. In the spring of 1887, when the question of settling the city debt was before the people for consideration, he was one of a committee appointed by the city council to consider the subject. In that capacity he demonstrated his ability for handling important public questions, and in April was elected to the city council from the Fifth ward. Upon the organization of the council he was made chairman of the finance committee and the satisfactory adjustment of the debt is due in a large degree to his valuable services. He also served as chairman of the water-works committee. Major Rosencranz was one of the largest contributors to the erection of the Young Men's Christian association building in 1890. He acted as treasurer of the building committee, and has since been treasurer of the board of trustees. He is a prominent member and officer in the Trinity Methodist Episcopal church; is a member of the Indiana Commandery of the Loyal Legion; Farragut Post, No. 27, Grand Army of the Republic; La

Vallette Commandery, Knights Templars, and wields a potent influence in all these organizations for their healthy advancement. Politically he is a Republican. He has three living children: Olive, a graduate of Wellesley college; Richard, a graduate of Cornell university; and Gertrude, now a student at Irvington, N. Y.

HARRY H. OGDEN, cashier of the West Side bank, Evansville, Ind., was born at Slaughterville, Webster county, Ky., Nov. 9, 1876, his parents being William C. and Margaret (Kuykendall) Ogden. The father was a merchant in Slaughterville, and died when Harry was about six years of age. The mother is still living at Slaughterville. Harry H. Ogden was educated in his native town. At an early age he learned the art of telegraphy and was for twelve years in the employ of the Louisville & Nashville Railroad Company at different points in the State of Kentucky. In 1899 he left the railroad and went to Davis, in the Indian Territory, where for about two years he was assistant cashier in a private bank, known as the Bank of Davis. In the fall of 1900 he returned to Kentucky and organized the Webster County bank at Clay. He was elected cashier of the bank and held the position until in 1902, when he came to Evansville and organized the West Side bank, of which he was made cashier. The officers of the bank at the present time are: Benjamin Bosse, president; George W. Warner, vice-president; Harry H. Ogden, cashier; H. F. Riechmann, assistant cashier. The board of directors consists of August Rosenberger, Jacob Fischer, Jacob Folz, Jr., Benjamin Bosse, Thomas Macer, Leon Curry, Frank Lohoff, G. W. Warner and H. H. Ogden. The West Side bank has been prosperous from the start, much of its success being due to the energy and tact of Mr. Ogden. It fills a much needed want for the citizens in what is known as the West side, a district with a population of about 15,000 people. In 1904 Mr. Ogden organized a bank at Haubstadt, a thriving little town in the edge of Gibson county, a few miles north of Evansville. He still holds an interest in this bank, though he has no official connection with it. He also still retains his interest in the Webster County bank. Few men at the age of twenty-eight years can claim the distinction of having organized three banks, all of which have been successful, yet such is the record of Mr. Ogden. He is a born financier and has a keen instinct, amounting at times almost to an inspiration, for discovering the financial needs of a particular locality. He is a member of the Masonic fraternity, the Benevolent and Protective Order of Elks, the Methodist Episcopal church, and the Evansville Business Men's association. The West Side bank belongs to the Indiana State and the American Bankers' associations. On Sept. 2, 1896, he was married to Miss Lissette McClusky of Florence, Ala., and they have one daughter, Jerrie Virginia, aged six years.

JOHN C. ZUTT, secretary and treasurer of the Evansville Mirror and Beveling Company, Evansville, Ind., was born in the city of Louisville, Ky., March 25, 1866. His parents, Daniel and Louise (Geis) Zutt, were both natives of Germany. The father came to the United States in 1851 and the mother in 1859, and they were married at Louisville on March 5, 1863. For many years Daniel Zutt followed the trade of butcher in Louisville, and died there in 1898, leaving two sons, Daniel and John C., who with the mother are still living. Daniel is a druggist in Louisville. John C. Zutt received his education in the Louisville schools, and before reaching his majority began his business career as a bookkeeper in the Falls City bank, where he remained for eleven years, or until the bank went into liquidation. In 1895 he came to Evansville and organized the Evansville Mirror and Beveling Company, with John Weber as president and himself as secretary and treasurer. This introduced a new industry into the city of Evansville, and it has come to be recognized as one of the substantial manufacturing concerns of that busy place, its success being largely due to the enterprise and business sagacity of Mr. Zutt. Besides his interest in this company Mr. Zutt is also connected with several other manufacturing concerns and holds stock in some of the leading banking institutions. He is a member of the Business Men's and Manufacturers' associations of Evansville, and is identified with every movement having for its object the advancement of the city's commercial standing. He was married on June 16, 1897, to Miss Elise Hartmetz of Evansville, and two sons have come to bless the union, viz: John Hartmetz, aged six years, and Daniel J., aged four.

SAMUEL G. EVANS, head of the well known mercantile establishment of S. G. Evans & Co., 328-330 Main street, Evansville, Ind., was born in Jackson county, W. Va., March 19, 1839, and is the son of E. S. and Ruami (Wright) Evans, the former a native of Virginia and the latter of Pennsylvania. The father, who was born at Morgantown, Va., in the year 1800, was an old time gentleman farmer. He died in his native state in 1876, and the mother died in Jackson county, W. Va., in 1882. Samuel G. Evans grew to manhood on his father's farm. After completing the course of study in the local schools he entered Washington college in Pennsylvania and graduated in 1861. For a short time after leaving college he studied law, and then came to Evansville as an employe of the Adams Express Company. In 1864 he took a position in the dry goods house of Jaquess, French & Co., with whom he remained for about two years, when he became the junior partner in the firm of Jaquess, Hudspeth & Co. In 1876, in connection with D. J. Mackey, he opened the business at 211 Main street, under the firm name of S. G. Evans & Co., which did well for four years, when, in 1880, the house of Evans & Verwayne was organized. The business of this firm increased from the beginning. In 1895 Mr. Evans acquired the interests of his partner and removed to his present location on the corner of Fourth and Main streets, where he has since conducted the business under the name of S. G. Evans & Co. Mr. Evans is practically the sole proprietor. Politically Mr. Evans is a Democrat, but is one of the kind who never makes himself offensive to his opponents, although never swerving from his settled convictions. He is a prominent member of the Masonic fraternity, being a Knight Templar, and belongs to the Business Men's Association. For years he has been one of the trustees of the Willard Library, and belongs to several societies for the advancement of science, among them being the American Association for the Advancement of Science; the Indiana Academy of Science; and the National Botanical Association. In 1867 he was married to Miss Louisa Hornbrook, who was born near Evansville in 1842, and is a descendant of one of the pioneer families.

FREDERICK BOCKSTEGE, president of the Karges Furniture Company, Evansville, Ind., was born in Germany, April 16, 1862. He learned the trade of cabinet maker in his native land, and at the age of nineteen years came to America. For several months he worked at his trade at Akron, O., and from there went to St. Louis, Mo., where he remained for about six months, at the end of which time he came to Evansville. During the first three years he was in Evansville he was employed as a cabinet maker in the furniture establishment of Joseph F. Reitz. Upon leaving Mr. Reitz he was for some time with George Mutschler in the planing mill, and when Mr. Mutschler was succeeded by Schnute, Dubber & Co. Mr. Bockstege remained about a year with the new firm. From that time until Feb. 1, 1889, he was in the employ of Stoltz & Karges. He then, in connection with A. F. Karges and John Jourdan, Jr., formed what has since become widely known as the Karges Furniture Company, of which he has been president ever since the organization. Mr. Bockstege started in life with the odds against him. When he came to America he knew no one in the country, and had no knowledge of the English language. A raw German boy, with no capital but his willingness to work and his mechanical skill, he has been almost phenomenally successful. His motto has ever been honest goods at reasonable prices, and the result is that the products of the Karges Furniture Company have found a ready sale on the market wherever they have been introduced. In 1898 Mr. Bockstege was one of the organizers of the Globe Furniture Company, of which he has been vice-president for the last three years. The following year he organized the Bockstege Furniture Company and has been president of it ever since. He is also interested in the West Side Bank, the Evansville Mirror and Beveling Company, and the West Heights Land Company. Few men in the city of Evansville occupy a higher place in the general esteem of the citizens than Mr. Bockstege. His industry and capacity for business are worthy of the highest emulation of young men, who can learn a useful lesson from his perseverance, which has been the secret of his success. Mr. Bockstege has been twice married. His first wife, to whom he was united on Oct. 30, 1884, was Miss Alwena Langele, of Evansville.

She died in 1887, leaving one child, and subsequently he was married to Miss Mena Seeger, also of Evansville. He has five sons and three daughters, viz.: Fred, Jr., Herman, Henry, John, Benjamin, Clara, Ida, and Anna. He is a member of the German Lutheran church of Evansville, and a liberal contributor to its good works.

JACOB MAYER, councilman at large, and one of the most popular caterers in the city of Evansville, Ind., was born at Rheinpfalz, Rhenish Bavaria, Jan. 8, 1850. During his boyhood he attended the schools of his native town, after which he learned the bakers' trade. Hence it can be seen that from his youth Mr. Mayer has been brought up to his business. After several years in his native town he determined to come to America and the latter part of 1868 found him in Evansville, which city has ever since been his home. The first ten years of his life in this country were spent as journeyman, working in the bakeries of Andrew Christ and Jacob Heblich. During that decade he saved his money and in 1878 started in the bakery business for himself at the corner of Second avenue and Ohio street. The genial German soon became popular with his customers and his business prospered in consequence. A few doors from his bakery he established a plant for making carbonated or mineral waters, which he operated for some time in connection with his bakery. Then he established the café and saloon at 317 Upper Second street, which soon came to demand so much of his time that he disposed of his other interests and devoted his whole attention to the café. While managing this popular resort Mr. Mayer formed acquaintances all over the city, and in 1897 he was induced to become a candidate for councilman at large on the Republican ticket. His service in the council added to his popularity and in 1901 he was re-elected for another term of four years, receiving the largest majority of any man on the Republican ticket. Mr. Mayer is one of the substantial citizens of Evansville and is the owner of considerable property. He is a member of the Masonic fraternity, the Ancient Order of United Workmen and the Benevolent and Protective Order of Elks, as well as some other fraternal organizations. Some years ago he was married to Elizabeth Schmidt of Evansville, and they have two children: Oscar and Carrie. The son is associated with his father in business, and Carrie lives at home with her parents.

WILLIAM HEYNS, president of the Heyns Furniture Company, of Evansville, Ind., was born in Germany in the year 1848, his parents being Louis and Mary (Page) Heyns. In 1866 the family came to America and located at Evansville. William began life as a cabinet maker and after coming to Evansville he found employment with the old firm of Bloomer & Honig, on Water street. Subsequently he was with Miller & Karges, now known as the Evansville Furniture Company, for about eighteen months, after which he went to St. Louis, where he was for two years with Aude Brothers. He then returned to Evansville and opened a retail grocery at the corner of Michigan street and Third avenue. Two years later he disposed of this business to accept a position as traveling salesman for the firm of Bloomer, Schulte & Reitman, selling furniture through the South. After three years on the road he resigned his position to become owner of a hotel at St. Wendell, Ind., which he successfully conducted for five years, when he returned to Evansville and started in the retail furniture business at 226 to 230 West Franklin street. That was in 1885, and he has continued in the business, adding to his stock until today the Heyns Furniture Company occupies the entire building from 224 to 230 West Franklin, besides a branch store at No. 208 Upper Third street. In the two establishments something like 60,000 square feet of floor space is occupied, and the stock of goods displayed is by far the largest and most varied of any similar concern in the city. The business was incorporated in 1901 with Mr. Heyns as president, and his son, John W., as secretary and treasurer. William Heyns and his children own all the stock with the exception of a small portion donated to the employes of the house. The growth of the Heyns Furniture Company has been remarkable, and it is mainly due to the thorough knowledge of the demands of the trade, the untiring industry and the high order of executive ability of Mr. Heyns. Besides the retail establishment the company also manufactures a line of high grade parlor furniture and is building up an extensive trade with the merchants in the surrounding towns. He was married in June, 1875, to Miss Anna Raben, daughter of Anton Raben. She died on Jan. 28, 1891, leaving the following children: Mary, John W., Lina, Winnie and Nettie. Mary is the wife of Ray Lannert; John W. is secretary and treasurer of the furniture company; and Winnie is an artist of more than ordinary ability, her natural talent having been aided by study in the Cincinnati Art school.

MARTIN KOEPKE, of Evansville, Ind., Indiana State agent for the Mountain Valley mineral waters, was born near the city of Berlin, Germany, Nov. 12, 1849. In 1865 he came to the United States and five years later located in Evansville, which city has ever since been his home. In early life he learned the trade of a harness maker, but in 1875 gave it up and embarked in the grocery and saloon business. Upon reaching his majority he cast in his lot with the Republican party, and has been an active worker in the cause of that organization. He was two years the councilman from the Third ward, and few men ever served in the city council who were more consistent, or more earnest in behalf of their constituents. In 1894 he was appointed deputy sheriff and in 1898 received the nomination of his party for sheriff. He was elected and at the close of his first term was re-elected, making eight years in all that he was in the sheriff's office, four years as deputy and four years as principal. His second term expired in 1902 and he soon afterward secured the local agency for the Mountain Valley waters, which come from a spring in the Ozark mountains, not far from Hot Springs, Ark., and have proved a fine remedy for stomach and kidney troubles, especially Bright's disease, as well as excellent for table use. His local trade grew to generous proportions and he was made state agent for the springs. By his energy and tact he is building up a good patronage throughout the state, particularly in the country adjacent to Evansville. Mr. Koepke is a member of the Independent Order of Odd Fellows, the Knights of Honor, the Improved Order of Red Men, and the Benevolent and Protective Order of Elks. He has been married three times, his first and second wives having died, and has five living children.

HARRY N. COOK, president of the Cook Grocery Company, Evansville, Ind., was born in that city, Nov. 8, 1857, his parents being Henry A. and Caroline J. (Clark) Cook, both natives of the State of New York. The family came to Evansville in 1852, where the father was for many years the leading retail grocer of the city. In 1901 the Cook Grocery Company was incorporated, with Harry N. Cook as president and William L. Hardigg as secretary and treasurer, and the official personnel of the company remains the same to the present time. The Cook Grocery Company is a model institution of its kind. Not only is it the largest and best appointed retail grocery in the city of Evansville, but it is certain it has no superior and probably not an equal in the State of Indiana. This superb establishment stands as a monument to the fine business qualifications, the indomitable energy, and the high integrity of character of Mr. Cook. In building up the concern Mr. Cook has given his city a wide advertisement and placed his name high on the roll of progressive business men of the country. For two years he was president of the Retail Merchants' Association of the state, and during the past three years he has been president of the Retail Merchants' Association of Evansville.

MARTIN EMIG, JR., proprietor of the Manhattan saloon, Evansville, Ind., was born in Germany, July 15, 1856. His father, John Emig, was a nail smith by trade, but in his later years followed farming. He died when Martin was but four years of age. The mother died in Germany in 1903 at the age of eighty-two years. While still in his boyhood Martin came to America and landed at Evansville on July 27, 1871, one day before he was fifteen years old. He had commenced to learn the blacksmiths' trade in his native land, but being young and rather small for his age, he was unable to obtain work in that line, so he sought and obtained a position as clerk in a dry goods store. He continued in this occupation for about eight years in Evansville, and in 1879 went to Piopolis, Hamilton county, Ill., where he conducted a general store for three years. At the end of that time he returned to Evansville and engaged in the retail grocery business for about five years, when he sold out to become a traveling salesman. On New Year's day, 1889, he opened a saloon on the corner of Third and Vine streets in Evansville. In 1894 he sold his business and for some time was a partner in a cigar manufactory. He then for some time had charge of Germania Hall, on Fourth street, and in 1899 purchased the elegant Manhattan saloon at No. 501 Main street, where he has since conducted one of the finest establishments of the kind to be found anywhere. Mr. Emig is a Democrat in his political associations and is always ready to do what he can to further the interests of his party. He is a member of the Catholic church, the Catholic Knights of America, and the Knights of St. John. As captain of the local company of the Uniform Rank, Knights of St. John, he won the first prize at the competitive drill at Columbus, Ohio, in 1903, and his company has frequently been awarded smaller prizes for its proficiency. He was married on May 11, 1881, to Miss Mary Jost, of Evansville, and they have five living children: Eva Catherine, Louisa, Rosa Barbara, Ferdinand J., and Henry A., all at home. Two children, Joseph N., and Leo, are deceased, the former dying at the age of six years and the latter at the age of seven and a half.

JOHN H. HUSTON, vice-president of the Kohinoor Laundry Company, of Evansville, Ind., was born on a farm in Miami county, O., June 9, 1840, his parents being David and Susanna Huston, both of whom are now deceased. He was reared on his father's farm in Miami county, receiving his education in the common schools. In August, 1862, he enlisted as a private in Company B, Ninety-fourth Ohio infantry, and served until the close of the war, being mustered out and discharged at Columbus in August, 1865, the regiment being one of the last to return home. While in the army he took part in the Atlanta campaign and in the famous march to the sea. At the close of the war he returned to the home of his parents, who had in the meantime removed to Paris, Ill., and for four years was a clerk in a grocery store there. He was then employed for about three years in the engineering department of the Louisville & Nashville Railroad Company. In 1874 he came to Evansville, his brother, E. P. Huston, being at that time the proprietor of the St. George hotel, the leading hostelry of the city. John H. Huston assisted his brother in the management of this house until the latter was made president of the Bank of Commerce of Evansville, when he assumed the entire management of the hotel. E. P. Huston finally sold his hotel interests and the subject of this sketch retired from the house when the new proprietor took charge. For several years he has been the vice-president of the Kohinoor Laundry Company, at No. 214 Locust street, one of the best equipped laundries in the country. Mr. Huston is a Republican in politics, and while his views on political questions are no secret, he has a host of friends among those of the opposite political faith. He is a member of the Evansville Business Men's association and is always ready to do his part in furthering any scheme for the advancement of the city's material welfare. He also belongs to the Grand Army of the Republic and to the Benevolent and Protective Order of Elks.

COL. CHARLES DENBY, lawyer, author and diplomat, late of Evansville, Ind., was born in Botetourt county, Va., June 13, 1830, and died suddenly of heart trouble at Jamestown, N. Y., while on a lecturing tour, Jan. 13, 1904. He graduated from the Virginia military academy in 1850 and came to Evansville three years later, where he made his first public address in 1854. His earnest manner, and the knowledge of public questions displayed in that speech, soon brought him into prominence, and for half a century he was a part of the warp and woof of the political events of his state and the nation. When the general assembly of Indiana met, in 1855, he was elected to a clerkship, and the following year he was elected to a membership in the lower branch of the Indiana legislature. During the latter part of President Buchanan's administration he was surveyor of the local port of Evansville for about two years, and in that position made an enviable record. Before coming to Indiana he had taken up the study of law, and after his admission to the bar he forged his way rapidly upward in his profession, being one of the popular lawyers in Southwestern Indiana within a very short time, meantime becoming interested in journalism in connection with John B. Hall, the publisher of the Evansville *Daily*

Inquirer. When the first mutterings of the Civil war were heard, before actual hostilities had begun, or a call for troops had been issued, Colonel Denby manifested his loyalty by organizing a company of home guards to be ready for any emergency that might arise. In September, 1861, this company was mustered into the Federal service as part of the Forty-second Indiana infantry, with Colonel Denby as lieutenant-colonel of the regiment. He served in that capacity until Oct. 10, 1863, when he was made colonel of the Eightieth regiment. While with the Forty-second he was in several severe engagements. At the battle of Perryville, Ky., Oct. 8, 1862, he was wounded on the lip and in the leg, had his horse shot from under him, and his clothing pierced by a number of balls that fortunately did him no further harm. He remained in command of the Eightieth regiment until his surgeon recommended his retirement from the service on account of disability, when he resigned and returned to Evansville, where he resumed the practice of law. Colonel Denby now became actively identified with the Democratic party and in every campaign was much sought after as a public speaker, because of his wide information concerning public questions, his forcible logic, and his earnest and convincing oratory. In his law practice in the years succeeding the war he was for some time in partnership with Daniel B. Kumler, the partnership being dissolved by the appointment of Colonel Denby as minister to China by President Cleveland, May 29, 1885. It was in this position that Colonel Denby's name became known from one end of the civilized world to the other. Assuming the duties of the position without a knowledge of the Chinese language or the customs of the people he soon won for himself a reputation unparalleled in the history of the diplomatic corps of the United States. Within three years he had so won his way to the hearts of the people of the Celestial Empire that when President Harrison was inaugurated, and after Colonel Denby had tendered his resignation to the new administration, the Chinese and the American citizens having interests in China were united in requesting the retention of Colonel Denby. His resignation, therefore, was never accepted and he continued to serve as the Chinese minister during the entire administration of President Harrison, and when Mr. Cleveland was again elected to the presidency in 1892 he was reappointed for four years more. After the inauguration of President McKinley he was retained in the position for over a year, so that his service as minister covers a period of more than thirteen years. The relations brought about between the United States and China by his efforts are like the pebble in the stream. The widening circles will keep growing until the uttermost parts of the two countries will be benefited by the friendly spirit that grows up out of the conditions established by his superb diplomacy. After retiring from the Chinese mission Colonel Denby was not permitted to long enjoy the quietude of a private life. He was a member of the President's commission to investigate the conduct of the Spanish-American war, and was appointed by President McKinley a member of the first Philippine commission in 1899. While in China Colonel Denby made a careful study of the laws, customs, commerce, and institutions of the Chinese, upon which subjects and the Philippine question he delivered many lectures in different parts of the United States, and contributed numerous articles to the leading magazines, by which future generations may enjoy the fruits of his labor. Colonel Denby's life was one of labor, and his work was not fruitless. Aside from the personal honors he reaped the world will long profit by his learning and diplomacy. His death came swift and probably painless, which to one of his active habits was a boon, avoiding the sufferings of a long illness and the galling stings of inactivity. While in the legislature in 1855 Colonel Denby formed the acquaintance of Miss Martha Fitch, of Logansport, Ind., a daughter of Graham N. Fitch, then United States senator, and in 1858 they were united in marriage. The widow and six children survive. Graham Fitch Denby, the eldest son, is a prominent attorney of Evansville. He married Olga Reis and they have one child, Martha Reis, born Aug. 16, 1901. Charles is now in Tien Tsin, China, as the representative of a firm of American manufacturers, and is also foreign adviser to the viceroy of the province of Pechili. He married Martha Orr of Evansville, and they have three sons: James, Charles and Edwin. Harriet Ethel is the widow of Gilbert Wilkes, who was a naval officer at the time of her marriage to him. He was commander of the Michigan naval reserves during the entire Spanish-American war on board the *Yosemite*. Later he became an electrical engineer at Detroit, Mich. He left two sons, Charles Denby and Gilbert. Wythe is a mining engineer at Juneau, Alaska. He married Lucia Hayes, of Milwaukee, Wis. Edwin is an attorney at Detroit, Mich., has been a member of the Michigan legislature, and was elected to Congress in 1904 from the Detroit District. He was also one of the reserves on the *Yosemite* during the Spanish-American war. Thomas Garvin, the youngest of the family, is connected with the Detroit branch of the Solway-Process Company and married

Esther Strong of that city. Although the widow and her children mourn the loss of the husband and father they have the consolation of knowing that he lived an untarnished life, and "joined the innumerable caravan" having the full confidence and esteem of his fellow-men.

Mrs. Martha Fitch Denby, the widow of Colonel Denby, now resides in the old homestead at No. 809 Upper Second street, Evansville. She was well fitted by nature to be the helpmate of such a husband, and to all of Colonel Denby's public functions she lent grace and dignity. At once the daughter and widow of two of Indiana's distinguished sons, she lives a retired life in the old home, hallowed by its cherished recollections, beloved by all her acquaintances, and a much sought for guest at all of Evansville's most exclusive society events.

THE HERCULES BUGGY COMPANY, of Evansville, Ind., with a capital stock of $300,000, and officered by W. H. McCurdy, president; W. L. B. Hawes, vice-president; Fred M. Hills, secretary

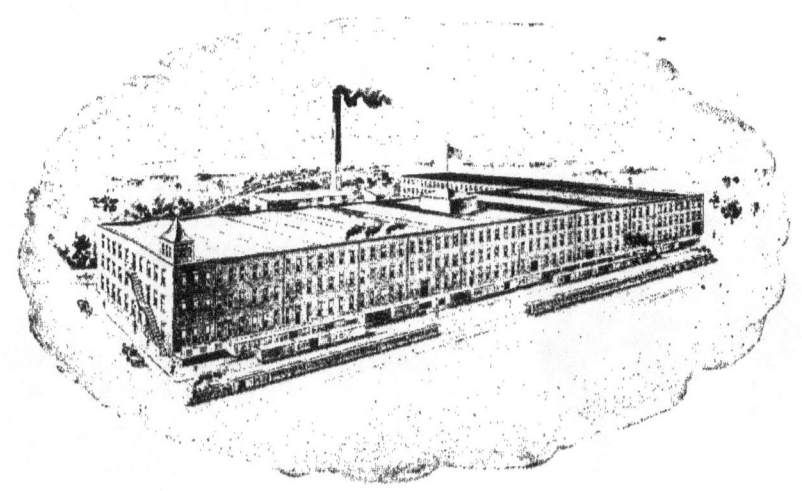

and treasurer, and John D. Craft, superintendent, was located at Evansville, in 1902, removing from Cincinnati, O. Before making this move, Mr. McCurdy and his able lieutenants made exhaustive investigations. After summing up their findings Evansville offered greater advantages as a place in which to locate a carriage factory in the way of cheap fuel, labor conditions and railroad facilities than any other point. Evansville is the only point east of the Mississippi river where the Southern, Southwestern, Western, Illinois and official classification applies, making it very advantageous in the way of rates in shipping out their finished product. The main factory of this company is 85 feet wide and 530 feet long, three stories high, built of brick. The warehouse is 114 feet wide and 130 feet long, three stories high, built of brick, making a total floor space of 180,000 feet, or nearly four acres. The factory is so located that switches from the Evansville & Terre Haute and Southern Railroad companies run on either side the full length of the factory. Every appliance in machinery, every method and every plan that works out economy in a carriage factory is already installed in this mammoth plant. The output of this company is placed in all parts of the United States, enabling them to keep the plant running the year around, as the off season in one locality means the season of heavy trade in another. The capacity of this concern is 150 jobs per day, or a complete vehicle every four minutes. Their normal output for the entire season through, however, is 35,000 jobs. It is predicted by those who ought to know best, that within three years the capacity of this company will be doubled, and it bids fair to be much the largest carriage factory in the world within a very short time.

W. H. McCURDY is of Scotch descent. He acquired a common school education, and then entered what was known in that day as an "academy for boys and girls." His early ambition was to be a mechanic. He served a short apprenticeship with a millwright, going to the top of the ladder within much less time than his associates. He continued at this trade until twenty-two years of age, then becoming tired of what he considered the "hum-drum" life of a mechanic, at so much per day, he locked his tool chest, never to be opened by him again. He quit his position, which was paying him good wages, and went forth to seek possibilities that might satisfy his ambitious desires. He filled many different positions, always leaving them of his own accord. He was very successful as a traveling salesman. It was in this capacity that he discovered his ability to take a fair measurement of men on meeting them, which has since been of great service to him during his business career. In 1879 he went West, and settled in Kansas

City, Mo. One year later he married Helen E. Hess, daughter of Mr. Alfred Hess of Cincinnati, O., and a native of New York state. Mr. McCurdy was engaged in the real estate and insurance business while in the West. In the year 1889 he again returned East with his family, and became interested in the Favorite Carriage Company of Cincinnati. He was elected secretary of this company, which position he held for five years. In 1894 he handed in his resignation, and severed his connection with this concern, organizing in the same year the Brighton Buggy Company under the laws of the State of Ohio. Mr. McCurdy's career as a manufacturer has been highly successful. Beginning with a very small capital, he has worked himself up to the position of one of the "Captains of Industry." Outgrowing his facilities in Cincinnati, where he was first located, he came to the city of Evansville in the year 1902, where he built a large brick factory, one of the most modern plants in the United States for the manufacture of vehicles. This business is now known as the Hercules Buggy Company, the name having been changed from the Brighton Buggy Company of Cincinnati. Each year, since the organization of the business in 1894, has shown a marked increase over the former year. Mr. McCurdy's skill in selecting the right kind of men, and his unquestioned executive ability, place him in the foremost ranks in the business community. The Hercules Buggy Company, of which he is president and the principal owner, has a floor space of nearly four acres, and a manufacturing capacity of 40,000 vehicles per annum. Mr. McCurdy has built a very large and commodious residence in the city of Evansville, located on Riverside avenue, where he has recently moved his family. He has also become identified with a number of enterprises in the city, including the banking interests and the street railway systems.

RAGON BROTHERS, wholesale grocers and proprietors of the Diamond Coffee and Spice Mills, Evansville, Ind., have been so long identified with that city's commercial life, and are so widely known through the Lower Ohio Valley, that their house has become one of the landmarks of Evansville. The Ragons are among the oldest families in the city. They came from Kentucky immediately after the war and established a wholesale grocery business, under the firm name of Ragon Brothers, the founders being Edward G. and Ferd H. Ragon, two of the most hard-working, energetic gentlemen who ever located in Evansville. The grocery trade of the city has always been one of the great factors in making Evansville an important commercial center, and few concerns have contributed more to this end than the firm of Ragon Brothers. For forty years, without a day's interruption, this house has gone steadily forward, increasing their own trade and widening the circle of Evansville's commercial influence. Ferd H. Ragon died some years ago, but the business went on and continued to increase under the management of his brother, Edward G., for twenty-five years, when he, too, was called to his final rest. Edward G. died Feb. 27, 1902, and his death removed from the business and social life of Evansville one of the most prominent figures, a liberal and willing contributor to the city's growth and welfare—one who will be remembered for many years to come as one of the most enterprising and public spirited of men. Since his death his son, Chester L. Ragon, has become the active head of the firm. In 1902 the business was incorporated, the present officers being Chester L. Ragon, president and treasurer; H. R. Dunavan, vice-president, and William Clarke, secretary. All these gentlemen have been connected with the business for many years, and know every demand of the trade. The policy of the firm has always been a conservative one, and under the present management its customers find no departure from its established usage. Chester L. Ragon was carefully trained to the business by his father, and upon the death of the latter took charge, conducting the business along the old lines. Even when incorporated no innovations were introduced, the old name being retained, and it is safe to predict that the house will stand for years to come, as it has stood for years in the past—the leader in the grocery trade of Evansville.

HENRY S. BENNETT, senior member of the insurance firm of Bennett, Hutchinson & Co., Evansville, Ind., was born in England, Feb. 22, 1836. In 1857 he came with his parents and the other members of the family to the United States. For several years he lived in the State of New York, but about the close of the Civil war came to Evansville, where he engaged in the insurance business, as manager of the insurance department of W. J. Lowry & Co. In 1872 he formed a partnership with Cyrus K. Drew, under the firm name of Drew & Bennett, and soon had a large insurance business. A branch office was established at Indianapolis, where a considerable volume of business was transacted. This branch office was later sold to Henry Coe. In 1882 Mr. Drew retired and was succeeded by I. H. Odell, the style of the firm becoming Bennett & Odell. In

1894 Mr. Odell was succeeded by Alexander Hutchinson, and the present firm name was adopted. Mr. Bennett has personally represented the Mutual Life Insurance Company of New York for thirty-six years, and enjoys the distinction of having written the only one hundred thousand dollar policy that was ever written in Evansville. In recent years he has given a good portion of his time to the adjustment of losses for some of the companies represented by his firm. This requires a rare tact and presence of mind, yet Mr. Bennett has fully demonstrated his ability in this line, as in all other departments of the fire insurance business. He has held the position of president of the Evansville board of fire underwriters several times during his career in the city and is undoubtedly the Nestor of fire insurance in Evansville, if not in the state. Politically Mr. Bennett is a Republican, and one of the kind who believes in not hiding his light under a bushel. For twelve years he was a member of the Evansville city council, and for twenty-five years he was chairman of the city, county or district committee, sometimes of all three at the same time. As chairman of the district committee he was a member of the State central committee, from the First Congressional district, and was a potent factor in shaping his party's policy in the State of Indiana. When he first took the political reins the First district, Vanderburg county, and the city of Evansville were all solidly Democratic. He was not daunted, however, by the conditions, but went to work to change the situation. For several years the First district has been represented by a Republican in Congress and both the city and the county are regarded as safely Republican on a straight party vote. Much of this change has been due to the intelligent, well-directed and persistent efforts of Mr. Bennett. Notwithstanding his success as a political leader he has never been a seeker for office, though he has twice been postmaster of Evansville; once to fill out an unexpired term under President Arthur, and a full four-year term under President Harrison, from 1889 to 1893. Mr. Bennett is well known in the fraternal circles of Southwestern Indiana, being a member of the Grand Army of the Republic, the Benevolent and Protective Order of Elks, and one of the charter members of Orion Lodge No. 35, Knights of Pythias, the first lodge organized in Evansville. On June 10, 1865, he was married to Miss Susan DeBruler, the adopted daughter of Dr. James DeBruler, formerly a prominent physician of Evansville, and they have four children, one son and three daughters living, and two sons dead.

MARCUS S. SONNTAG was born in Evansville, Ind., received his education in the public schools of that city and has, for the past four years, been a member of the board of education. He is regarded as one of the leading business men of the city. He is a member of the Evansville Business Men's association and, with others in this organization, has been active in bringing new industries to Evansville. He is president of the Union Investment Company, which has erected and sold more than three hundred homes in Evansville during the past ten years. This company has played a wonderful part in building up and beautifying the suburbs of the city and today is making it possible for many worthy citizens to secure their own homes. Mr. Sonntag is a director in the Old State National Bank, the largest and oldest financial institution in Southern Indiana, and has just taken a prominent part in the successful launching of the American Trust and Savings Company, a financial institution that is sure to cut a figure in the affairs of Southern Indiana. Associated with Mr. Sonntag in the organization of this new company was E. O. Hopkins, formerly occupying a high position in the railroad world and a man of large means and wide resources. Mr. Hopkins is president of the company and Mr. Sonntag vice-president. Mr. Sonntag is also a director and the secretary and treasurer of the Evansville & Eastern Electric Railway, the building of which line between Evansville and Rockport, Ind., was commenced on Sept. 6, 1904. In politics, Mr. Sonntag is a Republican and for years has taken a prominent part in the councils of his party. He stands high in the social, political and business life of the city and is a man of rare judgment, backed by an unsullied character. His opinions are often sought and generally heeded, for he is a man of conservative but tenacious disposition and usually safe to follow.

THE WILLARD LIBRARY, of Evansville, Ind., is the benefaction of Willard Carpenter, one of the most benevolent and public spirited men who ever lived in the city. He was a man of great native ability, progressive and energetic, and was deeply interested in the material prosperity and industrial development of the city where the greater portion of his long and useful life was passed.

In the public records of Evansville, in the old files of newspapers, his name is to be frequently seen, as having been associated with some of the progressive movements of his time. Men are yet living who knew him personally, and these living witnesses will corroborate the statement that he was always one of the leaders in behalf of good government and municipal progress. But, aside from his interest in the city's industrial and commercial thrift, he felt a deeper concern for the moral and intellectual advancement of his fellow-men. His contact with men in every walk of life, and his knowledge of public affairs, taught him that the highest destinies of a republic, where every man is a component part of the government, can only be realized through the liberal education of the masses. In his personal affairs he was eminently successful, accumulating a large fortune, and toward the close of his life he determined to do something for the city in which he had acquired his wealth. In his benevolence, as in all other matters, he was intensely practical. Entertaining the views he did it was but natural that his generous impulses should take the turn they did, and that he should endow a library. Had his object been the mere perpetuation of his own name; had he been actuated by the selfish motive of promulgating his own importance, his munificence might have found various channels better calculated to subserve such an end. Under date of Aug. 23, 1876, he addressed the following communication to a board of trustees selected by himself:

"Gentlemen:—I have intended for many years to devote to some public use a portion of the property and means which I have acquired by a long life of labor. I have, at various times, endeavored to benefit the community in which my life has been mostly spent, by inaugurating various enterprises. Legal difficulties, and other obstacles, have intervened to render inoperative schemes for the public good, which I have at various times undertaken to put in operation.

"After consultation with many gentlemen of this city, I have concluded without further delay to establish and endow a public library, to be located in a public park, on land owned by me, situate in the city of Evansville. I am induced to do this in the well-grounded hope that such an institution may become useful toward the improvement of the moral and intellectual culture of the inhabitants of Evansville, and collaterally to those of the State of Indiana; and also toward the enlargement and diffusion of a taste for the fine arts.

"The city of Evansville has reached in population and commercial importance a period in which such a scheme should, and I have no doubt will, meet with the hearty approval and assistance of the municipal authorities and all private citizens.

"In presenting to you the object I propose, I wish you to understand that the details proper to its organization and government and its future control and conduct are to be left to your judgment and discretion, and the perpetuity of that control I confide to you and your successor, to be appointed in the manner prescribed in this letter.

"But I desire to present my views in general of the object and purposes of the proposed institution, in order that by no possibility shall the property hereby donated ever be diverted to any other purpose; and that the result of much thought and labor on my part shall be commensurate with the high objects to be attained; and as a guide, and, as it were, an organic law for you, in the discharge of your duties.

"I have directed skilled attorneys to prepare a deed conveying to you the property therein described, estimated by me to be worth the sum of $400,000: the said deed to be signed and executed by my wife and myself. The property thereby conveyed lies in the limits of Evansville or contiguous thereto.

"I desire and direct that the building for the public library hereby proposed shall be located on that portion of the property designated in said deed which is generally known as Carpenter's field. The remainder of said tract of land known as Carpenter's field shall be forever kept as a public park. It shall be, at the discretion of the trustees, enclosed by a neat fence; and fountains, flowers, trees, grass-plats, and all the usual accessories of a park shall be provided and kept in order, so as to make the park a resort for the people for all time to come.

"I desire that the co-operation of the city in this scheme of a public park shall be secured, so that the square now owned by the city adjoining this tract of land shall be made subsidiary to the general purpose of promoting public health and popular recreation. The control of said public park under proper municipal regulations, shall remain with the trustees hereby appointed. You and your successors will constitute forever, a board of trustees, seven in number, to be maintained in perpetual succession for the accomplishment, preservation and supervision of the purposes for which the library and park are to be established. To you and your successors, therefore, by virtue of said deed and this instrument, I give full and exclusive power to take, receive and hold in fee simple, the said real estate in said deed particularly described, and to sell and convey in fee simple, at such times and for such prices as may be deemed advisable, all the said real estate except that which is particularly set apart for the said library and park, and out of the proceeds of such sale to erect a suitable building, to improve, ornament and adorn said park, and to purchase books, maps and works of art for the use of the people of all classes, races and sexes free of charge, forever. A permanent fund shall be created out of the proceeds of such sale for the support of the institution."

The trustees, to whom this communication was addressed, were Thomas E. Garvin, Alexander Gilchrist, Henry F. Blount, John Laval, Matthew Henning, and Charles H. Butterfield. These gentlemen accepted the trust, and on Aug. 23, 1876, the deed was executed and soon afterward was placed on record. A general expression of the public desire favored the naming of the library "The Willard Library," and the park "Willard Park." To this Mr. Carpenter gave his consent, and from that time until his death he worked hand in hand with the trustees to carry out the plan. He expressed his desire to see, in his own lifetime, the library in successful operation, "to embellish our city, to instruct and elevate the people, and to promote the growth of virtue and knowledge." As soon as a sufficient sum could be realized for the building fund Reed Brothers, architects, were commissioned to draw plans for a building, which in appearance is an ornament to the city. Its cost was about $80,000 and it was erected under the personal supervision of Mr. Carpenter, who, notwithstanding his advanced age, visited the building almost daily, and only two months before his death climbed to the top of the walls on a tour of inspection. The death of Mr. Carpenter occurred in November, 1883, before the library was opened to the public, though the building was practically completed and he had the satisfaction of seeing the happy fruition of his hopes. Owing to removals from the city, resignations, etc., some changes have been made in the board of trustees. The present board consists of Thomas E. Garvin, president; S. G. Evans, vice-president; O. F. Jacobi, treasurer; R. D. Richardson, secretary; Alexander Gilchrist, and John H. Foster. Miss Otilda Goslee is the librarian, and has been ever since the institution was opened, with Miss Katie Imbusch and Mrs. M. O. Flower assistants. The number of volumes in the library is about twenty-nine thousand, to which additions are constantly being made, and some valuable art treasures are now on the shelves.

Such, in brief, is the history of one of the public institutions of the city of Evansville. An institution of which every citizen is proud, and one which will stand as a more enduring monument than marble or bronze to the memory of its generous donor.

CAPTAIN LEE HOWELL, a prominent railroad man of Evansville, Ind., and president of the Evansville & Bowling Green Packet Company, was born on a farm in Lauderdale county, Ala., his parents having emigrated from the Carolinas some years before his birth. At the age of fifteen he began his business career as a clerk and bookkeeper in a general country store. Here he continued until 1862, when he enlisted in the cavalry service of the Confederate army, in Captain Philip Dale Roddy's company, which was afterwards organized into the Fourth Alabama cavalry regiment of Roddy's brigade and assigned to General Forrest's division, and served faithfully until the close of the war. Transportation had an attraction for him, and after the war he engaged in steamboating on the Tennessee and Ohio rivers, first as chief clerk and later as master and owner of packet steamers plying between Florence, Ala., Paducah, Ky., and Evansville, Ind. In the spring of 1872 he sold his steamboat interests to the Louisville & Nashville Railroad Company, and operated a steamer for that company between Danville, Tenn., and Florence, Ala., semi-weekly, for three years, when the company sold its river interests to the Evansville & Tennessee River Packet Company, and Captain Howell was appointed general agent for that company, with headquarters at Florence, Ala., looking especially after the interests of the company in the Tennessee river valley. Five years later he came to Evansville as general agent for the Louisville & Nashville railroad, and since that time has been one of the active business men of that busy city. In June, 1882, he was appointed general freight agent for the Henderson division. In the following November his jurisdiction was extended over the St. Louis division, and he has presided over the freight department of these two important divisions since that date. In addition to his duties in the freight department, he was acting superintendent of the St. Louis division and its branches from July 1 to Dec. 1, 1883. As the agent of a great railway corporation his first duty is naturally to subserve the interests of the company he represents. This he has done to the entire satisfaction of the company, at the same time contributing in divers ways to the material advancement of Evansville. By his broad and progressive policy as freight agent he has stimulated the coal mining industry along the line of the Henderson division, and a large portion of the products of the mines goes to Evansville and other points north of the Ohio river; and by his uniformly courteous treatment of all who come in contact with him he has made friends both for himself and his company. Captain Howell was one of the principal promoters of the Evansville, Suburban & Newburgh railway, an enterprise that has added in no small degree to the city's prosperity; was one of the founders of the town of Howell, which was named for him; and was instrumental in securing the location there of the great railroad shops, which have given steady employment at good wages to hundreds of Evansville's artisans. During the quarter of a century and more he has been engaged in the railroad business he has never forgotten the good old days on the river, and has always retained an affection for river traffic. This was manifested in the organization of the Evansville, Ohio & Green River Transportation Company in 1888, which established a permanent and reliable towboat service between Evansville and Green river points, and to which packet service was added in April, 1896, thus securing to Evansville a large share of the Green river trade. On Jan. 1, 1898, the packet portion of the equipment of the Evansville, Ohio & Green River Transportation Company, which at that time consisted of two first-class passenger and freight steamers, was merged with other interests into a new packet company, the Evansville & Bowling Green Packet Company, of which Captain Howell became, and is still president. The Evansville, Ohio & Green River Transportation Company and the Evansville & Bowling Green Packet Company have been very important factors in the development and building up of the entire Green river territory. During the present summer, the packet service of the Evansville & Bowling Green Packet Company was extended into Upper Green river as far as Brownsville, and as soon as the new government lock in course of construction just above Brownsville is completed, its service will be extended up to Mammoth Cave, which will give the entire Green and Barren river valleys within the zone of slack water navigation the benefit of regular and reliable packet service. The company in the spring of the present year contracted for the construction by the

Howard Shipbuilding Company, of Jeffersonville, Ind., of a new packet steamer, designed and built especially for the Green river trade. No expense has been spared to make this boat one of the best of her class plying on western waters, and it is safe to predict that she will be one of the most successful steamers that has ever plied on Green and Barren rivers, and no doubt will meet with the hearty support and fullest appreciation of the company's patrons. Captain Howell is entirely too modest a man to make any reference whatever to his work in connection with any of the interests he has represented, but he is especially proud of his connection with the Louisville & Nashville Railroad Company, and the fact that he has been one of the trusted lieutenants of the present president of the company, Mr. Milton H. Smith, from his first connection with the railroad, when Mr. Smith was general freight agent of that line, which extended from Louisville to Decatur, Ala., and from Bowling Green, Ky., to Paris, Tenn.; and that he has witnessed and rendered what assistance he could in the development of that company to its present position of the leading trunk line of the South. Captain Howell was married in 1867 at Tuscumbia, Ala., to Miss Emma Ottaway. To this union there have been born four children, only two of whom survive, Lee, Jr., of Evansville, and Emma, now Mrs. James Edward Cox, of Owenton, Ky.

HON. JAMES A. HEMENWAY, junior United States senator from Indiana, and since 1894 to his election to the U. S. senate the representative in Congress from the First district of Indiana, is a descendant of one of the oldest families in America. During the early colonial days a Ralph Hemenway came from the Old Country and settled at Shrewsbury, Conn. His descendants are numerous throughout the Eastern states. In the early part of the nineteenth century the grandfather of James A. Hemenway came from New York to Indiana, locating at Boonville, where the subject of this sketch was born March 8, 1860. He received his education in the public schools of Boonville, and with the exception of a few years has passed his whole life there. After leaving school he took up the study of law, and coming to the conclusion that the West offered better opportunities to a young lawyer than his native town, went to Ottumwa, Ia. For a time he gave up the law and was a clerk in the store of Field, Leiter & Co., of Chicago. Later he went to Harper, Kan., where he continued to study law, meantime being employed by a Harper firm in hauling cornmeal from that place to Wichita. While in Kansas he entered a family claim, but after occupying it for two years the land agents found out that he was not the eldest son and cancelled his title. Soon after this he returned to Boonville, where, with the assistance of an attorney named Scott Sisson, he completed his law studies and was admitted to the bar. He began practice at Boonville in 1885, and the following year was elected prosecuting attorney of the Second judicial circuit. An interesting story is told of how he won his first case. The attorneys for the defendant were old and experienced lawyers, who on this occasion were indiscreet enough to attempt to poke fun at the young prosecutor and criticize his methods. After several attacks of this character Mr. Hemenway rose and calmly said: "Gentlemen of the jury: While I have never had the experience of the gentlemen appearing for the defendant, I have been around the courthouse long enough to know that it is a fixed custom with some lawyers, when they have no case, to abuse their opponent." That settled it. The criticism was stopped and Mr. Hemenway won his case. His election as prosecutor in 1886, by a majority of over six hundred votes, in a circuit which was supposed to be reliably Democratic, gave him considerable prestige in the Republican councils in the First Congressional district. At the close of his first term as prosecutor he was re-elected, and in 1890 was chosen the First district member of the Republican State central committee. From this time on his political career has been steadily upward. In 1894 he became a candidate for the Congressional nomination and made a personal canvass in a majority of the counties constituting the district. His opponents were Frank B. Posey and Arthur Twineham, the former one of the best known attorneys of Evansville, and an orator of wide reputation, and the latter now mayor of Princeton, Ind. Mr. Hemenway was nominated and elected and has been returned to Congress at each subsequent election. When United States Senator Charles W. Fairbanks was elected to the vice-presidency, in 1904, Mr. Hemenway became a candidate for the senatorial toga as his successor. Several candidates entered the field against him, but a conference of these candidates and their friends, at Indianapolis, early in December, led to the withdrawal of all opposition, thus giving

Mr. Hemenway a clean field. He was married on July 1, 1885, to Miss Lydia Alexander, whose great-grandfather, Ratcliffe Boone, was the founder of the city of Boonville. He was also the first delegate in Congress from the Territory of Indiana, and afterward served several terms in Congress from the district now represented by Mr. Hemenway. Mr. and Mrs. Hemenway have three children: Lena Mae, eighteen years of age, is a student in Washington seminary; George, the only son, fifteen years old, is a student at the Washington College for Boys, and Estelle is seven years of age.

THOMAS WALSH, of Howell, Ind., the oldest master mechanic in the service of the Louisville & Nashville Railroad Company, was born at Preston, Lancashire, England, Jan. 12, 1844, his parents being William and Anna (Bamber) Walsh. His father was a mechanical engineer, and Thomas, after attending a private school until he was fourteen years of age, was placed as an apprentice with the firm of Claton & Bros., millwrights and engineers, proprietors of the Sho Works, to learn the trade. In June, 1862, he embarked for America and upon his arrival in this country worked for a short time at Fort Jarvis on the New York & Erie railroad. Next he went to Chicago, where he was for a little while connected with the Illinois Central; then to St. Louis as an employe of the Southern Foundry and Engine Company; and from there to Nashville in the service of the Nashville & Chattanooga Railroad Company. On May 15, 1863, he entered the employ of the Louisville & Nashville Railroad Company as a machinist and has been with that company ever since. In May, 1869, he was made foreman of new work, building new engines, etc., and in August of that year was made foreman of all engine work, new and repairing. On May 1, 1870, he was appointed master mechanic of the Memphis division, which had just been bought by the Louisville & Nashville, but in July following was transferred to Mount Vernon, Ill., to take charge of the line running from St. Louis to Nashville, which at that time was a recent purchase of the company. On this line he filled the position of master mechanic between Mount Vernon and Evansville, Ind., until July, 1879, when his jurisdiction was extended to the entire line. During the yellow fever epidemic of 1878 in Memphis the Louisville & Nashville was the only road that kept up communications with the stricken city. Mr. Walsh was at one time the only official of the road in the city. He had thirty-six engineers and firemen to die with the dread disease but he remained at his post of duty, his only helpers being a few laborers, as the machine department had been closed. By his heroic efforts the line was kept open and in working order, being the only one by which the city could obtain supplies of medicine and provisions, or by which doctors and nurses could be brought in or the convalescents carried out. In addition to his labors as a railway official he made a house to house canvass of a large part of the city giving aid to the sufferers. For his brave and unselfish conduct, Martin Langstaff, president of the Howard Aid Association, awarded him a gold medal. During that epidemic the highest death rate was two hundred and sixty in one day, although two-thirds of the population had left the city. On Dec. 24, 1889, the new shops at Howell were opened and Mr. Walsh was transferred to that point, the shops at Mount Vernon and Edgefield, Tenn., having been consolidated in the new establishment. Here he still remains in charge, having been in the employ of the Louisville & Nashville Company for more than forty years. This long career with one of the leading railway corporations of the country tells the story of his efficiency better than any words that could be used in writing a sketch of his life. It is unnecessary to say that his skillful services have been fully appreciated by the officials of that company, and that he stands high with the management of the road. Young men may read with profit the story of his life. Without murmuring at "hard luck" or wishing for some good position he has gone to work and hewed out his own career by his own industry and intelligence. Mr. Walsh was married in March, 1865, to Miss Mary Eliza Crumbell of St. Louis.

EDWARD F. YEARWOOD, chief train dispatcher of the St. Louis division of the Louisville & Nashville railroad, with offices in Evansville, Ind., was born at Mount Vernon, Ill., Sept. 13, 1872. His parents are both living, now residing in Evansville, where his father, Aaron L. Yearwood, is a carpenter in the employ of the Louisville & Nashville company. Edward F. Yearwood entered the employ of the railroad company as a messenger boy when he was ten years of age. He at once turned his attention to telegraphy and at the age of thirteen was given a place as an operator. From the beginning his advancement in the telegraphic department has been steady and certain, due to his correct habits and his thorough knowledge of the business. In 1891 he was made assistant train dispatcher, in the office at Evansville, where he soon demonstrated his fitness for such a responsible position, or even for one of greater importance. In due time he was promoted to the rank of dispatcher in the same office, and later was made chief dispatcher, his last promotion coming to him in 1902. He has therefore been for nearly fourteen years in the office, where he has completely mastered every detail of the business of train dispatching, assuring both celerity and safety in the transportation of freight and passengers. Mr. Yearwood is a member of the Benevolent and Protective Order of Elks, in which he is deservedly popular because of his genial disposition and his willingness to help in all the society's charitable work, as well as its social functions.

WILLIAM M. LUTZ, local freight agent for the Louisville & Nashville Railroad Company, at Evansville, Ind., and president of the Evansville local freight agents' association, was born at St. Jacobs, Madison county, Ill., Feb. 22, 1860. He is a son of Joseph and Rosina (Seibold) Lutz, both natives of Germany, who came to the United States with their parents and were married at Camden, N. J., in 1857. They are still living, residing at the present time in Clinton county, Ill., where the father is a prosperous farmer. Besides the subject of this sketch they have two daughters living: Louisa, who is the wife of O. D. Pitts, of Evansville, and Mollie, now Mrs. C. G. Benton, of Ashley, Ill. William M. Lutz was reared in the State of Illinois, and at the age of eighteen years entered the service of the Louisville & Nashville Railroad Company, as telegraph operator at Venedy, Ill. Afterward he was operator and agent at Okawville, Mascoutah, Ashley and Mount Vernon, Ill., until Dec. 1, 1895, when he was appointed to his present position. Mr. Lutz is also the local freight agent for the Louisville, Henderson & St. Louis railway, and for the past four years has been president of the Evansville local freight agents' association. He is also the Indiana member of the American Association of Local Freight Agents, and the committeeman at large for the state in that body. Although a comparatively young man he has been for twenty-six years in the railway service, all that time with the same company. That his work has been appreciated by the company may be seen in his repeated promotions to better positions. For twenty years he has been a Knight Templar Mason. On Dec. 24, 1884, he was united in marriage to Miss Nannie Belle Coffey, of Ashley, Ill., and they have two children: William Herbert, aged sixteen, and Mildred Lucile, aged fourteen years. In his intercourse with his fellow-men Mr. Lutz is uniformly courteous, and much of his success in his business is due to this trait of character.

LAWRENCE E. BARTER, of Mount Vernon, Ind., county clerk of Posey county, is a descendant of one of the pioneer families of that section of the state. The first of the name to settle in Posey county was John Barter, a native of Devonshire, England, a blacksmith by trade, who married Mary Foote, daughter of a distinguished English surgeon, and when well advanced in years came to America. Both himself and his wife died in Posey county. Their children were John, Richard, Edward, William, George, James, Jane, Mary and Phillipa. Of these Edward remained in England and died there; George died in Pennsylvania; the three daughters married and stayed in England, while the other four sons came with their parents to the New World. Richard, the second son, was born at the little village of Houl, in Devonshire, May 14, 1797, and was twenty-two years old when he came to America, in 1819. He crossed the Atlantic in a sailing vessel, landed at Philadelphia, made his way to Chambersburg, where he worked some time at blacksmithing, having learned the trade with his father before leaving England. After about four months in Chambersburg he went to Pittsburg, and in the spring of 1820 he came down the Ohio river on a flatboat to Mount Vernon, which was then a small village, having been settled but about four years. There he worked for a while at his trade and later added a stock of goods, managing both the general store and his blacksmith shop. In time he gave up blacksmithing entirely and devoted his entire attention to merchandizing. He accumulated considerable property about Mount Vernon, retired from active business about 1856, and died at his country home, a few miles north of Mount Vernon, on April 15, 1864. He married Martha Ann Aldridge, of Posey county, and the following children were born to this union: John M., Jane, James M., George, Richard Fulton, Henry Clay and Theodore Frelinghuysen. The mother of these children died on Dec. 17, 1846, and Mr. Barter married again in 1848, his second wife being Mary H., daughter of Capt. William Walker, of Evansville, who was killed at the battle of Buena Vista in the Mexican war. Three children were born to this marriage, viz.: Victoria, Elizabeth and Benjamin. John M. Barter, the oldest child by the first wife, was born at Mount Vernon in 1826. He received a good education, became his father's confidential secretary and business manager and later his partner. After his father's death he continued in mercantile pursuits for several years in Mount Vernon. His wife was Sarah Catherine Lichtenberger, of Mount Vernon, and to this marriage there were born the following children: Lawrence, Richard A., Charles, Edward, Martha, Ida and Catherine. Charles and Edward reside in Ridgway, Ill.; Catherine is the wife of Dr. Elwood Smith, of Mount Vernon, and the others are deceased. Richard A., the second son, was born at Mount Vernon and there grew to manhood, learned the trade of tinner and worked at it until his death in 1871. He married Miss Emma, daughter of Dr. L. D. Brooks, an old resident of New Harmony, Posey county, and one son, Lawrence E., the subject of this sketch, was born to the union. Lawrence E. Barter was born at New Harmony, March 28, 1871. A month later his father died. Lawrence was reared at New Harmony and received his education in the public schools there. Before reaching his majority he began life for himself as clerk in a store. He continued in this occupation until 1884, when he became bookkeeper for the New Harmony Banking Company, and remained with this concern for ten years, the last five of which he held the position of assistant cashier. During this time he served two terms on the board of trustees of the town, during the last two years of which he was president of the board, which position under the form of government made him virtually the mayor. He was the youngest man who ever held that position, yet during his term of office he secured a number of needed improvements. In 1902 he was a candidate for the nomination for county clerk before the Democratic convention, and, although this was his first entry into county politics, he was defeated by only seven votes. J. F. Blase, who secured the nomination, died soon after taking the office, and the county commissioners appointed Mr. Barter to the vacancy. He took charge of the office on Jan. 30, 1904, and at the Democratic convention of that year he was unanimously nominated to succeed himself. Mr. Barter is a Mason, a Knight of Pythias, to which order he has belonged for the last twelve years, and a member of the Benevolent and Protective Order of Elks. In all these orders he has a popular place because of his genial disposition and general good fellowship. He was married on April 15, 1896, to Miss Katherine Miller, whose father is an old resident of Posey county, and to this marriage there have been born two children, Richard Clinton and Isabelle.

FREDERICK A. MORLOCK, of Mount Vernon, Ind., treasurer of Posey county and a candidate for re-election, was born in that county, Dec. 16, 1868. He is a son of Christian and Christina (Willimann) Morlock, the former a native of Cincinnati, where he was born in November, 1835, and the latter of Posey county. Christian Morlock came to the county in 1850, bought a farm in Black township, and there passed the remainder of his life as a farmer. On Jan. 27, 1868, he was married to Miss Christina Willimann, daughter of Adam and Mary Willimann, both natives of Germany, but for a long time residents of Robinson township, Posey county. To this marriage there were born six children: Frederick, George, Mary, John, Edward and Emma. Frederick is the subject of this sketch; George, John and Edward are all farmers in the county; Mary is the wife of George Reinitz, of Black township; and Emma is the wife of William Cullman, residing in the same neighborhood. The Willimann and Morlock families are splendid representatives of that German-American citizenship which has been so important an element in the development of Posey county, the garden spot of Indiana. In these families none has played a more prominent part or more faithfully done his duty than Frederick A. Morlock. After receiving a good practical education in the common schools he embarked in the mercantile business at Hovey, a little village of Point township, but had the misfortune to lose his building and stock soon after starting by fire. In 1894 he was elected trustee of the township for a term of four years, but owing to the passage of an act by the legislature of 1897 his term was extended two years and his successor was not elected until 1900. In 1902 he was nominated by the Democracy for the office of treasurer and at the ensuing election was victorious. His administration of the office was evidently satisfactory to the people of the county, for in 1904 he was renominated without opposition. Mr. Morlock is a member of the Independent Order of Odd Fellows, the Benevolent and Protective Order of Elks, the Modern Woodmen, the Tribe of Ben Hur, the Court of Honor and the German Methodist Episcopal church. He was married on Jan. 8, 1890, to Miss Mary, daughter of Michael and Barbara Roos, both natives of Germany. Mr. and Mrs. Morlock have the following children: Lillie C., Erwin E., Louis A., Arthur G., Mary E., and Roose E. One son, Fred C., the second of the family, is deceased.

GEORGE HOUSTON CHAPMAN, M.D., one of the most successful physicians of Western Kentucky, was born in Morganfield, Ky., March 24, 1849. His ancestors on both sides of the house were distinguished people, notably his grandfathers, Doctor Chapman and Judge George Houston. Each of these gentlemen excelled in his line of work, accumulating large means and filling positions of great responsibility. Of Judge Houston it may be said that no other man stood higher among his fellows. The father of the subject of this sketch, Thomas Strother Chapman, was a highly educated man, very successful in business and frequently elected to responsible positions. Dr. Houston Chapman, after completing his academic education, entered Jefferson Medical college of Philadelphia, from which he graduated in 1873, with the highest honors. Immediately after graduation he sailed for London to spend six months in St. Thomas hospital with its fifteen hundred patients. Before returning home he visited the principal cities of the continent of Europe. Coming home fully equipped for his life's work, he began that work in earnest, and, by dint of close application and indefatigable industry, he has made a record of which he and his people have just cause to be proud. Doctor Chapman has written many articles on professional subjects, all of which were published in the prominent medical journals. His appointment as judge of surgical instruments at the World's Columbian Exposition was no trivial honor. In 1875 he married Miss Emma Homer. Two children were born to this union, Thomas Noel and Lena Taylor. The son holds a responsible position on the Southern Pacific railroad with headquarters at Houston, Tex. In politics the doctor is a gold standard Democrat. As secretary of the celebrated McDowell Medical society, he associated with the most distinguished members of his profession, and it is needless to state that he regards this office as the most exalted ever conferred upon him.

CHARLES I. MATTINGLY.

CHARLES IGNATIUS MATTINGLY, dealer in hardware, agricultural implements and vehicles, Uniontown, Ky., was born in that county, Nov. 28, 1848, and is a son of James E. and Margaret (Phillips) Mattingly, both natives of Kentucky, the former of Union and the latter of Webster county. The paternal grandfather, Jerry Mattingly, was a native of Maryland, blacksmith by trade and was one of the pioneers of Union county, settling near St. Vincents in 1811. His wife was a Miss Sallie Shanks before marriage. Both died in Union county. One of their sons, John L. Mattingly, married a Miss McGill, and this couple were the parents of James E. Mattingly, the father of the subject of this sketch. He was a farmer, a soldier in the Mexican war, a Democrat in politics, and both himself and wife were members of the Catholic church. They were married in Union county, but both died in Arkansas, she in 1878 and he about 1881. They had seven sons and two daughters, six of whom are still living. On the maternal side the grandparents of Mr. Mattingly were Andrew and Margaret (Parker) Phillips, both natives of North Carolina. He fought with Jackson at the battle of New Orleans. They came from North Carolina to Hopkins county, Ky., at an early day and there they passed the remainder of their lives. Charles I. Mattingly was educated at Uniontown and followed the vocation of a farmer until 1875, when he came

GEORGE E. MATTINGLY.

to Uniontown and for a time conducted a shoe factory on a modest scale. Later, he was in the hotel business, and was the builder of the Hotel Zora, which he sold in 1895 to engage in the present line. He has the largest establishment of the kind in Uniontown and enjoys a large patronage. His business naturally leads him to take an interest in agricultural matters and he is one of the stockholders of the Union County Fair association. He is a Democrat in politics, and was for ten years a member of the city council. He is regarded as a safe, conservative financier, and socially is a prince of good fellows. No man in Uniontown is more universally liked and esteemed than Charley Mattingly. He and his family are members of the Catholic church. In 1878 he was married at Uniontown, Ky., to Miss Josie Crane, a native of Livingston county, Ky. She is a daughter of George W. and Susan M. (Barrow) Crane, old settlers of the state. Both died at Uniontown, where the father was in the lumber business, and was for several years postmaster under Republican administrations. Mrs. Mattingly's maternal grandfather, John Barrow, was one of the pioneers of Logan county, Ky., coming from his native state of Virginia in an early day. Mr. and Mrs. Mattingly have had eight children, viz.: George Everett, now in business with his father; Margaret Zora, Mary Miskel, Tiny Catherine, deceased; Helen Agnes, Flora Annie, Charles Ignatius, Jr., and William Joseph. George Everett, the eldest son, attended St. Mary's college, Marion county, Ky., and graduated in 1895 from Gethsemane college in Nelson county, where he was awarded a gold medal for bookkeeping. For five years he clerked for Pike-Newman Dry Goods Company, of Uniontown, then three years with Bry & Bros. Cloak Company, of St. Louis, and is now in partnership with his father. Gifted with a wealth of shrewdness and common sense, he goes at everything he pursues with that energy and singleness of purpose that are bound to achieve success. He and his sister, Margaret Zora, are accomplished musicians, and were given the honor of playing for the Mardi Gras excursionists from Cincinnati to New Orleans on the steamer John K. Speed in 1899, the passengers on the steamer presenting Miss Mattingly with a diamond brooch as a token of their appreciation. While in St. Louis the son studied violin at the Beethoven conservatory of music in that city.

WILLIAM TEARE, mayor of Uniontown, Ky., was born in Ramsey, Isle of Man, in 1839. When a lad, only eleven years old, he emigrated to America, settling at Vandenburg, Meade county, Ky. At the early age of twelve years he began the life of a river-man and followed that avocation for ten years, experiencing many trials and hardships. It is certain, however, that this rough and hazardous life fitted him for his active and trying soldier life of four years.

Being an ardent supporter of the claims of the South in her dispute with the North, he was among the first of the Kentuckians to cast his lot with the South and to enter the Confederate army in August, 1861. He became a member of Company E, Tenth Kentucky cavalry, a regiment that saw as much active service as any other in the Confederate army. In 1862 he was wounded no less than three times, once in the memorable battle of Pittsburg Landing and twice in an effort of his regiment to capture a Federal gunboat. As soon as he recovered from these wounds he returned to his regiment and was wounded for the fourth time in the battle of Springfield, Tenn., in 1863. Surely he bears scars enough to establish the fact that he fought valiantly for a cause that he thought to be right. In Morgan's raid through Southern Indiana and Ohio he was taken prisoner and confined in Camp Douglas until February, 1865. He was paroled at Atlanta, Ga., in May, 1865. The first year after the war he spent in Texas, when he finally located in Uniontown, Ky., in December, 1866. He married Miss Catherine Wathen, to which union five children have been born, one of them being the wife of Benjamin Davison, an extensive coal operator. He filled the offices of constable and police judge before the people elected him to his present responsible position. In religious and political affairs Mr. Teare is quite liberal. He is an earnest Democrat, but in no sense a partisan. He is a public-spirited man, taking an active interest in everything that pertains to the healthful development of his home city.

GEORGE WALTER CLEMENTS, a well known farmer of Union county, Ky., and superintendent of the Uniontown wagon factory, was born in Washington county, Ky., July 7, 1870. His parents, George R. and Sallie (Clement) Clements, were both born in Kentucky, the former in Washington and the latter in Union county. The paternal grandparents were George R. and Anna (Hamilton) Clements. George R. Clements came from Virginia at an early day and settled in Washington county, where he died in 1872 and his wife in 1880. The maternal grandparents were Walter and Martha (Payne) Clement. George Payne, the father of Martha, came from Virginia and was among the pioneers of Union county. George R. Clements, the father of George W., is still living in Washington county, where he follows the vocation of a farmer. He is a Democrat and takes an active interest in politics. He and his wife were both members of the Catholic church. She died in 1874. They had ten children, five of whom are yet living. George Walter Clements was reared on a farm and has followed that occupation all his life. He was educated primarily in the public schools, afterward attending Cecilian college. He owns 375 acres of good land in Union county and is one of the progressive farmers of that section of the state. For some time he has been discharging the active duties of superintendent of the wagon factory, in which he is a stockholder. Politically he is a Democrat and he and his entire family are members of the Catholic church. Mr. Clements was married in 1895 to Miss Mary Pike, a daughter of Sylvester Pike, mentioned elsewhere in this work. To this union there have been born five children: Ignatius Loyola, Sarah Aileen, Mary Susan, George Forrest and Agnes Amelia.

CHARLES A. J. KELLENAERS, cashier of the Farmers' bank, Uniontown, Ky., was born in Holland, Dec. 12, 1862. He received his primary education in his native land and at the age of seventeen came to the United States, attended the Kansas State normal school and the Catholic normal school, of Milwaukee, Wis. For ten years he followed the profession of a pedagogue. In 1894 he came to Uniontown as a bookkeeper in the bank. His industry, fidelity, and quick intelligence won the approbation of his employers and when in 1902 the Farmers' bank was organized, buying out the old bank, Mr. Kellenaers was made cashier. He had previously been cashier of the old bank of Uniontown for about two years, and was largely instrumental in the organization of the Farmers' bank, in which he is a stockholder to a considerable extent. Politically Mr. Kellenaers is a Democrat and keeps thoroughly informed on the great questions of the day, though he is by no means an active politician. His highest aim is to intelligently discharge his duties as a citizen of his adopted country. In church matters he has adhered to his early training and is a member of the Catholic church. Mr. Kellenaers was united in marriage, in 1903, to Miss Ellen Lancaster, a young lady of many excellent qualities and womanly graces, of Calhoun, Ky., and one son, Joseph Theophilus, has come to bless this union.

SYLVESTER PIKE, a retired banker of Uniontown, Ky., was born in Meade county, of that state, April 30, 1830, and is a son of Joseph and Sarah (Howard) Pike, both natives of Washington county, Ky. Both of Mr. Pike's grandfathers came from England at an early date and settled in Washington county, where both lived to be very old. Joseph Pike received a common school education, but was by nature a close student. He and his wife were both members of the Catholic church. Of their seven children two are living. Sylvester Pike was educated at Rogers college. His early life was passed on the farm, and as his parents were in moderate circumstances he began life for himself with practically nothing at the age of nineteen years. His first business venture was as a lime burner, and it was in this business that he made the first start toward his fortune. He afterward followed farming for several years, buying more land occasionally until he was one of the most extensive land owners in the county. For more than twenty years he was interested in banking operations at both Uniontown and Morganfield. It has been said that he made more money in the banking business than any other man in Kentucky, and he is perhaps the wealthiest man in Union county today. He owns two fine residences in Uniontown, the wagon factory, a number of farms, and has given to his children about seventy-five thousand dollars. One thing can be said of Mr. Pike's wealth, and that is that every dollar was honestly acquired. He has always been very liberal and lenient toward his debtors and has shown his public spirit by being a contributor to every scheme for the upbuilding of the town. Mr. Pike is an active Democrat and is an enthusiastic supporter of his party's principles. In religious matters he is a Catholic of the broad gauge sort—one who believes in charitable works and actions. He was one of the heaviest contributors toward the erection of the fine Catholic church in Uniontown and personally supervised its erection. He was married in 1850 to Miss Sarah Newton, a native of Washington county, and they have had born to them seven children. George is deceased, Benjamin J. is a prominent merchant of Uniontown and has large farming interests in the county; Emma is the wife of R. E. Newman, a farmer of Union county; Agnes Maria is the Sister Superior of the

Catholic school at Whitesville, Ky.; William Dun is a priest at Fairfield, Ky.; Mary is the wife of G. W. Clements, a farmer of Union county, and Catherine is the wife of W. M. Morgan, whose farm is said to be the finest in the county. Mr. and Mrs. Pike are both living, having been married for fifty-five years, and in their old age they are enjoying the fruits of their industry and frugality of earlier years and the friendship and esteem of all who know them.

JOHN R. TAYLOR, a retired farmer and business man of Uniontown, Ky., was born in the county where he now resides, June 14, 1825. He is a descendant of some of the oldest families of Kentucky. His paternal grandparents, Jonathan and Ann (Berry) Taylor, were natives of Virginia, but came to Kentucky before the beginning of the nineteenth century. Jonathan Taylor had seven brothers in the Colonial army during the Revolutionary war. One of Jonathan Taylor's sons was Gibson B. Taylor, the father of the subject of this sketch. He was the youngest of the family and was born in Clark county, Ky., in 1797. He studied medicine and when he was about twenty years old located in Union county, where he married Mary Rives, a daughter of Burwell and Mary (Gilliam) Rives, who came from Virginia and were among the early settlers of Union county. Dr. and Mary Taylor had eleven children, ten of whom grew to maturity and five are yet living. In his day Dr. Taylor was one of the best known and most successful physicians of the county. He was an active Democrat and served one term as a member of the legislature. John R. Taylor was educated in the common schools and has been a resident of Union county all his life, part of the time as a merchant of Uniontown and part as one of the leading farmers of the county. For the last two or three years he has been retired from active business cares, enjoying the fruits of his industry and frugality of former years. Mr. Taylor is a Democrat politically and takes a keen interest in all questions relating to public policy. He is a consistent member of the Episcopal church. On April 14, 1863, he was married to Miss Bettie R. Givens, a daughter of Lyle and Polly (Waller) Givens, who were among the first settlers of Union county. Aaron Waller, the father of Polly, was one of the very first citizens of the county and was for many years prominent in its affairs. Mr. and Mrs. Taylor have had four children, only one of whom is now living. John Gibson, Mary, and Lyle are deceased, and Rives is the wife of Noel Berry, whose father, W. F. Berry, is mentioned elsewhere in this work.

ROBERT N. MERRITT, a carpenter and contractor of Uniontown, Ky., was born in Meade county of that state, June 15, 1842, and is a son of Nathaniel David and Harriet M. (Beven) Merritt, the former a native of Virginia and the latter of Nelson county, Ky. The paternal great-grandparents of Mr. Merritt came from Scotland. Three brothers came over at the same time; one settling in Virginia, one in North Carolina, and one in Ohio. Nathaniel D. Merritt came to Nelson county when he was a young man, there married Harriet Beven, a daughter of Nicholas Beven, one of the pioneers of the county. After his marriage he removed to Meade county and there both himself and wife ended their days. He died March 9, 1862, and she on Aug. 9, 1867. They had a family of six children, three of whom are still living. The parents and grandparents on both sides were members of the Catholic church. Robert N. Merritt attended the common schools in his boyhood and later took a course in the Bryant & Stratton Business College, graduating in 1861. The following spring he enlisted in Company E, Twelfth Kentucky cavalry, and served until the close of the war. He participated in the famous Morgan raid; was captured at Philadelphia, Tenn., Oct. 20, 1863, and held a prisoner until April 25, 1865; was five months in prison at Belle Isle, and at the famous Andersonville prison the rest of the time. He now draws a pension for disabilities incurred while in the service. After the war he took up the work of a carpenter and since then has been employed in the erection of some of the best buildings in the county. He and his family are members of the Catholic church, and he belongs to Post No. 206, Grand Army of the Republic, for the department of Kentucky. On April 1, 1867, Mr. Merritt was married to Miss Ann Melissa, daughter of Milton Greenwood, of Meade county, and to this marriage there have been born three children: Mary C. is dead; John N. married a Miss Maggie Nall and they had three children; one of his daughters married Robert Mattingly and died leaving one daughter, Annie May, now fifteen years old, and lives with her grandparents; his other two children were named Roy and Leo. Frances Belle, the youngest daughter of Mr. and Mrs. Merritt, is the wife of T. C. Below of Union county. John N. Merritt, the son, now lives in Missouri, where he is a contractor and builder, and is now postmaster of his town.

C. Z. CAMBRON, a distinguished lawyer of Uniontown, Ky., was born in that county, Aug. 12, 1864, and is a son of J. Matt and Ann D. (Wathen) Cambron, both of whom were born in Kentucky, the former in Washington and the latter in Union county. The great-grandfather of the subject of this sketch came from Maryland at a very early date and was the founder of the Cambron family in Kentucky. The grandfather, Raphael Cambron, came to Union county as a teacher, afterward becoming one of the largest farmers in the county, owning a farm of 530 acres, on which a daughter of his, Paulina Smith, now resides. On the maternal side Mr. Cambron's grandparents were Theodore B. and Susan (Buckman) Wathen, natives of Marion and Union counties, respectively. He was a farmer and carpenter by trade, and he and his wife both died in Union county. J. Matt Cambron was a farmer and an active Democrat politically. He died in 1866, but his widow is yet living. They had five children, four of whom still survive. The Cambron family are all Catholics, a bachelor uncle of C. Z.'s having given $25,000 toward the erection of the Catholic church at Uniontown. C. Z. Cambron was reared on the farm; attended the common schools and St. Mary's college, of Marion county, Ky.; came to Uniontown in 1855; was deputy county clerk under Capt. J. H. Wall; engaged in the dry-goods business; continued in that line until 1897; then took up the study of law; was examined by Hon. A. O. Stanley and S. B. Vance in 1900 and was admitted to the bar; has already taken a high rank as an attorney and was made city attorney in 1901, holding the office ever since. For several years he has been a notary public. Mr. Cambron was married on Nov. 17, 1885, to Miss Mary S., daughter of Robert L. and Rebecca (Ray) Byrne, both native Kentuckians, the former of Spencer and the latter of Union county. Mrs. Cambron's grandparents, William and Susan (Jarboe) Byrne, were early settlers in Spencer county, where he died, she spending her last days in Union county. On the maternal side her grandparents were Alexander G. and Mary (Kinslow) Ray, both natives of Washington county. The great-grandfather, John Ray, was a native of Ireland, settling in that county in 1813. Mrs. Cambron has one brother living—R. G. Byrne, an attorney of Uniontown. Mr. and Mrs. Cambron have five children:

Robert T., a student at St. Mary's college and a graduate of the commercial course of Gethsemane college; Willie Mary, Charles Ray, Louis R. and Rebecca.

ROBERT WESLEY CRABB, a retired business man of Uniontown, Ky., a son of S. F. and Mary A. (Mathews) Crabb, was born in Charleston, Miss., Sept. 25, 1848. His father was a native of North Carolina and his mother of Virginia. They were married in Mississippi, where both died in the same year—1858. He was a planter, an extensive slaveholder, somewhat active in politics as a Democrat, and both parents were Methodists in their religious faith. The Crabb family is of German extraction, the American branch having its origin in three brothers who came from Germany in the sixteenth century and settled in New York, North Carolina and Virginia. The Mathews family is of old Virginia stock, the grandfather of Mr. Crabb having come from that State to Mississippi in the early part of the nineteenth century. Robert W. Crabb is one of a family of nine children, only two of whom survive. Until he was ten years of age he lived on his father's farm. At the age of fourteen years he became a courier in the Confederate service and later enlisted in Capt. W. F. Burk's company, Company E, Forty-seventh Arkansas cavalry, under Col. Lee Crandall, and served until the end of the war. After the war was over he came to Uniontown, where for twenty-seven years he was engaged in the hardware and implement business, becoming one of the best known and most widely patronized merchants of the place. For a number of years he served as mayor of the city and was internal revenue collector under President Cleveland's administration. During the four and a half years that he held the position he collected over half a million dollars. In 1900 he retired from active business, though he looks after his property, being a large real estate owner, and is the secretary and treasurer of the Confederate Mining Company, of Globe, Ariz. Mr. Crabb has accumulated every dollar he has by his industry and close attention to his business. He married Betty Edwards Delany, daughter of Judge S. D. Delany, formerly of Union county, but later went to Texas and died there. Mr. and Mrs. Crabb have had five children, three of whom are living: Davis D. married Kate Morris and lives in Uniontown; W. V. lives in Louisville, and Lista is at home.

D. E. CAULTON, superintendent of the National Coal and Oil Company, of Uniontown, Ky., was born in the Province of Ontario, Canada, June 7, 1868, and is a son of Dr. F. G. and Lorinda Jane (Elliott) Caulton, the father a native of England and the mother of Canada. Doctor Caulton was educated in his native land; graduated in medicine in New York City, and is still engaged in practice in Canada at the age of seventy-three years. He and his first wife had five children, only two of whom are living: Frederick C., a wealthy grain and stock dealer of Nebraska, and the subject of this sketch. Their mother died in 1875 and their father married a second wife by whom he has two children living. The paternal grandfather of Mr. Caulton was a native of England and a prominent Baptist minister. He spent his last days in Canada. D. E. Caulton received a good education in the Canadian schools and began life as a civil engineer. For about seven years he was engaged at Cleveland, then two years at Chicago; came to Louisville and engaged in general engineering work until 1898; then became superintendent of the coal company at Uniontown, now a part of the National Coal and Oil Company. Mr. Caulton is an expert in his line of work and in addition to his technical knowledge of engineering has fine business qualifications. He was married at Morganfield, Ky., in 1902, to Miss Emma Prentice, daughter of George A. Prentice, one of the leading lawyers of Morganfield, and they have one daughter, named Marion Elliott. Mr. Caulton and his wife are members of the Episcopal church.

H. E. WHITLEDGE, M.D., a promising young physician of Uniontown, Ky., was born in Henderson county, of the same state, Feb. 20, 1875. For several generations his ancestors on both sides have lived in Henderson county. His paternal great-grandfather was one of the first settlers, and his grandfather, whose name was William Whitledge, was a native of the county. C. C. Whitledge, a son of William, married Margaretta Cottingham, the daughter of Thomas and Sarah (Minton) Cottingham, both of whom were natives of Henderson county, and she is still living there. Thomas Cottingham was a tobacco merchant, and was the son of Isom Cottingham, one of the first settlers of the county. Both of Doctor Whitledge's parents are still living in Henderson county, where the father is engaged in the business of farming and tobacco buying. He is an active Democrat, a member of the Masonic fraternity, and he and his wife both belong to the Methodist church. Doctor Whitledge was educated at the Corydon high school and graduated from the medical department of the University of Louisville in 1897. He first began practicing at Oakland City, Ind., but three years later came to Uniontown, where he has built up a lucrative practice and has a high standing, both with his professional brethren and with the public. He is a member of the American and Kentucky State Medical associations and the Medical society of Union county. In political matters Doctor Whitledge was reared a Democrat, but in local elections he votes for the man rather than for the party candidate, believing that good government depends upon the selection of honest and capable officials. In fraternal circles he is well known, being a member of the Free and Accepted Masons, the Independent Order of Odd Fellows, the Knights of Pythias and the Benevolent and Protective Order of Elks. He was married in 1898 to Miss Edith Snyder, a native of Newburg, Ind., and they have one daughter, Elizabeth May, now four years of age.

JAMES E. BUCKMAN, head of the J. E. Buckman Grocery Company, of Uniontown, Ky., is a native of that county, having been born there on Feb. 21, 1860. His father, L. M. Buckman, was a native of Marion county, Ky., a contractor and builder, and an active Democrat in his day. He died some years ago in Union county and his widow, whose maiden name was Jane Wathen, is still living there. She is a daughter of Stanns and Mary (Davenport) Wathen, both natives of Virginia, but came in their early lives to Kentucky. The paternal grandfather, William Buckman, was one of the pioneers of Marion county, Ky. L. M. and Jane Buckman had eleven children, five of whom are yet living. James E. was educated in the St. Rose parochial school of Uniontown and for several years after leaving school clerked in a drug store and later in a hardware store. About fifteen years ago he embarked in the grocery business and in 1897 the Buckman Grocery Company was established. Since then it has had the lion's share of the grocery trade of Uniontown and the surrounding country. The success of the company is due largely to the fact that it does a strictly cash business and sells goods for the smallest possible margin of profit. It has been a potent factor in educating the people of Uniontown of the uselessness of the credit system, in which the honest patrons of a concern must pay the debts of the dishonest ones in the higher prices necessary to cover losses by bad debts. Mr. Buckman has been successful in life. He owns a number of houses and lots in the city, a small farm just outside the town, and property in Arkansas. His dealings with his fellow-men have been distinguished by punctuality and a strict adherence to the spirit and letter of his obligations. He was married on Sept. 25, 1898, to Miss Fannie Mayfield, a popular and accomplished young lady of Union county. The Buckman family are all members of the Catholic church and contributors to its charitable work.

JOHN MARAMAN BUCKMAN, collector, Morganfield, Ky., is a son of William Dunbar Buckman, and was born in Nelson county, Ky., March 13, 1830. He takes his middle name from the family name of his mother. (For ancestry, etc., see Sketch of B. Z. Buckman.) John M. was educated in the common schools and at St. Joseph's college, Bardstown, Ky. In early years he worked as a carpenter, and was also interested in agricultural pursuits. At one time he owned a farm near Morganfield, but after the death of his wife, on Aug. 11, 1890, he sold it and came to Morganfield, where he has since been occupied in his present line of business. In that time thousands of dollars have passed through his hands, but his accounts are always found correct, which is all that need be said regarding his character as an honest man. Mr. Buckman is one of the active Democrats of Union county. From 1859 to 1863 he was deputy sheriff and sheriff and held the position of chief deputy under Sheriff R. S. Spaulding for two years. He has served for years as county assessor and has held other important and responsible positions. In church matters he is a true Catholic, to which church his family all belong. Mr. Buckman was married on Jan. 4, 1860, to Miss Mary A. Clarke, a daughter of Thomas James and Frances (Marshall) Clarke, of Morganfield, where they settled about 1836. He died in 1850 and his wife in 1887. Mr. and Mrs. Buckman had born to them ten children: Mary Clarke, Laura Mary, Frances Catherine, Samuel Edward, John Hamilton, William Clarke, Ann Elizabeth, Benedict Joseph, Charles Marshall and Ida Lillie. All are living except Laura, Ann Elizabeth and Charles Marshall.

BENEDICT ZACHARIAH BUCKMAN, a retired merchant and business man of Uniontown, Ky., was born near Leonardtown, St. Mary's county, Md., March 27, 1834. He can trace his ancestry back to early emigrants from England and Ireland. His paternal great-grandparents, John Baptist and Nancy (Drinker) Buckman, were natives of Lincolnshire, England, who came to Maryland at an early date. A son of this couple was Charles Buckman, the grandfather of the subject of this sketch. He was born in Maryland in 1752 and died in Washington county, Ky., in 1832. One of his sons was William Dunbar Buckman, who married a Miss Maraman, and these were the parents of Benedict Z. Buckman. The maternal grandparents were Zachariah and Ann (Howard) Maraman, the former a native of Ireland and the latter of Maryland. Her parents came from France. A brother of Charles Buckman served in the war of the Revolution. William Dunbar Buckman was a farmer and mechanic. He came to Kentucky in 1796 and settled in what was then Washington, now Marion county. About 1852 he came to Union county, where he died Aug. 21, 1864. His wife died on April 28, 1845. Benedict Z. Buckman was reared on the farm, attending the subscription schools of that day, where he managed to pick up a good practical education. He began life as a clerk in a grocery; was elected constable when he was twenty-one and served two years; came to Uniontown in 1858 and went to work in a dry-goods store; was deputy sheriff from 1860 to 1862; enlisted in the Confederate army in Johnson's regiment of Kentucky cavalry; fought at Milton, Tenn., and in numerous skirmishes in that state and Kentucky; was with Forrest at Chickamauga; fought under Wheeler after the capture of General Morgan; was captured on the Tennessee river in 1864, and paroled at Nashville; commissioned to raise a company, but the war being almost at end the company was never organized. After the war Mr. Buckman came to Uniontown and took a position in the grocery store of Byrne & Chapman. This concern changed hands while he was there but he remained with the firm until March, 1873, when he bought an interest in the grocery business of S. A. Davis & Co. The following January he bought the entire stock and a little later formed a partnership with William Albert, as Albert & Buckman, and this partnership lasted until April, 1876. Mr. Buckman was made police judge in the following August and served until February, 1878, when he resigned to return to the grocery business with J. C. David. In November of the same year Mr. David sold out to Thomas J. Pike, and in June, 1879, the firm was succeeded by J. A. Mason & Co. Mr. Buckman was then assistant postmaster for some time, after which he was in the sewing machine business for several years. He was then with C. H. Blanford & Co. for some time; formed a partnership with Abram Davenport which was dissolved in 1889; then sold out and went to Maxonmill, where he was in the grocery business and assistant postmaster; was next in business at Paducah for about two years; came to Uniontown again in 1892; worked for the firm of J. H. Chapman & Son for a while, and from November, 1898, to February, 1903, he was a partner and manager of the J. O. Buckman grocery business. Since then he has lived retired. Mr. Buckman is a Democrat of the rock-ribbed variety, and he and his family are members of the Catholic church. He was married, May 8, 1871, to Miss Mary E., daughter of Raphael T. and Elizabeth (Watt) Cissell, of Morganfield. Her father was born in Marion county, Ky., and her mother in Ireland. Mr. and Mrs. Buckman have had no children of their own but they have reared several adopted children.

JOSEPH E. LILLY, M. D., clerk of the circuit court of Union county, Morganfield, Ky., was born in Nelson county of that state, March 3, 1850. His parents, W. Newton and Ellen (Clark) Lilly, were both natives of Nelson county, the former born in 1810 and the later in 1817. He was a mechanic and died in 1865. His widow is still living, aged eighty-seven years. The Lilly family are all Catholics. Of the thirteen children born to W. Newton and Ellen Lilly, six are living. The ancestors of Doctor Lilly were among the pioneers of Nelson county. His great-grandparents, John and Sallie (Newton) Lilly were natives of Maryland, but came in their youth with their parents to Nelson county, which John Lilly represented in the legislature after he reached manhood. He died in New Orleans. The paternal great-grandparents were Clement and Nellie Clark, who came to Nelson county when their son William, the grandfather of Doctor Lilly, was but four years old. They were natives of Maryland. William Clark married Susan McGill. Doctor Lilly was educated at St. Joseph's college at Bardstown; studied medicine at Louisville; came to Morganfield, where he practiced for about twelve years with excellent success; was elected magistrate in 1894; elected circuit court clerk in 1897 and re-elected in 1903; is now serving his second term in that office; is a prominent worker in the Democratic party in Union county; proprietor of the Parsons hotel, one of the oldest and best known places of entertainment in Morganfield; is one of the prominent Catholics of Union county, and is, all round, a representative Kentuckian. In whatever he undertakes he is successful because he brings to the enterprise rare tact, a quick intelligence, an indomitable energy and a strict reliability. Such qualities must of necessity win, not only success, but the esteem and friendship of those with whom he comes in contact. Doctor Lilly was married on Jan. 13, 1875, to Miss Maud Parsons, daughter of Henry C. and Catherine (Smith) Parsons. Her father was born in Marion county, Ky., but went to Louisville with his parents, J. G. and Mary A. (Lilly) Parsons, while still in his boyhood. His father was born in Mason county in 1799 and his mother in Nelson county in 1805. The great-grandfather of Mrs. Lilly was Clement Parsons, a native of Virginia, who died in Washington county, Ky., in 1830. He married a Miss Elizabeth Forrest of Maryland. She died in 1860. Henry C. Parsons was a clerk in early life; later followed agriculture; came to Union county in 1861, where he farmed until 1866, when he engaged in the hotel business at Caseyville; bought the hotel he now owns in Morganfield, and has been manager of the Parsons House most of the time since. He and his wife had six children, three of whom are now living. The maternal grandfather of Mrs. Lilly was John A. W. Smith, of Green county, Ky. He married a Martha Robinson, daughter of Thomas Robinson, a native of Virgina, who settled in Taylor county, Ky. Mrs. Parsons, the mother of Mrs. Lilly, died in March, 1901. To Dr. and Mrs. Lilly there have been born nine children. Those living are Harry N., Joseph E. Jr., Percy A., Catherine, and Thomas.

AARON WALLER CLEMENTS, county judge of Union county, Morganfield, Ky., was born in that county, March 8, 1853. He is a son of Aaron and Lucy Casey (Johnson) Clements, both natives of Union county, where the father was for many years a well known farmer, an active Democrat, a prominent member of the Masonic fraternity, and of the Christian church. He died on Dec. 28, 1889, and his widow is still living at the age of eighty-three years. She is a member of the Christian church. The paternal grandfather of Judge Clements was Leonard Clements, mentioned elsewhere in this work, and the maternal grandfather was George Johnson, an early settler of Union county. He was a farmer; a Whig until that party was dissolved, and then a Democrat; served as sheriff and jailer of the county; kept hotel at Morganfield for many years, and was one of the leading citizens of the county. He married Nancy Reeves, who was a native of Morganfield and passed her entire life there. Judge Clements was educated in the common schools and at Princeton college; followed farming for several years; served as road supervisor from 1886 to 1890; elected sheriff in 1897; took the office in 1898 and served four years; was elected county judge in 1901, and is now holding that position. He is one of the leaders of the Democratic party in his county and is always active in promulgating its principles. He is one of the substantial citizens of the county, owning three houses and lots, besides other property in Morganfield and three farms near Uniontown. In 1900 he was made a Mason in Morganfield Lodge No. 66; has been a member of the Independent Order of Odd Fellows ever since 1878, when he joined Humane Lodge No. 37 at Morganfield, and belongs to the Ancient Order of United Workmen and the Christian church. On May 27, 1885, Judge Clements was married to Miss Sallie A. Tuley, a native of Uniontown, Ky., and a daughter of W. P. and Julia (Orme) Tuley. Her father was a native of New Albany, Ind., and was a saddler by trade. He was an active Democrat in his day. Both of Mrs. Clements' parents are deceased. To Judge and Mrs. Clements there have been born six children, viz.: Baldwin Johnson, Edward Tuley, Lillian Ethel, Lucy Casey, Clarence Berry, and Earl Chester.

JAMES S. BLUE, a well known grocer of Morganfield, Ky., and mayor of the city, was born in Caldwell county, Ky., Jan. 29, 1848. His parents, John R. and Pernesia (Glenn) Blue, were both natives of the same county, where the father was a farmer and a prominent Whig before the war. He died in 1864, the mother having died some ten years before. They had four children, all of whom are living. The paternal grandfather, James Blue, lived in Union county in the early part of the nineteenth century. He was sheriff of the county along in the twenties and in 1830 removed to Caldwell county, where he died in 1848. The maternal grandfather was David Glenn, a native of Lyon county, Ky., but who died in Caldwell county in 1864. James S. Blue received his education in the common schools of Caldwell county, where he lived until he reached his majority. In January, 1871, he came to Union county and there farmed for several years, after which he located in Morganfield. He was marshal of the city for two years, constable for four years, and sheriff for three years. For the last eleven years he has been in the grocery business, and is now serving his third year as mayor of the city. Politically Mr. Blue is an unswerving Democrat, always willing to do his part to achieve a victory for his party, and in 1904 was nominated for sheriff of the county. He is a member of Morganfield Lodge No. 66, Free and Accepted Masons, and he and his wife belong to the Presbyterian church. Mr. Blue was married in April, 1878, to Miss Lou Hughes, of Union county, and to this marriage there were born five children. Two sons died in infancy and those living are Bessie G., Camille, and Willis. Mrs. Blue departed this life in March, 1888, and in the succeeding October Mr. Blue was married to Miss Bessie Hughes, a sister of his first wife. Four children have been born to this marriage, viz.: James Barber, George E., Charles David, and Sarah McGoodwin.

GEORGE LUCIAN DRURY, junior member of the law firm of Drury & Drury, Morganfield, Ky., was born in Union county of that state Dec. 12, 1875, and is a son of George H. and Ellen (Harris) Drury, both natives of the county. The family is descended from Philip Drury, a native of London and a member of the family from which "Drury Lane" took its name. He came to America at an early date and settled in Maryland, where the great-grandfather of the subject of this sketch was born. His name was Bernard Drury. Ignatius Drury, the grandfather, was born at Leonardtown, St. Mary's county, Md., Oct. 23, 1806; came to Marion county, Ky., when he was ten years old; married Lydia O'Nan, a native of Davis county, and settled in Union county in 1820; followed the brickmasons' trade; was a member of the Catholic church, and died July 9, 1887. The maternal grandparents were Truman and Virginia (Pratt) Harris, both native Kentuckians, the former born in Nelson county, March 1, 1817, and the latter in Jefferson county, Sept. 19, 1819. He died in January, 1860, and she is still living. They came to Union county in their infancy, where he followed farming and was for many years a justice of the peace. The great-grandfather on the mother's side was Benjamin Harris, born near Baltimore; married Innocent Ann Wight and came to Union county in pioneer days. James Pratt, the father of Virginia Pratt, was born in Virginia in 1785 and died in Union county in 1856. He served in the war of 1812, came first to Union county in 1814, and settled there in 1826. George H. Drury, the father of George L., now resides near St. Vincent, Union county, where he is engaged in farming on the old homestead. His wife is also living. They had four children: William Truman, George L., Mary Allie, and Boyd Harris. The eldest was born Oct. 12, 1871; was educated in the public schools and the State university at Lexington; studied law at Morganfield; was admitted to the bar on July 9, 1896, and is now the senior member of the firm of Drury & Drury. Mary Allie was born May 10, 1878, and was married on Jan. 15, 1902, to Thomas C. Bingham, of Henshaw, Ky., and has two children: George Henry and Margaret Ellen. Boyd Harris died in infancy Aug. 7, 1880. George L. Drury graduated from the Morganfield high school in June, 1895; taught school for three years; began the study of law in February, 1898, and graduated from the Louisville law school on April 28, 1899; was admitted to the bar the following day; formed a partnership with his brother on May 15, and has since practiced in Morganfield. Although both members of the firm are young men they have a high standing at the bar and are on the road to a successful business. Both are close students and good judges of human nature, and this combination rarely fails to make a good lawyer. Neither is married, both are Democrats and members of the Catholic church. George L. was a candidate for county attorney in 1901, but was defeated by a small margin.

MATHEW ROBERT WALLER, a retired farmer of Union county, Ky., living near Morganfield, was born in the county, April 21, 1833. Shortly after the close of the Revolutionary war his grandfather, John Waller, came from Virginia, where he was born, and settled in Washington county, Ky. In 1811 he decided to remove to Union county, and on the way he was captured by the Indians and held a prisoner for two years before he found an opportunity to escape. He married a Miss Small, who died in Union county. One of their sons was Aaron Waller, the father of Mathew R. He was born in Washington county in 1789, came with the family to Union county in 1811 and died there on Feb. 5, 1851. He married Mary Allison Givens, a native of Hopkins county, and they had eight sons and two daughters. Four of the sons and both of the daughters are yet living. The four living sons are John Givens, William, Mathew Robert, and Robert A. Mathew Robert Waller received such an education as the common schools of his youthful days afforded and followed the vocation of a farmer until 1858, when he located in Morganfield and engaged in business. In 1861 he enlisted in the Confederate army in company F, First Kentucky cavalry, joining the army at Bowling Green. He served through the entire war, taking part in numerous engagements, among them the battle of Chickamauga and the military operations around Atlanta. Near that city he was captured and held as a prisoner of war at Camp Douglas, Chicago, Ill., for seven months. After the war he embarked in the business of a general store-keeper at Morganfield and continued in that business for sixteen years, at the end of which time he sold out and returned to farming. For two years he was president of the National Bank of Union county, and is now one of the directors of the bank. He lives in a beautiful home about a mile from Morganfield and still takes an active interest in all questions affecting the general welfare of the county. Politically he was a Democrat until 1896, and since that time has been independent. Mr. Waller has been twice married. In October, 1866, he was married to Addie Forman, and to this union there were born three children: Alfred Forman, Martha Lizzie and William Robert. Addie Waller died on May 5, 1880, and on March 2, 1882, Mr. Waller was married to Miss Camilla B. Hughes, of Union county. Mr. Waller is a man who is universally respected by his acquaintances and is regarded as one of the best citizens of the county. He and his wife are both members of the Methodist Episcopal Church South.

J. MATT CAMBRON, one of the leading liverymen of Morganfield, Ky., is a son of J. Matt and Ann D. (Wathen) Cambron, and was born in Union county, Ky., Dec. 29, 1864. (See sketch of C. Z. Cambron.) He was reared on a farm and received his education at St. Mary's college in Marion county, Ky. Until he was twenty-four years of age he followed the vocation of a farmer. He then went into a dry goods store and was a salesman in that line for twelve years. Then for about a year and a half he was in the grocery business in Morganfield and since giving up that occupation has been engaged in the livery business. Mr. Cambron has been measurably successful in whatever he has undertaken. He is a man of industrious habits, good judgment and sterling honesty. In his various undertakings he has had the good will and support of his friends and acquaintances, which he fully appreciates. Politically he is one of the solid and reliable Democrats of Union county, and is always ready to defend his political opinions. In church matters he remains true to the teachings of his parents, and is a consistent member of the Catholic church. Mr. Cambron was married in 1894 to Miss Isabel Clayton, a native of Davis county, Ky., and a daughter of T. N. Clayton, a well-to-do farmer of that county, an active Democrat and a member of the Catholic church. The mother of Mrs. Cambron was a Miss Vance of Davis county, where she died a few years ago. To Mr. and Mrs. Cambron there have been born six children: Sue Emma, James Will, Roy Jerome, J. Matt and Mary Bell, twins, and Edward Smith.

HON. WILLIAM MOUNT BERRY, sheriff of Union county, Morganfield, Ky., was born in Hopkins county of that state, May 16, 1848. His parents, Thornton and Elizabeth (Edwards) Berry, were both natives of Kentucky, the former of Nelson and the latter of Shelby county. Thornton Berry was born in 1817; received a common school education; read medicine with Dr. James Bassett of Providence, Ky.; attended the medical college at Louisville; practiced in Union county; and died there in 1877. He was a prominent Free Mason, a Democrat, a Presbyterian, and his wife was a member of the Methodist church. She was born in 1826, and died in Union county in 1893. They had five sons and two daughters, and two sons and the daughters are now living. The paternal grandparents of William Berry were Albert Judson and Nellie (Bean) Berry, the former born in St. Charles county, Va., in 1786, and the latter was a native of Maryland. They came to Kentucky and settled first in Nelson county and later in Union, where both passed their last days. He was with General Jackson at the battle of New Orleans. The maternal grandparents were natives of Simpson county, Ky., where they passed their whole lives. William Mount Berry was educated in the common schools and has been a farmer the greater part of his life. He now owns a good farm near Sturgis. Politically he is one of the most active Democrats in Union county. He has served as a delegate to different state conventions and in 1904 was a delegate to the national convention at St. Louis. For ten years he held the office of justice of the peace; was in the legislature in 1896-97; served four years as deputy sheriff under A. W. Clements, and was elected sheriff in 1902. His term as sheriff does not expire until 1906. He has served as chairman of his county campaign committee for several campaigns, and while justice of the peace was district committeeman most of the time. He is a member of Morganfield Lodge No. 66, Free and Accepted Masons; Humane Lodge No. 37, Independent Order of Odd Fellows, at Morganfield; Silver Lodge No. 68, Knights of Pythias, at Sturgis, and of the Sturgis lodge of the Golden Cross. He is a member of the Cumberland Presbyterian church, and one of the elders of his congregation. His wife is a Baptist. Mr. Berry was married in 1870 to Miss Mary Jane Gatlin, of Union county, and they have three children: Archie Logan, received his education in Sturgis and Caseyville and is now in the insurance business in the former town; Van Reese, attended the common schools and the Sturgis high school, and now holds the office of deputy sheriff, under his father; Lora, attended the public schools of Sturgis and finished her education at the Providence college in Webster county.

JAMES BASIL AUSTIN, a successful farmer, living near Waverly, Ky., is a descendant of some of the oldest and most highly connected families of the state. His grandfather, James Austin, was born near Harper's Ferry, Va., married a Miss Howard, of that state, and in 1790 settled in Washington county, Ky. Shortly afterward he visited his native state and on his return brought back with him a pint of clover seed, which was the introduction of red clover into the State of Kentucky. His wife died in Washington county about 1830 and some two years later he removed to Union county. About the same time Basil Railey and his family settled in the same neighborhood. His wife was Miss Elizabeth Spalding, and both were natives of Marion county. James Basil Austin is a son of Thomas A. and Mary Ann (Railey) Austin, the former born in Washington county, Oct. 15, 1810, and the latter in Marion, March 2, 1812. They were married in Union county, July 26, 1836. Thomas A. Austin was educated in the common schools and at St. Rose's convent. Prior to 1850 he was a prominent Whig, but after that time he affiliated with the Democratic party. He and his wife were both members of the Catholic church, as were their parents. Of nine children, one died in infancy, Victoria died in later life, and the other seven are still living. They are James B., the subject of this sketch; Mary Ann; Francis X., who served under Johnston in the Confederate army during the war and now lives in Mississippi; Margaret, Thomas, John H., now living in Henderson, and Benedict J., of Waverly. The mother of these children died on Nov. 29, 1856, and the father on March 13, 1864. James B. Austin was born in Union county Sept. 1, 1837; was educated in the common schools; brought up as a tiller of the soil, which has been his vocation through life. While other farmers may have more land than he few have farms in a better state of cultivation. He owns seventy acres of good land near Waverly, upon which he carries on a general farming business. Mr. Austin is an unswerving Democrat in his political faith and for more than twenty years held the office of magistrate. He and his family are members of the Sacred Heart Catholic church, of St. Vincent. He was married in 1864 to Miss Mary Ellen Yates, daughter of William and Maria (Montgomery) Yates, of Washington county, and to this marriage there have been born the following children: George Edward, Mary Geraldine, Charles Martin, James Heman, Robert Aaron, Anna C., and William Joseph. All are living except George Edward and William Joseph. The children of James Austin, the grandfather of the subject of this sketch, were: Ambrose, who died in Graves county, Ky.; Benedict, a candidate for delegate to the constitutional convention of 1850, was shot and killed, while making a speech in Paducah, by Judge Campbell, of that city; John, a soldier in the war of 1812, fought at the battle of New Orleans, and died in Washington county some years afterward; Thomas A., the father of the subject; Catharine and Sallie, who died single; Theresa, who married Benedict Smith, removed to Illinois, and there died; Rosa, who died in Union county as the wife of Edward Yates. All were useful members of society and the training given them by their parents has been handed down to the present generation, for not many men can be found with higher ideals or firmer moral convictions than James Basil Austin.

W. C. COFFMAN.

W. C. COFFMAN, an old and honored resident of Union county, Ky., and one of the leading farmers in the vicinity of Morganfield, was born in Hopkins county, of that state, June 29, 1829. He is a son of Isaac and Mary A. (Harbor) Coffman, both natives of Kentucky, the father of Mercer and the mother of Woodford county. After their marriage they settled in Hopkins county, where they passed the remainder of their lives. He died in 1875 and she in 1885, both at advanced ages. Their children were Hiram, Isaac S., Huldah, Annie, Elisha J., Joel H., W. C., Mary, James R., Mildred and Lutitia, the last two being twins. Hiram married Mary A. Ashby; Isaac married Elizabeth Lynn; Huldah married George Whitsell, and after his death, Godly Shite; Annie married James Lynn; Joel married Sarah Springfield, and after her death, a widow named Jones, a sister to his first wife; Mary married John Springfield; James married Nancy Springfield, and after her death, Eliza Buchanan; Mildred married Frederick Hartman, and Lutitia John Neiswonger. The paternal grandparents of these children were Isaac and Annie (French) Coffman, he a native of Maryland and she of Scotland. They were among the pioneers of Hopkins county. The maternal grandfather, Amos Harbor, married a Miss Husted. He died in Tennessee and she in Woodford county. W. C. Coffman received a common school education and in 1852 came to Union county, where he has been engaged in farming ever since. He has

MRS. MARTHA COFFMAN.

helped every one of his living children to obtain good farms. In politics he is a rock-ribbed Democrat and in former years took an active part in political contests. In more recent years he has left the arduous labor of the campaign to younger men, though he never fails to do his duty on election day. Mr. Coffman was married in 1846 to Miss Martha Ashby, who was born in Hopkins county, Oct. 18, 1824. To this marriage there have been born eight children: Mary Jane, Annie E., Sarah Catherine, Will Ignatius, James Edward, Richard

Franklin, Henry Clay and Robert Lee. All are living except James Edward, who died in infancy, and Henry Clay. Nearly threescore years have passed since Mr. and Mrs. Coffman entered the marriage relation. And now in their old age they are enjoying the fruits of their industry and frugality of former years, surrounded by their children and a large circle of friends who love them for their many amiable qualities.

JOHN C. WOLFLIN, a farmer living near Waverly, Union county, Ky., was born in that county, June 22, 1855. His father, Casper Wolflin, was born in Germany in 1831. When he was about fourteen years of age he came with his father to the United States, his mother having died when he was a child. Christopher Wolflin, the grandfather of John C., was a shoemaker by trade. After living for some years in Union county he went to Indiana and there died. He had six brothers who came to America, and he was married six times. Of his children only two are living: Casper, who lives near Louisville, and Wilhelmina, living at Mount Vernon, Ind. Casper Wolflin grew to manhood in Union county, where he learned the distillers' trade, which has been his occupation through life. He married Mary Alvey, a native of Union county, and a daughter of John C. and Eliza (Bright) Alvey, pioneers of the county. Casper and Mary Wolfin had twelve children, eight of whom are still living. John C. Wolflin was educated in the Uniontown schools, and learned the distillers' trade with his father, but gave it up for the business of farming. In 1889 he bought the farm he now owns, consisting of about seventy acres, near Waverly, and this farm he has brought to a high state of cultivation. Mr. Wolflin also has a threshing outfit and threshes much of the grain that is raised in Union county. He is a stanch Republican in his political views and takes a keen interest in the political movements of the country. He is a member of Humane Lodge, No. 37, Independent Order of Odd Fellows, at Morganfield, and is always ready to assist in the benevolent work of the order. On May 18, 1875, Mr. Wolflin was married to Miss Paulina, daughter of John N. Griggs, mentioned in this work, and to this marriage there have been born nine children. Mamie, Nellie and Robert are deceased. The living children are Alice, Griggs, Nannie, John, Herman, and Ella. Mr. Wolflin was reared a Catholic, and his wife is a member of the Methodist Episcopal church.

JOHN N. GRIGGS.

JOHN N. GRIGGS, a well known farmer living near Waverly, Union county, Ky., was born in the neighborhood where he now resides, March 19, 1830, and is a descendant of pioneer families who came from Maryland and North Carolina. His paternal grandfather, Clem Griggs, came from North Carolina in 1820, and settled in Union county, where he died about 1864. His wife, whose maiden name was Melvina Hall, died before he came to Kentucky. About the same time John and Martha (Burgher) Culver came from Maryland and located in the same neighborhood. John Culver was a veteran of the war of 1812, and his father-in-law, Nicholas Burgher, served in the American army in the Revolutionary war. Rolin Griggs, a son of Clem Griggs, married Mary Culver, and this couple had nine children, the subject of this sketch being the only one now living. Rolin Griggs was an active Democrat in his day, and was interested in the affairs of the county. His wife was a devoted member of the Baptist church. John N. Griggs was educated in the common schools and has all his life followed the vocation of a farmer. Until 1886 he lived within a half mile of the town of Waverly. In that year he bought the farm known as the Milton Young farm, consisting of 254 acres, and located four miles from town. In this farm he has one of the best in the county and he takes a commendable pride in keeping it up to the standard of the best farms in that section of the state.

MRS. LAVINIA GRIGGS.

Mr. Griggs is a public spirited citizen, believes in good roads, good government, and takes an interest in political matters. He and his wife are both members of the Methodist Episcopal church. He was married on Aug. 17, 1852, to Miss Lavinia Minton, a native of Henderson county, Ky., and a daughter of Gilford and Nancy (Elliott) Minton, the father a native of North Carolina and the mother of Maryland. On coming to Kentucky they settled first in Logan and later in Henderson county, where both passed to their rest. Mr. and Mrs. Griggs have had ten children. Three died in infancy; Alice and

Nannie died later; and those now living are Martha, Rolin, Paulina, **John** and Robert.

W. H. COMPTON, a well known farmer near Waverly, Ky., was born in Washington county of the same state, April 15, 1830. He is a son of Benjamin and Margaret (Smith) Compton, both of whom were natives of Washington county, where they were married, at Springfield, in 1832, and shortly afterward removed to Union county. There the father became an extensive farmer and slave owner. He took an active interest in the affairs of the county as a Whig before the war, and after that time he affiliated with the Democratic party. He died in 1877, at the age of seventy-four years, and his wife departed this life in 1882, aged seventy-eight. Both were devout members of the Catholic church. They had five children who grew to maturity, but the subject of this sketch and Mrs. Isabel Roberts are now the only ones living. W. H. Compton was reared on a farm and received his education in the public schools. From his early manhood he has been engaged in farming, in which occupation he has been eminently successful, being now the owner of 1,600 acres of land, all of which has been accumulated by his industry and well-directed efforts. He is an extensive stock raiser. Although a Democrat in his political affiliation he has no desire to join the ranks of the office seekers, notwithstanding he has all the qualifications of a successful official. He wisely prefers the certain returns from a well conducted farm to the precarious emoluments of a political career. The atmosphere with which he has been surrounded most of his life has given him broad views of both politics and religion, and while he is Democrat from principle he is, for the same reason, extremely liberal in his religious views.

JAMES W. HARRIS, one of the largest farmers and land owners of Union county, Ky., and a stockholder in the People's bank, of Uniontown, was born in the county where he now resides, Aug. 4, 1839. His father, William Truman Harris, was born in Nelson county in 1817, and his mother, whose maiden name was Virginia Pratt, was born in Gallatin county, Ky., in 1819. He died in 1860 and she is now living with the subject of this sketch, at the advanced age of eighty-five years. William T. Harris was a Jackson Democrat in his day and was a magistrate for several years. His father was Benjamin Harris, a native of Maryland, who came to Nelson county at an early day, and in 1825 settled in Union county. He married Innocent Ann Wight of Maryland. The maternal grandfather, James B. Pratt, was a native of the Old Dominion. He served in the war of 1812 and was wounded in the service; was mustered out in 1815; married Louisa Thompson, a native of Virginia, and settled in Gallatin county, Ky., in 1817. In 1828 they came to Union county and there passed their last days. He died in 1856 and she in 1865. William T. and Virginia Harris had a family of fourteen children, eight of whom are still living and all are over fifty years of age. Both parents were members of the Methodist church and he was a prominent Free Mason. James W. Harris was educated in the public schools and at St. Mary's college. His life work has been that of a farmer and he is one of the most progressive in the county. He owns eight hundred and forty acres of fine land and keeps fully abreast of the times in agricultural progress. Prior to 1896 he was a power in the Democratic party, but since then he has been independent in his political affiliations. He is a member of Morganfield Lodge, No. 66, Free and Accepted Masons, and of the Methodist Episcopal church. His paternal ancestry came from Ireland and his mother's people from Wales. This combination of Welsh and Irish blood has produced some of the best citizenry of the United States. Mr. Harris is no exception. He is strong, self-reliant, with Irish wit and Welsh courage, but withal a gentleman whom every one respects for his many sterling qualities.

JAMES THOMAS MARTIN, a farmer and stock raiser, residing near Waverly, Ky., was born in Union county of that state, Aug. 15, 1865. His parents were Lafayette and Jane V. (Austin) Martin, both natives of Union county. Lafayette was the son of John Martin, who settled in Union county some time in the thirties and there reared a family of nine children, all of whom are now deceased. During the Civil war Lafayette Martin served about a year in Captain Barnett's company, in the Confederate service. He was a farmer all his life in Union county, was a stanch Democrat, and he and his wife were both members of the Catholic church. He died in 1868 and his wife, who was a daughter of Thomas A. Austin, mentioned elsewhere in this work, died in 1896, aged fifty-six years. Of their three children James

Thomas is the only one now living. He was educated in the common schools and brought up to the life of a farmer. At the present time he has 425 acres of good land, upon which he successfully carries on a general farming business, his specialty being the feeding of hogs for market. Mr. Martin is a Democrat in his political opinions, but he is not an active politician. He and his family are members of the Sacred Heart Catholic church and are liberal supporters of its charitable works. In 1859 he was married to Mary N. Buckman, daughter of Charles N. Buckman, and they had two children, Joseph and Mary, twins. Joseph died in infancy. Mrs. Martin passed to her rest on April 29, 1890, and in 1899 Mr. Martin was united in marriage to Miss Nettie Bowling, of Davis county, Ky. To this union have been born three children: William Lafayette, deceased; Catherine Gertrude and James Bernard. Mr. Martin is looked upon as one of the most up-to-date farmers in the vicinity of Waverly. As a citizen he has a high standing in the community where he resides as a man of industrious habits, an accommodating disposition, and an unimpeachable integrity. He believes in modern progress, good roads, good schools, and his influence is always on the side of every movement for the promotion of the moral and material advancement of his fellow-men.

EDWARD F. ROBERTS (deceased) was born in Breckenridge county, Ky., in the year 1832, and died on his farm near Waverly, in Union county, on the last day of January, 1890. He was a son of Edward and Clara (Manning) Roberts, both of whom were native Kentuckians. The father died in Breckenridge county and the mother in Union. Both were members of the Catholic church. Edward F. Roberts received a good education in the public schools. In 1856 he came to Union county, where he was married in 1860 to Miss Sarah Isabel Compton, a daughter of Benedict Compton, one of the leading citizens. To this union there were born seven children, all living, viz.: Benjamin, Catherine, John, Mary E., Susan, James and Anna. John married Tillie Clements, daughter of Martin Clements, of Uniontown, and has two children, Pearl C. and Margaret Frances; Catharine married Clement M. Hancock, of Henderson, and has one son, Clyde Edward; Mary E. is the wife of Dudley Phipps, of Carlisle county, and Anna is the wife of James T. Speaks and the mother of one son, Edward Francis. At the time of his death Mr. Roberts was the owner of 190 acres of fine land, which still belongs to his family, and was reckoned one of the well-to-do farmers of Union county. He was a Democrat in politics and took a commendable interest in all matters pertaining to public policy. In church matters he was a devoted member of the Catholic church, to which Mrs. Roberts still belongs and takes an interest in its good works. In all his dealings with his fellow-men during his life Mr. Roberts was conspicuous for his spirit of fairness and his reputation for truthfulness. It has been said of him that "his word is just as good as his bond," and the good name he transmitted to his children is a prouder inheritance than lands and houses.

JOHN B. CRUZ, a farmer near Waverly, Ky., and a director in the Waverly Coal Mining Company, is of French extraction, his father, Peter J. Cruz, having been a native of France. At the age of seventeen years the latter came to America, with the monks who had educated him, and located in Washington county, Ky. There he married Matilda Abell and about the year 1815 settled in Union county. In his early life Peter J. Cruz formed a partnership with Richard Spaulding and for several years they followed the occupation of trading and flatboating on the river. Upon giving up this vocation Mr. Cruz settled down to the life of a planter, became the owner of 700 acres of fine land and a number of slaves. He was always a Democrat in his political views, and both himself and wife were members of the Catholic church. John B. Cruz was born in the county where he now resides on Oct. 21, 1828. He was reared on a farm, educated in the common schools, and his principal occupation through life has been that of a tiller of the soil. In 1887 he bought a farm of 192 acres, to which he has added until he now owns 365 acres. This farm is well improved and is in a fine state of cultivation. Besides his farming interests Mr. Cruz is one of the principal stockholders and one of the directors in the Waverly Coal Mining Company, as already mentioned. In both political and religious matters he has followed after his father, being a Democrat and a Catholic, to which church his entire family belongs. Mr. Cruz was married in 1852 to Miss Arametta Wathen, daughter of Francis and Rosalie (Clements) Wathen, old settlers of Union county, where both passed their last days. To Mr. and Mrs. Cruz there have been born eleven children: William A. and two daughters, each named Rosalie, are deceased and those living are Peter J., Matilda A., Mary L., Emma D., Susan M., John B., Francis W., and Carrie C. All are married except Francis W., who lives at home with his parents. Mr. Cruz is a man of fine business ability. What he has he has made himself, by his industry and intelligent efforts. He enjoys the confidence and esteem of his neighbors and in every way is one of the representative men of his county.

ULYSSES SHERMAN BISHOP, a well known farmer, three and a half miles east of Morganfield, Ky., was born in the county where he now resides on Feb. 8, 1865, his parents being John P. and Rebecca N. (Hawkins) Bishop. Both parents were natives of Jefferson county, Ky., where the father was born on Dec. 22, 1823, and the mother on May 1, 1843. Both grandfathers, Daniel Bishop and Jacob Hawkins, were also natives of that county. John P. Bishop located in Union county, near Morganfield, in 1854, and there followed farming until his death on April 10, 1893. At the time of his death he was one of the well-to-do farmers of the county, being the owner of about 600 acres of land. For a number of years he held the office of justice of the peace. In politics he was a Republican and in the stormy days just before the Civil war he was a stanch Union man. He was a member of the Masonic fraternity and with his wife belonged to the Christian church. He was twice married, the subject of this sketch being one of the seven children born to the second marriage. By his first wife he had three children. Ulysses S. Bishop was educated in the common schools, the Caseyville high school, and a commercial college at St. Louis. With the exception of two years he has followed farming ever since he reached manhood. During the two years mentioned he was engaged in mercantile pursuits at Henshaw, a small town in the western part of Union county. He now owns 163 acres where he lives and has one of the best improved farms in the county. Mr. Bishop is a Republican in his political views and takes a laudable interest in all questions pertaining to the public weal. He is a member of

De Koven Lodge, No. 577, Free and Accepted Masons, and with his family belongs to the Christian church. On June 17, 1891, he was married to Miss Anna, daughter of W. B. Henshaw, whose father, George Henshaw, came from Virginia at an early date and settled in Union county. To this marriage there have been born three children: Catherine R., Robert H., and J. Wesley.

WILLIAM WALLER, a farmer living about four miles west of Morganfield, Union county, Ky., is a native of that county, having been born there Feb. 18, 1828, his father being Aaron Waller, an old resident of the county, of whom mention is made elsewhere in this work. William Waller was reared on his father's farm, assisting in the work of raising the crops during the summer seasons and attending the common schools during the winter months, thus securing a good practical education. Upon arriving at manhood he began life as a farmer and has followed that occupation all his life. Mr. Waller is one of the successful farmers of Union county. He owns 500 acres of good land, well improved and the most of it under cultivation. Politically he is a Democrat and while he takes an interest in public questions it is always more as a citizen than as an office seeker. In 1856 he was united in marriage to Miss Elizabeth Muir, the daughter of W. Muir, a native and old resident of Nelson county, Ky., and the year following his marriage located on the farm where he now resides. Consequently he has been a resident of the neighborhood where he lives for almost half a century, and in that time has been identified with almost every movement to secure better roads, better schools, etc. Mr. and Mrs. Waller are both members of the Methodist Episcopal Church South and consistently practice the precepts of their faith in their daily conduct. They are the parents of the following children: William M., a farmer in Union county, living on the old homestead; Aaron, a grain dealer of Henderson, Ky.; Claude, an attorney of Nashville, Tenn.; Jasper, a farmer, living at home with his parents; Margaret, wife of Henry Hughes, of Paducah, Ky.; Mary, at home with her parents, and one who died in infancy. All the children who reached maturity are useful members of society, due in a great measure to the Christian teaching of their parents.

GEORGE S. WILSON, a promising young attorney of Sturgis, Ky., is a descendant of some of the most prominent families of Union county. His grandfather, John Wilson, was a native of

England, but came with his father when sixteen years of age to the United States. After living for a while in New York, Ohio, and Illinois, he settled in Union county about the year 1851 and died there in 1863. He married Matilda Brackett, who died in 1885. Of their ten children six are living. John Wilson was a miner in his early life, but after coming to Kentucky he followed farming as long as he lived. One of his sons, William Wilson, was born in Illinois, Nov. 7, 1839. He received the greater part of his schooling after the family removed to Union county, and began life as a clerk in a store. Later he was engaged in merchandizing at Caseyville, was for a time in the livery business and was also interested in steamboating, having charge of a steamer. He served for four years as deputy sheriff and sheriff of the county, is a prominent member of the Masonic fraternity, belonging to Kelsey Lodge, No. 659, Union Chapter, Royal Arch Masons, No. 54, and Alida Commandery, Knights Templars, No. 21. He and his wife are members of the Cumberland Presbyterian church, though his father was an Episcopalian. William Wilson was married to Martha A. Collins, daughter of Dr. James and Eleanor Ann (Pitman) Collins, both natives of Virginia, and early settlers in Union county. Doctor Collins died in 1867 and his wife in 1883. William and Martha Wilson are the parents of the following children: Addie Belle, John W., one who died unnamed, James C., Herbert Lee, Emma P., and George S. John W. is deceased. George S. Wilson, the youngest of the family, was born at Caseyville, Union county, Nov. 14, 1876. His elementary education was acquired in the public schools of Union and Henderson counties, and on June 7, 1900, he was graduated from the law department of Cumberland university, at Lebanon, Tenn. Shortly after leaving college he established himself at Sturgis, where he commenced the practice of his profession. He has already built up a good practice, extending to Union and adjoining counties, and has a growing clientage. Mr. Wilson is one of the active young Democrats of his section of the state and in 1904 was the candidate of his party for representative to the legislature. He has probably inherited some of his love for Democratic principles from his father and grandfather, both of whom were inflexible supporters of that party's doctrines. In fraternal circles he is a well known figure, being a member of the Knights of Pythias and the Independent Order of Odd Fellows, holding his membership in both orders in the lodges at Sturgis. In 1901 he was married to Miss Virginia L. McGill, of Webster county, and to this union there have been born two children: George S. and Henry McGill. Mr. Wilson is a member of the Cumberland Presbyterian church and his wife is a Baptist.

P. H. WINSTON, of Sturgis, Ky., a prominent member of the Union county bar, is a native of that county. For several generations on both sides his ancestors have been a part of the warp and woof of the Commonwealth of Kentucky. His grandfather, Maj. William Winston, was a native of Hanover county, Va. He came in early manhood to Boone county, Ky., and subsequently became the owner of large tracts of land in Boone, Fleming and Union counties. About 1835 he settled in Union county and there passed the remainder of his days. His wife was a Miss Martha Mosby, also a native of Virginia. She died at Caseyville in 1858, aged seventy-two years. One of their sons was Dr. G. V. Winston, the father of the subject of this sketch. He was born in Henrico county, Va., March 8, 1821; graduated from the medical department of the old Louisville university under the first Doctor Yandell; began practicing at Covington; later came to Union county, where he continued to practice until 1885; and died on Nov. 24, 1896, aged seventy-five years. In politics he was an unflinching advocate of Democratic principles; was a man of great public spirit, and was a prominent member of the Masonic fraternity. He married Elizabeth Byers Dix, a daughter of Clarendon Dix, a native of Illinois. Her mother was Amelia Byers, a native of Mason county, Ky., a daughter of Col. James Byers, who was born in Maryland and died in Mississippi. The wife of Colonel Byers was Anna Maria Johnston, a sister of Albert Sidney Johnston, the famous Confederate general who was killed at the battle of Shiloh. Dr. G. V. Winston and his wife were the parents of twelve children. Seven sons and two daughters are still living. One of the sons is P. H. Winston, the subject of this sketch. He was born in Union county, May 13, 1876, and was reared to manhood on a farm. After completing the course in the public schools he took up the study of law and in June, 1900, graduated from the law department of Cumberland university at Lebanon, Tenn. Immediately after leaving college he established himself at Sturgis and commenced the practice of his profession. He has already won a high place at the bar and is looked upon as one of the coming lawyers of Kentucky, a state that has produced some of the greatest legal lights of the nation. Mr. Winston is an unswerving Democrat in his political opinions and is well informed on all public questions. He is a member of Kelsey Lodge, No. 659, Free and Accepted Masons, and of Silver Lodge, No. 68, Knights of Pythias. On Oct. 28, 1903, he was united in marriage to Miss Elizabeth Luttrell, of Hickman, Ky.

Another son of Dr. G. V. Winston is Isaac Dix Winston, M.D., who was born in 1874; educated in the common schools and the Sturgis high school; graduated from the medical department of the University of Nashville in March, 1900, and has since practiced his profession in Sturgis, where he has already established a lucrative practice. He is a member of the same lodge of Knights of Pythias as his brother, and belongs to the Christian church. Politically he is a Democrat.

W. L. MARKWELL, D.D.S., a rising young dentist of Sturgis, Ky., is a native of Union county, having been born near the town where he is now in business, Oct. 7, 1877. His father, Charles W. Markwell, was born in Bullitt county, Ky., but came to Union county when a young man and located on a farm not far from Sturgis. When the town was laid out he erected the first dwelling there and engaged in business as a grain dealer. For some time he was associated with the old Sturgis Milling Company as a buyer of wheat. He married Belle Davis, a daughter of Lewis Davis, who was born in Union county in 1822. Her mother was Lewis N. Whitecotton, a daughter of George N. and Nancy (Young) Whitecotton. George N. Whitecotton was born in Prince William county, Va., Oct. 27, 1802, and came to Union county when about twenty years of age. He died July 19, 1889. His wife was born Nov. 10, 1797, and was a daughter of Christopher Young, who spent most of his life in Union county. Lewis Davis, the maternal grandfather of Dr. Markwell, was a son of William and Druzilla (Falkner) Davis, the former born in Fayette county, Ky., June 12, 1791, and the latter born in the same county, Feb. 3, 1793. They settled in Union county soon after their marriage. He died there on July 4, 1862, her death having previously occurred on Aug. 19, 1844. William Davis's father was John Davis, who settled in Union county in 1819. Dr. W. L. Markwell received his education in the public schools of Sturgis and in 1903 graduated from the Louisville college of dentistry. Immediately upon leaving college he established an office for the practice of his profession in Sturgis and has built up a lucrative business. As a dentist he has acquired the reputation of being one of the best in the county and his painstaking methods of doing his work have won for him the patronage of the best class of people. Like his father before him, he is a Democrat, though he thinks more of his professional duties than of political preferment. In religious matters he has accepted the faith of his honored parents and belongs to the Baptist church.

SAMUEL LEWIS CLEMENTS, a farmer of Union county, Ky., living near Morganfield, is a descendant of some of the oldest families of that county. His grandfather, Edward Henson Clements, came from St. Mary's county, Md., and settled in Union county in 1802. At that time Patrick Clements, the father of Samuel L., was about six years of age, having been born in the year 1796. He grew to manhood in Union county. Upon reaching manhood he became a farmer, the farm he formerly owned now belonging to the subject of this sketch. Patrick Clements received such an education as the schools of that early day afforded, but by self-study he became one of the best informed men in his neighborhood. He was a Democrat in his political views and with his family belonged to the Catholic church. He was twice married. His first wife was Christina, daughter of Dr. Bernard Smith. She was born in St. Mary's county, Md., July 24, 1801, and came in childhood with her parents to Union county. She died in 1847, the mother of eight children, two of whom are still living. His second wife was Matilda Hite, also a native of Maryland, and to this marriage were born two children, both living, one being the subject of this sketch. Patrick Clements died on Dec. 15, 1869, and his wife on July 29, 1870. Samuel L. Clements was born April 29, 1852, was reared on the farm, attended the common schools in his boyhood and later the Christian Brothers' school at Dayton, O. Upon arriving at manhood he adopted the life of a farmer and is now the owner of 485 acres of fine land. Like his father, he is a Democrat and a Catholic, and is one of the progressive and respected citizens of the community in which he lives. He was married on Feb. 24, 1873, to Miss Catherine Cambron, a daughter of Logan and a granddaughter of Zeph Cambron, a sketch of whose brother, Raphael, appears elsewhere in this work. Her grandmother was a Miss Grundy and her mother a Miss Truman. Samuel and Catherine Clements have had the following children born to them: Lewis P., Annie, Charlie, Logan, Samuel, Gertrude, Mary, Nicholas, and Franklin, living, and two who died in infancy.

REV. CYRIN THOMAS, pastor of Sacred Heart Catholic church, St. Vincent, Ky., was born in Grant county, Ind., Jan. 1, 1853. His parents, Enoch G. and Jane (Votaw) Thomas, were both born in Wayne county, Ind., and now live in Huntington county of that state. His grandfather, Jesse Thomas, was born Sept. 9, 1796; went from Wayne to Grant county at an early date, and died at Marion. He married Hannah Cox, who was born Aug. 15, 1798. She also died at Marion. On the maternal side his grandparents were Daniel and Mary (Hampton) Votaw, the former born in Loudoun county, Va., Aug. 7, 1783, and the latter in Fayette county, Nov. 22, 1787. Daniel Votaw died in Kansas, Aug. 18, 1871, and his wife in Wayne county, Ind., May 17, 1827. Daniel Votaw was a son of Isaac and Ann (Smith) Votaw. Isaac was born in Virginia, Jan. 29, 1744, and died in Columbiana county, O., Oct. 12, 1817. His wife was born in Bucks county, Pa., July 20, 1746, and died in Columbiana county, Jan. 23, 1834. Enoch G. Thomas has been a farmer, mechanic and miller and is now eighty-one years of age. He and his wife have been married sixty-one years. They are the parents of twelve children, only three of whom are now living. Rev. Cyrin Thomas was reared on a farm and graduated from St. Meinrad seminary in Spencer county, Ind. After completing his education he spent some time in South America and in 1896 came to Kentucky. For about eighteen months he was pastor of the church of SS. Peter and Paul at Danville, and since Nov. 4, 1897, has been in charge of the Sacred Heart church of St. Vincent. His parish numbers about 300 families and under his ministration the church has prospered. Father Thomas is popular in the community where he lives and his popularity is not confined to the members of his church.

J. W. HITE, one of the largest farmers in the vicinity of Waverly, Union county, Ky., was born near Uniontown, in that county, Dec. 13, 1853. He is a son of George and Anna (Fenwick) Hite, and a grandson of Peter Hite, who was one of the pioneers of the county. (For account of the family history, see the sketch of W. P. Hite.) George Hite was born in Union county, was educated in the common schools and in later years was a large farmer and slave owner. He was always an ardent Democrat and a member of the Catholic church. He and his first wife were the parents of nine children, seven of whom are still living. After the death of his first wife he was married to Mrs. Spaulding, the widow of Charlton Spaulding, and one daughter was born to this union. His second wife died and he was married a third time, his last wife being Marian Helon. J. W. Hite was reared to manhood on his father's farm. After attending the common schools he spent some time at St. Mary's college. Upon completing his education he commenced life as a farmer, and has continued in that occupation through life. He is the owner of 575 acres of good land and his farming is carried on according to the latest and most approved methods. Mr. Hite has won considerable reputation as a breeder of Shorthorn cattle. In his political and religious affiliations he has followed in the footsteps of his sire, being an unwavering adherent to Democratic principles and a member of the Catholic church. On Feb. 4, 1879, he was united in marriage to Miss Mary Lewis Cruz, a daughter of John B. Cruz, whose sketch appears in this work. To this marriage there have been born the following children: John B., Gertrude, Araminta, Emma, William F., Anna Florence, Samuel R. and Paulie.

REV. ROBERT CRANEY, pastor of St. Ann's Catholic church, Morganfield, Ky., was born in the city of Louisville, Feb. 15, 1859, his parents being Dennis and Tirzah (Norman) Craney. His parents were both born in Ireland, married in that country, and soon afterward came to America, settling in Louisville, where both died, the father in 1889 and the mother in 1895. Rev. Robert Craney acquired his elementary education in the public schools of his native city, after which he graduated from St. Joseph's college at Bardstown, and finished with a course at Preston Park seminary. He left school in 1885, and from that time until 1889 was pastor at various places in the State of Kentucky. In 1889 he came to Morganfield and assumed pastoral charge of St. Ann's parish, in which there are about 150 families. Here for almost fifteen years he has toiled in the vineyard of the Master, rejoicing with those who rejoice and sympathizing with those who mourn, but always having a praiseworthy solicitude for the spiritual welfare of his people. In civic life Father Craney is an exemplary citizen. He takes an interest in all questions touching the public weal, and never hesitates to perform his duty to the whole people as he sees it. Politically he is a conscientious supporter of Democratic principles and affiliates with that party.

WILLIAM PETER HITE, a farmer, living near Waverly, Union county, Ky., was born Nov. 12, 1840, in the neighborhood where he now lives. His grandfather, Peter Hite, was born in Germany, but came in early life to the United States, located in Union county, and there became an extensive farmer and slaveholder. He married Polly Clements, a native of Washington county, and both died near Hitesville. In his day Peter Hite was one of the leading Democrats of the county, was widely known and a citizen of considerable influence. One of his sons was John Hite, the father of the subject of this sketch. He was reared on the farm, educated at St. Mary's college, and in later life became a large land and slave owner and a prominent citizen. He married Ann Frances Pike, a daughter of William and an aunt of Sylvester Pike. Her mother was a Miss Susan Mills. Her parents settled in Marion county in 1828, and both died there. John Hite and his wife were the parents of six children, three sons and three daughters. Two sons and two daughters are still living. The mother died on April 9, 1880, aged sixty-nine years, and the father on March 26, 1887, at the age of seventy-three. William P. Hite received his elementary education in the common schools, after which he attended St. Mary's college. In May, 1861, he enlisted in Company C, Fourth Kentucky infantry, and served four years, taking part in some of the hottest engagements of the war. At Shiloh he received two severe wounds. After the war he returned to his home and took up the occupation of farming, which he has followed through life. At the present time he is the owner of 320 acres of good land, well improved and in a high state of cultivation. Like his father and grandfather, he is identified with the Democratic party, and held the office of magistrate for a period of twelve years. He has also accepted the religious faith of his ancestors, who were members of the Catholic church, and with his family belongs to that denomination. On Nov. 5, 1867, he was united in marriage to Miss Sarah Catharine, daughter of Benjamin and Priscilla Jane (Mills) Thomas. Her parents lived in Marion county, where she was born, but during the war removed to Union county. Her father died at Morganfield Sept. 21, 1904. Her mother died in Marion county, and her father was afterward twice married. William P. and Sarah C. Hite have had the following children: Mary, who married John Hancock and died leaving two sons and two daughters; John, who died in infancy; Anna, married William Wathen and afterward died; B. J., a farmer near Morganfield; Florence C., who married C. C. Hardesty. She and one of her two children are yet living.

IGNATIUS WATHEN, a well known farmer, living near Waverly, Union county, Ky., was born on the farm where he now lives, March 3, 1856. He is a son of Theodore Wathen, mentioned elsewhere in this work. Ignatius Wathen was educated in the common schools and at Gethsemane college. Upon reaching manhood he became a farmer and has followed that vocation all his life. He now owns 182 acres of the old homestead, and is one of the well-to-do farmers of his neighborhood. He takes a commendable interest in public affairs and is identified with the Democratic party on all political questions. On Dec. 3, 1887, he was married to Miss Mary Ann, daughter of Morris and Margaret Ann (Hancock) Griffin, of Henderson county. The ancestors of Mrs. Wathen were among the early settlers in that county. Morris Griffin was born in Ireland, but came to this country when he was about twenty-five years of age and spent the rest of his life in Henderson county. His wife was a daughter of Joseph and Mary (Quinn) Hancock, who lived and died in Henderson county, where they were well known and universally respected. Mrs. Wathen died on Aug. 20, 1902, leaving four children: Margaret Griffin, Paul Ignatius, Ruth Elizabeth and Julia Adell. She was a member of the Methodist church, but Mr. Wathen is a Catholic, and is interested in the many worthy charities of his church.

JOHN MILTON RONEY, a prominent citizen of St. Vincent, Union county, Ky., was born at Lebanon, in that state, Aug. 16, 1830. His parents, Edward and Elizabeth (Wright) Roney, were both born in Marion county, the father at Lebanon and the mother near there. His grandfather, Roger Roney, was born in Ireland, but came in early manhood to America and located near Lebanon on a farm now owned by the subject of this sketch. He died at Lebanon about the year 1879, aged seventy-nine years. His wife lived to be ninety-three. They had three sons and three daughters. One daughter and two of the sons are still living. John M. Roney grew to manhood on a farm, attended St. Mary's college, after which he learned the carpenters' trade, and in 1855 came to Union county, where he has ever since lived. For several generations his ancestors have been identified with the Catholic church. He was brought up in that faith and has always been interested in the welfare of his church and her institutions. His zeal in this cause led to his being made general manager of the St. Vincent academy in 1861, a position he has held ever since that date, and the duties of which he has discharged with ability and enthusiasm. Mr. Roney is interested in several of the leading financial institutions of the county, notably among them being the People's bank of Morganfield, the Farmers' bank of Uniontown, and the Waverly bank at Waverly. In political matters he affiliated with the Democratic party until 1896, when, being at variance with the party's declarations on the money question, he went over to the Republicans.

WILLIAM G. LINDLE, M.D., of Sturgis, Ky., one of the most prominent physicians and surgeons of Union county, is a descendant of old North Carolina and Virginia families, who were among the early settlers of Kentucky. His grandfather, Jacob Joseph Lindle, was born in the year 1798. He married in Spencer county, Ky., a Miss Elizabeth Redmond, and in 1852 removed to Union county, where he died in 1856. One of the sons born to this marriage was Jacob William Lindle, the father of the subject of this sketch. He was born at Fairfield, Nelson county, May 1, 1828, received his education in that county, and on July 16, 1850, married Hannah Beasley

Reynolds in Spencer county. Three years later he removed with his family to Union county and there passed the remainder of his life. In 1864 he built Lindle's mill, and two years later began selling goods there, but discontinued the business after a time to engage in other pursuits. He also owned and operated a distillery and had a good farm in the Lindle precinct, which was named in his honor. In politics he was a stanch Democrat and he was a member of the Masonic fraternity. His death occurred in 1894. His widow is now living at Sturgis, in the eighty-third year of her age. Their children were Richard Mitchell, William Green, Belle, Maggie Green, Jacob Beasley, Robert Dimmett, Anna and Lavinia. On the maternal side Doctor Lindle's grandfather, Greenbury Reynolds, was born in North Carolina in 1806, came to Spencer county in 1825, and in 1853 settled in Union county, where he died. His wife was Nancy Vance Cogshill, a daughter of John and Hannah (Beasley) Cogshill. Her father was a native of Culpeper county, Va., married his wife near Frankfort, Ky., and died in Spencer county in 1839. Richard Reynolds, Doctor Lindle's great-grandfather, was a native of North Carolina. He married Anna Holmes in that state, and shortly afterward settled in Kentucky. Dr. William G. Lindle was born on a farm about three miles from Sturgis. His elementary education was acquired in the common schools. In 1877 he went to Valparaiso, Ind., as a student in the Northern Indiana normal school, and graduated from that institution the following year in the teacher's course. He then taught for about ten years in the schools of Union county and at Eldorado, Ill., leaving the latter place in 1887 to enter the Kentucky School of Medicine at Louisville, where he graduated on the roll of honor in 1888. Soon afterward he commenced the practice of his profession at Otisco, Ind., where he did a successful business for about five years. In 1892 he took a post-graduate course in the New York Polyclinic Institute and at the same time took special courses in diseases of women and children; eye, ear, nose and throat; nervous diseases and obstetrics. He then returned to Sturgis, bought several lots at the corner of Sixth and Adams streets, built a handsome residence and office and has since practiced his profession there. In 1898 he again went to New York and took a review term in the Polyclinic hospital. The same year he took a major operating course in surgery under Dr. A. G. Gerster, of Mt. Sinai hospital, and an operating course in gynecology. Doctor Lindle is rightly regarded as one of the most progressive physicians in his section of the state. He is fully up to the times in all new discoveries relating to his profession, and has a large and lucrative practice. He is well known in Masonic circles, being a member of Kelsey Lodge No. 659; Union Chapter No. 54, Royal Arch Masons, and Alida Commandery No. 21, Knights Templars. He is also a member of the Ancient Order of United Workmen and the Golden Cross, and belongs to Chanty Lodge, Independent Order of Odd Fellows. In religious matters he belongs to the Christian church and is a consistent practitioner of the tenets of his faith. He married some years ago Miss Mary Ellen Kirk, who was reared in Union county. She died on June 18, 1903.

B. F. HUMPHREY, M.D., an eminent young physician of Sturgis, Union county, Ky., was born near that town on March 3, 1877. His parents, J. B. and Cordelia Ann (Nall) Humphrey, are both natives of McLean county, Ky., were married in that county, and in 1872 removed to Union county, where they still live on a farm about five miles from the town of Sturgis. They are the parents of seven sons and three daughters, all living but one son. The father is an influential man in the community where he resides. He takes an active interest in political affairs as a Democrat and is a member of the Masonic fraternity. He and his wife are both members of the Baptist church. Dr. B. F. Humphrey received his primary education in the public schools, and in 1897 graduated from Bethel college at Russellville, Ky., with the degree of Bachelor of Sciences. He then took up the study of medicine and in 1901 received the degree of M.D. from the medical department of the University of Louisville. The same year he located at Sturgis and began the practice of his profession. Although one of the youngest physicians in the county he has won a high standing, both with his brother doctors and the public, and is on the high road to professional success. He is a member of Silver Lodge No. 68, Knights of Pythias. On Feb. 3, 1903, Doctor Humphrey and Miss Lillian Russell were united in marriage. She is a native of Paris, Tex., where her father, Thomas Russell, is a retired business man. Her mother was Annie Henry, born in Union county, a daughter of Thomas and Mary (Hawkins) Henry, old settlers of Union county, where her father was a prominent farmer and slaveholder before the war. To Dr. Humphrey and his wife there has been born one daughter, whom they have named Dorothy Russell. Both himself and wife are members of the Baptist church.

WILLIAM BURNETT GOAD, a retired farmer of Sturgis, Union county, Ky., was born in that county in June, 1861. He is the only child of John Bail and Rebecca (Gatling) Goad, both natives of Hopkins county, where the grandparents, John and Rachel Goad, were among the early settlers, coming from Virginia. John and Rachel Goad had three children, two sons and a daughter, all now deceased. In his day he was one of the large land and slave owners of Hopkins county. A few years before the Civil war the parents of William B. Goad settled in Union county, where the father owned a farm of 300 acres at the time of his death, which occurred on July 26, 1896. He was one of the prominent Democrats of the county and he and his wife were members of the Baptist church. She died in August, 1899. Her father, Ephraim Gatling, was also one of the pioneers of Hopkins county. William B. Goad attended the public schools in his boyhood and later Bethel college at Russellville, Ky. For a number of years he followed the vocation of a farmer and was also interested in buying and selling horses. In 1902 he retired from the active conduct of his farm and came to Sturgis. Here he built one of the finest residences in the town and is one of the prominent citizens. He is a member of the Independent Order of Odd Fellows and the Knights of Pythias, holding membership in both bodies at Sturgis. His wife is a Baptist and he is a constant attendant at her church. About the time that he settled in Sturgis he became one of the organizers of the First National bank of that place, was one of the first board of directors and later vice-president, but is not now connected with the institution. On Feb. 25, 1891, he was married to Miss Lulu Harris, a native of Union county. Her father is J. D. Harris, a prominent citizen of Sturgis, a son of Thomas and Mahala (Redmond) Harris, and came with his parents from Spencer county when he was about four years old. His paternal grandfather, Webb Harris, was born in Virginia and was one of the early settlers of Spencer county. He was one of the organizers of the bank above referred to, and was its first cashier. He belongs to Kelsey Lodge, No. 659, Free and Accepted Masons; Union Chapter, No. 54, Royal Arch Masons, and Alida Commandery, No. 21, Knights Templars. His wife was Miss Nancy O. Jones, a daughter of W. H. Jones, a native of Union county. She is a member of the Christian church. Mr. Goad still owns his farm of 400 acres and looks after its management. He is one of the public spirited men of Sturgis and is always in favor of any movement for the general advancement of the interests of the town.

WILLIAM H. NUNN, M.D., a popular and successful physician of Henshaw, Union county, Ky., comes of one of the old pioneer families of the state. About the beginning of the last century his paternal grandparents, Ira and Sarah (Langston) Nunn, came from their native state of Georgia and located in Crittenden county. There he became one of the leading citizens, and at one time owned something like 3,000 acres of land in that and Union counties. They died in Crittenden county and their remains rest in the little cemetery on the old Nunn homestead. They were both members of the Methodist church. One of their sons was Thomas L. Nunn, the father of Dr. Nunn. He was born in Crittenden county, was educated in the common schools there, became a successful farmer and one of the prominent men of his neighborhood. He served as master of Zion Hill Masonic lodge and won considerable reputation as an orator. He married Sarah C., daughter of Robert H. and Pernicia (Young) Haynes, who were also pioneers of Crittenden county. The maternal grandmother of Dr. Nunn was a member of the Georgia family of Livingstons, dating back to colonial days, Alexander Stephens being a relative. Thomas L. Nunn and his wife had ten children, seven of whom are still living. He died on the old homestead on Jan. 16, 1880, and was buried in the cemetery already mentioned. His widow is still living near Marion, aged seventy-three years. Dr. W. H. Nunn was born near Marion, Ky., Sept. 10, 1854. After acquiring a common school education he commenced teaching and followed that occupation for several years, reading medicine in the meantime. On Feb. 22, 1881, he was graduated from the medical department of the University of Tennessee at Nashville, and soon afterward began practicing near his home in Crittenden county. In 1891 he located at Henshaw, where he has established a lucrative practice. Dr. Nunn is a member of the Ohio Valley and Kentucky State Medical associations and of the Union County Medical society. His professional standing is of the very best and his reputation as a citizen is that of a patriotic, public spirited and law abiding man. He is a prominent member of the Masonic fraternity, belonging to Shiloh Lodge, No. 453, at Grove Center; Union Chapter, No. 54, Royal Arch Masons, at Sturgis; and Alida Commandery, No. 21, Knights Templars. On Jan. 27, 1891, he led to the altar Miss Ida J. King, of Crittenden county, and to this union there have been born two children, Olga Lucile and J. Proctor. Dr. Nunn and his family belong to the Methodist Episcopal church.

HENRY RICHARDS DYER, a merchant of Henshaw, Union county, Ky., was born in that county, Jan. 18, 1857. His grandfather, William Dyer, came from Virginia at a very early date and aided in locating the county seat of Union county at Morganfield. He married a Miss Harris, a native of the county, and both died near Morganfield. One of their sons was Harvey Dyer, the father of the subject of this sketch. He was born and reared in the county, married Mrs. America Bingham, widow of James C. Bingham, also a native of the county, and devoted the greater part of his life to agricultural pursuits, owning a farm of 465 acres near Henshaw. He attended the common schools, and, starting in at the age of eighteen years, he became a fine Latin scholar under the instruction of Professor Johnson. He and his wife were members of the Cumberland Presbyterian church. They died within two weeks of each other, her death occurring on Oct. 16, 1872, and his on Nov. 1st. They had six children. Three died in infancy and three are living, viz.: W. C., a resident of Dekoven; Henry R., the subject of this sketch; and George, who has been a mail clerk on the Illinois Central railroad for a number of years. The maiden name of the mother of these children was America Henry. Her father, Patrick Henry, was a native of Ireland, a pioneer of Union county, and died near Caseyville, where he was a large land and slave owner before the war. She had one son by her first marriage, S. H. Bingham, of Henshaw, whose sketch appears in this work. Henry R. Dyer obtained his education in the common schools and a select school at Caseyville, under W. C. Dimmitt, and until 1899 followed farming for a livelihood. In that year he formed a partnership with J. V. Runyan in the mercantile line, and has since been engaged in that business at Henshaw. Mr. Dyer is one of the most active Democrats in the county. In this he has followed the example of both his father and grandfather, who were prominent in the councils of that party. He served as magistrate from 1886 to 1890; was road supervisor from 1890 to 1894; and for several years has been district committeeman. He is a prominent member of the Masonic fraternity, belonging to Shiloh Lodge, No. 453, of which he was worshipful master for ten years; Union Chapter, No. 54, Royal Arch Masons, at Sturgis; and to the Ancient and Accepted Scottish Rite. He is a member and for several years has held the office of elder in the Christian church. Mr. Dyer has been married three times: First to Miss Allie Evans, of Lyon county, on Jan. 29, 1878, and who died in March, 1882, leaving one daughter, Jennie; second, to Miss Katie Bishop, of Union county, on May 2, 1884, and who died on May 16, 1888, leaving one son, Harry; third, to Miss Sallie, daughter of Hugh Nunn, an old resident of Union county, on April 29, 1890, and to this union there have been born two children, Mary Casey and Henry Richards, Jr. Katie Bishop was a daughter of John P. Bishop, whose sketch appears in this work. The present Mrs. Dyer is a member of the Cumberland Presbyterian church.

J. P. BISHOP, M.D., of Henshaw, Union county, Ky., is one of the popular and promising young physicians in that section of the state. He is a native of the county; a son of John P. Bishop, mentioned elsewhere in this work; was educated in the elementary branches in the common schools of his native county, and grew to manhood on his father's farm. In 1897 he was graduated from the South Kentucky college, at Hopkinsville, and soon afterward began the study of medicine. In May, 1901, he graduated from the medical department of the University of Cincinnati, O. Shortly after receiving his degree he located at Henshaw, where, by his close attention to business, his genial disposition and sympathetic nature, he has built up a practice of which a physician of more mature years might well feel proud. Dr. Bishop is a member of the Kentucky State Medical association and the Medical society of Union county. In fraternal circles he belongs to the Modern Woodmen of America; in religious matters he is a member of the Christian church, and in politics he is a Republican in whom there is no guile. In 1903 he was a delegate from Union county to the Republican state convention, and is always interested in promoting the principles and success of his party. Notwithstanding his pronounced political activity he does not permit any political matters to interfere with his professional duties. He is one of those physicians who understand the true nature of the Hippocratic oath, and no call from the afflicted is turned aside. Dr.

Bishop is a student of everything pertaining to his noble calling. He realizes that the mere possession of a diploma does not make a physician and that there is much to be learned after the doors of the university close behind the graduate. With this view, and the fact that he has a laudable ambition to enroll his name among the eminent men of his profession, it will not be surprising if the future confers still greater honors upon him. In addition to his professional duties he is interested in business enterprises; is secretary and treasurer of the Henshaw brick and tile works; holds the office of town clerk and treasurer, and is always interested in every movement to promote the general welfare of Henshaw.

JOHN B. NUNN, a farmer, living one and a fourth miles east of Sturgis, Union county, Ky., was born in that county, Nov. 16, 1859, his parents being Hugh and Mildred (Whitecotton) Nunn. (See sketch of Dr. W. H. Nunn for an extended account of the family ancestry.) Hugh Nunn spent the greater part of his life in Union county, where he followed the occupation of farming. He was a prominent Democrat and for twenty years held the office of magistrate. He was twice married. His first wife was a Miss Hughes, and to this union there were born two children, both now deceased. His second wife was a daughter of George Whitecotton. She was born in Jefferson county, Ky., but came with her parents to Union county in her girlhood. She died on Sept. 26, 1876, the mother of ten children—eight daughters and two sons—all living but one. Hugh Nunn died on June 1, 1887. He and his wife were both members of the Cumberland Presbyterian church. John B. Nunn was reared on the farm and educated in the public and private schools of Union and adjoining counties. He now owns and occupies the old Whitecotton homestead, that formerly belonged to his mother's parents. In politics he is an active factor in shaping the affairs of the Democracy of Union county, and now holds the office of deputy county assessor. He is a member of Kelsey Lodge, No. 659, Free and Accepted Masons; Silver Lodge, No. 68, Knights of Pythias; and of the Independent Order of Odd Fellows at Sturgis. On Dec. 27, 1882, he was united in marriage to Miss Sarah C., daughter of William S. Martin, an old resident of Union county, who died in 1883. To this marriage there have been born the following children: G. W., Casey S., Clifton A., Georgia S., Byers A. and Cantrell. Mr. and Mrs. Nunn belong to the Cumberland Presbyterian church at Sullivan.

SILAS HENRY BINGHAM, a prosperous and well known farmer, living about one and a half miles from Henshaw, Union county, Ky., is of Irish ancestry and a descendant of one of the old colonial families. About the middle of the eighteenth century, John Bingham and two brothers came from the Emerald Isle to America. One of the brothers settled in Pennsylvania and the other two finally located in Ohio. All were soldiers in the American army during the Revolutionary war, and all reared large families. One of John Bingham's sons was Silas, the grandfather of the subject of this sketch. He was a millwright by trade and married Martha A. Cranston. After his death at Athens, O., his widow went to Trigg county, Ky., and there passed the remainder of her days. James C. Bingham, a son of this marriage, was born at Athens in the year 1817. He learned the trade of millwright with his father and followed that occupation the greater part of his life. He was an active Whig in politics and was a member of the Methodist church. He married America Henry, a daughter of Alexander and Nancy (Richards) Henry, the former a native of Virginia and the latter of Union county. Alexander Henry was of Irish parentage, his parents, William Henry and wife, coming from that country and locating in Hopkins county, Ky., where both died. James Bingham and his wife had two sons, one of whom died in infancy, and the other is the subject of this sketch. The father died in Trigg county on Nov. 11, 1847, and his widow subsequently married Edwin H. Dyer. (See sketch of Henry R. Dyer.) Silas H. Bingham was born in Trigg county, Oct. 16, 1843. He received his education in the public schools. On Oct. 19, 1861, three days after he had reached the age of eighteen years, he enlisted in Company G, First Kentucky Confederate volunteer cavalry, and served until June, 1865. In that time he was in the battles at Perryville, Murfreesboro, Stone River, Missionary Ridge, Resaca, Big Shanty, Washington, Ga., around Atlanta, and in many minor skirmishes. After the war he returned to his native state, and on April 5, 1866, married Miss Margaret Gardner, a native of Spencer county and a daughter of Benjamin Sidney Gardner, an old resident of the county. Her father died in California about the close of the war. To this marriage there were born the following children:

Mary Irene, Thomas C., Louisa, James H., William E., John B., America, Margaret and Laura S. Mary Irene and Margaret are deceased. The mother of these children died on March 30, 1901, and Mr. Bingham married Ollie Holt, of Union county. His first wife was a member of the Catholic church and his children have been brought up in that faith. His present wife is a Methodist. Mr. Bingham now owns about 170 acres of land. In politics he is an unflinching Democrat; served sixteen years as magistrate and eight years as county assessor, and has served his party eight years as chairman of the Democratic county central committee. He is a member of the Knights of Honor, which is the only fraternal society to claim him as a member.

JOHN S. WINSTON, a farmer of Union county, Ky., was born Nov. 20, 1852, on the farm where he now lives, three miles from the town of Sturgis. His father, William Winston, was a native of Hanover county, Va., but came to Union county in early life and there passed the remainder of his days. He had the advantages of some of the best schools in Virginia and was a highly educated man. After coming to Kentucky he became a farmer on a large scale, owned several slaves and was an influential citizen. In politics he was a Democrat; was a member of the Masonic fraternity, and in religion was a member of the Christian church, in which he held the office of elder for a long time. His wife was also a member of the same church. He married Eliza Lawson, a native of Union county, and to this union there were born three children. One died in infancy; Willie was killed by accident; and John S. is the subject of this sketch and the only survivor. The mother of these children is still living in Union county. John S. Winston grew to manhood on the old homestead, a fine farm of 400 acres, which he now owns, and is one of the up-to-date farmers of his community. He takes a keen interest in all matters pertaining to public policy and for years has been the member from South Sturgis of the Democratic central committee. His aid can always be depended on to win a Democratic victory at the polls. In fraternal matters he is a member of the Independent Order of Odd Fellows, belonging to the lodge at Sturgis, which is one of the best in the state. In 1873 he was married to Miss Jennie, daughter of John Waskom, an old settler of the county. Her mother was a Miss Lisk. She died in November, 1904. Mr. and Mrs. Winston have two daughters: one the wife of Dr. Handley, of Sturgis, and the other the wife of Thomas Williams, of Corydon, Ky.

JAMES T. BISHOP, an old resident of Union county, Ky., residing on his farm near Sturgis, was born in Jefferson county, of that state, June 27, 1828. His grandfather, Lawrence Bishop, was a native of either Pennsylvania or Maryland and came to Bullitt county, Ky., at a very early date, where he spent the remainder of his life. His son Daniel married Catharine McKowan, widow of A. McKowan, and this couple were the parents of James T. Bishop. The mother's maiden name was Patterson. By her first marriage she had four children, none of whom are now living. Of the four children born to her second marriage the subject of this sketch is the only survivor. James T. Bishop was reared on a farm and has been a tiller of the soil through life. He received his education in the public schools of his native county and later came to Union. For more than fifty years he has been a member of the Masonic fraternity. He was made a Mason in Bullitt county, but now holds his membership in Kelsey Lodge, No. 659, of Sturgis. Since the war he has been a Republican, and he and his family belong to the Christian church. Mr. Bishop has been twice married. In 1854 he was married to Miss Judith Jackson, of Bullitt county, and to this marriage there were born ten children, nine of whom are still living. His first wife died in 1882, and about two years later he was married to Mrs. Annie (Brump) Hopkins, the widow of Dr. Hopkins. She has one child by her last marriage, Arthur Leroy Bishop. The children born to Mr. Bishop by his first wife are Albert D., John W., James C., Newton, Laura, Elydia, Daniel W., Dora, Addie and Clarence, all living except Laura. Mr. Bishop is a splendid example of a self-made man. Beginning life in a humble way he has prospered by his industry and the exercise of his intellectual faculties, until he is today one of the leading farmers in the community where he lives. He owns nearly 240 acres of fine land, well improved and in a high state of cultivation, all of which has been accumulated by his own energy.

GEORGE W. McKEAIG, a farmer of Union county, Ky., living about three miles from the town of Sturgis, is descended from one of the old colonial families. His great-grandfather, Harrison Mc-

Keaig, was an Indian fighter of note in the early settlement of the country. Harrison McKeaig's son Samuel married Lydia Fields, a native of Bullitt county, Ky., and they settled not far from the city of Louisville. In the same neighborhood lived John Smith and his wife, whose maiden name was Betsey Hall. John Smith was at the battle of Tippecanoe and took part in the war of 1812. John H. McKeaig, a son of Samuel and Lydia, was born in Jefferson county, Ky., received his education in the public schools there, married Sarah A., daughter of John and Betsey Smith, and in 1871 removed to Union county. He was prominent in politics as a Democrat, was a member of the Masonic fraternity and belonged to the Methodist church. He died in 1893, aged eighty years. His wife died in Jefferson county in 1862. They had ten children, seven of whom are still living. George W. McKeaig, one of the sons, was born near Louisville, Jan. 13, 1847. After the regular preliminary training in the public schools he attended high school and finished his education at Belgrove academy. For some time he was employed on public works in the State of Ohio, after which he engaged in the edge tool business. He was in Evansville, Ind., for about three years, and came to Union county at the same time as his father. Since 1890 he has been engaged in farming. He now owns a little over eighty acres of land, having recently sold 100 acres. Mr. McKeaig was one of the commissioners to arrange the Union county exhibit for the Louisiana Purchase exposition at St. Louis in 1904, and won a medal for corn grown upon his farm. Politically he is a Democrat, and, while firm in his convictions, is not an aspirant for public office. In 1875 he led to the altar Miss Julia Lockhart, of Union county, and to this marriage there have been born six children, viz.: Alma, Clyde, Della, Elbert, Durward and Orville. Clyde and Orville are deceased. Mr. McKeaig and his family belong to the Baptist church.

JOHN WHITEHEAD, SR., who since 1868 has been superintendent of the mines at Dekoven, Union county, Ky., was born Dec. 17, 1836, in Cheshire, England. In 1840 he came with his parents, William and Elizabeth (Lewis) Whitehead, to America. His father had been a mine foreman in England, and upon coming to this country he settled in Schuylkill county, Pa., where he found employment at his old occupation. He died in that county, was buried at Port Carbon, and in 1854 the widow with her six children came to Union county. Two daughters remained in Pennsylvania and one died in infancy in England. John Whitehead obtained his education in the common schools, and at the age of eight years commenced working in the mines during his vacations. When he came to Union county he began working in the mines at Dekoven, and in 1857 was placed in charge of the outside business of the Kentucky Coal Company. Since then he has been connected with different companies and since 1868 has been general superintendent of the Dekoven mines, as already mentioned. Mr. Whitehead has been brought up to the business of mining coal, and few men have a better understanding of all the details of the work. For threescore years he has been connected with mines, beginning at the bottom and working his way up to his present position. Politically he is a Republican, but can hardly be called an active politician. In church relationship he and his wife are Baptists. His father was a Whig and a Presbyterian. Mr. Whitehead is well known in the fraternal organizations of Dekoven, being a member of the Free and Accepted Masons, the Independent Order of Odd Fellows, and the Knights of Honor. He has been twice married. His first wife was Miss Margaret Stephenson, a native of Scotland, and to this union there were born seven children. Two died in infancy; William and Elizabeth died later in life, and John, James and Margaret are living. His second wife was Ellen Yeakey, of Union county. The children of this marriage are Annie, Charles, Susan Ellen and Henry.

CLAYTON PERCIVAL NOGGLE, manager of the Ohio Valley Coal and Mining Company's store at Dekoven, Union county, Ky., is a native of the "Buckeye State," having been born at Greenfield, Huron county, O., Dec. 23, 1865. He is a son of George W. Noggle, a sketch of whose life appears elsewhere in this work. His education was acquired in the schools of Havana and Plymouth, O., in Union county, and in 1884 he graduated from the commercial college at Evansville, Ind. Upon completing his education he entered the employ of the Ohio Valley Coal and Mining Company as a clerk and has gradually worked his way upward to the position of general manager of the store, which position he has held for the last three years. Mr. Noggle is a fine example of what can be accomplished by industry and perseverance. At the age of nineteen he began his business career. Instead of waiting for some friend to secure him a position through personal influence, without regard to his merit, he took what was offered him and by energy and the exercise of his intellectual faculties demonstrated that he was worthy of promotion.

It is very rarely that such men fail to receive their deserts, and today he occupies a confidential position, is trusted by his employers with weighty business matters, handles large sums of the company's money—all because he has proven himself capable and trustworthy. Mr. Noggle is a Republican in his opinions, but is not an active politician. He is prominent in Masonic circles, being a member of Kelsey Lodge, No. 659; Union Chapter, No. 54, Royal Arch Masons; and Alida Commandery, No. 21, Knights Templars, all of Sturgis. In 1895 he was united in marriage to Miss Margaret Wallingford, of Marion, Ky., and to this union there have been born two children: Dudley Clayton, born Feb. 28, 1896, and Leona Mildred, born Oct. 28, 1902.

GEORGE WASHINGTON NOGGLE, cashier and paymaster for the Ohio Valley Railroad and Mining Company, at Dekoven, Union county, Ky., was born in Greenfield township, Huron county, O., April 26, 1839. His ancestors came from Germany during the colonial days, his great-great-grandfather, Ezra Banghart Noggle, having been a soldier in the American army during the Revolutionary war. His father, Jacob Noggle, was born at Chambersburg, Pa., in 1813, but removed in childhood with his father, Joseph Noggle, to Westmoreland county of that state, then to Wayne county, O., and in 1822 to Huron county. In 1834 he married Jane Gibbs and settled on a farm in Greenfield township, though at that time there was really no farm there, their cabin standing in the woods. He cleared the farm and lived there until his death in 1884. He and his wife had three children: one who died in infancy; Fannie, now a Mrs. Ransom, of Chicago; and the subject of this sketch. The mother of these children died at the home of her daughter in Chicago in 1902, aged eighty-three years. Both parents are buried near the old home in Huron county. George W. Noggle was educated in the common schools of Huron county. In 1861 he married Emma Alice Kelsey, who was born in the same neighborhood as himself, and soon after his marriage enlisted in the Third Ohio cavalry. The regiment was assigned to Buell's command and was in numerous skirmishes, but took no part in the larger military operations of the war. While in the service he was permanently injured by being crushed between some horses, and after thirteen months of service was discharged. Upon returning home he went to Cleveland, where he was for four years in the employ of the Lake Shore & Michigan Southern Railroad Company. He then returned to Huron county, and for the next seven years was engaged in merchandizing. At the end of that time he removed to Plymouth, O., where he remained until 1876, when he came to Union county as manager of the store for the Ohio Valley Railroad and Mining Company. This position he held until 1902, when he came into his present place. Mr. Noggle is prominent in Masonic circles, being a member of the lodge, chapter, council and commandery. For six years he was eminent commander of Alida Commandery, No. 21, Knights Templars, of Sturgis. He is also widely known as a musician, having been connected with a brass band in almost every place he has ever lived. In 1881 he organized the Dekoven cornet band, and since that time has been connected with it. Previous to that time he had organized several bands. Mr. Noggle owns property in the city of Cleveland, and is one of the substantial men of the community in which he lives, being noted for his business sagacity and public spirit. He and his wife are both members of the Baptist church. They have had two children: Harry died at the age of seven and a half years; Clayton P. is mentioned elsewhere in this work.

SAMUEL PRATT STURGIS, secretary and general manager of the Ohio Valley Coal and Mining Company, Dekoven, Union county, Ky., is a native of Indiana, having been born in the city of Fort Wayne, March 20, 1855. He is a son of Dr. Charles Edmund and Louisa (Ewing) Sturgis, the former a native of Maryland and the latter of Miami county, O. They were married at Logansport, Ind., and went to Fort Wayne in early life. At that time Indians still inhabited that part of the country, and Doctor Sturgis practiced his profession in the old fort from which the city took its name. He continued to practice there for many years, and was one of the most noted physicians in Northern Indiana. The town of Sturgis, Mich., was named in his honor. In politics he was one of the leading Democrats of his section of the state, representing Allen county in both branches of the Indiana legislature. His last service to his party was in 1868, when he was a delegate to the national convention that nominated Seymour and Blair, as he died on Nov. 24 of that year. During the Civil war he was a surgeon and had charge of the drafting of men for the service. His wife died at Fort Wayne, March 10, 1886. Of their twelve children two sons and two daughters are still living. Doctor Sturgis was also a prominent member of the Masonic fraternity, and he and his wife were Old School Presbyterians. Samuel Pratt Sturgis received his early education at Fort Wayne. After the death of his father he went to Louisville, Ky., where he attended the public schools for two years, and finished with a commercial course in the Bryant & Stratton business college. For the next five years after leaving school he was with the firm of Green & Green, two years as collector and three as a traveling salesman. In 1876 he came to Union county, as a bookkeeper for what is now the Ohio Valley Coal and Mining Company, and has ever since been connected with that corporation, rising to his present position through his energy and fine business qualifications. In connection with Percival Gates Kelsey he promoted the Ohio Valley railroad and was the first secretary of the company. This road was backed financially by Capt. Samuel S. Brown, a Pittsburg millionaire, sometimes called the "Coal King." Mr. Sturgis is president of the Union County Fair association and the Ohio Valley Axle Company of Dekoven. As a compliment to his interest in developing the resources of Union county, the town of Sturgis was named in his honor. In addition to his many other business connections, he is a licensed steamboat pilot and a notary public. In political matters Mr. Sturgis is a Democrat, but does not take an especially active part in party work. In fraternal circles he occupies a prominent place, especially in Masonry. In this order he is a member of Kelsey Lodge, No. 659; Union Chapter, No. 54, Royal Arch Masons; Etta Council, No. 58; Alida Commandery, No. 21, Knights Templars; Louisville Consistory, Ancient and Accepted Scottish Rite, and Corsair Temple, Nobles of the Mystic Shrine, of Louisville. He is also a Knight of Honor, holding his membership at Caseyville. In 1878 he was married to Miss Lymna Orvillet Kelsey, a sister of Dr. P. G. Kelsey, of New York City. Arthur P. Kelsey, a son of Dr. Kelsey, is manager of a large farm for the Ohio Valley Coal and Mining Company. Mr. and Mrs. Sturgis are members of the Baptist church.

JOHN T. GRAHAM, a prominent farmer and an extensive dealer in fine stock, was born in Union county, Ky., April 28, 1859. He is the son of James and Alice (Ginety) Graham, both natives of Ireland, who came to the United States about the year 1840, and settled in Union county, Ky. James Graham was a farmer, a Democrat and a member of the Catholic church. He and wife had ten children, of whom six are still living. He died at his home in 1868, and was followed by his wife in 1892. The subject of this sketch received a fair common school education in his native county. Reared on a farm, he chose farming as his life's work. His farm is located one and one-half miles from Dekoven. While managing the home place, he finds time to cultivate a large tract of land, which he rents of the Ohio Valley Coal and Mining Company. He is very successful as a breeder of Polled Durham cattle and Poland-China hogs, both of which he raises on a large scale. Mr. Graham first married Miss Lottie Oakes, of Union county, Ky., and by her had seven children, five still living. Those living are James P., John W., Leonard R., Orville and Arthur. Mrs. Graham was a kind, loving mother and a devout Catholic. She died Nov. 17, 1902. Jan. 20, 1903, Mr. Graham married Mrs. Mary Stephenson, of Union county, Ky. To this union three children have been born: William, Ella and Alma. He is a stanch Democrat, an earnest Catholic and an Odd Fellow. Push, energy and effort have made Mr. Graham a decided success in his chosen calling.

JEFFERSON D. PRIDE, a prominent and successful farmer of Union county, Ky., living near Bordley, is a native of that state, having been born in Logan county, April 7, 1861. He is a son of James S. and Piety (Porter) Pride, to whom six children were born, all living. The paternal grandparents were Francis and Elizabeth (Mearl) Pride, natives of North and South Carolina respectively. The maternal grandparents were David and Martha (Johnson) Porter. James S. Pride was a native of Tennessee. He was married three times. His first wife was a Miss Ann Eliza Crawford, by whom he had four children, three of whom are yet living. His second marriage was to Miss Porter, already mentioned. His third wife was a Miss Harriet Hardy, a native of Tennessee, and to this marriage were born five children, four of whom survive. Francis Pride was a wealthy land and slave holder and a very successful business man. The subject of this sketch has doubtless inherited some of his business ability, as he is the owner of 200 acres of the finest land in Union county, well stocked and improved. He was reared on a farm and has been brought up to the business, receiving his education in the common schools. All his life has been passed in Union county, where he is well known and has a high standing in the community where he lives. Politically he is a Democrat, and while he takes a laudable interest in public affairs he is by no means an active politician. In fraternal matters he belongs to Bordley Lodge No. 390, Free and Accepted Masons. His parents were both devoted members of the Baptist church and contributed to its good works. In 1892 Jefferson D. Pride and Miss Margaret Walker were united in marriage. She is a native of Kenton county, Ky.

J. W. WATSON, M.D., a prominent and highly successful physician of Bordley, Ky., was born in Union county, of that state, March 11, 1863. He is the son of Thomas and Amelia (Youngs) Watson, both natives of Kentucky, he of Henderson and she of Union county. Thomas was the son of Jacob Watson, a native of Kentucky, who died in Henderson county at the age of eighty-eight years. The wife of Thomas Watson was a Miss Nancy Robina Handley before her marriage. She died near Corydon, Ky. The maternal grandfather of the subject, D. M. Youngs, was a native of Christian county and died in Union county about 1889. The maiden name of the grandmother was Louisa Jane Pritchett. Dr. Watson's father was a blacksmith, wagon-maker and a Democrat. He died June 7, 1893. His wife still lives at Bordley, Ky., aged sixty-four years. She is a devout member of the Christian church. Their marriage was blessed with seven children, five of whom are living. The subject of this sketch was reared in Henderson county and received his literary education in the schools of Corydon and Providence, and on June 21, 1894, graduated from the Kentucky School of Medicine of Louisville. In 1904 he took a post-graduate course in the Chicago Clinical School of Medicine. For three years he practiced medicine at Wanamaker, Webster county, Ky. For the past seven years he has enjoyed an extensive and lucrative practice at Bordley. His high standing as a physician is vouched for by the fact that he holds membership in the following medical societies: The Kentucky State and Ohio Valley Medical associations and the Union County Medical society. He is a member of Bordley Lodge No. 390, Free and Accepted Masons; St. Luke's Lodge, No. 204, Independent Order of Odd Fellows, and Ideal Lodge of the Tribe of Ben Hur. On Dec. 15, 1895, he married Miss Frances Parker of Webster county, and had one child by her. It died in infancy. His wife died Feb. 11, 1898, and he married, the next year, Miss Lucretia B. Fryer, the daughter of George W. Fryer of Bordley. Three children have blessed this union, viz.: Muriel Juanita, Lettie Echert, and Letcher. The ownership of 177 acres of fine land near Bordley makes Dr. Watson a comparatively rich man.

MONTGOMERY GRASSHAM, a blacksmith of Salem, Ky., was born in Roane county, Tenn., March 19, 1843. He is the son of Nehemiah Grassham and the grandson of John and Sarah (Woolsey) Grassham, both natives of Roane county, where they lived and died. Montgomery Grassham came to Crittenden county, Ky., with his parents when eight years old, where he resided until Dec. 14, 1868. He then removed to Salem, Livingston county, and farmed for several years. Since then he has followed his trade uninterruptedly for thirty-three years. He is a Democrat in politics, an Odd Fellow and a member of Salem Lodge No. 81, Free and Accepted Masons. In 1861 he married Miss Lucy Caroline Grimmett of Monroe county, Tenn., daughter of Samuel and Fannie (Rankin) Grimmett, who came to Crittenden county, Ky., in 1851. One child was born to this marriage, Josephine, who died Sept. 3, 1864. His wife dying in March, 1864, Mr. Grassham, on Jan. 17, 1865, married Miss Martha Elizabeth Mahan, daughter of William and Sarah (Potten) Mahan, the former a native of North Carolina and the latter of Livingston county, where both died. By his second wife Mr. Grassham has had nine children. The first was born Oct. 17, 1865, and died in infancy. The second child, Martha Caroline Grassham, is now the wife of Dr. C. E. Percell, of Paducah, Ky. She has the double honor of having held the first state certificate and of having taught the first graded school in Livingston county. She graduated from the Lebanon, O., normal and for several years was a noted teacher. This family has two children, named Ewart Edison Grassham and Sarah LaVerne. The third child is Charles Cario Grassham, born March 20, 1871, and now a successful lawyer at the

Smithland bar. Emma, the fourth child, was born Dec. 8, 1872, and died December 19 of the same year. Anna Dean, the fifth child, was born Oct. 7, 1874, and died November 27 following. The sixth child was Lucy Elizabeth, who was born Oct. 13, 1875, and died Nov. 17, 1878. The seventh child, Sarah Doc., was born March 23, 1878. William Montgomery, the eighth child, was born at Salem, March 1, 1882. Kit Oliver, the youngest, was born Feb. 12, 1884.

J. T. WOOLFE, a prominent miller of Salem, Ky., was born in Caldwell county, of that state, Aug. 11, 1849. His parents were W. H. and Matilda (Baker) Woolfe, both born in Caldwell county. W. H. Woolfe was the son of Alfred and Polly (Bond) Woolfe, the former a native of North Carolina and the latter of Caldwell county. The maternal grandparents of J. T. Woolfe were Wiley and Nancy (Howard) Baker, natives of North Carolina and Kentucky respectively. Both died in Caldwell county. The grandfathers on both sides of the house were farmers and Democrats. The Bakers and the Woolfes are earnest Baptists. W. H. Woolfe received a common school education and has followed farming for a living. He came to Crittenden county in 1851 and now resides about eight miles east of Marion, where his wife died in 1897. This family reared nine children, of whom seven are living. The father was a Democrat and during the war, a magistrate. J. T. Woolfe was reared on a farm in Crittenden county and had the benefit of a common school education. At the age of seventeen years he went into the sawmilling business, which he followed for five years. From that time up to 1891 he followed farming and stock raising. Selling his farm he next engaged for four years in the hardware business in Fredonia, Caldwell county, after which he came to Salem and purchased a small saw and grist mill. In 1892 he built a new flour mill, and since that time has built up an extensive business. On Dec. 5, 1872, he married Miss Sarah A. Drennan, the daughter of David Drennan, born and reared in Kentucky. Her mother was also a Kentuckian by birth. Their parents came either from Virginia or North Carolina. Mr. and Mrs. Woolfe had six children, all living. They are Rosalie, Nettie, Elmer, Cleveland and Byron at Berea, Ky., and George in Mississippi. Mr. Woolfe, like his ancestors, is a Democrat and a Baptist. His wife, who was also a devout Baptist, died Nov. 29, 1903.

ROBERT H. GRASSHAM, an eminent physician of Livingston county, Ky., was born in that county, April 28, 1868. He is the son of Philip and Catherine (Grimmett) Grassham, both natives of Tennessee, the former born Dec. 27, 1827, and the latter June 6, 1828. Philip was the son of Nehemiah and Mary (Clark) Grassham, the former a native of Kentucky and the latter of Tennessee. They were married June 20, 1822, and settled in Crittenden county March 10, 1851, where his wife died Aug. 20, 1858, and he ten years later. Samuel Grimmett, the maternal grandfather of Doctor Grassham, was a native of Virginia. He married Miss Fannie Rankin, both of whom spent their last days in Tennessee. Philip Grassham was educated in the public schools of his home county. In 1851 he came to Crittenden county and engaged in merchandizing and dealing in tobacco. In 1869 he became a Republican, having been a Democrat up to that time. He was a Mason and attended the Christian church, of which he was an active member. They had eight children, of whom five are still living. Those living are: Phillip, Sallie, Nettie, for seven years postmistress at Salem; Lizzie and Robert H. Philip Grassham died Oct. 25, 1902, and is survived by his widow. Dr. Robert H. Grassham, after completing his common school education, entered the Madisonville, Ky., Normal School and Business college, from which he graduated in 1886. He graduated from Miami Medical college, Cincinnati, O., in 1890. Beginning the practice of his profession immediately after graduating he has built up an extensive and lucrative business. The doctor is a member of the Southwestern Kentucky Medical association; also of the American Medical association. He is a Royal Arch Mason and a member of Salem Lodge No. 81, Free and Accepted Masons. On Oct. 8, 1902, he married Miss Margie Gore of Crittenden county.

J. A. PIERCE, farmer and stock raiser, near Salem, Ky., was born in Jefferson county, Tenn., Dec. 16, 1842. He is the son of Stanton Pierce, a native of Russell county, Ky., whose wife was Miss Mary Bettis, a native of Jefferson county, Tenn. Stanton was the son of Jeremiah and Jane (Hall) Pierce, both natives of Russell county. He died in that county and she in Crittenden county. He was a farmer, a Whig, and a Baptist. His wife was a member of the Primitive Baptist church. The maternal grandfather of J. A. Pierce was Eli Bettis, a native of North Carolina, whose father came to America from Italy in an early day and died in Jefferson county, Tenn. Eli Bettis came to Kentucky, locating in Crittenden county about the year 1865, and died there in 1869. His wife, Dorthula (Lewis) Bettis, was born in Virginia and died in Crittenden county. The father of the subject of this sketch received a common school education and learned the trade of blacksmith. From blacksmithing he went to farming, but is now retired from active business and resides in Crittenden county. He and his wife had five children, four of whom are living. The mother died July 4, 1902, aged seventy-nine years. J. A. Pierce was reared and educated in Tennessee. At the age of seventeen years he came to Crittenden county, and from there in 1884 moved to Livingston county, where he has since resided. Mr. Pierce is interested in the Pierce-Elder Hardware Company of Salem; is the owner of 600 acres of fine land and follows general farming and stock raising; is a Baptist and a Democrat. On Nov. 8, 1863, he married Miss Elvira Oliver, who was born in Trigg county, Ky., Dec. 28, 1845. She is the daughter of John W. and Mary Jane (Gee) Oliver, the former born Nov. 17, 1814, and the latter Oct. 7, 1826. John W. was the son of Walter and Mary (Winn) Oliver, both natives of Virginia, whence they came to Kentucky in an early day. The father of Mary Jane Gee was Anderson Gee, who came from Virginia to Crittenden county, where he and his wife both died. John W. Oliver was a farmer. Politically he was a Democrat, and both himself and wife were identified with the Baptist church. They were the parents of thirteen children, of whom four are living. His first marriage to Miss Station was blessed with three children, one of whom is living. J. A. Pierce and wife have had the following children: Willis C., Walter, John, Wirt, Oscar, Richard, who died Nov. 21, 1878; Marion and James. Willis C. Pierce, the eldest son, is a prominent Baptist minister, a graduate of Logan college, of Russellville, Ky., and the Louisville Theological seminary. He began preaching at the age of nineteen years and is now located at Orlinda, Tenn. Prior to going to Orlinda he filled the pulpit of the Baptist church at Catlettsburg, Ky., for seven years, and was for several years at other places in Kentucky.

BENJAMIN R. GARNETT, a prominent farmer residing near Salem, Ky., was born in Boone county of that state, Jan. 13, 1847. He is the son of Benjamin E. and Elizabeth (Ryle) Garnett. Benjamin was born in Barboursville, Knox county, Ky., and his wife in Boone county of the same state. The paternal grandfather, Wesley Minor Garnett, was born in Virginia and moved to Knox county, Ky., in an early day, where both he and his wife died. The maternal grandfather of the subject, William Ryle, died in Boone county, Ky. His wife was a Miss Frances Jack before her marriage. The father of Benjamin R. Garnett received a liberal education and became a very successful teacher. He also learned the carpenters' trade, thus doubly preparing himself for life's work. His education also fitted him for the duties of steamboat clerk, which calling he followed for a time. He and wife had a family of eight children, of whom two sons are yet living. He died July 7, 1861, and his wife in September, 1878. Benjamin R. Garnett was reared at Hamilton, Ky., where he received a common school education. He came to Crittenden county in 1873, and settled on a farm near Salem, in 1887. In the course of time, by dint of hard work and successful management, he became the owner of the farm on which he first settled. It consists of 100 acres of the very best of land and is located two miles north of Salem. On Aug. 18, 1863, he enlisted in company B, Thirtieth Kentucky mounted infantry, and served with it until April 19, 1865, when he was mustered out by virtue of the close of the war. In 1871 he married Miss Martha Patmor, a native of Boone county, by whom he had seven children, six still living. The names of the children are Jonathan W., deceased; James B., John S., Walter H., Louella, Thomas D. and Ray. The family worships with the Christian church.

C. C. DORROH, a prominent and highly successful farmer near Pinckneyville, Livingston county, Ky., was born in that county Aug. 16, 1828. He is the son of William and Mary (Stone) Dorroh, the former a native of Alabama and the latter of Kentucky. They settled in Caldwell county in an early day and both died there. William Dorroh was a farmer by occupation, a Democrat in politics, and in religion was a Baptist. He and his wife were members of the New Bethel Baptist church, where both are buried. The maternal grandfather of C. C. Dorroh was John Stone, who died in Caldwell county, and the grandmother was a Miss Baker. The subject of this sketch attended school in his native county, receiving a fair education. In December, 1845, he married Miss Nancy Dyson, a native of Caldwell county. They first located in Marshall county, but after eleven years came to Livingston county, where he now resides. Here he purchased and cleared a farm of 206 acres, and so thoroughly has his work been done that he can justly boast of the ownership of one of the most productive farms in the county. His work shows what a man of enterprise and push can do in the line of farming. All that he has he has earned himself, never having received a dollar from his father with which to begin his life's work. In politics Mr. Dorroh is a Democrat, but in no sense a partisan. He and his wife have for years been active members of the Baptist church. They had nine children, only three of whom are living, viz.: William F., Edwin and Richard. The names of those deceased are Mary J., Frank F., Ellen, Charles, Willis and James.

M. R. NEAL, an ex-Confederate soldier of Pinckneyville, Livingston county, Ky., was born at Shady Grove, Crittenden county, of that state, in 1842. He is the son of Thomas and Almina (Sims) Neal. Thomas Neal was born in North Carolina and came to Crittenden county, where he died at the ripe age of eighty-four years. The mother was born in Caldwell county, Ky., and died at Shady Grove at the age of seventy-two. Their marriage was blessed with seven children, of whom three are still living. Thomas Neal was a Democrat in politics. His life's work was farming, to which he applied himself diligently and achieved success. The subject of this sketch was brought up on a farm and educated in the common schools of his native county. He chose farming as the most fitting occupation, and went to work with the view of owning a farm himself. He has been successful enough to be able to boast of the ownership of seventy-five acres of the most valuable land in his section of Kentucky. In 1862, when his native state was divided on the question of secession, he enlisted in company C of the Tenth Kentucky Confederate cavalry and served under General John Morgan in his celebrated raid into Southern Indiana and Ohio. He, along with many others, was captured at Buffington's Island and held a prisoner for eighteen months. In 1865 he married Miss Elsie

J. Parsons, of Jackson county, Ill., and this union has been blessed with six children, of whom three are dead. Those living are Alvin, John B. and Delevann. Frank, Mary and Buddy are the names of those deceased. In church matters Mr. and Mrs. Neal are actively identified with the various lines of work of the Baptist church.

L. P. MITCHELL, of the firm of P. H. Styers & Co., was born in Graves county, Ky., Aug. 24, 1861. He is a son of R. P. and Mary J. (Watson) Mitchell, both natives of Tennessee. In 1869 they came from Tennessee to Graves county, Ky., from which county they removed to Livingston county, same state, in 1876. Here he died in 1890, and his wife four years later. R. P. Mitchell was the son of Matthew and Martha (Taylor) Mitchell. Matthew Mitchell came to Tennessee from Virginia in an early day. He was a minister of the Methodist Episcopal church. Both he and his wife died in Tennessee. The maternal grandfather of the subject was William Watson, who was born in Tennessee and came to Kentucky about the year 1854, settling first in Webster and afterwards in Graves county, where he and his wife, also a native of Tennessee, both died. The father of L. P. Mitchell was trained in the common schools of his native county. By self-study he fitted himself for teaching and preaching, in both of which he excelled. He was a Royal Arch Mason and an Odd Fellow. He and his wife reared a family of six children. The father died March 13, 1890, and the mother, Dec. 28, 1894. L. P. Mitchell was reared on a farm, educated in the common schools of his native county and Bethel college, Tenn. After working on a farm for a time he gave his attention to saw-milling and threshing and, in 1891, embarked in the mercantile business at Lola, Ky. Selling out this business he, in 1903, became a member of the firm of P. H. Styers & Co., doing business in the same line. His father had also been in business for some years at Lola, a town which was named after a sister of Mr. Mitchell. In his business undertakings he has been very successful and has managed his earnings so well that he now owns a farm of 250 acres of fine land, upon which he does a general farming and stock raising business. He is a Democrat and a member of Carrsville lodge, No. 665,

Free and Accepted Masons. On March 31, 1892, he married Miss Ida M. Adams, of Livingston county, Ky. She is the daughter of Richard Adams, an early settler of that county. Mr. Mitchell and his wife have had four children, whose names are Lois, Carmen E., Morris and Inez. All except Carmen E. are living. Lola's first postmaster was the father of the subject of this sketch. All that Mr. Mitchell possesses he has made himself. Beginning in 1890 with a capital of $200, he is now rated as one of the wealthiest men in his county.

P. H. Styers, the senior member of the firm, was born in Marshall county, Ky., Sept. 17, 1868, his parents being Martin and Mary (Rose) Styers, the former a native of North Carolina and the latter of Tennessee. They were married in Marshall county, where the mother died in 1899, and where the father is still living as a retired farmer. P. H. Styers was educated in the common schools of Marshall and Graves counties and at the age of twenty-three years became a teacher. In 1892 he was appointed to a position in the revenue service and served about a year. In 1894 he embarked in the mercantile line in which he has been ever since, the partnership with Mr. Mitchell being formed in 1903. He was married in 1893 to Mrs. Ida Kennedy, whose maiden name was Fowler, a granddaughter of James Fowler, of Crittenden county. Her father, John Fowler, was also a native of that county. Mr. and Mrs. Styers have two children, Gladys May and Hobart.

SILAS JACKSON MOSS, pilot and steamboat captain, of Pinckneyville, Ky., was born in Livingston county, of that state, Feb. 29, 1852. He is the son of Ralph and Fannie (Ramage) Moss, who came to Livingston county in an early day. The maternal grandfather was Jackson Ramage, who came to Livingston county with his parents and who is buried on the old homestead there. Ralph Moss was a pilot and steamboat captain by profession and served on boats plying the Ohio, Mississippi, Cumberland and Illinois rivers. He married in Livingston county, Ky., and had a family of five children: Silas Jackson, the subject of this sketch; Alice, Thomas, Lizzie and Lee Milins, the last two named being dead. While working on the Mississippi he was in New Orleans soon after the battle there on Jan. 8, 1815. In politics he was a Democrat. His wife died April 18, 1885, and he on Dec. 14, 1895. Silas J. Moss received his early education in the public schools of his county. At the age of seventeen years he began to make his own living. Beginning at the bottom, he has worked himself up to the position of pilot and captain of boats running from Evansville, Ind., to Cairo, Ill., and from Cairo, Ill., to Nashville, Tenn. On Aug. 10, 1870, he married Miss Savilla Parker, born near Salem, Ky., Sept. 15, 1849, and the daughter of Mack and Typhena (Lindley) Parker, both natives of Kentucky. Mack Parker was the son of Jonathan and Dorothy (Burgess) Parker, both of whom died in Livingston county. Typhena Lindley was the daughter of Joseph Lindley, a native of England, who came to America when twenty-two years old and settled in Pennsylvania, where he married Miss Savilla Benjamin. From Pennsylvanina they came to Fleming county, Ky., where the wife died. He died in Illinois. Silas J. Moss and his wife have had six children: George L., Mildred, Russell, Lyon C., Lizzie D. and Francis T. Of these Lyon C. is a steamboat pilot and George and Russell farmers. All are natural musicians. Captain Moss is independent in politics. He, his wife and youngest daughter are members of the Missionary Baptist church.

JOHN S. LOWERY, a successful farmer residing near Salem, Ky., was born in Caldwell county, Ky., March 9, 1836. He is the son of John and Grace (Ordway) Lowery, both natives of North Carolina, the father born Feb. 26, 1806, and the mother Aug. 5, 1807. The paternal grandfather was James Lowery, a native of North Carolina, who came to Kentucky in an early day, spending the remainder of his life in Crittenden, Hopkins and Caldwell counties. He died in the last named county at the extreme old age of one hundred years. John and Grace Lowery came to Crittenden county quite early, where they both died. Their marriage was blessed with eleven children, six of whom are living. John Lowery was a farmer, a Democrat and a member of the Cumberland Presbyterian church, of which his wife was also a devout member. John S. Lowery was reared on a farm, received a fair education in the common schools of his county, and has made farming his life's work. Finding 300 acres too large a body to cultivate profitably, he sold a portion of his farm. He is a Democrat and a Cumberland Presbyterian. On Nov. 10, 1859, he married Miss Polly Ann Butler, of Crittenden county, who was born Sept. 4, 1844. This union resulted in the birth of ten children, of whom four are living. They are: Daniel Allen, Charles Owen, Nora Ella and William Smith. Mrs. Lowery died Dec. 14, 1901, and on April 20, 1902, he married Mrs. Lura Pryor, *nee* Cossey, who has one daughter, Leota Agnes, by her former husband. Mr. and Mrs. Lowery have two children, named Odell and Wilma.

J. J. TYNER.

JOSEPH JOHN TYNER (deceased), late a well known cooper, carpenter and farmer of Livingston county, Ky., was born in Cheatham county, Tenn., Feb. 4, 1822, his parents being Memory and Elizabeth (Everett) Tyner, both natives of Virginia. Memory Tyner died in Mississippi and his wife in Illinois. They were blessed with a family of five children, all deceased except Martha. Joseph J. Tyner was about eight years of age when his father died, and he was reared by a Mr. George Wilson of Tennessee. He received a common school education and began life as a farmer. About the close of the Civil war he came to Livingston county, where he lived the rest of his life. In the meantime he had learned the trades of carpenter and cooper, and after coming to Livingston county he worked at these occupations with such success that he soon acquired a competency sufficiently large to enable him to retire from active business. He lived a retired life for many years. In politics he was an ardent Democrat, having an abiding faith in the principles of that party. In 1892 he married Miss Adeliah Jane Clark, who was born in Roane county, Tenn., Aug. 29, 1849, and with her parents, G. M. and H. G. (Grimmett) Clark, immigrated to Kentucky when she was but three years of age. Her mother was a daughter of Joseph and Fannie Grimmett, mentioned elsewhere in this work. G. M. Clark was a son of John and Sarah (Stevens) Clark, both born in Virginia,

MRS. J. J. TYNER.

and died in Roane county, Tenn. The father of John Clark was an Englishman, who came to this country at a very early day, settling first in Virginia and removing later to Sevier county, Tenn. G. M. Clark was a blacksmith by trade and a Democrat in his political views. When he first came to Kentucky in 1852 he settled in Crittenden county, but in 1868 removed to Livingston county, where he died Oct. 13, 1875, aged fifty-three years. His wife died in 1893, aged sixty-eight. They had ten children: Ruth Caroline, Samuel Grimmett, deceased; Adeliah Jane, Martha Livonia, Philip

Andrew, Sarah Frances, deceased; John Stevens, Isaac Willie, a lawyer and editor of the *Livingston Democrat;* Charles Tollifaro, a Baptist minister; and one who died in infancy. Mr. Clark and his wife were Baptists, as were all their children, Mrs. Tyner having been a member of that church for thirty-eight years.

AARON LINDLEY CHARLES, a retired farmer of Tylene, Ky., was born in Tennessee, Sept. 19, 1841. He is the son of John and Amy (Lindley) Charles, the former a native of Tennessee and the latter of North Carolina. John was the son of Richard and Martha (Beyford) Charles, both natives of Tennessee. Richard was a local Methodist minister. He and his wife died in Tennessee. The maternal grandfather of the subject was Joshua Lindley, a native of North Carolina, who came to Tennessee about 1835, where he lived the rest of his life. His wife was Nellie Lindley, who died in Texas at the advanced age of ninety-two years. John Charles was a wheelwright by trade, a Democrat in politics and for fifty years a member of the Methodist church. He and his wife had five children, two of whom are living. His first wife died in 1856. He then married Mrs. Sarah E. Gains, by whom he had four children, three still living. Mr. Charles died in Livingston county, Ky., where he had resided since 1851. When ten years old Aaron L. Charles moved with his parents to Crittenden county, Ky. In 1858 he removed to Livingston county, where he has since lived. He now lives a retired life at Tylene, enjoying the fruits of his thrift and industry. He has been the owner of 300 acres of the best land in the county, which alone places him in easy circumstances. He is a Democrat, a Granger and a member of the Methodist Church South. On March 28, 1867, he married Miss Ellen Frances Bunton, the daughter of James and Mary Ann (Owen) Bunton. Her father was a native of Tennessee and her mother of London, England, whence she came with her mother, Mary (Trotter) Owen, when sixteen years old, to the United States, settling in Livingston county, Ky., where she died in 1884. Mary Ann Bunton had four children by her first marriage, two of whom are yet living. She was married a second time, to Jesse Bunton, a brother of her first husband, and had seven sons by this marriage, of whom three are living. Two of her sons were physicians. Henry Wallace Bunton and his brother, J. W., were both ministers of the Methodist Church South. Mary E., the sister of Mrs. Charles, is now a widow, residing at Tylene. Mrs. Charles has another brother, Dr. Fred Bunton, a physician, living in Caldwell county, Ky. Mr. and Mrs. Charles have eight children, six of whom are living. They are W. E., Laura A., M. B., F. F., Ella and Lola. Mary Ann and Gideon Berry are dead.

WILLIS BRYANT CHAMPION, a merchant of Pinckneyville, Ky., was born near Green's Ferry, or Vicksburg, in Livingston county of that state, March 31, 1858. He is a son of James Mansfield and Sallie Ann (Brown) Champion, the former a native of Livingston county, born near Salem, and the latter born near Baltimore, Md. The paternal great-grandfather, Willis Champion, was born and reared in North Carolina, married in that state, and came to Kentucky in 1812, settling near the old Salem church, where he and his wife both died and are buried in that old church yard. His son, Willis, the grandfather of the subject of this sketch, was about ten years old when the family came to Kentucky. He grew to manhood in Livingston county, married Vinecia Hardin, and both passed their whole lives in the county, he dying Aug. 7, 1876, and she in August, 1869. On the maternal side the grandparents were Peter and Maria (Smullen) Brown, who came from Maryland and settled near Green's Ferry, where both died. James M. Champion, the father, was educated in the common schools, was a farmer by occupation and in the agitation just preceding the Civil war was a firm Union man. He was a member of the Baptist church for many years before his death, which occurred in 1867. He and his wife had two children, Willis B. and Maria Alice. The mother and sister now live with the subject at Pinckneyville, the former being a member of the same church to which her husband formerly belonged. Willis B. Champion received a common school education and at the age of sixteen years was stricken with paralysis. That was in July, 1874. In October, in company with his mother and sister, he started for California to regain his health, leaving Kentucky on the 13th of the month and arriving at Soledad, one hundred and fifty miles south of San Francisco, on the 29th. He soon regained sufficient strength to go to work and began cutting wood for some of the ranchers. Later he was employed in the livery business and then with the Godshaw & Brianstein Company, butchers, of San Francisco, where he worked his way up to $120 a month. On July 22, 1876, they left California and on August 6 reached Birdsville, Ky., where Mr. Champion went to work on a farm for Sidney J. Mitchell. For two years he worked at saw-milling and farming on a little farm formerly owned by his father. In January, 1881, he sold this farm and bought a tract of land near Cedar Grove, where he engaged in farming until 1890. He then engaged in getting out staves, railroad ties and lumber and continued in this line until 1897, being in the employ of the Powell, Lord Tie Company until 1893 and after that time with the Ayer & Lord Tie Company until 1897. In 1895 he engaged in the mercantile business at Kuttawa, where he had gone in 1892, and also had a branch store at Dover, Tenn. The Dover establishment was discontinued in 1898, and the business removed to Pinckneyville, where he has ever since carried on a successful business. In May, 1899, he removed his family to Pinckneyville, though he still conducted the store at Kuttawa until January, 1900. He then started a store at Vicksburg, or Green's Ferry, but removed it to Sheridan in the month of March, 1904, where it is still running as a branch. He is still interested in getting out railroad ties, and is also the owner of a $5,000 farm and of 250 acres on the river at Pinckneyville and runs it in connection with his other pursuits. In the panic of 1893 he lost over $4,000, taking everything he had except about one thousand dollars, so that all he has has been practically accumulated since then. But Mr. Champion is not easily discouraged. He has worked for as little as twenty-five cents a day and knows what it is to be without the luxuries of life, though he is now a well-to-do man owing to his untiring industry and correct judgment. Politically he is a Democrat and while he takes an interest in public questions he can hardly be classed as a politician. He has been twice married; first on June 6, 1892, to Rosa Forest Hardin, of Livingston county, and after her death he married, on Feb. 4, 1903, Miss May Hurley, of Pinckneyville. By his first wife he had three children: May and Maud, twins, born Feb. 17, 1894, the former dying on May 20, 1894, and the latter only five days later; and Willis Elbert, who died in infancy. His first wife was a member of the Methodist Episcopal church, to which he also belongs, and his present wife is a Missionary Baptist.

JOHN WILLIAM PENN, a prominent farmer residing near Salem, Ky., was born in Coffee county, Tenn., Sept. 15, 1847. He is the son of Thomas and Hulda Cawkins (Stewart) Penn, the former a native of Georgia and the latter of Tennessee. Thomas was the son of John D. and Jane (Deney) Penn, both natives of Virginia. He died in Georgia and his wife in Tennessee. He was a blacksmith and wagonmaker. The maternal grandfather of John W. Penn was John Stewart, a native of Tennessee. At the close of the Civil war Thomas Penn became a Democrat, having been a Whig prior to that time. He and his wife had six children, of whom three are yet living. The mother died on Lookout Mountain, Ga., in 1858, and he then married Miss Jane Arnold, by whom he had four children, three still living. John W. Penn was reared on a farm, was educated in the common schools of his county and at Hillsboro, Tenn., after which he learned the carpenter trade and settled in Livingston county, Ky., in 1873, where he has resided ever since. Mr. Penn is also interested in farming. In politics he is a stanch Democrat. In 1873 he married Miss Margaret A. Kirk, of Crittenden county, which marriage has been blessed with nine children: Maud Allie, Fred H., Annie F., Myrtle Leoda, Ellen E., Pearl May, Orlena, Paulina and Ida Bell. Of these Orlena and Paulina are twins. All are living except Ellen E. Maud Allie, the oldest child, is married to George A. Simpson, a farmer; Fred H. married Miss L. Sunderland; Annie F. is the wife of E. C. Brasher, a farmer, and all three live in Crittenden county. Mr. Penn enlisted in Company G, Twenty-fourth Tennessee, of Cheatham's division, in 1863 and served until the close of the war.

CHARLES R. STEVENS, farmer and manager of fire-clay mines, Salem, Ky., was born in Princeton, Ky., Sept. 27, 1844. He is the son of Herrington and Mahala B. (Stemmons) Stevens, the former a native of Caldwell county and the latter of Logan county, both in Kentucky. Herrington's father was one of the pioneer settlers of Caldwell county, Ky. Herrington Stevens received his education in the public schools and Princeton college, Princeton, Ky., and devoted his whole life to the ministry. He and his wife had six children. Of this number four are still living. He was a Whig in politics and died Sept. 25, 1856. His wife survived him many years, dying July 2, 1872. Charles R. Stevens came with his parents when only four years old to Crittenden county, Ky. In 1874 he removed to Livingston county, where he has engaged in farming, being the owner of 350 acres of land near Salem. He has made Salem his home for the past fifteen years. In 1903 the Stevens-Tunnell fire-clay mines were opened and operated by the Western Clay and Mining Company of Kewanee, Ill. Mr. Stevens discovered these mines and has been the agent of the company for three years. While attending to this work he does not neglect his farming interests. He is a stock-holder and director of the Salem National bank. In politics he is a Democrat. He served one term as justice of the peace in Crittenden county, and has been nominated by his party for the fourth time as justice of the peace in Livingston county, where a nomination is equivalent to an election. Mr. Stevens is a Royal Arch Mason and worshipful master of Salem lodge, No. 81, Free and Accepted Masons. On Dec. 17, 1871, he married Miss Martha C. Tyner, a daughter of Thomas R. Tyner, an early settler of Livingston county, who died in 1888. Mr. and Mrs. Stevens have had three children: Mary Burton, now Mrs. C. W. Mitchell of Salem; Myra T. and John H., the last-named a merchant of Salem. The parents are members of the Methodist Church South. W. C. Tyner, a brother of Mrs. Charles R. Stevens, was born in Montgomery county, Tenn., Oct. 28, 1843. He was reared on a farm and educated in the public schools of Salem; owns and manages a farm of 240 acres two miles east of the town; pays especial attention to stock raising, a business in which he is remarkably successful; is a Democrat, a Mason and a member of the Methodist Church South. On Sept. 16, 1868, he married Miss Josephine Hodge, the daughter of A. B. Hodge, of Crittenden county, Ky. Mr. and Mrs. Tyner have been blessed with three children: Blanche, Felix and Jesse.

O. C. LASHER, of Smithland, Ky., editor of the *Livingston County Banner*, was born in that county, near Carrsville, Nov. 11, 1874, and is the son of W. B. and Elizabeth (Rhodes) Lasher, both natives of Perry county, Ind. W. B. Lasher came to Hampton, Livingston county, in 1873, where he resided, following the business of farming. He was a member of the Democratic party, and his wife was an active member of the Methodist church. They had eight children, all of whom are still living. The paternal grandfather of the subject of this sketch, Abraham Lasher, settled in Perry county, Ind., where he followed the occupation of farming. A strong Democrat, he served his county as sheriff for one term. The maternal grandfather, Henry Rhodes, a native of Perry county, Ind., removed to Livingston county, Ky., in 1873. He followed farming and flat-boating, carrying hoop poles and other products as far south as New Orleans.

His wife, Brunetta (Spencer) Rhodes, was born in Perry county, Ind., and is still living. O. C. Lasher was reared near Carrsville until sixteen years of age, when he moved to Hampton with his parents. He was educated at Hampton academy and the Southern normal of Bowling Green, Ky., receiving the degree of B. S. from the latter institution in 1899. One year later he graduated from the Bowling Green Business college. From 1892 to 1899 he taught in the Livingston county schools; came to Smithland in 1900 and served as county superintendent of schools for one year, having been appointed to that office. Here he began the study of law in the office of Bush & Grassham, and three years later was admitted to the bar, attorneys J. M. Morton and Henry Hughes being the examiners. For eighteen months he was associated with Rid Reed in publishing the *Livingston County Banner,* and Jan. 1, 1904, became sole proprietor of said paper. Mr. Lasher is a Democrat in politics, and holds membership with the Ancient Order of United Workmen and the Knights of the Maccabees. For one year he taught the science and business branches in the Bardstown county educational college.

CHARLES C. GRASSHAM, one of the most prominent young lawyers of Western Kentucky, was born in Salem, Ky., Nov. 20, 1871. He is the son of Montgomery Grassham, a sketch of whose life will be found elsewhere in this work. Charles C. was educated in part at Salem, after which he attended McCulley's school at Madisonville, Ky., finishing at the National normal university of Lebanon, O. For five years he was engaged in teaching, beginning at the unusually early age of fifteen. While teaching he read law, and at the age of twenty years entered the office of Capt. J. W. Bush and John K. Hendrick of Smithland, Ky. On Oct. 8, 1891, he was admitted to the bar at Smithland, where he soon enjoyed a successful and lucrative practice. Since 1896 he has been associated with Capt. J. W. Bush, his father-in-law. Mr. Grassham in his practice represents the following corporations: The Illinois Central Railroad Company, the Hillman Land and Iron Company, the Eagle Fluorspar Company, the American Lead and Zinc Company. The Western Clay and Mining Company, the Pittsburg Fluorspar Mining and Manufacturing

Company and the Ayer & Lord Tie Company. In politics Mr. Grassham is affiliated with the Democratic party. He has served as election commissioner of Livingston county, as assistant elector of the First congressional district of Kentucky in 1900, and as elector of the same district in the campaign of 1904. He is now serving as aid-de-camp on Governor Beckham's staff with the rank of colonel. He is an Elk in the Paducah lodge and an entered apprentice Mason in the Smithland lodge. On Aug. 19, 1896, he married Miss Corrie Bush, daughter of his law partner, Capt. J. W. Bush. To this marriage two children have been born: Roscoe Bush Grassham, who died Nov. 21, 1900, and Pauline Bush Grassham, who was born Jan. 29, 1900. After a residence of fifteen years in Smithland, Mr. Grassham has just moved to Paducah, Ky., where he will no doubt extend his practice so auspiciously begun at Smithland. Few young lawyers of his experience can boast of such a wide practice as he enjoys.

WILLIAM I. CLARKE, lawyer, was born in Dycusburg, Crittenden county, Ky., Sept. 17, 1862. He is the son of George Madison Clarke, mentioned elsewhere in this work. He received his early training in the common schools of Livingston county, Salem academy and the National normal institute of Madisonville, Ky. On June 4, 1891, he graduated from the Cumberland university of Lebanon, Tenn., with the degree of Bachelor of Laws, and was admitted to the practice of law in the States of Tennessee and Kentucky in the same year. He has been actively engaged in the practice of law at Smithland ever since. For one year he was in partnership with C. C. Grassham, when, until Jan. 1, 1905, he practiced alone. Then the firm of Clarke & Hendrick was formed, composed of Mr. Clarke and Alfred Grayot Hendrick. Mr. Clarke takes an active interest in the politics of his county. In 1894 he resigned the office of police judge of Smithland to take that of county attorney of Livingston county, which position he held until 1898. In 1898 he was appointed master commissioner of the Livingston circuit court, which position he held till 1904. In 1897-98-99, also in 1904, he was editor and publisher of the *Livingston Banner*. In 1905 he and Frederick Cowper established the *Livingston Democrat*.

He is a member of the Baptist church and takes an active part in all church work, being clerk, superintendent of the Sunday school and secretary of the church building committee. At present he is serving as chairman of the Democratic county committee. On Nov. 27, 1895, he married Miss Emma J. Weldon of Livingston county, daughter of William and Sarah (Lloyd) Weldon, one of the pioneer settlers of Livingston county, who died at Pinckneyville, Ky., in 1896. He is survived by his widow, now eighty-one years old. William I. Clarke and his wife have two children: Carter Weldon, born Oct. 20, 1896, and Mildred Ferguson, born Aug. 21, 1903.

ALFRED GRAYOT HENDRICK, of the law firm of Clarke & Hendrick, of Smithland, Ky., was born in that city, May 2, 1878. In an early day his grandparents, William and Susan (Bennett) Hendrick, came from North Carolina to Kentucky, settling first in Logan county, but after a short residence there moved to Todd county. John K. Hendrick, a son of this couple, and the father of Alfred G., was born in North Carolina in 1851. He was reared in Logan and Todd counties; received his primary education in the common schools, after which he was under the private instruction of Professor Shields for a time and then attended Bethel college at Russellville. Upon leaving college he went to Crittenden county, where he engaged in teaching in the public schools and also served some time as deputy sheriff. He then came to Livingston county, read law with his uncle, Judge Caswell Bennett, and was admitted to the bar. Shortly after his admission he formed a partnership with Capt. J. W. Bush and practiced for several years. He then served two terms as county attorney, one term in the state senate, and in 1894 was elected to Congress from the First district of Kentucky. After retiring from Congress he opened a law office in Paducah and has practiced there ever since. In 1877 he was married to Miss Louise, daughter of A. A. and Mary (Hunt) Grayot, of Livingston county. Her father was born in France, was a pharmacist, a prominent Free Mason, and was for many years postmaster at Smithland, where he died. Hon. John K. Hendrick and his wife have had the following children: Alfred G., the subject of this sketch; William R., a real estate man of Paducah; Cavit, deceased; Harry D., and Nellie. He belongs to the Independent Order of Odd Fellows and the Ancient Order of United Workmen, and is always active in furthering the interests of the Democratic party. Alfred G. Hendrick was reared in Smithland, received his elementary education in the public schools there, and attended the high school department of the Washington, D. C., schools, while his father was in Congress. When the family returned to Kentucky he took the teacher's course and fitted himself for that profession. For three years he was a successful teacher, when he laid aside that calling to take up the study of law. After reading for a year in the office of his father and J. C. Hodge he took a course in law and English at the Washington and Lee university at Lexington, Va. Immediately after leaving college he was admitted to practice in Calloway county, Kentucky, by an examination in open court under Judge Thomas P. Cook, the examination being conducted by Wells & Wells. Since his admission Mr. Hendrick has been actively engaged in the practice of his profession. The firm of Clarke & Hendrick was formed in January, 1905, and is composed of two of the most brilliant and energetic young men in Western Kentucky. Both are close students of everything pertaining to their chosen calling and fitted by nature and training for successful lawyers. Those who know them best predict for the firm a bright future. In politics Mr. Hendrick is a Democrat, as his father and grandfather before him were, and takes an active part in the work of his party, now holding the position of secretary of the county central committee. In religious matters he is quite liberal and is not identified with any church organization.

WILLIAM FREDERICK COWPER, a successful lawyer of Smithland, Ky., was born in Livingston county, of that state, Dec. 8, 1875. He is the son of Richard Ballard Cowper, a sketch of whose life appears elsewhere in this work; was reared on a farm and received his common school education in the Smithland schools. In 1895 he graduated from Bethel college. After graduating he taught school for two years and served as deputy sheriff under his father for one year. He began the study of law in the office of John K. Hendrick, and was admitted to the bar in December, 1898; soon built up a lucrative practice, which he continues to enjoy; is a Democrat, a Baptist and holds membership in Smithland Lodge, No. 138, Free and Accepted Masons. At the early age of twenty-four years he was elected police judge of Smithland. In June, 1898, he married Miss Flora Seyster, daughter of Capt. J. V. Seyster, a brief mention of whom appears in connection with this sketch. Mr. and Mrs. Cowper have two interesting children, named Esther and William Frederick. Together with Mr. W. I. Clarke Mr. Cowper owns and edits the *Livingston Democrat,* a paper established by these gentlemen at the beginning of the present year. Mr. Cowper is now serving as a member of the Democratic county committee.

Capt. J. V. Seyster, the father-in-law of the subject of this sketch, was born in Livingston county Aug. 2, 1823, and was there reared and educated. He is the son of David and Rebecca (Evans) Seyster, who came from Virginia to Kentucky about the year 1820, settling in Livingston county. Captain Seyster was for many years engaged in river navigation, working himself up from cabin boy to captain of a steamer. Later he took up the mercantile business and followed it for ten years, at the same time acting as agent of the Cairo Packet Line.

L. H. COTHRON, farmer, and postmaster at Smithland, Ky., was born within two miles of Grand Rivers, Livingston county, Ky., Jan. 20, 1868. He is the son of Morris and Pernecia (Fulks) Cothron, both natives of Kentucky; the former of Caldwell and the latter of Lyon county. The paternal grandfather of the subject, Thomas Cothron, came from Scotland to the United States in an early day, and located finally in Livingston county. The maternal grandfather was Noah Fulks. Morris Cothron began very poor in life, without even the advantage of an ordinary education, and yet accumulated more than a thousand acres of land on the Cumberland river, which he sold to the Grand Rivers Company. A Democrat before the war, he became a strong Republican after its close. Two of his brothers, Robert and William, served in the Federal army and both died while in service. He and his wife were members of the Christian Union church. He died Dec. 29, 1892, and is survived by his widow. There were born to this couple nine children, five of whom are still living, four sons and one daughter. L. H. Cothron was reared on a farm and was educated in the public schools of Livingston county. For four years he was in the retail liquor business and then followed farming until 1903, when he was appointed postmaster at Smithland. He is a member of Mangum Lodge, No. 21, Independent Order of Odd Fellows, of Paducah, Ky., and of the Knights of the Maccabees. He and his wife are actively engaged in church work, both being members of the Baptist church. In 1890 he married Miss Lizzie Wilson of Livingston county, the daughter of G. M. Wilson and the granddaughter of Charles and Martha Ann Wilson, pioneer settlers in the county. Both died at an advanced age. Three children have been born to Mr. and Mrs. Cothron: Effie May, born July 24, 1891; Thomas Hollis, born Sept. 11, 1893; George Morris, born Feb. 22, 1898. Two and one-half miles southeast of Smithland is located the old Mose Broomfield and T. J. Ward place, a farm of 200 acres, whose proud owner is no other than Mr. Cothron himself.

JOHN W. BUSH, a prominent lawyer of Smithland, Ky., was born in Eddyville, Lyon county, of that state, June 3, 1836. He is the son of Dr. Reuben R. and Louisa (Williams) Bush, the former born in Potosi, Mo., in 1810, and the latter in Lyon county, in 1820. John Bush, the father of Reuben R., was a native of Virginia, who went from that state to Missouri in an early day. In 1820 he removed to Princeton, Ky., where he died in 1830. He was a prominent physician and surgeon in his time; was identified with the Whig party and the Methodist Episcopal church. His wife was a Miss Elizabeth Roland, a native of Virginia, who died in Missouri. The maternal grandfather of Captain Bush was John Williams, born in Newbury, S. C., where he died in 1825. His widow, Sarah (Young) Williams, afterwards married a Mr. Jones of that state, and died there in 1865. Dr. Reuben R. Bush was reared and educated in Missouri, whence he came with his father to Kentucky. In 1861 he removed to Fredonia in Caldwell county. Three years later he came to Smithland, where he died in 1879. His wife died just two weeks later. Dr. Bush served as a surgeon in the Federal army and practiced medicine in Kentucky for forty years. He was a Whig before the war and a Republican afterwards. Both he and his wife belonged to the Methodist Episcopal Church South. They had ten children, only two of whom are living, Capt. John W. Bush, the oldest, and George Bush, the youngest. William R. Bush, a brother of Captain Bush, was a lieutenant in the Federal army and died while in the service. Captain Bush was reared on a farm and educated at Bethlehem academy. In 1856 he began to read law in the office of W. P. Fowler of Smithland. A year later he was admitted to the bar at Eddyville, where he practiced his profession until 1858, when he moved to Missouri. After an absence of two years in Missouri, where he practiced law, he returned to Kentucky in 1860, and afterwards enlisted in Company G, Forty-eighth Kentucky volunteer infantry of the Federal army, and served as captain until November, 1864. Returning home he resumed his law practice at Smithland, where he has since enjoyed a lucrative business. Twenty young men have read law in his office, all of whom are doing well. While never an aspirant for office, he has always taken an active interest in politics as a Democrat, making speeches for that party in various states. He is a Knight of Honor and a member of the Methodist Episcopal Church South. His wife, whom he married in 1857, was a widow, her maiden name having been Sarah E. Holloway. They had two children, named William R. and James, the latter dying in infancy. William R. Bush was educated at Lexington, Ky., and choosing the law as his profession he located at Gainesville, Tex., where he built up a successful practice. Returning to Kentucky he served one term in the legislature and died of consumption in 1892, aged thirty-four years. The first wife of Captain Bush died in 1860. One year later he married Miss Sarah A. Watkins, of Lyon county. This marriage has been blessed with ten children, seven of whom are living: Elizabeth Harris, a widow of Smithland; Pat. H., sheriff of Livingston county; C. H., superintendent of mines; Jettie, wife of J. A. Crenshaw, cashier of the bank, Newbern, Tenn.; Corrie, wife of C. C. Grassham, a distinguished attorney of Paducah, Ky.; Janett, wife of Dr. Robert Rivers of Paducah, and Frank M., train dispatcher on the Illinois Central railway at Calvert City, Marshall county, Ky.

R. B. COWPER, liveryman and farmer, was born in Livingston county, Ky., Feb. 20, 1851. He is the son of William and Polly (Hawkins) Cowper, born respectively in Virginia and Kentucky. The father of the subject of this sketch came to Livingston county from Virginia when a lad eight years old. He received a liberal education and filled acceptably several positions of trust, among them being the offices of county judge and justice of the peace. In 1850 he was a delegate to the constitutional convention of the State of Kentucky. In religious matters both he and his wife were identified with the Baptist church. Of the six children born to their marriage the subject is the only one living. Both parents were twice married. Two of the children, both daughters, born to his mother by her first marriage are still living. The father died in 1857 and the mother in 1871. R. B. Cowper was reared on a farm and educated in the common schools of his county. The fact that he has held a number of public offices demonstrates that he has taken an active part in politics. For three years he served as assessor of Livingston county, after which he was elected sheriff of that county, serving four years. In 1901 he embarked in the livery business, without, however, neglecting his farming interests. He was nominated by the Democratic party for jailer in 1904. In 1875 he married Miss E. E. Nelson, the daughter of Washington Nelson, of Livingston county. Mr. and Mrs. Cowper have had three children: William Frederick; Christiana Richard, wife of Gilbert Presnell, of Paducah, Ky., and David. Mr. and Mrs. Cowper are earnest Baptists and take a deep interest in all branches of church work.

CHARLES H. WILSON, one of the most successful attorneys practicing at the Smithland, Ky., bar, and a member of the firm of Bush & Wilson, was born in Livingston county, of that state, Aug. 11, 1872. His grandfather, Charles Wilson, came to America from Sweden in 1826, locating at Smithland, where he died in 1864. His wife, Martha Ann Walker, whom he married in 1840, lived until 1903. They had a family of eleven children, of whom five are now living. He was a Democrat in politics, a farmer by occupation, owning a large tract of land, and, with his wife, identified with the Baptist church. His maternal grandfather, Reuben Coffer, born May 5, 1789, came from Virginia to Lyon county, Ky., where he died June 20, 1853. On Feb. 19, 1824, he married Elizabeth Ann Brewer, a native of Christian county. In politics he was identified with the Whig party. He was a farmer, and, with his wife, a member of the Baptist church. They had seven children, of whom two are living. The parents of Charles H. Wilson were George Martin and Millie Frances (Coffer) Wilson, the former born in Livingston county Oct. 17, 1841, and the latter in Christian county

Feb. 9, 1844. George W. Wilson was educated in the public schools of Livingston county, one of his teachers having been Capt. J. W. Bush. His occupation was farming and stock raising, in which he was remarkably successful. He now lives a retired life on his farm of 1,000 acres. The Democratic party has a strong supporter in the person of Mr. Wilson, who served in the Confederate army, and as constable and coroner of his home county. Mr. and Mrs. Wilson had eleven children, of whom seven are living. They are: Lizzie, wife of L. H. Cothron, a sketch of whose life appears elsewhere in this work; Charles H.; George Martin, Jr., whose life sketch also appears in this work; Thomas Henley, a farmer and stock dealer; Hattie May; Martha Ann and Harry Winfred. His wife dying June 2, 1896, Mr. Wilson, in November of the same year, married Mrs. Delia Fort, who has borne him one son, Floyd A. Charles H. Wilson, the subject of this sketch, received his common school education in the public schools of Livingston county. In 1894 he graduated from Princeton collegiate institute of Princeton, Ky., his wife graduating in the same class. Beginning the study of law in the office of Col. J. C. Hodge, of Smithland, he was admitted to the bar Dec. 5, 1895. For two years he served as city attorney of Smithland, when he was elected attorney of Livingston county. In 1901 he was re-elected and is now serving in that capacity. Mr. Wilson is a memper of Smithland Lodge, No. 138, Free and Accepted Masons, and of the Knights of the Maccabees, being commander of Smithland Tent, No. 120. In politics he is a Democrat and in church relationship a Baptist. He married Miss Saidee Eliza Polk, born in Louisville, Ky., April 21, 1873. She is the daughter of Dr. Edward Theodore Polk, a distant relative of ex-President James K. Polk, and his second wife, Emma Sophronia (Hooten) Polk, who was born in Louisville Oct. 19, 1853, and died Aug. 19, 1875. By his first wife, Elizabeth (Marshall) Polk, Doctor Polk had three children: Elizabeth Marshall, wife of George Fulton, who was born Jan. 4, 1843, and died Aug. 30, 1899; Betsey Marshall, wife of Capt. Alexander Lawson, who was born Jan. 6, 1845, and Attorney John R. M. Polk, who married Miss Addie Rice of Louisville, Ky., was born Sept. 19, 1851, and died Dec. 24, 1894. His wife died about five years later. On the death of his second wife, Doctor Polk married her sister, Mrs. Eliza Hooten, the widow of Captain Frisbee, and by this marriage to Captain Frisbee she has one daughter, Ella Frisbee Coleman, the wife of Benjamin Tyler Coleman, of Middletown, Ky. She was born May 9, 1872, and has two sons, Frisbee and Charles Tyler Coleman. Dr. Polk was born in Woodford county, Ky., June 12, 1813, and died Feb. 27, 1891, in Jefferson county, Ky. His third wife, Eliza Ann Polk, was born in Louisville, Ky., Sept. 23, 1843, and still survives. Charles H. Wilson and wife have had a family of four children. They are Ruby Frances, deceased; Ella Christine; Mildred Kathleen, and Sarah Pauline.

GEORGE MARTIN WILSON, JR., one of the most successful young men of his county, was born in Livingston county, Ky., April 6, 1877. His grandfather, Charles Wilson, came to America from Sweden in 1826, locating at Smithland, where he died in 1864. His wife, Martha Ann Walker, whom he married in 1840, died in 1903. They had a family of eleven children, of whom five are now living. He was a Democrat in politics, a farmer by occupation, owning a large tract of land, and, with his wife, identified with the Baptist church. His maternal grandfather, Reuben Coffer, born May 5, 1789, came from Virginia to Lyon county, Ky., where he died June 20, 1853. On Feb. 19, 1824, he married Elizabeth Ann Brewer, a native of Christian county, Ky. In politics he was identified with the Whig party, was a farmer by occupation, and, with his wife, a member of the Baptist church. They had seven children, of whom two are living. The parents of George Martin Wilson, Jr., were George Martin, Sr., and Millie Frances (Coffer) Wilson, the former born in Livingston county Oct. 17, 1841, and the latter in Christian county Feb. 9, 1844. Mr. Wilson was educated in the public schools of Livingston county, one of his teachers having been Capt. J. W. Bush. His occupation is farming and stock raising, in which he has been very successful. He is a stanch Democrat, and was a soldier in the Confederate army. He now lives a retired life on his farm of 1,000 acres. Mr. and Mrs. Wilson had eleven children, of whom seven are living. They are: Lizzie, wife of L. H. Cothron, a sketch of whose life appears elsewhere in this work; Charles H., whose sketch also appears in this work; George Martin, Jr.; Thomas Henley, a farmer and stock dealer; Hattie May; Martha Ann and Harry Winfred. His wife died on June 6, 1896, and Mr.

Wilson, in November of the same year, married Mrs. Delia Fort, who has borne him one son, Floyd A. The subject of this sketch was educated in the common schools of Livingston county, graduating from the Smithland graded school in 1896. In 1898 he received from Mr. R. B. Cowper (high sheriff) the appointment of deputy sheriff of Livingston county, and was again made deputy sheriff under Mr. P. H. Bush in 1901, which position he still holds. On Sept. 3, 1904, the Democratic party nominated him for the office of high sheriff. On Dec. 29, 1901, he married Miss Linnie Belle Crewdson, who was born in Pope county, Ill., and came when a child with her parents, Green and Susan (Scott) Crewdson, to Livingston county. Green Crewdson died in Louisville, Ky., in 1893 and was followed by his wife in October, 1901. Two children were born to this family: Harry J. Crewdson of Smithland, Ky., and Linnie B., the wife of the subject of this sketch. George Martin Wilson, Jr., is the father of two sons, Cecil Crewdson and Charles Edwin. The grandfather of Mrs. Wilson, Rev. J. W. Crewdson, a noted Baptist minister of Illinois and Kentucky, died in Livingston county about 1895. Hon. S. R. Crewdson, circuit judge of the Seventh Kentucky district (Russellville), is a great-uncle of Mrs. Wilson.

WILLIAM THOMAS THRELKELD, of Smithland, Ky., jailer for Livingston county, was born in Crittenden county of that state, Jan. 31, 1849. He is a son of Willis and Sarah (McCullum) Threlkeld, the former a native of Virginia and the latter of South Carolina. They came to Kentucky in 1848, where the father became a prosperous farmer and stock dealer, owning a large amount of land and a number of slaves. He took an active part in politics as a Democrat; was for a number of years deputy county clerk; was a member of the Masonic fraternity and the Independent Order of Odd Fellows, and was a regular attendant at the Baptist church, to which his wife belonged. They had a family of three sons and three daughters. One son, Dr. John B. Threlkeld, is a prominent physician of Salem and a stockholder in banks at that place, Marion and Dawson Springs. He is one of the directors of the bank at Salem. The mother died in 1855 and the father married Susan Foster. To this second marriage there were born one son and two daughters, one daughter now living. He died on May 2, 1864. The paternal grandfather, Thomas Threlkeld, was a Virginian who came in an early day to Allen county, Ky., removed from there to Crittenden county and died near Salem in 1850.

He was married three times. His first wife was a Miss Duncan and to this marriage were born two children: the father of the subject of this sketch and Jeannette, who married P. C. Barnett and is now deceased. The second wife was also a Miss Duncan and the third a Mrs. Hodge. No children were born to the second and third marriages. The maternal grandfather of Mr. Threlkeld was Aaron McCullum, a native of Ireland. He died about 1862 and his wife in 1870. William T. Threlkeld was educated in the public schools and upon reaching manhood became a farmer. He now owns a fine farm of 500 acres on the Ohio river, three miles from Smithland, where he carries on a general farming business and devotes considerable attention to stock raising. Ever since he became of age he has been active in promoting the interests of the Democratic party. In 1897 he was elected jailer for the county and re-elected in 1901. He is a member of Smithland Lodge, No. 138, Free and Accepted Masons, and Carrsville Lodge, No. 145, Independent Order of Odd Fellows. In 1882 he married Miss Viola, daughter of W. and Sallie (Davis) Thomas. She was born in the State of Tennessee, her parents both being natives of that state, but removed to Livingston county about 1874. Her father was a farmer, a prominent Democrat, a Free Mason, and both her parents belonged to the Christian church. During the war her father served in the Confederate army. He died in 1876 and his wife in 1892. Mr. and Mrs. Threlkeld are both members of the Christian church. Their children are Lucy Maud, Sallie, Willis, Lula, Leon and Lillian, the last two being twins.

PATRICK H. BUSH was born in Livingston county, Ky., Feb. 26, 1870. He is the son of Capt. J. W. Bush, a sketch of whose life appears elsewhere in this work. Patrick was reared in Smithland and educated in part in its public schools. He also attended Bethel college at Russellville and Kentucky State college at Lexington. After farming for a time he engaged in other pursuits. For two years he was a bookkeeper for the Grand Rivers Iron Company, and then for eighteen months worked in a railroad office at St. Louis, Mo. The Democratic party honored him with an election to the office of sheriff of Livingston county, Ky., in 1901. In 1904 he was nominee of the same party for the office of county clerk. Mr. Bush is a member of Smithland Lodge, No. 138, Free and Accepted Masons, and belongs to the order of Knights of the Maccabees. On Sept. 14, 1893, he married Ola Mitchell, of Livingston county, daughter of William and Julia Mitchell, both deceased. To this marriage three children were born: Virginia Ogela, Edgar Bryan and Mary Musa. Mr. Bush has been quite successful in every enterprise that he has conducted. His frequent election to positions of great trust shows that he enjoys the confidence and esteem of his fellow-men. In addition to a fine farm near Grand Rivers, he owns valuable property in Florida.

GEORGE W. LANDRAM, of Smithland, Ky., clerk of the Livingston county court, was born in that county July 6, 1859. He is the son of Hubbard and Clara E. (Barlow) Landram, the former a native of Culpeper county, Va., and the latter of Hawesville, Ky. Hubbard Landram, after operating a gold mine in Virginia for nine years, came to Livingston county, Ky., in 1840, where he resided until his death in 1877. He was an engineer and was in chief control as such for two years at White's old furnace in Livingston county until the furnace ceased operation. He was also a blacksmith, a farmer and a slaveholder. In religious matters he was identified with the Baptist church. He married his first wife, Mahala Darnell, in Virginia and to this union were born two sons who grew to manhood. They were William, a soldier in the Confederate army, who died in Camp Douglas, at the age of seventeen years, and Joseph L., a carpenter, who died in Texas in 1886. He married the second time in Kentucky and had a family of five children: two died in infancy; Agnes died at the age of four years, and Hubbard at the age of three; the subject of this sketch being the only one now living. The mother of these children died in 1879, and was interred beside her husband in the old "Landram" cemetery on the Smithland and Dover road, ten miles from Smithland. George W. Landram was reared on a farm and in the blacksmith shop, and what little education he received was obtained in the public schools of the county, and one five months' term in "Hambleton" college at Elizabethtown, Hardin county, Ky., where he was under the care of Prof. J. W. Heagan. He learned the trade of wagonmaker and blacksmith. Under Cleveland's first administration he was appointed to an office in the internal revenue service at Owensboro, Ky. When Mr. Cleveland was elected the second time, Mr. Landram received the appointment of postmaster at Grand Rivers, Ky., which place he filled until August, 1897. During his term as postmaster he served as railroad agent for the Illinois Central and as express agent for the American and Southern Express Companies. Prior to this time he had suffered the loss of three fingers from his right hand, in a saw mill accident, and in 1892 he lost his left arm from blood poisoning; in spite of these terrible misfortunes he with a single finger and thumb discharged all the duties of these various positions, without aid or assistance from any one else. In 1897 he was nominated and elected on the Democratic ticket as clerk of the Livingston county court, and moved to Smithland in November, of that year. In 1901 he was renominated and re-elected to the same office. In addition to holding the office of county court clerk, he was, in 1904, at the April term of the Livingston circuit court, appointed by Judge J. F. Gordon as master commissioner and receiver of said court. During all the years, from 1898 to 1904, except the year 1901, he has been the chairman of the Livingston county Democratic campaign committee. He is a member of Smithland Lodge, No. 138, Free and Accepted Masons, and a member of the First Baptist church of Grand Rivers, Ky. In 1879 he married Miss Rebecca A. Driskill of Livingston county. Five children were born to this union: Clarence E., now an ensign in the United States navy; Ora Evelyn, assistant music teacher in the South Carolina Co-educational Institute; Lula A. G., wife of V. D. Presnell, a merchant of Smithland, Ky., and the mother of Bernadette; Beulah Ethel, who died in infancy, and Andrew Hudnall. After the death of his first wife in 1888, Mr. Landram married Miss Dora A. Mitchusson of Livingston county. Five children have been born to this marriage; Hubbard J.; John Lawson; Anna Blanche; Ellis Coleman, and George Wheeler. Notwithstanding the fact that time, from a physical standpoint, has dealt rather heavily with Mr. Landram, he looks upon the bright side of the picture of life, and stands as a living example to the young men of the age, that "Where there is a will there is a way." He pushes along the road of life as though he was blest with all the hands and arms that are given to any man, and never grumbles or complains of his misfortunes. He is greeted daily by many, who assure him that if they were in his place they would give way to despondency and discouragement, but he does not look at matters in that light. He has many friends in the county and state, and also has many enemies, who take great delight in abusing him, but he is never disconcerted by them, and gives no attention to their criticisms; he says life is too short to allow your enemies to disturb you, but enjoy the confidence of your friends and leave your enemies to take care of themselves.

THOMAS EVANS, of Smithland, Ky., judge of the county court of Livingston county, was born in Caldwell county of that state, May 3, 1861. He is the son of Ezer E. and Frances E. (Dawson) Evans, both natives of Christian county, Ky. The former was born on Sept. 8, 1838, and the latter on May 7, 1840. Ezer E. was the son of Ezer and Susan (Lindsay) Evans, the former born in North Carolina in 1792, and the latter in Kentucky in 1798. Ezer Evans died and was buried at Saltillo, Tenn., in 1838, and his wife died in Caldwell county in 1865. The paternal grandfather of Thomas Evans was Jesse Evans, who came to North Carolina from Wales in an early day, and died at Florence, Ala. The maternal grandfather, James W. Dawson, was a native of Virginia, who went to Tennessee and from there came to Christian or Trigg county, Ky., dying near Mayfield in Graves county in 1879. His wife, Sallie (Washburn) Dawson was born in Virginia and died in Christian county, in 1841. Ezer E. Dawson was educated in the common schools of his native county and learned the trades of millwright and wagonmaker. He came to Livingston county in 1867, and on January 14 of that year located at Salem. He was killed in a railroad accident at Malvern, Ark., Jan. 31, 1885. He was a Democrat, a Mason, an Odd Fellow, and he and his wife were members of the Christian church. They had eight children: four reached manhood and womanhood, and four died in infancy. Those now living are, Mrs. Dora Sherrill of Stevensville, Tex.; Charles Evans, principal of the Marion high school, a graduate of the Normal university of Lebanon, O., an active worker in the Young Men's Christian Association, an institute instructor for the State of Kentucky, a Democrat, a Knight of Pythias, and a member of the Christian church. He married Miss Mattie Blue, a daughter of the late John W. Blue, Sr., one of Marion's most popular lawyers. Two children have blessed this union, Charles Blue and Edward C. Thomas Evans, the third surviving child, was educated in the public schools of Salem, learned the trade of blacksmith and engaged in the hardware business in conjunction with his trade. In 1894 he was elected sheriff of Livingston county, and served one term. In 1897 he was elected judge of the county court, receiving 321 more votes than both of his opponents, notwithstanding the fact that they were prominent politicians of the county. He was re-elected to this important office in 1901, and three years later (1904) received the nomination of the Democratic party for the same office. His ability and energy are shown by the construction of twenty-one steel bridges which span the streams of his county as monuments to his memory. On Nov. 26, 1885, he married Miss Lelia Miles of Crittenden county, a daughter of Richard and Sallie (Barnett) Miles. The former died in 1874. The widow was born in Crittenden county, and still survives. Richard Miles, Jr., was a son of Richard Miles, Sr., and the grandson of William Miles, who came from Virginia to Crittenden county, where he died. Richard Miles, Sr., was a farmer by occupation, served as sheriff of the county for eight years, and died near Salem. Richard Miles, Jr., was a farmer, a Democrat, deputy sheriff of the county under his father, and a Mason. He was drowned at the mouth of Deer Creek, Crittenden county, in March, 1874. The wife of Mr. Evans is a member of the Christian church, to which he himself inclines. They have one child, Elaine, who was born Aug. 2, 1893.

GIBSON AARON RUDD, farmer, stock raiser and justice of the peace, was born in Union county, Ky., Oct. 31, 1866. He is the son of Joseph K. and Elizabeth (Taylor) Rudd, the former a native of North Carolina and the latter of Union county. His maternal grandparents were Aaron and Nancy Taylor, the former coming to Union county in an early day, where he died. Joseph K. Rudd was reared and educated in his native state and came to Union county when a young man. He and his wife were the parents of eleven children, of whom six are still living. He died June 21, 1897, and is survived by his widow, who still resides in the old homestead in Union county. In his day he was an active Democrat, an Odd Fellow, and with his wife belonged to the Methodist Episcopal Church South. The subject of this sketch was reared on a farm and was educated in the common schools of Union county. After engaging for a time in farming he was for three years in the grocery business as a member of the firm of McKinley & Rudd, at Commercial Point. Quitting the grocery business he returned to the old homestead. In 1896 he came to Livingston county, where he, with N. B. Robinson, managed the T. T. Barnett farm under the firm name of Rudd & Robinson for three years. He then bought a farm in Panhandle precinct of Livingston county, where he is now engaged in farming and dealing in stock. On Feb. 1, 1905, he accepted a position with the Ayer & Lord Tie Company, with headquarters at Smithland, Ky. In politics Mr. Rudd is a stanch Democrat. Gov. W. O. Bradley appointed him a justice of the peace to fill out an unexpired term. He was twice elected to the same office and is at present the incumbent of this office. He is a member of the Humane lodge, No. 37, Independent Order of Odd Fellows of Morganfield.

JAMES A. CLOPTON, a successful merchant of Smithland, Ky., is a native of that city and is a descendant of one of the old Virginia families. He can trace his ancestry back to one William Clopton, who was born in the Old Dominion, of English ancestry, Sept. 9, 1764. He married Betsey, daughter of John and Elizabeth Hale, and one of their sons was Reuben Ford Augustus Clopton, the great-grandfather of the subject of this sketch. Reuben Ford Clopton was engaged in mercantile pursuits, was an ardent Whig, and both he and his wife, Elizabeth, were members of the Methodist Episcopal church, as were all the members of the Clopton family. This couple had a son named Reuben F., who was born on March 18, 1795. He grew to manhood in Virginia, married Mary Ann Taylor, and in 1833 came to Kentucky. After stopping for a while at Franklin and Princeton he finally settled in Livingston county, where he died on Aug. 20, 1845. His son, Reuben A., was born at Felixville, Cumberland county, Va., Jan. 24, 1823, and was therefore ten years of age when his parents came to Kentucky. Upon reaching man's estate he married Catherine Harris, who was born at Princeton, Caldwell county, Ky., Oct. 15, 1828. Their marriage occurred on Nov. 4, 1847. The father of Catherine Harris died when she was a mere child, while on a business trip south. Her mother died at the age of thirty, leaving her and four sisters orphans, and she was reared by Dr. Miles of Salem. For fifty-six years Reuben A. Clopton was engaged in mercantile pursuits. For more than fifty years he dealt with the firm of E. Q. Smith, manufacturers of furniture, Evansville, Ind., and in the last days of his business career dealt exclusively in furniture. Although he met with many reverses, he died free from debt. From the commencement of his business career in 1847 he made it his rule to owe no man more than he could pay and to suffer no one to owe him more than he was able to lose. During the war he was associated with a Mr. Wiley in the clothing business at Murray, Calloway county, and after the war he formed a partnership with W. C. Ellis at Smithland. Subsequently he was in business by himself until his death, which occurred Sept. 10, 1903, at Evansville, Ind., where he had gone for medical treatment. His wife died on April 27, 1904. During the war he and ten other young men of Livingston county were arrested and taken to Louisville as military prisoners but all were released through the influence of Henry F. Givens. Later he was drafted but hired a substitute. The children of Reuben A. and Catherine Clopton were thirteen in number, of whom five are now living, viz.:-Mrs. T. F. Bunton, of Smithland; J. T., of Evansville, Ind.; J. D. and James A., of Smithland, and Maria A., wife of John T. Watson, a patent broker. James A. Clopton was born Sept. 24, 1868, and reared in Smithland, where he received his education in the public schools. After clerking for some years for his father and other parties he, in 1890, embarked in the confectionery and fancy grocery business, which has ever since been his vocation. In 1897 he received the appointment of trustee of jury funds for Livingston county at the hands of Judge T. J. Nunn, to which office he was reappointed in 1903 by Judge Fleming Gordon. He is a Democrat and a Knight of the Maccabees. On May 20, 1891, he married Miss Katie Metcalf of Union county, who was born Jan. 1, 1872. She is the daughter of Frank and Hannah Metcalf, formerly of Union county, but now of Paducah, Ky. The children of this marriage are Leonard, James, Lorena, Winfield Schley, Willard Caroline, and Katie Harris. Of these James A., Lorena and Katie Harris are deceased.

ZED A. BENNETT, superintendent of Livingston county, Ky., schools, was born in that county March 13, 1874. He is the son of Roland and Mina (Aydelott) Bennett, both natives of Livingston county, the father born Sept. 11, 1849, and the mother May 10, 1857. Roland Bennett is the son of Alfred Bennett, who was born in Livingston county in 1808, his father being Nathan Bennett. Alfred Bennett's wife, whose maiden name was Susan Stringer, was born in Georgia in 1810. She died Nov. 26, 1904, being in her ninety-fifth year. She was the daughter of Leonard Stringer, a Baptist preacher, teacher and doctor. He was a Revolutionary soldier and was intimately acquainted with George Washington; preached in a pulpit once occupied by John Wesley, and was a close friend of Andrew Jackson. He was in prison when Cornwallis surrendered, having been captured by the British. He had two sons in the war of 1812, under General Andrew Jackson. Susan Bennett was made a member of the National society of the "Daughters of the American Revolution," only one month before her death, she being the only real daughter in the State of Kentucky at that time. After the marriage of Alfred and Susan Bennett, which occurred in Livingston county, they went to Illinois and spent one year there, but returned at the end of that time to Livingston county and lived there until death. They were members of the Baptist church and were the first subjects baptized between the Tennessee and Cumberland rivers. The maternal grandfather of Zed A. Bennett, Zed Aydelott, was born in Illinois and came to Livingston county, with his parents, where he lived and died. His wife was Miss Lucinda Spell, a native of Livingston county, the daughter of Wiley Spell, a pioneer of the same county, where both died. Roland Bennett was reared and educated in Livingston county; is a farmer by occupation and a Democrat in politics. His wife died in 1882. They had four children, the subject of this sketch being the eldest. He was reared on a farm and educated in the common schools of his native county; Smithland graded schools; Hampton academy; and Marion high school. He taught six years, having taught in the country schools and also at Pinckneyville and Salem, both in Livingston county. He was elected county superintendent of schools by the Democratic party, to fill out the unexpired term of H. V. McChesney, who was elected state superintendent of public instruction. In 1901 Mr. Bennett was re-elected and still holds the office. He has the distinction of being the only man living "between the rivers" who ever got a majority of the votes on the "north-side" of Cumberland river, over a man living on the north side. He received every vote in his home precinct but one. In addition to his duties as county superintendent of schools, Mr. Bennett is interested in the life insurance and real estate business. On Dec. 24, 1902, he married Miss Melville Glenn of Marion, Ky. She is the daughter of Francis Marion and Susan E. Glenn, both natives of

Caldwell county. The husband died at Marion in March, 1896. Mrs. Bennett was a graduate of the Marion high school and a student of Stetson university of Florida. She taught in the Marion graded schools and the Ohio Valley Baptist college of Sturgis, Ky. She died Aug. 30, 1904, being only twenty-one years of age. She had a host of friends who bowed in grief at her death. Mrs. Bennett was known far and wide as a woman of great beauty, queenly bearing and possessing a wonderful versatility of mind. She was one of the most devout Christian characters the world ever knew, and took a leading part in the church. Mr. Bennett says the greatest honor of his life was the winning of her heart and hand and he loves to be called Melville Glenn's husband. Mrs. Bennett and her husband were members of the Baptist church, she having been converted and joined the church at fourteen years of age and he at the age of fifteen.

LEE B. DAVIS, clerk of the circuit court and ex-officio recorder of deeds, Cairo, Ill., was born in Marion county of that state, Feb. 27, 1873, his parents being James P. and Amanda (Benham) Davis. The father was born in Kentucky, July 3, 1831. In 1854 he came to Cairo, but later went to Missouri, where he remained until 1867, when he returned to Illinois and located on a farm near Salem in Marion county. The mother was born near Crawfordsville, Ind., in 1832. Her first marriage was to a Mr. Ramsey, by whom she had two children: Hiram E. Ramsey, a farmer near Odin, Ill., and Mrs. Eudora Dursky, living not far from Salem. Two children were born to her second marriage: Mrs. May Aird and the subject of this sketch, both living in Cairo. The mother died in 1892 and the father is now living, at the age of seventy-three years, with his son. Lee B. Davis received his education in the Salem schools, graduating from the high school in 1891. Upon leaving school he went to Alexander county, of which Cairo is the county seat, and engaged in teaching. This occupation he followed for nine years, the last six of which he was principal of the graded schools at Willard. He resigned this position to take charge of the clerk's office, to which he was elected in the fall of 1900. He was re-elected in the fall of

1904, his second term beginning on December 5th. Mr. Davis is a Democrat in politics, and the fact that he has twice been elected clerk of Alexander county, which is strongly Republican, attests his popularity. In 1900, when he was first elected, the Republican national ticket carried the county by over 1,000 majority. At that election he defeated, by a small majority, a man who had held the office for sixteen years, but in 1904 he carried the county by 450, while the Republican national ticket received a majority of more than 1,500. He has made a record as an efficient and conscientious official, and has won the regard of his fellow-citizens, as his second election plainly shows. Mr. Davis is a Royal Arch Mason and a member of the Fraternal Order of Eagles. He was married on March 28, 1893, to Miss Adelia Pickett, of Alexander county, and they have three daughters: Dorothy, born Oct. 3, 1895; Beulah, born March 6, 1897; and Leota, born June 11, 1903.

JAMES S. ROCHE, of Cairo, now sheriff and ex-officio collector of taxes of Alexander county, Ill., was born in Pulaski county, of that state, on Christmas day, 1852. He is a son of Michael and Ellen (Murphy) Roche. The father came to Pulaski county from the State of New York in 1848, and was for many years a contractor in the employ of the Illinois Central Railway Company. He died Sept. 16, 1882. The mother died just one year later, Sept. 16, 1883. Sheriff Roche and a sister, Mrs. Anna Sitphin, of Jonesboro, Ark., are the only surviving children. James S. Roche grew to manhood and received his education in his native county. Upon reaching his majority he engaged in fruit farming, which he conducted successfully until 1884, when he bought a farm on the Mississippi river, about twenty miles above the city of Cairo, and removed to Alexander county. Since then he has made several purchases of the land adjoining his farm until he now owns nearly 1,200 acres, practically all of which is under cultivation. Few farms in Southern Illinois are better stocked with implements, machinery, live stock, etc., or in the character of buildings and other improvements. Although Mr. Roche fills the office of sheriff and has his temporary residence in Cairo he still retains the management of this farm, employing men to do all the work under his personal direction. Ever since attaining his majority he has been an ardent Republican, and has held several minor offices. Soon after he was twenty-one he was elected justice of the peace in Pulaski county, and after holding this office for several years, was county commissioner for one term, just before he removed to Alexander county. In the fall of 1902 he was elected sheriff for a term of four years by a handsome majority, though a portion of the Democratic county ticket was elected. Sheriff Roche was married in 1884 to Miss Maggie Atherton. To this marriage were born three children: Francis D., aged seventeen years; Leslie B., aged fifteen, and Leon, aged twelve. The mother of these children died in 1894, and in 1896 Mr. Roche was united in marriage to Miss Mattie Martin, one of Alexander county's best known and most popular school teachers.

JOHN A. MILLER, late one of the leading jewelers of Cairo, Ill., president of the board of county commissioners and of the Merchants' League, was born at Coblentz on the Rhine, Germany, June 17, 1840. His parents, Andrew and Gertrude Josephine (Adams) Miller, were both natives of Germany, though the mother's father, Christian Adams, was the great-grandson of an English gentleman who came to Germany from his native land, and whose descendants continued to live in Germany. Andrew Miller, the father of John A., was a cabinet-maker by trade, and in later life, before coming to America, he operated a factory for the production of fine furniture. He was an inventor of considerable note, among his inventions being the process of gluing together numerous strips of different kinds of woods for the purpose of bending into almost any shape desired. This process led to the manufacture of the now celebrated Vienna chair. He was also the inventor of the differential roller system, for malting purposes, and equipped the first malt mill in Germany with this process, operating it for some time after its completion. In addition to his other business undertakings he was the manufacturer of veneers for fine furniture. The name was originally spelled "Mueller," but after coming to America Andrew Miller changed the spelling to the English form. In April, 1854, the family left their native land for America, and landed at New Orleans in December of the same year. Their destination was St. Louis, but owing to ice in the Upper Mississippi they were compelled to remain in New Orleans until the following spring. John A. Miller was one of a family of five children, viz.: Joseph Augustus, Christian William, Gertrude Josephine, John Andrew, and Christian. Soon after their arrival in St. Louis Christian, the youngest child, died of measles, and not long afterward the mother fell a victim to the cholera. Joseph A. died on Dec. 28, 1904, at Providence, R. I. He was one of the chief engineers in the construction of the Union Pacific railway, and later a patent attorney making a specialty of electrical cases. Christian William served in the Union army during the war and died at Milwaukee, Wis., in 1893, where he was superintendent of the construction of the national soldiers' home. Gertrude Josephine married G. A. Staff, and died at her home in St. Louis in 1900. After the death of the mother the father went to Alton, Ill., where he had a son living, and died there in 1859, at the age of sixty-one years. John A. Miller attended school from the age of five years to the age of thirteen in his native land, with a vacation of six weeks each year. After coming to St. Louis he entered the jewelry store of Benjamin Grane, corner of Fourth and Locust streets, as an apprentice and served four years. Mr. Grane was succeeded by the present well known house of Mermod & Jaccard. While serving his apprenticeship Mr. Miller attended night school, where he acquired a good English education. In 1858 he went to Alton, where he obtained a position as clerk in a jewelry store and worked there until the commencement of the war. He then went to Springfield and offered his services to his adopted country, but was rejected on account of his physical appearance, the government officers deeming him unfit for military duty. Soon after he returned home he learned that he could get into the army by going to Cairo. He accordingly went there, but being overtaken by a spell of sickness he was never mustered in. However, he went with General Prentiss on the Cape Girardeau expedition, but soon returned to Cairo, where he accepted a position in the jewelry establishment of David Ford. After a year with Mr. Ford he went to Paducah and opened a jewelry store of his own. There he did a prosperous business for twenty years, part of which time he was president of the Western Watch Manufacturing Company, of Chicago, which was organized for the manufacture of watches, but never succeeded in establishing itself on a paying basis. In 1881 Mr. Miller came to Cairo and from that time until his death was engaged in the jewelry business in that city.

By trade he was a practical watch maker, attained prominence as a scientist and inventor, was one of the leading promoters of distributing weather signals and was a member of the American Association for the Advancement of Science. His practical knowledge of the business, and his careful attention to details, soon enabled him to build up a large patronage. He employed a number of skilled workmen and there was nothing in the jewelry line too pretentious for him to undertake. Nearly all the railroads that center at Cairo employed him as their inspector, because of his well known skill in repairing and adjusting fine watches. The visitor to his store, on looking around at the large and well selected assortment of jewelry, clocks, watches and silverware and optical goods, might well imagine himself to be in one of the leading establishments of some large city. Mr. Miller was a Republican in his political views, and took a keen interest in public affairs. He was twice elected county commissioner and at the time of his death was president of the board. Before his election as commissioner he was for twenty years a member of the Cairo school board. He served as president of the Merchants' League from its organization several years ago. For a number of years he was interested in the good roads movement, and as commissioner did much to improve the public highways of Alexander county. Each time he was elected to any public office it was without his solicitation or personal effort. As an advocate of the improvement of the Ohio and Mississippi rivers he attended nearly every meeting of the associations to discuss the proposition. In fraternal circles Mr. Miller was a member of the Knights of Pythias and the Ancient Order of United Workmen. During the years 1894-95 he was grand chancellor of the Knights of Pythias of Illinois, the highest office of the order in the state. In business, political or fraternal matters Mr. Miller never dallied with duty. Whatever he found to do was done promptly and to the best of his ability. It was to these traits of character he owed his success. People learned to depend upon him and were never disappointed. He was married on June 19, 1862, at St. Louis, to Miss Katie F., daughter of John Lohrum, who was the pioneer street paving contractor of that city. To this marriage there were born the following children: John A., who holds a responsible position in the jewelry store; Hattie, wife of George Petter, who has charge of the optical department of the business; Minnie, a teacher in the Cairo public schools; and Adele, now bookkeeper in the jewelry store established by her father. All received good education, being graduates of the high school, and Adele studied music in the Boston conservatory. In 1899 Mr. Miller visited his birthplace in Germany, after an absence of forty-eight years. While he had the true German sentiment in his love for the traditions of the Fatherland; there was none who had a higher conception of the duties of American citizenship, or who stood more ready to discharge such duties. He died suddenly of heart disease, Jan. 7, 1905, and his remains were cremated at St. Louis two days later.

DR. JOHN JUDSON JENNELLE, a prominent dentist of Cairo, Ill., and a member of the board of county commissioners of Alexander county, was born at Le Roy, Genesee county, N. Y., Aug. 3, 1850. His father, John Jennelle, was a native of Canada, born near Quebec in 1818. He learned the trade of tinner and was connected with that and the hardware business all his life, working for years in the city of Toronto, after which he came to the United States, locating at Albion, N. Y. He was of pure French Canadian stock, his ancestors coming from France, and he did not learn the English language until after he went to Toronto. Shortly after he came to New York he was married to Miss Elvira Barter, of Albion, a native of Heuvelton, St. Lawrence county, where she was born in 1821. Their children were: George William, Joanna, Adelaide E., John Judson, Joseph Abel, Silas Edgar and David. George William enlisted at Buffalo in the regular army about the outbreak of the Civil war. Being a musician, he joined one of the largest regimental bands in the service, being stationed at Fort Preble, Portland Harbor, Me., Hart Island, N. Y., Washington, D. C., and San Antonio, Tex., where he was mustered out after a continuous service of six years, and died at Pontiac, Mich., in March, 1880. Joanna and David both died in childhood in New York. In May, 1870, Adelaide E. married Mr. O. C. Morris of Pontiac and died at Orchard Lake, Mich., April, 1900, surviving her husband some twenty years. Joseph Abel lives in St. Louis, Mo., and Silas Edgar, in Pontiac, where the family went in 1865. The father died in Detroit, July 18, 1901, and the mother at Pontiac, July 3, 1904. The boyhood of Dr. Jennelle was passed in his native village. After removing to Michigan with his parents he decided to study dentistry, and before he was seventeen years of age he entered the office of Dr. J. A. Harris of

Pontiac, under whose skillful instruction he mastered all departments of the profession during the three years of his apprenticeship. In 1870 he came to Illinois, locating at Duquoin in Perry county. Four years later he came to Cairo, where he practiced for two years, when he returned to Duquoin. In 1885 he again took up his residence in Cairo and since that time has practiced his profession there with unvarying success. Dr. Jennelle is one of the pioneer dentists of Southern Illinois. In 1881 he was appointed a member of the Illinois state board of dental examiners by Governor (now Senator) Cullom, and served as such four years. He is a member of the Illinois State Dental society, which he joined in 1887 and in which he has held various official positions. It was through his influence the society held its meeting in Cairo in 1888, memorable in the fact that this meeting was the first and only one ever held by the society south of Springfield in its fifty years of existence. At this meeting Dr. Jennelle was elected vice-president. Although years have elapsed since Dr. Jennelle first began the practice of dentistry, he has not allowed himself to fall behind the procession in the march of dental progress, on the contrary, has always been in the van, keeping in touch with all the improved methods and appliances relating to the science of dentistry and dental surgery. His office is one of the best equipped in this section of the country. In political affairs he is an unswerving Republican, and has held various offices in local and municipal governments. While living at Duquoin he served six years as member of the board of education; was also city clerk, city treasurer, and alderman. Since coming to Cairo he has served as alderman seven years; was the candidate of the Citizens' League for mayor in 1903, but was defeated by the so-called "liberal element"; and in the fall of 1904 was elected a member of the board of county commissioners. On Aug. 6, 1874, Dr. Jennelle was married to Miss Lucy E., youngest daughter of Dr. Lewis Dyer, a prominent physician of Duquoin and a veteran of the Civil war, having entered the service as surgeon of the Eighty-first Illinois volunteers in 1861; was with General Grant in all the important engagements in the Mississippi Valley, and when mustered out had attained the rank of division surgeon. To this marriage there have been born the following children: John Judson, Jr., now thirty years of age and secretary and treasurer of the W. W. Herron Lumber Company, Mobile, Ala.; Marion and June. On Dec. 30, 1902, John J. was married to Miss Edith, daughter of Maj. Edwin W. Halliday, a prominent citizen of Cairo, Ill., and a Confederate veteran of the Civil war. On June 2,

1903, Marion was married to R. E. Given, a civil engineer of Memphis, Tenn., a member of one of the old families of Kentucky and whose grandfather founded the city of Paducah, Ky. All the children have had the advantage of good schooling and are fitted to occupy any station in society to which they may be called. Miss June is still at home.

JAMES H. GALLIGAN, cashier of Alexander County National bank, was born in Cairo, Nov. 11, 1866. He is the son of Andrew J. Galligan, a prominent and well known contractor late of Cairo, who died in 1887. His father was born in Ireland and came to the United States with his parents when quite young. He was reared and educated in Trenton, N. J., and located in Cairo during the Civil war. The mother of the subject was Anna Callahan, also a native of Ireland, crossing the Atlantic with her parents. The father and mother met in Cairo and were married in 1864. They had a family of seven children, of whom James H. is the eldest. The mother, a widow, still survives, her home being with James, who was reared and educated in Cairo. He quit school at eighteen and entered the Alexander County National bank as a messenger boy. He has practically grown up with the bank, for he has been with it constantly since he was eighteen and has filled every desk and position in the bank from that of messenger boy up to cashier. He has held the last position for seven years. The great popularity of this well known financial institution, its high degree of success, and the confidence it has of all the people of Alexander county are largely due to the high personal standing, well known integrity and wide popularity of Mr. Galligan. His inflexible honesty and fine financial ability as well as his uniform courtesy to the public have made him one of the most popular and thoroughly respected bank officials in Alexander county. This bank was originally the Alexander County bank, which was organized in 1875 with a capital of $25,000. In 1887 it was made a national bank and its capital was increased to $100,000 and its name changed to the Alexander County National bank. In 1889 the Alexander County Savings bank was organized under the laws of the State of Illinois with a capital of $50,000. It was organized by the officers and directors of the Alexander County National bank and its business is conducted in the same building. Mr. Galligan is also cashier of the savings bank. On Sept. 18, 1895, Mr. Galligan married Miss Jennie Spalding of Zainesville, O. She died May 9, 1903, leaving one daughter, Marie Helen Galligan, now six years old. In politics Mr.

Galligan is a Gold Democrat. He is now serving his second term on the board of education. He is an active member of the Benevolent and Protective Order of Elks. It is needless to state that Mr. Galligan is one of the foremost men of Cairo.

REED GREEN is a lawyer of Cairo, Ill.; was born at Mount Vernon, Ill.; is the son of William H. and Ann Letitia (Hughes) Green, who were natives of Kentucky, both of whom are dead. He was educated in the public schools at Cairo, and afterwards attended the Illinois State normal university at Normal, and the Southern Illinois State normal university at Carbondale. He taught school in Cairo for two years. During those two years he read law and afterward attended the Wesleyan law school at Bloomington, Ill., and was admitted to the bar in 1886, since which time he has been engaged in the practice of law at Cairo. Soon after the beginning of the practice he was elected to the lower house of the general assembly of Illinois for two terms; afterwards served four years in the State senate. For the past ten years has been devoting his entire attention to the general practice of law at Cairo.

CHARLES REED, the widely known and popular proprietor of the Palmer House, Paducah, Ky., was born in that city, Nov. 4, 1842. He is a son of William H. and Elizabeth (Segenfelter) Reed, the former a native of Virginia and the latter of Germany. William H. Reed came to Paducah in his early manhood and there followed the occupation of contractor and builder until his death, which occurred while Charles was still in his childhood. The mother died in 1862, leaving the subject of this sketch the sole survivor of his family. Charles Reed received his education in the schools of Paducah. When the Civil war commenced he cast his lot with the Confederates by enlisting in the Third Kentucky infantry, under General Tihlman. His company was afterward mounted and assigned to the cavalry division commanded by the celebrated General Forrest. He served until the close of the war, more than half of the time in Forrest's command, and fought in some of the greatest battles of the historic contest, among them being Shiloh, Corinth, Brice's Cross Roads and Harrisburg. Entering the army in his nineteenth year, he was but little past his majority when he was mustered out and returned to Paducah. Soon after the war he engaged in the hotel business as the proprietor of what was known as the European House. This he conducted until 1876, when he became the proprietor of the Richmond, which was at that time the leading hotel of the city. He was one of the organizers of the Palmer House company, and when the house was opened in 1892 it was with him as the manager. The house is a fine four-story structure, modern in its construction, contains one hundred and sixteen rooms and cost about one hundred and thirty-five thousand dollars. In its furnishings and appointments it is one of the finest hostelries in the Lower Ohio Valley. The same company which erected this hotel also built the Kentucky Theater, one of the best equipped houses of entertainment between Cincinnati and the mouth of the Ohio. Mr. Reed has been successful in the hotel business mainly because he possesses all the essential qualifications of the ideal Boniface. Always attentive to details, the little things that contribute to the comfort of his guests are not overlooked; upon arrival at his house the guest is greeted with a smile and a kind word; during his stay he is made to feel at home, and upon his departure he receives the invitation to call again—not in that perfunctory way so common to many hotel men, but with a sincerity that shows his patronage is appreciated by the house. Mr. Reed may also be mentioned as one of the public spirited men of Paducah. He takes an interest in every movement for the upbuilding of the city, or in the proper administration of municipal affairs. For many years he has been one of the leading Democrats of the city. From 1881 to 1889 he served as mayor, his administration being noted for its progressive, and at the same time conservative policy, and for the high order of executive ability he displayed in looking after the city's interests. At the present time he is the president of the board of aldermen. Through all the years since the war he has cherished the memory of his military service, though the cause for which he fought was lost. He is a member of the United Confederate Veterans, and is a member of the staff of Gen. Bennett H. Young, commander of the Kentucky division. Time has dealt kindly with him and he is one of the best preserved of the veterans of the Civil war. Colonel Reed, as he is popularly known, is also a member of the Independent Order of Odd Fellows and is a Knight Templar Mason. On Feb. 9, 1868, he was united in marriage to Miss Jessie B. Wood. She died in 1890, leaving one daughter, Emma L.

HON. WILLIAM BAKER GILBERT, one of the oldest and most eminent attorneys of Cairo, Ill., is a descendant of an English family, some of whose members were distinguished characters in English history. The first of the name to come to America came from Norfolk and settled in Connecticut at an early date. Judge Miles A. Gilbert, the father of William B. Gilbert, was born at Hartford, Conn., Jan. 1, 1810, his father being Merit Gilbert, one of the many descendants of the first immigrants in Colonial days. Miles A. Gilbert came west in 1832 and settled at Kaskaskia, Ill. Subsequently he was one of the original projectors and founders of the city of Cairo. In 1846 he removed to Missouri and laid out the town of St. Mary's, in Sainte Genevieve county. There he held the position of presiding judge of the county court for many years. He died at his home, "Oakwood," St. Mary's, Jan. 21, 1901, in the ninety-second year of his age. He married Ann Eliza, the eldest daughter of Hon. David J. Baker, ex-U. S. senator and a prominent lawyer of Kaskaskia. Her brother, David J. Baker, was for a number of years chief justice of the Illinois supreme court. William Baker Gilbert, the subject of this sketch, is the eldest son of this marriage, and was born at Kaskaskia, Sept. 24, 1837. He was educated at Shurtleff college, Upper Alton, and after leaving school studied law with his grandfather Baker at Alton, and with Krum & Harding of St. Louis. In 1859, a little while after he attained his majority, he was admitted to practice in the Missouri courts. In September of that year, he entered the senior class of the Harvard law school, and graduated with the class of 1860, receiving the degree of Bachelor of Laws. The following year St. Paul's college, of Missouri, conferred on him the degree of Master of Arts. Shortly after graduating from Harvard he commenced practice at Ste. Genevieve, Mo., as the partner of Hon. John Scott. In the spring of 1862 he removed to Alton, where he formed a partnership with his uncle, Judge Henry S. Baker, and practiced there until 1865, when he removed to Cairo as the junior member of the firm of Haynie, Marshall & Gilbert, the two senior members being Gen. Isham N. Haynie and Judge B. F. Marshall. This association lasted but a short time, when, Judge Haynie having died and Judge Marshall, on account of bad health, retiring, Mr. Gilbert found himself possessed of a large corporation clientage, as well as a large admiralty and general practice. He was admitted to practice in the Federal district courts in 1866, and to the supreme court of the United States in 1873. In that high tribunal he has frequently conducted important cases, and he has been often quoted as an authority on admiralty law. June 1, 1867, he formed a partnership with Judge William H. Green, under the firm name of Green & Gilbert. Subsequently his younger brother, Miles Frederick Gilbert, and Reed Green, son of Judge Green, were taken into the firm and were members thereof until Jan. 1, 1902, when they both withdrew, leaving the two seniors the sole members of the firm as originally established. The firm of Green & Gilbert existed for over thirty-five years, and until finally dissolved, by the death of Judge Green on June 6, 1902. It was probably the oldest law firm in the state. Few law firms in the state have played a more important part in litigation, and the names of Green & Gilbert appear frequently in the reports of the Illinois supreme court. Upon the death of Judge Green Mr. Gilbert formed a partnership with his eldest son, Miles S. Gilbert, under the style of Gilbert & Gilbert, which succeeded to a large part of the business of the old firm. The firm of Gilbert & Gilbert has a large corporation practice, and enjoys the distinction of being one of the leading law firms of Southern Illinois. Among their clients can be named the Illinois Central railroad, the City National bank, the Enterprise Savings bank, the Cairo Water Company, trustees of the Cairo Trust property, trustees of the W. P. Halliday estate, and various other prominent corporations and firms of Cairo. For almost half a century Mr. Gilbert has been engaged in the practice of his profession, and he is still a prominent figure in the litigation of Southern Illinois. There has been no admiralty suit of importance in that section of the country that he has not been retained therein by either libellant or defendant, during the past thirty years. From 1877 to 1894 he held by successive annual appointments the position of corporation counsel for the city of Cairo, and during the same period of seventeen years he was retained as special counsel for Alexander county. For nearly forty years he has been attorney for the Illinois Central railroad.

His entire legal career has been marked by dignified bearing in the courts, courteous demeanor toward his brother practitioners, great care in the preparation of his cases, and intense earnestness in behalf of his clients. A distinguished member of the Southern Illinois bar once said of him: "William B. Gilbert has been connected with much of the important litigation, especially in corporation law, for a quarter of a century. He has won for himself very favorable criticism for the careful and systematic methods which he has followed. He has strong powers of concentration and application, and his retentive mind is often spoken of by his professional colleagues. As an orator he stands high, especially in the discussion of legal matters before the court, where his comprehensive knowledge of the law is manifest, and his application of legal principles demonstrates the wide range of his professional acquirements. The utmost care and precision characterize his preparation of a case, and have made him one of the most successful attorneys of Cairo." This compliment from a fellow lawyer, and one who is competent to judge, tells the story of Mr. Gilbert's professional life and conduct as well as volumes could express. In political matters he is conservative. While affiliating with the Democratic party he has never become an active politician, and has steadfastly refused to be a candidate for public office. In his religious views he is an Episcopalian, and for over thirty-five years has been vestryman and one of the wardens of the Church of the Redeemer, of Cairo. Mr. Gilbert was married on Oct. 18, 1866, to Kate, eldest daughter of Amasa S. Barry, of Alton. To this marriage there have been born three sons, Miles Safford, William Candee, and Barry, and a daughter who died in infancy. His beautiful home at Cairo is called "Greenway," after the ancient seat of the Gilberts in England.

Miles Safford Gilbert, the eldest son, was born in Cairo, Sept. 2, 1868. He was educated in the public schools of his native city; graduated from Racine college in 1889; read law in his father's office; entered the Harvard law school in 1890, and graduated with high marks and a degree of Bachelor of Laws in 1893. The same year he received his license from the Illinois supreme court, and began practice in Chicago, first with the firm of McCurdy & Job, and in 1896 with his brother, William C. Later he went to Cairo, where, upon the dissolution of the firm of Green & Gilbert by death of Judge Green, he became the associate of his father, as already stated. He is a Republican in politics and a member of the Episcopal church, being superintendent of the Sunday school. On Oct. 4, 1899, he was married to Miss Helen E. Judson, of Evanston, Ill., and they have two children: Judson, born Feb. 22, 1901, and Helen, born Nov. 11, 1902.

William Candee Gilbert, second son of William B. Gilbert, was born at Cairo, Jan. 7, 1870. In the matter of education he attended the same schools as his elder brother, and often in the same classes. He graduated at the same time from Racine college, winning the gold medal which distinguished him as the "Head of the college." He also read law two years in the office of his father until he entered the class of 1893, in its second year, in the Harvard law school, and graduated with his brother in 1893, receiving the degree of Bachelor of Laws. Soon afterward he and his brother formed the law firm of Gilbert Bros., in Chicago, which firm continued until his brother removed to Cairo. William C. is still in practice in Chicago. He has among his clients, and is general attorney for, the Paepcke-Leicht Lumber Company, Chicago Mill and Lumber Company and other large corporations. He is an Episcopalian, a member of the Harvard club, of Chicago, and the Country club, of Evanston, where he resides. In politics he is a Republican and takes an active interest in civic affairs. He is well known in Masonic circles, and has filled important offices in that order. On Oct. 8, 1902, he led to the altar Miss Ethel T. Ogden, of Fort Atkinson, Wis.

Barry, the youngest son of William B. Gilbert, was born at Cairo, May 16, 1876. He graduated from the literary or classical and legal departments of the Northwestern university, of Evanston, from the former in 1899 and the latter in 1901 with degree of LL.B., and at the head of his class. While in college he was the recipient of several valuable oratorical prizes. In the law department his two theses—*"Law of Independent Contractors in Illinois"* and *"The Right of Asylum in the Legations of the United States in Central and South America"*—were deemed by the dean of the school to be of such merit as to deserve publication — the former in the *Chicago Legal News* and the latter in the *Harvard Law Review.* He was admitted to the bar in June, 1901; married to Miss Mary R. Peterson of McGregor, Ia., Oct. 15, 1901; began practice at Cedar Rapids, Ia., June, 1901, with the law firm of Griman & Moffit, where his knowledge of the law, natural talent, indefatigable energy, close application and pleasing address soon brought him into such prominence that in 1903 he was offered and accepted the office of professor of law, one of the important professorships, in the college of law in the Iowa State university, which office he still holds, discharging the duties thereof, as teacher and one of the faculty of the law college, with credit to himself and satisfaction to the university. He is a Republican in politics and a member of the Episcopal church. It has been well said of him, "He belongs to a race of lawyers and is a chip of the old block." He is also an enthusiastic "Beta" and one of the alumni of that fraternity.

EDWARD A. BUDER, president of the Alexander County National bank, Cairo, Ill., was born in the village of Zeidler, Austria, Nov. 4, 1839, and is the son of Florian and Rosalia (Pitschman) Buder. His father and mother had a family of five sons, of whom Edward is the second. Their names were Anton, Edward A., William, Gustave and Reinhold. In 1853 the father, having met with reverses, came with his three elder sons to the United States with the object of preparing a home and then sending for the wife and the two younger children. They first settled at Hartford, Conn., where Edward A. found employment in a large silverware establishment owned by the Rogers Bros., which is still a well known house. The father and eldest son Anton later went to Milwaukee, whither the mother and two younger children joined them late in the fifties. Soon afterward the family removed to St. Louis, Mo., whither Edward and William had gone directly from Hartford in 1858. This united the family in St. Louis. There the father died in 1863 and the mother in 1883. Of the five sons Anton, Edward and Reinhold are still living. In St. Louis Edward A. found employment in the jewelry establishment of E. Jaccard, founder of the immense jewelry house of Mermod & Jaccard, the largest and finest in the West. He remained with him four years. Upon the outbreak of the Civil war he enlisted in the Union army in the Third Missouri infantry for three months, but served six months. In the fall of 1861 he came to Cairo, where he has ever since conducted a jewelry establishment. He is now the pioneer jeweler of Cairo and has one of the finest and best equipped jewelry stores in Southern Illinois. Mr. Buder has been very successful in his business and is now the head and front of some of Cairo's most important financial institutions. He is president of the Alexander County National bank, the Alexander County Savings bank, and the Citizens' Building and Loan association. He is prominent both as an Odd Fellow and an Elk. He has been married twice. His first wife was Susanna Williams of Cairo, who died leaving two daughters, Rosalie and Mary. He afterward married his present wife, Wilhemina Kaufman of Cairo. There are four children by this marriage; Edward A., Jr., who married Nellie Smith and is now employed in his father's jewelry store; Otto, who is married and lives in St. Louis; Minnie and Flossie, both of whom are still at home.

CAPT. JONATHAN CLAY WILLIS, a coal dealer and one of the oldest residents of Metropolis, Ill., is a descendant of one of the earliest English settlers in America. The family really originated in Wales, but about the middle of the seventeenth century seven brothers of the name came from England and settled in different parts of the United States. Capt. Richard Willis, a descendant of one of these brothers, was a native of North Carolina. He served with distinction in the Revolutionary war, where he won his title of captain, and after the establishment of the United States government was a planter in his native state until his death. One of his sons, whose name was also Richard, was born in North Carolina in 1767. In early manhood he went to Tennessee, where he married Miss Catharine Brigman, and continued to live in Sumner county, Tenn., until 1833, when he removed to Gallatin county, Ill., and died there in 1840, at the age of seventy-two years. He was a teacher and shoemaker by occupation; in politics he was a Jackson Democrat, being a personal friend of "Old Hickory"; and fought under that noted general at the battle of New Orleans. His wife died in 1837. They had twelve children, Capt. Jonathan C. being the eleventh of the family and the only one now living. He was born in Sumner county, Tenn., June 27, 1826, and was seven years old when his parents came to Gallatin county. At the age of sixteen years he removed to Elizabethtown, Ill., and in 1843 located at Golconda, in Pope county. After working a farm for a few years, he took up flat-boating on the Ohio and Mississippi rivers, which occupation he followed for six years. It was while engaged in this business that he was first called Captain Willis. After filling several minor offices, he was, in 1852, elected sheriff of Pope county and re-elected in 1856. In February,

1859, he married Miss Fannie E. Ward, a native of Ireland, who came to America and settled at Cairo, Ill., in 1851. Her father died while crossing the ocean and was buried at sea. Her mother died in Cairo. They had six children, two of whom are living. After the death of her mother the wife of Captain Willis removed to Union county, Ky., where they were married in 1859. Five children have blessed the marriage: Richard W., a river man; Thomas E., cashier of the First National bank of Metropolis; John G., a stock farmer; Jay Clay, a partner of his father in the coal business and steamboat agent, and Fannie E., wife of Fred P. Davenport, D.D., of Memphis, Tenn., a distinguished minister of the Episcopal church. In 1859 Captain Willis came to Metropolis, where he has since resided. Here he engaged in the wharfboat and commission business until 1890. Since 1873 he has also been engaged in flour milling, but for the last two years has given his attention principally to the coal business. During the Civil war he served for a short time as quartermaster of the Forty-eighth Illinois regiment, but by being thrown from a horse was disabled for service. In 1868 he was elected to the Illinois legislature and served one session. In 1869 he was appointed collector of internal revenue for the thirteenth district of Illinois, which position he held for thirteen years. During this time he served one term as mayor of Metropolis. In 1886 he was elected county judge and served one term. He also served one term as railroad and warehouse commissioner and two terms as a member of the county board. Although admitted to the bar in 1856 he has never followed the practice of law. In Masonry he has taken an active part, being both a Royal Arch Mason and a Knight Templar. Captain Willis is not identified with any church, but is quite liberal in his religious views. His father was a Baptist and his mother a Presbyterian.

JUDGE WILLIAM S. DEWEY, county judge of Alexander county, Ill., and eldest son of Capt. E. S. Dewey, was born in Irvington, Ill., on Aug. 25, 1869. He was but three years old when his father removed to Cairo. After completing his public school education in the Cairo city schools he entered the Sioux Falls university, at Sioux Falls, S. D., from which he graduated in the classical course with high rank in June, 1889. Returning to Cairo he began the study of law in the office of the Hon. Walter Warder, and was admitted to the bar June 20, 1892. He soon won a good practice. However, in 1894 he was elected to the office of county judge, as a Republican. He received a majority of over six hundred, something unusual in his county. In 1898 he was re-elected to the office at a time when all of the Republican candidates on the county ticket except himself and the clerk were defeated. In 1902 he was elected to the office for the third time without opposition, receiving every vote that was cast for county judge. When first elected judge he was but twenty-five years old, which gives him the record of being one of the youngest county judges in the United States. At the expiration of his present term he will have served twelve years, each term being four years. He is a member of the Knights of Pythias and Masonic fraternities, in both of which he takes a very active part. At present he is secretary of the Republican county central committee and a member of the Republican committee of the Fiftieth Illinois senatorial district. On June 14, 1904, he married Miss Katherine Klier of Cairo.

MILES FREDERICK GILBERT, a prominent lawyer of Cairo, Ill., was born in Alton, Madison county, of that state, Sept. 11, 1849. The genealogy of the family can be traced back to some of the most distinguished characters in English history, whose names have been conspicuous in literature, science and art. The family was first represented in America by five brothers, who emigrated from Norfolk county, England, at an early date, and settled, one in Virginia, one in Massachusetts and three in Connecticut, near the present cities of Hartford and New Haven. It is to this branch of the family that the father of the subject of this sketch, Judge Miles A. Gilbert, born in Hartford, belongs. He was long a resident of Kaskaskia, the first capital of Illinois, and also one of the pioneers of Cairo, entering from the government land on which that city now stands. Subsequently he removed to Ste. Genevieve county, Mo., where for sixteen years he served as judge of the county court. He was a man of superior ability and on the bench discharged his duties with marked impartiality. He died at his home in St. Mary's, Mo., June 21, 1901, aged ninety-one years. His wife, Mrs. Ann E. Gilbert, died July 14, 1893. Miles Frederick Gilbert, the subject of this sketch, was educated in the public schools of Alton, Ill. Afterward he entered Washington university, St. Louis, Mo., but on account of ill health was forced to leave that institution before graduation. Subsequently he was enrolled among the students of the Pennsylvania military college at Chester. On the completion of his literary education in that institution he entered the law department of Harvard university, from which he graduated with the degree of LL.B., June 29, 1869. Prior to entering Harvard he had read law in the office of Haynie, Marshall & Gilbert, well-known attorneys of Cairo, and had been admitted to the bar in 1868. Jan. 1, 1870, he began the practice of his chosen profession as a member of the firm of Green & Gilbert. In 1875 he was licensed to practice law in the various federal courts, and in 1892 before the supreme court of the United States. He is now district attorney for the St. Louis & Southwestern railway. In addition to the practice of law Mr. Gilbert is now administering successfully the interests of the Loan and Improvement association, being president of that corporation. He is a prominent and influential member of the Episcopal church, in which he is serving as warden and vestryman. For many years he has annually represented his parish in the diocesan synod and for nineteen years the diocese at the general convention of the American church, serving on the committee on constitutional amendments. For ten years he has been chancellor of the diocese, the bishop's legal adviser, and was in October, 1904, elected one of the judges of the court of review of the Fifth judicial department of the American church, including five states. While a strong advocate of the principles of the Democratic party, he has never been an aspirant for official honors. For twelve years he served as a member of the board of education of the Cairo public schools, before elevation to its presidency, during which time he did much to elevate their standard and to increase their efficiency. Fully appreciating the great work that Mr. Gilbert has done for the schools, the people have re-elected him president of the board for nine successive terms, being twenty-one years in the cause of education. On Oct. 18, 1871, Mr. Gilbert married Miss Addie Louise Barry, of Alton, youngest daughter of the late Amasa S. Barry, formerly of Alton and later of Chicago. They have two living children: Mrs. Nellie Gilbert-Halliday and Edward Leigh Gilbert, the latter now a well-known business man of Cairo. Strong in his individuality, Mr. Gilbert never lacks the courage of his convictions. There are, however, as dominating elements in this individuality, a lively human sympathy and an abiding charity, which, taken in connection with the sterling integrity and honor of his character, have naturally gained for him the respect and confidence of his fellow-men.

CAPT. EDMUND SABIN DEWEY, an old and prominent citizen of Cairo, Ill., and an ex-clerk of the circuit court of Alexander county, was born in Berkshire county, Mass., Nov. 10, 1836. He is the son of Oliver Dewey, who was born July 24, 1805, in Massachusetts, and died in Bond county, Ill., March 14, 1901. He was a farmer by occupation. Oliver Dewey was the son of Edmund Dewey, who died Nov. 9, 1842, aged seventy-four years. He too was a farmer. The latter was the son of Paul Dewey, who was born in 1739 and died in 1827. Paul Dewey was the son of Israel Dewey, who was born March 3, 1712, and died May 23, 1773. Israel Dewey was the son of Thomas Dewey who was born June 29, 1662, and died March 15, 1758. He in turn was the son of Jedediah Dewey who died Jan. 26, 1727. Jedediah Dewey was the son of Thomas Dewey, who emigrated from Sandwich, county of Kent, England, to Plymouth, Mass., in 1632. Thomas was of sturdy English Puritan stock. In 1638 he removed to Windsor, Conn., where he died April 27, 1648. His son, Jedediah, returned to Massachusetts, where for the most part the succeeding members of the family resided. Oliver Dewey, the father of Edmund S., who belonged to the seventh generation removed from Thomas Dewey, the emigrant, removed from Massachusetts to Aurora, Ill., in 1853. Later he removed to DeKalb county, Ill. On April 14, 1829, Oliver Dewey married Eliza Sabin, who died in DeKalb county, Ill., Dec. 10, 1893. She was born in Massachusetts June 17, 1807, being eighty-six years of age at her death. She and her husband lived together as man and wife for more than sixty-four years. Their marriage was blessed with six children whose names were as follows: Robert King, born Aug. 25, 1830, a resident of Greenville, Bond county, Ill.; Edmund Sabin, whose name heads this memoir; Hannah Josephine, born April 8, 1838, now Mrs. Charles H. Sabin, of Lee, Berkshire county, Mass.; Oliver Burdette, born July 12, 1840, who served as a private in an Illinois cavalry regiment in the Civil war and who died May 24, 1895; Charles Ansel, born Sept. 17, 1842, now living in DeKalb county, Ill.; Mira Eliza, now Mrs. Andrew Beveridge of South Dakota, who was born April 6, 1849. Eliza Sabin, the mother of this subject, was the daughter of Origen Sabin, who was born Dec. 20,

1771, and died Jan. 18, 1857. Origen was the son of Ziba Sabin, who was born in August, 1749, and died in 1825. Ziba was the son of Israel Sabin who died at Norwich, Conn., in 1782. Admiral George Dewey of the United States Navy and the hero of Manila is a member of the same family, having descended from Josiah Dewey, the second son of Thomas Dewey, while Edmund S. Dewey is a descendant of Jedediah Dewey, the fourth son of the same Thomas Dewey. In England the Dewey family was of good rank and standing, possessing a coat of arms. Edmund S. Dewey, the subject of this sketch, came to Illinois from Massachusetts in 1853. He was then a lad of seventeen years. He received a liberal education and in early manhood taught school for several years both before and after the Civil war. In 1860 he left home and after teaching a term in St. Clair county, Ill., went to Greenville, Ill., where he clerked in a store until July, 1862. This position he resigned to enlist in the Union army. In 1862 he enlisted as a private in company F, One Hundred and Thirtieth Illinois infantry. Almost immediately, however, he was made sergeant-major of his regiment and very soon thereafter was promoted to the position of adjutant with the rank of first lieutenant. Toward the close of the war, after his regiment had suffered disaster on the Red River campaign under General Banks, the remnant was consolidated with the Seventy-seventh Illinois infantry, when he was made captain of Company C of this regiment. He served with this rank until after the surrender at Appomattox. However, before he was finally mustered out, the old One Hundred and Thirtieth Illinois was reorganized, and he resumed his old position as its adjutant. He was mustered out of service at Springfield, Ill., August, 1865. Captain Dewey received his first wound at Vicksburg, May 19, 1863. He was wounded the second time at Jackson, Miss., shortly after the surrender of Vicksburg. After the war he returned to Greenville, Ill., where for three years he served as deputy circuit clerk of the county. He was then four years instructor in mathematics in the Illinois Agricultural college at Irvington. In 1872 he came to Cairo where he has since resided. Since coming here he has served as circuit clerk of Alexander county for fourteen years, retiring in 1900. Captain Dewey is a member of the Grand Army of the Republic, of the Royal Arch Masons and of the Knights Templars. On June 14, 1868, Capt. Dewey married Maria Jane French, daughter of David Patten and Mehitable (Foster) French, of Greenville, Ill. She was born at Goffstown, N. H., July 12, 1847, and died at Cairo, Ill., Jan. 29, 1889. She came to Illinois with her parents in 1853, her father becoming pastor of the Baptist church at Jerseyville, Ill. Here the family resided until 1862, when they removed to Greenville, Ill. From 1864 to 1866 her father was president of Almira college, a female seminary located at Greenville. Here the wife of Captain Dewey completed her education, giving especial attention to music, for which she had marked ability. After her marriage she moved to Irvington, Ill., where her husband was a teacher and her father president of the Illinois Agricultural college. She was a lineal descendant of William French, who came to this country from the town of Billericay, Essex county, England, in 1635 and settled in Massachusetts. She belonged to the eighth generation of French settlers, all of her ancestors in this country being residents of Massachusetts and New Hampshire. She was a member of the Baptist church, the Women's Relief Corps, the Women's Club and the Library Association. Her death occurred on Jan. 29, 1889, at Cairo. To Captain Dewey and wife were born seven children, viz.: William Sabin, Aug. 25, 1869; George French, Nov. 19, 1870; Charles Beveridge, Nov. 27, 1872; Jennie Elizabeth, Dec. 22, 1874; John Myron, Nov. 2, 1877; Mira Josephine, Nov. 2, 1877; Robert Edmund, Nov. 25, 1879. Edmund S. Dewey was married the second time on Nov. 25, 1890, at Lebanon, Ill., to Mary Agnes Lytle, daughter of Francis W. and Florida Martin (Routte) Lytle. Captain Dewey is an elder in the Presbyterian church of Cairo and in political matters is a Republican.

ERNEST H. RIGGLE, of Cairo, Ill., county jailer of Alexander county, was born on a farm in that county, about sixteen miles north of the city, March 22, 1876. He is a son of Jacob and Jennie (Atherton) Riggle, the former a native of Franklin county, Pa., and the latter of Alexander county, Ill. The father was born Dec. 22, 1833, and died July 26, 1895. For many years prior to his death he was a farmer in Alexander county. The mother was born Oct. 12, 1843, and is still living on the old Riggle homestead. They had a family of ten children, seven of whom, five sons and two daughters, are still living. Ernest H. Riggle grew to manhood on the farm where he was born. He received his education in the country schools. After the death of his father he aided in the management of the farm, until appointed to his present position by Sheriff James S. Roche in December, 1902. On Jan. 4, 1900, he was married to a first cousin, Ettie May Riggle, a daughter of Joseph and Susannah (Garman) Riggle and a native of Henry county, Ind., where she was born Feb. 7, 1868. To this marriage there have been born three children, viz.: Ethel Marguerite, born Sept. 28, 1900; Homer Garman and Herbert Atherton, twins, born April 25, 1903. Politically Mr. Riggle is a Republican. He is a modest, unassuming gentleman, who goes about his business with a determination to succeed, and possesses all the essential qualifications of the successful turnkey.

CAPT. JOHN HODGES, of Cairo, Ill., familiarly known to his friends as Capt. "Jack" Hodges, was born in that county, Aug. 19, 1836. He is the son of John Hodges, a native of Tennessee, who died in 1862. The paternal grandfather, Edmond Hodges, a Tennesseean, removed to Alexander county, Ill., in an early day and located at Unity. The mother, now deceased, of Captain Hodges was Margaret Hunsaker before her marriage. Eleven children were born to this union, of whom the captain is the oldest, seven yet living. In his youth and early manhood he was employed in his father's store. In 1860 he was elected to the office of sheriff of Alexander county; was repeatedly re-elected to this office and in all held it for more than twenty years. He enjoys the distinction of having served as sheriff longer than any other one who ever held that office in this county. He was first elected county treasurer in 1859, but resigned this office to run for sheriff. After serving one term in this office he was then elected city marshal, a much more lucrative office in those days, and held it for two terms. For ten years he was engaged in mercantile pursuits. In 1876, at the request of the sheriff, Captain Hodges became his deputy, serving two years. In 1878 he was again elected sheriff and held the office for eight consecutive years. In 1890 he was again elected sheriff and served four years. In 1898 he was once more elected to the office, serving four more years. He might in all probability have held the office continuously but for the fact that the law now makes the sheriff ineligible to succeed himself.

Captain Hodges is an Elk and a Democrat. July 25, 1858 he married Josephine I. Wicker, who died Nov. 7, 1902, leaving five children —three sons and two daughters. June 1, 1903, he married Miss Capitola Nelson, of Caseyville, Ky., and to this union one son, Herbert Nelson Hodges, aged about six months, has been born.

CHARLES FEUCHTER, JR., vice-president of the Alexander County National bank of Cairo, Ill., and senior member of the firm of Feuchter Bros., wholesale liquor dealers, was born in Cairo, Nov. 2, 1863. He is the elder son of Charles Feuchter, Sr., a prominent and well known citizen of Cairo; was reared and educated in Cairo, supplementing his public school training by a course in the Eastman Business college of Poughkeepsie, N. Y., from which institution he graduated in 1881. Returning to Cairo he was variously employed for a short time when he entered the employ of the Illinois Central Railroad Company in its local freight office. He held a position with this road for ten years, passing through many promotions. He was finally made cashier, which position he resigned in 1890 to accept the position of cashier and chief clerk in the local freight office of the Iron Mountain railroad. Holding this position until Feb. 1, 1891, he resigned to embark in business for himself. He formed a partnership with his younger brother, William Feuchter, and under the firm name of Feuchter Bros., purchased the wholesale liquor business formerly conducted and owned by the late Judge F. Bross. Feuchter Bros. have prospered, making their business one of the leading wholesale industries of Cairo. A few years ago the firm purchased the extensive two-story and basement brick business block, corner Sixth and Ohio streets, all of which is occupied by their business. Mr. Chas. Feuchter, Jr., is president of the Cuban Cigar company; is a director of the St. Louis & Cairo Railroad Company; the Citizens' Building and Loan association; a member of the Alexander club; of Safford Lodge 67 Independent Order of Odd Fellows, of which he is a past noble grand; is a past exalted ruler of Cairo Lodge No. 651 Benevolent and Protective Order of Elks, and is a member of the Knights of the Mystic Krew of Comus, a local order of Cairo. He is also a member of the commercial club of Cairo. William Feuchter, junior member of the firm of Feuchter Bros., was born at Cairo, Sept. 11, 1866. He is the younger son of Charles Feuchter, Sr., of that city. William Feuchter received his education in the Cairo schools. For several years in early life he was employed by the Andrew Lohr Bottling Works of Cairo. In 1888 he became the manager of the wholesale whisky house of Judge F. Bross. In 1891 he formed a partnership with his brother Charles, purchasing the business of Judge Bross, which business they have largely extended. Mr. William Feuchter is secretary and treasurer of the Cuban Cigar Company. He is a member of the Cairo Lodge 651 Benevolent and Protective Order of Elks, the Knights of the Mystic Krew of Comus, and is a charter member of the Alexander club. The parents of the Messrs. Feuchter are still residing in Cairo and the two sons, both single, make their home with them.

JOHN M. LANSDEN, a member of the legal profession, of Cairo, Ill., was born in Sangamon county in that state, Feb. 12, 1836. His parents, Rev. A. W. and Mary M. Lansden. came to that county in 1835, from Wilson county, Tenn. He worked on the farm, attended the village and district schools during the fall and winter, prepared for college at Virginia, Cass county, Ill., and on Sept. 15, 1858, entered the freshman class of Cumberland university at Lebanon, Wilson county, Tenn. Being somewhat in advance of his class in most of their studies, he was able to prepare and recite the lessons in both the freshman and sophomore classes, and at the beginning of his second year was admitted to the junior class. In the junior and senior classes, of about forty members, he stood third in mathematics and second in all other branches. Owing to the disturbed condition of the country following the election of Mr. Lincoln to the presidency and the probable early suspension of college work, he left Lebanon, in January, 1861, and went to Jacksonville, Ill., where he entered the senior class of Illinois college, and there graduated June 20, of the same year. His studies in the institutions mentioned were those usually prescribed for the classical course in most colleges. After leaving college, he engaged in teaching in Menard and Sangamon counties, and subsequently took the superintendency of the public schools at Centralia. In 1864, he entered the Albany law school, of Albany university, New York, from which he graduated May 25, 1865. While there he was chosen president of the class which embraced all of the one hundred and twenty members of the law school. Judge Thomas A. Moran, of Chicago; Judge Irving G. Vann, of the court of appeals of New York; Judge Samuel D. Hastings, of Wisconsin, and many others who have become prominent in the profession, were members of his class. After being admitted to the bar in both New York and Illinois, in the year of his graduation, he went to Cairo in 1866, where he began the practice he has continued uninterruptedly to the present time. He was a member first of the firm of Olney, McKeaig & Lansden, and afterward of the firm of Omelveny & Lansden, the senior partner of which was the Hon. Harvey K. S. Omelveny, who subsequently removed to Los Angeles. In 1874, he formed a partnership with the Hon. David T. Linegar, which continued nearly to the time of the latter's death in 1885. The Hon. John H. Mulkey, prior to his election to the supreme bench, was associated with them for a time under the firm name of Mulkey, Linegar & Lansden. In 1887 Judge Lansden and Angus Leek formed the present firm of Lansden and Leek. Mr. Lansden's practice has been chiefly of a general nature, in the State and Federal courts in Illinois, and for some years past in Missouri and Kentucky. He and the firm of Lansden & Leek, for twenty years, have been district counsel for the Mobile & Ohio Railroad Company, for the States of Illinois, Missouri and Kentucky. For many years he has been the attorney and counselor of the Alexander County National bank and the Alexander County Savings bank, of Cairo. He was admitted to practice in the United States supreme court some years ago; has confined himself very closely to his profession; has taken little part in politics; has held no offices except those of city attorney, mayor and treasurer of schools, and has acted for the most part with the Democratic party. He was married Sept. 25, 1867, to Effie Wyeth Smith, a daughter of the late David A. Smith, of Jacksonville. They have six children: David Smith, Mary Gallaher, Effie Allan, Emma Louise, John McMurray and Margaret Lansden, all of them, except John, graduates of the Cairo high school. David is also a graduate of Princeton, class of 1891; Mary of the Southern Illinois normal, class of 1890, and John of Rose Polytechnic institute, Terre Haute, Ind., class of 1898. David has been with his father in the practice of law since 1894. The family's church relations have always been with the

Presbyterian church, as have been the ancestors of Mr. and Mrs. Lansden for a very long time. He has belonged to no secret society except the college Greek letter society of Alpha Delta Phi, Cumberland Chapter, 1861.

CAPT. BELFIELD BERKSHIRE BRADLEY, of Cairo, Ill., was born at Petersburg, Ky., Sept. 13, 1855. He is the son of Capt. Dillon Bradley, an old Ohio and Mississippi river steamboat captain, who was accidentally drowned in the Ohio river April 22, 1876, by having his skiff capsized by a steamboat. He was born at Madison, Ind., in 1812. The mother of the subject was Mary Ann Toomey, born at Dayton, O., in 1814, dying in Trimble county, Ky., in 1884. Six children were born to this union: Henry Clay, James Dillon, William S., Amanda, Mary E., and Belfield Berkshire, the subject of this sketch. Only two sons are now living— Henry Clay Bradley, an ink manufacturer of Cincinnati, O., and the subject. James Dillon Bradley learned the saddler's trade and for twenty-five years was engaged in that business at Rocheport, Mo., where he died in the early eighties. William S. Bradley enlisted in the Confederate army, serving under Gen. John Morgan, and was killed at Mt. Sterling, Ky., while in active service. Amanda was married to Mr. D. C. Peck and died in Trimble county, Ky., July 7, 1904. Mary E. Bradley never married and died in Trimble county, Ky., in 1898. Captain Bradley spent his boyhood days in his native town. At the age of sixteen he left home and became an office boy in a box factory in Cincinnati, the property of his brother, Henry Clay. Prior to this he had earned his first money by ferrying people across the Ohio river at Petersburg in a skiff. At the age of eighteen years he borrowed $400.00 and with the money bought a small steam passenger boat, thus starting the first passenger packet line between Lawrenceburg and Aurora, Ind. This boat was named the *Water Witch*. Later it was succeeded by another called the *Western Wave*, which he sold just before buying the *Little Queen*, a somewhat larger boat. With this boat he for several years plied the river between Rising Sun and Lawrenceburg, Ind. He then had the *Charles L. Grant* built to order, but soon found her too heavy a boat for the Upper Ohio at all seasons of the year. Making a trip to New Orleans on this boat he disposed of her to good advantage. Returning to Petersburg he purchased a half interest in the steamer *P. D. Dale,* with which as its captain, he plied the Ohio for two years between Madison and Patriot, Ind. His next purchase was the tow-boat *W. B. Cole,* with which for two years he engaged in the coal trade. This boat proving too small, he disposed of it and bought, in Pittsburg, a much larger one, the *Geo. W. Stone.* He had as partners in the *Geo. W. Stone* the Huntington and St. Louis Tow-boat Company, of Cincinnati, the partners' interest being two-thirds. In 1891 he sold his interest to his partners and came to Cairo, where for a year he was the manager of the Huntington and St. Louis Tow-boat Company. In 1892 he bought the *Nellie Speer* together with several barges, using them in the lumber and log trade on the Ohio and Mississippi rivers until Jan. 1, 1900, when he sold out to the Monongahela Coal & Coke Company of Pittsburg, Pa. He then entered the employ of that company and has been its local manager, at a handsome salary, at Cairo ever since. Captain Bradley is an Elk, a Knight of Pythias, a member of the Cairo board of trade and a charter member of the Alexander club. In politics he is a Democrat and in religious matters leans toward the Christian church. On Nov. 16, 1888, he married Miss Isabella Hull McAroy, of Rising Sun, Ind. One son has blessed this union, Master Fred, now fifteen years old.

H. E. HALLIDAY, president of the H. L. Halliday Milling Company and the Halliday Elevator Company, of Cairo, Ill., was born in that city Aug. 8, 1872, being the eldest son of the late Henry L. Halliday, founder of the milling company, who died in 1895, a sketch of whom appears elsewhere in this work. H. E. Halliday, familiarly known to his friends as "Harry," graduated from Racine college of Racine, Wis., and immediately after graduation became connected with the H. L. Halliday Milling Company. Beginning at the bottom of the ladder, as a mere employe, he rolled barrels. Later he became a clerk and held various positions, his object being to familiarize himself with every phase of the business. Upon the death of his father in 1895 he succeeded to the presidency of the concern, which position he still holds. As the nominal head of the family and manager of the H. L. Halliday estate, Mr. Halliday in 1897 built what is known as the Halliday elevator, organized the company and became its president. This property was destroyed by fire in 1898. The following year the present large elevator was begun and completed in 1900. It has a capacity of 500,000 bushels of grain and is capable of handling 100 car loads a day. It is fully equipped with machinery for handling grain from the boats on the Ohio river and for loading river boats for export trade. Mr. Halliday is a member of the board of trustees of Racine college, of the Alexander club, a director of the St. Louis & Cairo Railroad Company and a member and director of the Cairo Board of Trade. On April 8, 1897, he married Miss Nelly Gallagher, of Zanesville, O., and three children have blessed this union: Henry E., Jr., Eleanor and Russel.

HENRY L. HALLIDAY (deceased), one of the most prominent citizens of Cairo, Ill., in his day, a miller of wide and unsullied reputation, was born in Pomeroy, Meigs county, O., March 7, 1842, and died at his home in Cairo, Sept. 2, 1895. His father was a native of Scotland, and his mother of Ohio. In 1856 he settled in Wayne county, Ill., where he remained for several years. Then he engaged with his older brothers in steamboating on the Ohio and Mississippi rivers until 1860, when he came to Cairo. Thrown out of employment by the breaking out of the Civil war, Mr. Halliday went to LaCrosse, Wis., where he clerked in the freight depot of the LaCrosse & Milwaukee railroad. The close of navigation threw him out of work there and he returned to Cairo, where he entered the service of Captain Hatch, chief quartermaster of Gen. U. S. Grant. Mr. Halliday remained in the quartermaster's department until 1862, serving successfully under Captain Hatch, Captain Baxter and Colonel Dunlap. At this time his older brothers organized the firm of Halliday Bros., whom Henry served for some years as bookkeeper and cashier, when he was admitted to the firm. He remained with this firm until Jan. 1, 1895, when he organized the H. L. Halliday Milling Company, of which he became president. In 1898 the George Mayo mill was sold under foreclosure and the Halliday Brothers, to protect their interests in the shape of money advanced Mr. Mayo, were compelled to take charge of the property. From that day until his withdrawal from the firm Mr. Halliday gave his attention to that branch of the business in connection with the grain business of the firm. The H. L. Halliday Milling Company operates a mill of 700-barrel capacity, its products being sold principally in the South and Southwest, where they have an excellent reputation. Mr. Halliday was not only a representative citizen of Cairo, but also of Southern Illinois, where his name was a synonym for honesty and integrity. In banking affairs he was equally prominent, being vice-president of the City National bank of Cairo. He was an honor to the milling industry and belonged to a generation of millers notable for great achievements, both in the making of flour and the development of American trade. He took a deep interest in national milling affairs, being a frequent attendant at the conventions of the Millers' National associations, where he made many friends by his unassuming but no less real worth. His natural bent of mind led him at all times to stand for what was progressive and for the best and most worthy interests in civic affairs. Owing to the geographical position of his mill, his field of operation was somewhat limited. By a thorough understanding of his business environment, by a conscientious attention to his business interests and by an irreproachable rectitude in his dealings, he built up a reputation second to no other man engaged in the milling business. His death was truly a heavy loss to his fellow millers as well as to the world at large. On March 7, 1867, Mr. Halliday married Miss Laura Evans, of Batavia, O. He had four children: Mrs. E. H. Capen, St. Louis, Mo.; Mrs. L.-H. Kelsey, Chicago, Ill.; H. E. and Douglas Halliday, of Cairo.

DOUGLAS HALLIDAY, secretary and treasurer of both the H. L. Halliday Milling Company and the Halliday Elevator Company, Cairo, Ill., is a native of that city. He is the youngest child of the late H. L. Halliday, whose sketch appears elsewhere in this work. His early training was received in the public schools of his home city, after which he entered the preparatory department of St. Paul's school, an Episcopal institution of learning in Concord, N. H., where he studied three years. This preparatory work was done to enable him to enter Yale, but the sudden death of his distinguished father in 1895 changed his plans entirely. Instead of entering Yale, he returned home and went to work for the H. L. Halliday Milling Company and learned the business from its very foundation. After holding various positions he was in 1899 made secretary and treasurer of the company. This important and responsible position he has up to this time filled with superior ability. His success in this position led to his appointment to a like position in the Halliday Elevator Company, one of the largest concerns of its kind in Southern Illinois. In 1902 he married Miss Emma Halliday of New Orleans, one of the most popular young ladies of that Southern metropolis.

SAMUEL HASTINGS, wholesale dealer in feed, Cairo, Ill., was born in Noble county, O., March 31, 1850. He is the son of Hezekiah and Anna (Ball) Hastings, both of whom were born in Ohio. His father for many years followed merchandizing, farming and stockraising with marked success, and is still hale and hearty at the advanced age of eighty years. His mother, daughter of Jonas Ball, died in Illinois in 1885. The paternal grandfather of this sketch was Samuel Hastings, of English birth, who upon coming to the United States located in Ohio. The subject of this sketch is the oldest of nine children. Those living are Noah H., James W., Jonas, Ira, Samuel, Cora and Nannie. Noah and Jonas are farmers in Clay county, Ill.; James is a merchant in New Orleans; Ira is associated with the subject of this sketch in business; Cora is an artist and photographer in Denver, Col.; Nannie is the wife of Rev. O. S. Gard, a Methodist minister of Steamboat Landing, Col. At the age of five years Samuel moved with his parents to Jasper county, Ill., where he was reared on a farm. After graduating from McKendree college, Lebanon, Ill., in 1872, he taught school for three years in Clay county, Ill. For the next five years he devoted his time and energy to stockraising and farming in that county. In January, 1884, he removed to Cairo, where for the next seven years he was associated with the wholesale feed firm of Thistlewood & Co., being the manager of the business until 1890. During this time Mr. Thistlewood, the senior member of the firm, was in Kansas. In 1891 he embarked in the wholesale feed business for himself, since which time he has built up a large and lucrative business in the buying and selling of hay, oats and corn. Because of his success and prominence he is a leading member of the board of trade. In politics he is a Republican. For four of the six years that he served on the board of county commissioners, he was chairman; served as alderman for two years; was for four years a member of the board of trustees of the Southern Illinois hospital for the insane. Being a member of the Methodist church he takes an active part in religious affairs. On Sept. 24, 1876, he married Miss Anise Burney, of Clay county, Ill., and to this union four children have been born: Leila May, Anna Maud, Oris B. and Mary Alice. Leila, a graduate of the Northwestern university of Evanston, Ill., is a successful teacher of music in Cairo; Anna Maud, a graduate of Cumnock's School of Oratory of Evanston, is a very successful teacher of elocution, having taught that subject in the high school; Oris B. is now a member of the junior class of the Northwestern university, and Mary Alice, the youngest, just twelve years old, is a member of the eighth grade of the city schools. With marked success in business and with such an interesting family to gladden his days, Mr. Hastings has just cause to be proud and happy. Honored and respected by all who come in contact with him, whether in a business or social way, his lot is indeed one to be envied.

GEORGE H. PENDLETON, superintendent of the Cairo elevator, Cairo, Ill., is a native of Indianapolis, Ind., having been born in that city Jan. 21, 1871. He is the son of the late R. C. J. Pendleton, of Indianapolis, who throughout his career followed railroad pursuits. Later in life he was made an adjuster of the Phœnix Insurance Company, of Brooklyn, N. Y. Maine was the native state of his father. During the Civil war he served as an ensign in the United States navy. He not only served throughout the war but remained in active service several years after its close. When he severed his connection with the navy he located in Indianapolis, Ind., where he spent the remainder of his life, dying at the age of sixty-eight. A few years before the war he married Miss Hannah Davis, a native of the same state. His wife still survives, being a resident of Indianapolis. George H. Pendleton, the subject of this sketch, was next to the youngest in a family of six children— five sons and one daughter. He was educated in the public schools of Indianapolis and those of Rutland, Vt. While attending the Rutland schools he made his home with an uncle. At the age of sixteen he set out to learn the moulders' trade in the Indianapolis car shops, following this calling about three years. When twenty years old he entered the employ of the firm of William P. Harvey & Co., of Baltimore, and went to work as a shoveler of grain in an elevator belonging to that firm at Kankakee, Ill. This marked the beginning of his elevator life. He has been in the employ of that firm and its successors ever since. William P. Harvey & Co. were succeeded by the firm of Carrington, Hannah & Co., it in turn was succeeded by Carrington, Patten & Co., and finally by Bartlett, Frazier & Carrington, of Chicago, the last named being his present employers. Beginning at the very bottom Mr. Pendleton has worked his way up to a responsible and lucrative position. He has done service in elevators in Kankakee, Chicago and Cairo. For five years he was superintendent of the Danville elevator of Chicago, which had a capacity of about 500,000 bushels. For the past two years he has been superintendent of the Cairo elevator at Cairo, Ill., the property of the Illinois Central Railroad Company, and leased to the firm of Bartlett, Frazier & Carrington. This elevator is the largest in Southern Illinois, having a capacity of 750,000 bushels of grain. It was built in 1881. Mr. Pendleton is an active member of the board of trade of Cairo and of the Benevolent and Protective Order of Elks. On Aug. 12, 1897, he married Miss India, daughter of Samuel M. Orr, of Cairo.

JOSEPH B. REED, proprietor of the Cairo Foundry and Machine shops, Cairo, Ill., was born in Lowell, Mass., March 16, 1831. He is the son of Thaddeus Reed, a native of Massachusetts, who died when Joseph was only six years old. The mother was Catherine Dow, a native of Maine. She died in Boston, Mass., at the age of seventy-six. After the death of Thaddeus Reed she was married to a Mr. Ballard, a newspaper man of Boston. Joseph B. Reed had one brother, Charles Reed, who died in the early fifties while en route to California as a home seeker, and one sister, Miss Phoebe Ann Reed, of Boston. The late Henry S. Reed, of St. Louis, Mo., once president of the National Bank of Commerce of that city, was a half brother of Joseph B. Reed, being the son of his father by a former marriage. Joseph B. was reared in Lexington, Mass., whither his parents removed from Lowell when he was a child. In early life he learned the machinists' trade in Lawrence, Mass. At the age of twenty-five he went to Cumberland, Md., where for two years he was superintendent of a machine shop. In 1856 he went to St. Louis, Mo., where for many years he was proprietor of the Laclede foundry and machine shops. He came to Cairo, Ill., in 1864, upon the solicitation of the United States government for the purpose of establishing a machine shop to do repair work on the government river fleet. Upon coming here he founded the present Cairo foundry and machine shops which have been in continuous operation ever since and are among the oldest and most successful machine shops on the Ohio river. During the war he built a number of tugs for the government when General Fremont was in command of the Western army. These tugs were built at the foot of Carr street on St. Louis levee, and used for tenders for the large boats. He also built at the same time two for the Wiggins Ferry Company of St. Louis to be used in the harbor, two for Joe Gartside of St. Louis and two for Captain Sam Brown of Pittsburg, used in Memphis and New Orleans harbors for jobbing and towing coal. Mr. Reed is sole proprietor of the works. He is also sole proprietor of the Cairo iron and machinery supply store in Cairo, which was established in 1871. Mr. Reed is a Republican, but in no sense a politician. In religion he is a Presbyterian. On Dec. 13, 1856, he married Helen S. Stickney of Beverly, Mass., who yet survives. They have had six children, two of whom died in infancy. The four living ones are Joseph H. Reed, of Chicago, where he is employed in a large heavy hardware house; Helen S. Reed, a teacher in the Iowa State college at Ames; Frank S. Reed, associated with his father in Cairo, and Miss Sarah Alice Reed who is at present teaching elocution and history in the Cairo high school.

JOHN T. RENNIE. As the sole owner of the extensive Vulcan Iron Works, of Cairo, Ill., John T. Rennie enjoys a wide reputation among the proprietors of the great machine works of this country. His father who so successfully conducted the business up to the date of his death has been succeeded by his son. When the subject of this sketch was but a year old his father moved to Cairo, where the son has been reared and educated. He became actively connected with the business established by his father and of which he is now the sole proprietor, having bought the interest of the other heirs. Mr. Rennie makes it his chief business to supply steamboats with all needed machinery on the shortest notice possible. It is needless to state that the son has conducted the business with the same zeal and energy that characterized his father's management. Push and progressiveness count here as well as in any other successfully conducted business. Mr. Rennie is an active member of the Benevolent and Protective Order of Elks, being one of the trustees of that order. He married Miss Clara Chambers and this union has been blessed with one son, Master Roswell Rennie. Few men have done more than Mr. Rennie to build up their home city. Fully up to date and constantly striving to improve his business, it is not to be wondered at that he has proved so successful.

MAJOR EDWIN W. HALLIDAY, a retired merchant of Cairo, Ill., was born in Meigs county, O., May 11, 1836, his parents being Samuel and Eliza (Parker) Halliday. Samuel Halliday was born in Scotland, and his wife was a native of what is now Meigs county, O. He graduated from the University of Edinburgh at the age of nineteen years, and at once came to the United States, crossing the Atlantic in 1818. His mother and six brothers followed him to this country two years later, his father, Alexander Halliday, having previously died in Scotland. Upon reaching the United States he at once proceeded to that part of Gallia county, O., that is now Meigs county. There he held the office of county auditor for twenty-one years, after Meigs county was created, a record which for length of service has never been equaled in that county. In 1855 the family removed to Wayne county, Ill., where the wife and mother died on Feb. 18, 1861, in her fifty-sixth year. The following children were born to Samuel and Eliza (Parker) Halliday: William P., who was born July 21, 1827, and died Sept. 22, 1899; Jane, born Jan. 29, 1830, married Rufus Putnam Robbins and died April 28, 1885; Samuel B., born July 19, 1832, and died Dec. 1, 1868; Edwin W., the subject of this sketch; Eliza, born Aug. 2, 1839, married on Dec. 25, 1862, to Charles T. Hinde of the Spreckles Brothers' Commercial Company of San Diego, Cal., and died April 24, 1899; Henry L., the founder of the H. L. Halliday Milling Company of Cairo, born March 7, 1842, and died Sept. 2, 1895; Thomas Wyatt, the youngest son, born June 10, 1844, and died at Cairo on Sept. 18, 1892, and Mary C., born on April 2, 1847, and is now a resident of Georgia, where she is recognized as a cultured and refined lady of large means and considerable financial ability, as well as a philanthropist of the most liberal type. Three years after the death of his first wife Samuel Halliday returned to Ohio and married Mrs. McKnight, an old acquaintance. To this marriage one daughter was born, Jean by name, who is now the wife of John

W. Ewing, county clerk of Gallia county, O., residing at Gallipolis. Samuel Halliday died in that county on Aug. 25, 1880, in his eighty-first year. Samuel B. Halliday had four children, three sons and one daughter, all living in Cairo. They are: Ada, the wife of John S. Aisthorpe, cashier of the City National bank; William R., Edwin C., and Horace H., all prominent business men of Cairo. Thomas Wyatt was the fifth son of Samuel Halliday. In 1862 he and his brothers, Henry L. and Thomas W., came to Cairo and were associated with their brothers, William P. and Samuel B., in the grain and commission business, started by the two last named, under the firm name of Halliday Brothers, and at that time in a flourishing condition. In 1866 he married Charlotte Josephine Taylor the daughter of Col. S. Staats Taylor. After ten years' connection with the grain business he sold his interest to the other members of the firm, to accept a position with his father-in-law in the management of the Cairo Trust Company. A man of vast capabilities and possessed of rare business instincts, he was well versed in the law. While not a politician he was successful in politics. He represented his district in the legislature of the state as a member of the lower house of the general assembly; served as a member of the state board of equalization; on the board of county commissioners and as mayor of the city of Cairo. In the latter position he endeared himself most to the people, standing shoulder to shoulder with them in the struggle for municipal supremacy. He was first elected in 1883 and served continuously until his death on September 18, 1892. This length of service, and the wonderful progress in the material welfare of the city during his incumbency, attest his ability and popularity. His ability as a financier was so well known and so widely recognized that President Cleveland tendered him the position of comptroller of the currency, which flattering offer Mr. Halliday declined because of his loyalty to Cairo and his love of home. He left his family $25,000 life insurance, a beautiful home and other real estate. Better than all else, he left them the heritage of a good name. Major E. W. Halliday, the subject of this sketch, left home in 1852 at the age of sixteen years. From that time until 1862 he served as clerk or master on Ohio and Mississippi river steamboats. In 1862 he entered the Confederate army at Memphis, Tenn., joining the cavalry regiment of Gen. N. B. Forrest as a private. Forrest was then only a colonel, not having yet become famous. Major Halliday served with Forrest until the latter's promotion to the rank of brigadier-general, when he was detailed for staff duty under Gen.

Lloyd Tilghman, with the rank of major. He served with General Tilghman until the latter was killed at the battle of Champion Hills, when he took his commander's remains to Vicksburg and interred them there. Major Halliday remained in Vicksburg during the siege and on the fall of the city was taken prisoner and paroled. After his release from parole until the close of the war he served in the commissary department of the Confederate States of America, having charge of manufacturing. At the close of the war he rejoined his brothers at Cairo, which place has ever since been his home. He was a member of the firm of Halliday Brothers, composed of William P., Samuel B., Edwin W., Henry L. and Thomas W. Halliday. The firm, by carrying on various business interests, amassed a fortune. The Halliday family is not only the most numerous family in Cairo, but decidedly the most conspicuous in a business sense. It has been identified with the establishment and successful operation of many of the most important business enterprises and institutions of Cairo and vicinity, which have served as the life blood of the business affairs of the city. Maj. E. W. Halliday is the only surviving one of the five brothers. In 1903 he retired from active business, leaving the management of the Halliday institutions and enterprises to younger representatives of the family. He was married on June 28, 1864, at Macon, Ga., to Miss Emma Witherspoon, of Memphis, Tenn., who yet survives together with nine children, three sons and six daughters, five of whom are married. The Major and his wife have seven grandchildren.

CAPT. WILLIAM P. GREANEY, teller in the Alexander County National bank, Cairo, Ill., was born Feb. 19, 1869. He is the son of the late James Greaney of Cairo, who died in 1890. William P. quit school at the early age of eleven years and went to work to fight life's battle. For ten years (1880 to 1890) he was in the employ of the New York Store Mercantile Company, a large wholesale and retail house of Cairo. Beginning as cashboy, on a salary of a few dollars a week, he was regularly promoted to higher positions and finally was made bookkeeper of the concern. He held this position until Jan. 7, 1891, when the establishment was completely destroyed by fire. On Jan. 21, 1891, he became bookkeeper in the Alexander County National bank. In 1902 he was promoted to the still more responsible position of teller in that bank. Being a successful business man he was called upon by his fellow-citizens to serve them for six years in the city council. For two years he filled the responsible position of city treasurer, and for the past four years he has filled the position of deputy city treasurer. In religious affairs he has always been identified with the Catholic church, of which he is a devoted member. He is also an active member of the Benevolent and Protective Order of Elks. On Nov. 14, 1894, he married Miss Loretto Carroll of Cairo. Two interesting and lovable girls have been born to this union: Gertrude Lynette and Margaret Marian, aged nine and six years respectively. Captain Greaney is captain of Company K, Illinois National Guard, which company he organized in 1904.

CHRISTOPHER BECK, president of the Cairo Brewing Company, Cairo, Ill., was born in Germany, June 11, 1860. He is the son of Conrad and Catherine Beck, both of whom are living, now residing in St. Louis, Mo. The subject of this sketch attended school in Germany until he was fourteen years old. After quitting school he was employed for four years in learning the wine, whisky and brewing business in his native country. In 1879 he emigrated to the United States, being the first of his immediate family to come over the ocean. The following year he was followed by his father, mother, two sisters and one brother, who located in St. Louis, Mo., where they still reside. His first work in this country was in a brewery in Wheeling, W. Va., where he worked for nine months. In the spring of 1880 he came on westward to St. Louis, Mo., where he at that time spent one year, a part of the time in the employ of the Lemp Brewing Company and the remainder of the year in a wholesale whisky house. In the spring of 1881 he went to Leadville, Col., at the time of the great silver excitement, where he remained for about eleven years in the wholesale whisky business. In December, 1892, he returned to St. Louis to become one of the organizers of the Columbian Distilling Company, and was made secretary and treasurer of the concern. He held this position until 1897, when he organized the Union Brewing Company of St. Louis, of which, for the next three years and a half, he was president. Selling his interest in this company to Otto F. Stifel in 1902, he spent a brief time in recuperating his health, which had become somewhat impaired, and in March, 1902, he came to Cairo, purchased a site for a new brewery and set out at once to build. On the last day of the following September the Cairo Brewing Company was organized with Mr. Beck as president, a position he yet holds. The buildings, located on the corner of Fourth street and Commercial avenue, were completed and fully equipped with the most modern and up-to-date machinery, and the result is the present fine brewing plant, one of Cairo's best institutions as well as a substantial improvement to the city. The capital stock of the Cairo Brewing Company is $200,000, a majority of the stock being held by Mr. Beck. He is an active member of the Benevolent and Protective Order of Elks and the Knights of Pythias.

JOHN B. GREANEY, secretary and treasurer of the New York Store Mercantile Company, of Cairo, Ill., was born in that city Nov. 21, 1873. He is the second son of the late James Greaney; was educated in the public schools of his native city, graduating from the high school department in 1892, at the age of eighteen years. Immediately after leaving school he went to work as assistant shipping clerk of the New York Store Mercantile Company, with which well known firm he is still connected. He filled various minor positions with such ability and fidelity that his promotion naturally followed, until now he holds one of the most important positions in the gift of his employers. As bookkeeper and traveling salesman he discharged his duties so well that he was made a stockholder in the company. At the election of officers after his promotion he was made secretary and treasurer, which position he still holds. This rapid advancement demonstrates the possibilities open to any young man of intelligence and enterprise. The firm, in which he is now a partner, is one of the largest business concerns of Cairo, its trade being both wholesale and retail. Mr. Greaney is a stockholder in and one of the organizers of the Bank of Moscow, at Moscow, Ky. The fact that he is an active member of the Benevolent and Protective Order of Elks, the Travelers' Protective Association, the Alexander club, and the Knights of the Mystic Krew of Komus shows that he is prominent in social and fraternal circles. On Oct. 21, 1903, he was united in marriage to Miss Kathryn Moran, of Cairo, and one daughter, Kathryn, was born to this union Aug. 13, 1904.

EBERHARD BUCHER, of the Bucher-Woodford Packing Company of Cairo, Ill., was born in Germany, March 4, 1857. His father, Alois Bucher, a farmer, died in Germany in 1883. His mother came to the United States and joined her children in Cairo in 1885, and died there in 1895. The historic city of Ravensburg, in the kingdom of Wurtemberg, Germany, is the birthplace of Mr. Bucher. He learned the butchers' trade in his youth in Switzerland, and came to the United States in 1880, being the first of his family to emigrate to this country. His mother, four brothers and two sisters came later. His brothers living in Cairo are Joseph and Carl Bucher. Silas Bucher, another brother, lives at Mounds, Ill. Stephen, a fourth brother, is a farmer near Freeport, Ill. His sisters are Mrs. Theresa Becker, of Freeport, and Mrs. Mary Love, of Sparta, Ill. Upon coming to this country Eberhard first worked for a year in a sausage factory in Cincinnati, O., and then in 1881 came to Cairo. Here he worked at his trade six months and then started a meat market at Clinton, Ill., but at the end of three months sold out and returned to Cairo, where he has since lived. After spending a year in the saloon business he sold out in 1883 and started a meat market here which he conducted successfully for several years. He made considerable money in this business and in 1892 embarked in the meat packing business as a partner in the firm of Bucher Bros. & Co. In 1901 he bought the interest of his brother Joseph and that of the company in the business. On Sept. 1, 1903, he sold a half interest to B. F. Woodford, and on Jan. 1, 1905, a stock company was formed and the business incorporated under the firm name of the Bucher-Woodford Packing Company, with Mr. Bucher as president and Mr. Woodford as secretary and treasurer. The capital stock was fixed at $50,000. It is the only meat packing industry in Cairo. Mr. Bucher is an active member of the Catholic church. On April 14, 1884, he married Miss Dora Duncker of Cairo. To this union five children have been born: Carl E., Eberhard Silas, Mary Martha, Anna and Dora, aged respectively nineteen, eleven, sixteen, thirteen and eight years. Mr. Bucher's career demonstrates clearly what can be accomplished by push and perseverance.

BENJAMIN F. WOODFORD, secretary and treasurer of the Bucher-Woodford Packing Company of Cairo, Ill., was born in Syracuse, N. Y., Aug. 1, 1855. He is the son of Alanson Woodford, a native of New York, of English parentage, and whose occupation was farming and thoroughbred stock breeding. He removed from New York to Whiteside county, Ill., in 1867. There the father spent the remainder of his life, dying March 22, 1884, aged seventy-two years. The mother of the subject before her marriage was Mary Elizabeth Lawrence, a native of New York State. She was the daughter of Eusephus Lawrence, a native of Connecticut and the son of John Lawrence, an Englishman by birth. The mother died in September, 1885. There were four children born to this union, of whom the subject of this sketch is the youngest. The other three are James E. and Alanson A., of Burlington, Kas., and Mary Elizabeth, who died in infancy. From this sketch it will be seen that only the three sons are left. Benjamin spent his youth on his father's farm in Whiteside county, Ill., graduated from the Rock Falls high school at the age of eighteen and then went to work as an assistant to his father in the breeding and trading of fine stock and in general farm work. He acquired an interest in his father's business on reaching his majority, and it was conducted under the management of Alanson Woodford & Son, until the father's death. Their specialty was the breeding of thoroughbred Poland-China hogs and Shorthorn cattle. Shortly before his father died Benjamin F. engaged in business for himself by purchasing a meat market at Rock Falls, Whiteside county. In 1886 he traded his interest in this business for a 240 acre farm in Lee county, Ill. He then devoted himself for a time to trading and dealing in live stock. In 1888 he entered the employ of T. M. Sinclair & Co., of Cedar Rapids, Ia., a large packing concern whose export trade in fine meat products is probably equal to that of any other firm in America. He was with this well-known house for two and one-half years, being its buyer most of the time. He resigned this position in 1891 and purchased a fine market in Cedar Rapids. A few months later he sold this business to accept a lucrative position with Swift & Co. of Chicago. He remained with this firm seven years in all. Beginning as salesman he soon worked his way to the front and was finally given a highly responsible position with the house. For one year he was in the employ of the Hammond Packing Company, a period sandwiched in between two periods with Swift & Co. Early in 1900 he entered the employ of Armour & Co. as traveling salesman. On May 7, 1902, he came to Cairo as manager of the Cairo branch of the concern, a position which he held until Sept. 1, 1903, when he resigned against the urgent solicitation of the house. Declining a liberal salary, he embarked in the packing business on his own account. He had purchased a half interest in the packing business of Eberhard Bucher, and it was to give his entire attention to this enterprise that he resigned his position with Armour & Co. On Jan. 1, 1905, the Bucher-Woodford Packing Company was organized with a capital stock of $50,000, Mr. Eberhard Bucher becoming president and Mr. Woodford secretary and treasurer. This concern does an extensive business in the packing and jobbing of beef, pork, veal, mutton and provisions. Mr. Woodford has recently identified himself with the Masonic order.

WILLIAM NICHOLS BUTLER, one of the three judges of the First circuit of Illinois, was born in Green Lake county, Wis., Aug. 16, 1856. He is the son of Comfort Edgar and Celestia Ann (Carter) Butler. With his father he removed to Columbia county, Pa., where the family resided until the breaking out of the Civil war. The father first enlisted in the Thirty-first Pennsylvania volunteer infantry and afterward in the Seventy-ninth regiment of the same state, fighting gallantly in the defense of the Union. During the father's absence in the army the family resided with friends and relatives in Canandaigua, Ontario county, N. Y. A few years after the close of the war the family removed to Texas, but not liking the country returned to the North, locating at Anna, Union county, Ill., where William grew to manhood, attending school, clerking in stores, working at the carpenter and printing trades and teaching school. On June 7, 1879, he graduated from the University of Illinois at Champaign, having paid his own way out of money earned by teaching and working at his trades. After graduating he determined to enter the legal profession. The same steadfast persistence that characterized him in his efforts to obtain an education is one of the chief secrets of his success in life. After reading law in the office of Monroe C. Crawford, of Jonesboro, Ill., he, in the fall of 1881, entered the Union College of Law in Chicago, being a classmate as well as seatmate of Hon. W. J. Bryan. The following fall he entered the senior class of the Albany, N. Y., law school, receiving therefrom the degree of Bachelor of Laws, May 25, 1883. In August of the same year he came to Cairo as a clerk in the internal revenue service under Gen. Charles W. Pavey, holding the position one year. On Sept. 10, 1884, he was nominated by the Republican party for the office of state's attorney of Alexander county and triumphantly elected. He gave such general satisfaction that he was re-elected in 1888, 1892 and 1896. The only defeat that he suffered was in the year 1900. These repeated marks of confidence in him by his fellow-citizens afford the best comment on his efficiency and faithfulness to duty. For six years he was honored with the chairmanship of the Republican central committee of Alexander county; also served as chairman of the congressional district committee; the Republican judicial committee of the First district and the committee of the First supreme court district. Mr. Butler was at the head of the judiciary committee of the supreme court district when his fellow-townsman, David J. Baker, was elected a member of the supreme court. This fact is worthy of mention because it was the first and only time that a Republican was elected from this district, and because it was the first time in the history of the state that the supreme court was Republican. Interested in the welfare of the public schools of Cairo, Mr. Butler has served on the board of education for six years. From December, 1884, to February, 1886, Mr. Butler was the senior member of the firm of Butler & Linegar, the firm being dissolved by the death of David T. Linegar. He was then associated with W. H. Boyer, but this connection was also terminated by the death of his partner. In the multiplicity of honors which Mr. Butler has enjoyed none has been more highly appreciated by him than that of the presidency of the alumni association of the University of Illinois, in which capacity he has twice acted. For one year he was adjutant of the Ninth regiment, Second brigade, National Guards of Illinois, ranking as captain. On the death of Joseph P. Roberts, one of the three circuit judges in this, the First circuit, in October, 1903, a vacancy on the bench occurred. Mr. Butler was one of the seven candidates for the nomination and was chosen on the sixty-fourth ballot. The election took place on Dec. 12, 1903, his opponent being Monroe C. Crawford, his preceptor in the beginning of his legal studies, and resulted in the election of Mr. Butler by a majority of 2,181 votes. He at once qualified, and is now serving in that capacity. As a lawyer Mr. Butler has been eminently successful, having among his clients some of the largest establishments in Cairo. His practice extended to the highest courts of the state and nation. Thoroughly qualified and eminently fitted for the position he now holds, Mr. Butler has fully demonstrated that no mistake has been made in his election, for he is administering the duties of this exalted office as successfully as he cared for the interests of his clients when practicing law. On Oct. 28, 1882, Mr. Butler married Miss Mary Mattoon of Fairbury, Livingston county, Ill. The names of the children are as follows: Comfort Straight, born in 1887; William Glenn, in 1889; Franklin Mattoon, in 1892; Mary, in 1894; Helen, in 1897 and John Bruce in 1900.

JOSEPH W. WENGER, commercial agent for the Illinois Central railway, Cairo, Ill., was born in Lacon, Marshall county, Ill., Sept. 28, 1851. He is the son of Dr. Elias Wenger, born in Rockingham county, Va., in June, 1821. In 1855 Doctor Wenger graduated from Rush Medical college, Chicago, and practiced medicine in Northern Illinois for thirty-two years, dying Aug. 29, 1887. He served as a member of the Illinois legislature in the year 1862-63, and at the time of his death was president of the Illinois State Medical society. The mother of Joseph W. was Eliza Smith, born in Augusta county, Va. She was married to Elias Wenger in that state and died in 1879. Joseph W. Wenger is the fourth of seven children—four sons and three daughters, all living. He was educated in the public schools, and at the age of twenty entered the employ of the Illinois Central Railway Company at Gilman, Ill., serving in the capacity of switchman and clerk for three or four years. In 1873 he entered the office of the general freight and passenger agent of the Gilman, Clinton & Springfield railroad, at Springfield, where he was a clerk for two years. From Springfield he went to Peoria, Ill., where he served until 1879 as clerk in the general freight office of the Toledo, Peoria & Western Railroad Company. He then re-entered the service of the Illinois Central as clerk in the freight office at Cairo, where he has been ever since. In 1882 he was made chief clerk in the superintendent's office. In 1887 he received the appointment of commercial agent, his present position. Thus it will be seen that he has been in the continuous employ of the Illinois Central for twenty-five years, and its commercial agent for eighteen years. He is a Royal Arch Mason, a Knight Templar and a Shriner, and is an ex-president of the Alexander club. He is actively affiliated with the Hoo Hoo order, a fraternity whose members are made up of the railway men and lumber men throughout the United States and Canada. Mr. Wenger is a Democrat in politics and a vestryman in the Episcopal church. On Sept. 28, 1881, he married Miss Mary Bainbridge Taylor of Cairo. She is the daughter of Augustus F. Taylor, a former well known citizen of Cairo, and granddaughter of Col. Samuel Staats Taylor, who was very prominent in the early history of the city. Mr. and Mrs. Wenger have three children: Joseph Bainbridge, of Chicago; Miss Alice Mary and Kenneth Taylor. The mother of Mrs Wenger was the late Phoebe Alice Taylor, who for many years held the office of county superintendent of schools of Alexander county. The brothers and sisters of Mr. Wenger are Mrs. Mary E. Danforth of Washington, Ill.; Mrs. Louise A. Craig of Twin Lakes, Col.; Abram A. of Ogden, Utah; Charles P. of Cairo, Ill.; Daniel B. of Trinidad, Col.; and Mrs. Nellie Pennewill of Kankakee, Ill.

ELMER SMITH, passenger and ticket agent of the Big Four, Iron Mountain and Missouri Pacific railways, at Cairo, Ill., was born at Allendale, Wabash county, Ill., June 28, 1876. He is the son of Dr. James E. Smith, a practicing physician of Mt. Carmel, Ill. Dr. J. E. Smith was born in Campbell county, Ky., Dec. 11, 1838, being the son of Geo. W. Smith. The doctor graduated from the Eclectic Medical Institute of Cincinnati, Ohio, in 1877. During the Civil war he served three years as private and hospital steward with the Ninety-eighth Illinois regiment of Wilder's brigade. Since 1877 he has practiced his profession in Wabash county, Ill. The mother of the subject was Nancy Howey, of Arkansas, born Feb. 27, 1846. She is the daughter of John and Eliza (Axton) Howey, and is still living. Of the eight children born to this union five survive: Mrs. Zillah Klindera of Tipton, Tulare county, Cal.; Elmer, Morris and Mattie (twins), and Vera Grace. Morris is baggage agent of the Big Four and Iron Mountain at Cairo. Mattie is now Mrs. E. L. Holsen of Allendale, Ill. Elmer Smith, the subject, learned telegraphy at the age of seventeen, and for several years served at various places as operator on the Cairo division of the Big Four. In 1897 he became night operator and ticket agent at the Union Station, Cairo. In 1898 he entered the office of C. L. Hilleary of St. Louis, assistant general passenger agent of the Big Four, where he served as stenographer and assistant city ticket agent for a year and a half. On Feb. 1, 1901, he assumed the duties of his present position as passenger and ticket agent of the Big Four, Iron Mountain and Missouri Pacific railways at Cairo. He holds membership in the following societies: Elks, Royal Arcanum and Knights of the Mystic Krew of Komus. On Oct. 21, 1901, he married Miss Grace Hewitt, daughter of Mr. and Mrs. R. A. Hewitt of Cairo, Ill. Two children, Helen Hewitt born Aug. 7, 1902, and Elmer, Jr., born Feb. 28, 1905, have blessed this marriage.

H. T. STEPHENS, local freight agent of the Big Four railway at Cairo, Ill., was born in the village of Normanda, Tipton county, Ind., Oct. 13, 1860. He is the son of Philip S. and Elizabeth B. (Huston) Stephens, now residents of Lapel, Madison county, Ind. His father was born near Goshen, O., April 10, 1830. The mother was born near Mechanicsburg, Ind., Dec. 25, 1840. To their marriage, solemnized April 29, 1857, there were born three children, only two of whom survive, the subject of this sketch and A. M. Stephens of Lapel, Ind. H. T. Stephens was reared in Indiana and educated in the public schools of that state. He first learned the trade of carriage painter. Laying this aside he served for a time as hotel clerk. Finally he drifted into railroading. His first position was that of clerk in a freight office at Union City, Ind., for the Cleveland, Columbus, Cincinnati, Chicago & Indianapolis railroad. He has been engaged in railroad work ever since in the constant employ of the above named road and its successor, the Big Four. When in 1888 the C. C. C. & I. was absorbed by the Big Four he went with it. All of his work has been in the freight department. He has been stationed at Cairo since Jan. 11, 1890. After serving nearly three years as cashier he was on Dec. 1, 1892, promoted to the position of freight agent, which he still holds. He is a member of the American Association of Freight Agents. In Masonry he ranks high, being a Royal Arch Mason, a Knight Templar and a past master, past high priest and past eminent commander of that order. In politics Mr. Stephens is a Republican. April 4, 1886, he married Miss Alethea C. Winslow, of Marion, Ind. They have one child, Kathryn, aged nine years.

JOSEPH STEAGALA, the proprietor of Uncle Joe's hotel, restaurant and saloon, was born in New Orleans, La., Feb. 13, 1839, and came to Cairo with his parents in 1854, having previously worked as a river man for three years. In 1857 Joe Steagala helped to organize the first fire department in Cairo, a volunteer relief department, which continued until 1865, when he became a charter member of the "Rough and Ready" fire company, and from that day to this he has been a member of the company. During the period of nine years that Mr. Steagala served as chief the department was handled more ably and economically than it had been handled before or has been handled since. When the position became a salaried one he promptly resigned. This is one of Uncle Joe's traits. Whatever he does for the community he does for the pure love of the town and not for pay. We doubt if there is another town in the country that can boast of a man who gives up his time and money, and to a certain extent neglects his business, to attend to the duties of a position while it is a voluntary service and then resigns it as soon as there is any pay attached to it. In 1866 Mr. Steagala moved to Hickman, Ky., where he resided for thirteen years. During these years he paid his dues and was a member in good standing of the "Rough and Ready" fire company of Cairo. In 1879 he returned to Cairo and opened up his present place of business on the corner of Sixth street and Commercial avenue. He was first elected justice of the peace in 1885 and is still serving his city in that capacity. He served the First ward as alderman in 1894 and has two or three times been brought out by his friends and admirers as an independent candidate for mayor. Mr. Steagala has at all times been identified with every movement which had for its object the bringing of people to Cairo, and of keeping them. He is a member in good standing of nineteen secret societies, to each of which he gives more of his time and money than does any other member. He is at present a director of the Cairo Baseball club, and was one of the active promoters of the Central League. Among the various business enterprises that Mr. Steagala has been connected with can be mentioned the broom factory on Tenth street, operated by him two years, a sewing machine store on Commercial avenue, managed by Mr. Steagala for three years, and the widely popular "Uncle Joe's Hotel," on the levee, which he opened in 1889 and in which he himself placed the electric light plant. Without any display or any notoriety, Joe Steagala has quietly and unobtrusively dispensed thousands of dollars in Cairo in worthy charity. Personally he is a quiet, unassuming gentleman, with whom it is a pleasure to have business and social relations. He is known by every man, woman and child in the town, and while he may have enemies we doubt if there is any other man in town who has more or warmer friends than has "Uncle" Joe Steagala.

L. P. PARKER, manager of "The Halliday," Cairo, Ill., as well as of the Hotel Gayoso, Memphis, Tenn., was born in Bradford county, Pa., Nov. 24, 1848. He came to Illinois with his parents when but ten years of age. On Nov. 15, 1880, he came to Cairo and at once took charge of the Halliday House. He has been associated with that fine and popular hostelry ever since, fully twenty-four years. In these years he has made a reputation as a successful hotel man second to none in the country. Mr. Parker is widely known as a very practical hotel man. He is also manager of the Hotel Gayoso, Memphis, Tenn., the first hotel in that city and one of the best and most thoroughly equipped, popular resorts in the South. Mr. Parker became manager of this hotel Aug. 1, 1898. On July 4, 1899, this fine property was destroyed by fire. Immediately after the fire the Memphis Hotel Company was organized with Stuyvesant

Fish, president of the Illinois Central Railroad Company, as its president and J. S. Aisthorpe of Cairo, Ill., as secretary and treasurer. Upon the site of the ruins a fine, new, modern hotel building was erected, which was completed and opened to the public on May 1, 1902. This hostlery is known as the Hotel Gayoso and is easily one of the finest hotels in the Mississippi Valley. Mr. Parker's eldest son, A. L. Parker, is assistant manager, while a younger son, B. S. Parker, is manager of the Istroama Hotel at Baton Rouge, La. Maynard, the third and youngest son, is a professional violinist, being instructor on the violin at the Freeze Conservatory of Music, Los Angeles, Cal. Mr. Parker has just cause to be proud of his own standing in the hotel world, as well as that of each of his progressive, wide awake sons.

CHARLES E. GREGORY, proprietor of the Cairo Monument Company, Cairo, Ill., was born at Fredericktown, Madison county, Mo., July 31, 1879. He is the son of Col. Felix G. and Hannah A. (Anthony) Gregory, both of whom were born and reared in Fredericktown, Mo. The father died there July 3, 1899, aged fifty-nine. The mother still survives. Throughout his business career the father followed the livery and hotel business. Colonel Gregory served as a colonel in the Confederate army. His father, also named Felix G., was a native of Virginia, but with his brother Serrel emigrated from Virginia to Kentucky and later located in Missouri. The Anthony family, too, has been quite prominent both politically and socially in the State of Missouri. Among the members of the family today are E. D. Anthony, a prominent attorney; Robert Anthony, an ex-circuit judge of Fredericktown, and William Anthony, a prominent commercial lawyer of Farmersburg. Charles E. Gregory, is the youngest of eight children—four sons and four daughters. His brothers and sisters are: William T., a merchant of Baxter Springs, Kan.; Martin P., a farmer of the vicinity of Farmersburg, Mo.; John F., a Missouri Pacific passenger engineer residing at Alexandria, La.; Mrs. Bird Isibell, of Colorado; Mrs. Bertha E. Zeran, of Farmington, Mo.; Miss Lizzie F., who still resides with her mother, and Mrs. May Bell McGrew, of Galena, Mo. Charles E.

Gregory was reared at Fredericktown and graduated from the Marvin Collegiate institute of that place at the age of twenty years. On the death of his father he assumed the management of the Gregory hotel and conducted it successfully for two years. On the sale of the property in September, 1901, he devoted a year of his time to the study of music. In 1903, he came to Cairo and bought the property of the Cairo Monument Company, of which he is still the proprietor. On Nov. 12, 1904, he added to his business the Zeran Marble & Granite Works, formerly owned by his brother-in-law, John S. Zeran. This institution is the only one of its kind in Cairo and does quite an extensive business, both wholesale and retail. Its sale of building stone is also quite large. It secures its granite for the most part from its own granite quarries, located near Farmington, Mo., a granite which is being extensively used throughout the United States as a substitute for the imported Scotch granite. Mr. Gregory is an enthusiast on the subject of music and always manages to spare some of his time to the cultivation of that subject. He takes delight in church choir singing and sings the part of tenor in the Methodist church of his home city.

MRS. M. E. FEITH, proprietress of the largest undertaking establishment of Cairo, Ill., located at No. 1101 Washington avenue, was born in that city Dec. 28, 1872. She is the daughter of the late Dennis Coleman, one of the early residents of Cairo, who died Sept. 17, 1904, at the ripe age of eighty-two years. He was born in Ireland, came to the United States at the age of eighteen and located in Cairo, in 1858. There he was married Feb. 12, 1872, to Mary DeNeen, also a native of Ireland. She died Sept. 12, 1890. There are three children living: Mrs. Mary E. Feith and John Coleman of Cairo, and Mrs. Josie Watkins, of Mt. Carmel, Ill. Mrs. Feith has lived in Cairo all her life. She graduated at the age of seventeen from Loretta academy, a Catholic institution, and on Oct. 21, 1891, was married to William E. Feith, a well-known undertaker, proprietor of the Feith undertaking establishment on the corner of Eleventh street and Washington avenue, the oldest establishment of the kind in the city, having been started on this corner by his father, Nicholas Feith, in 1865. William E. Feith was born in Cincinnati, O., Aug. 18, 1865, coming to Cairo with his parents when quite a small child. He died Aug. 12, 1899, leaving to his wife's care the management of the undertaking business and the rearing of three children born to them. The children are: Chester

J., born May 28, 1894; Mary Loretta, born June 10, 1896, and Anna Marie, born Aug. 20, 1898. One other child, a son, the first born, was William E. Jr., born July 19, 1892, and died Feb. 13, 1899. Upon the death of her husband Mrs. Feith, by force of necessity, assumed charge of the business, and has since conducted it very successfully, in a manner which gives it first place among like establishments of Cairo. She certainly deserves great credit for the ability she has shown, and all the more so, when it is recalled that at the time of Mr. Feith's death she had only a meager knowledge of the business. She is now a licensed undertaker, having completed a course in embalming since her husband's death. At the time Mr. Feith died he had in course of erection on the corner of Eleventh street and Washington avenue a large, two-story brick undertaking establishment to take the place of an old frame building which had done such good service for years. Mrs. Feith completed this structure without delay, equipping it throughout in the most modern style. Her equipment includes two funeral cars, one ambulance and other vehicles, together with two fine teams, and the stock displayed in her salesrooms embraces everything from the plainest coffin to the most pretentious casket.

GEORGE J. BECKER. There are few better examples of the success that awaits the young men of the present generation who are willing to work, giving all of their time and efforts to advancing either their own business interests or, if employed, the interests of their employers, than is afforded by the successful career of George J. Becker, president of the Andrew Lohr Bottling Company, of Cairo, Ill., who has, by sheer hard work, constant application and untiring energy, raised himself from the bottommost round of the ladder to his present position at the head of the largest institution of its kind in the United States. Born in Cincinnati, O., Feb. 22, 1855, the son of John and Catherine Becker, natives of Bavaria, to which source can be attributed the taste for music later displayed, the subject of this sketch was at three years of age deprived of a father's help and guidance, and in 1863 his mother married Joseph Lehmes, a citizen of Cairo. Shortly afterwards George had his first view of that city from the deck of a Cincinnati packet. Since that day, the boy and afterwards the man, has spent his entire life actively engaged in the various occupations which have always been along similar lines. His mother, after losing her second husband, died at Cairo, Sept. 15, 1888, leaving besides the subject of this sketch one daughter by her second marriage, now Mrs. Emma Brisbin, wife of Henry Brisbin of St. Elmo, Ill. Young George obtained such schooling as was possible at that date, employing himself out of school hours as a helper in various restaurants and cafés along the then busy Ohio levee. Leaving school at the age of twelve years, he shortly afterwards entered the employ of Mr. Henry Breihan, where he acquired his first knowledge of the soda water business. He remained with Mr. Breihan in the capacity of bookkeeper and afterward manager until he accepted a position with Mr. Andrew Lohr, at that time conducting a modest bottling plant. Into his new vocation Mr. Becker threw his entire personality, and by force of hard work, not only became vice-president of the newly incorporated company in 1889, but ten years later, reorganized the company, Mr. Lohr retiring, and as president and general manager of the new corporation, of which Dr. J. J. Rendelman of Cairo is secretary, he has added to, improved and modernized the entire plant, until today there stands on the site of the little bottling shop of 1879 an immense factory covering an entire city block in length, with a large warehouse across the street from the main plant, and an equipment as complete as can be obtained, with electricity as the motive power, the company having a complete plant of its own, and with every device known to the bottling business utilized. The products of this institution have been characterized by that on which Mr. Becker prides himself; viz., absolute purity of ingredients, the best of everything, and thorough cleanliness throughout every branch of manufacture. Mr. Becker has been singularly blessed as regards his family, for since Sept. 16, 1880, when Miss Maggie Hines, of Cairo, and himself were united in the bonds of wedlock, five children, two sons and three daughters, have blessed the union, the oldest son, Harry, being at present assistant to his father in the management of the multifarious details of their immense business. Mr. Becker early in life displayed an extraordinary talent for music and for many years was prominent as a violinist in local musical circles. In the palmy days of the local volunteer fire companies, Mr. Becker was an active member, finding thereby another use for his favorite element—water. Mr. Becker is an Odd Fellow, a member of the local lodge of

Elks, an active member of the Cairo Commercial club, and belongs to various other societies. Upon being asked what motto he had held before him in his busy life, the answer characteristically was: "What is worth doing at all, is worth doing well."

WILLIAM KLUGE, a prominent citizen and business man of Cairo, Ill., was born in Germany, July 30, 1837. His parents having died when he was still in his childhood, his mother's brother, Conrad Leodige, brought the lad to America with him when only twelve years of age. The family landed at New Orleans in 1849, where William lived with his uncle for ten years. In 1859 he came to Cairo, which city has ever since been his home. His first work after coming to Cairo was that of clerk in a grocery store. After serving his employer faithfully for a year in this capacity he embarked in the grocery business for himself, and, with slight interruptions, has been engaged in that line ever since with unvarying success. For about thirty years he conducted an extensive wholesale and retail business at the corner of Sixth and Commercial avenues. His present place of business is on the corner of Nineteenth and Poplar streets. In the building and development of the present electric street railway system of Cairo he was one of the leading spirits, and was for many years president of the company. In 1902 he sold his street railway interests and retired from the presidency. Mr. Kluge is a director in the Alexander County National bank and is identified with other movements and institutions that have for their object the advancement of the city's commercial interests. In 1866 he married Annie Feith, and to this union was born one daughter, now Mrs. Edith Walsh, of Cairo. Mrs. Kluge died in 1875 and some three years later he married Katherine Feith, a sister of his first wife. One son was born to this marriage, but died when about five years of age. Mr. Kluge is deservedly popular with the enterprising citizens of Cairo, for few have done more to bring the city up to its present standing as an industrial and commercial center. Whenever he thought he was right he never faltered, but has always been firm and consistent in the advocacy of correct principles. His motto has ever been *sans peur et sans reproche,* and his life has been a living exemplification of that motto.

ANTHONY P. EHS, one of the prominent merchants of Cairo, Ill., was born in that city, Aug. 19, 1865. He is the son of Peter and Dora Ehs, both natives of Germany, and now deceased. Anthony is the only son living. His three sisters are Mrs. Lena Koehler and Mrs. Mollie Davis, of Cairo, and Elizabeth Ehs, of Paducah, Ky. He was reared and educated in his native city, and at the early age of fourteen years he began his successful business career as cash boy in the New York store. He remained with this firm in the capacity of cash boy and clerk for about nine years, when he began business for himself. In his present business, that of general merchandizing, he has been actively engaged for fully fifteen years. His store is located at 2009 and 2011 Washington avenue. Mr. Ehs is a director of the Weber Dry-Goods Company and vice-president of the Cairo Candy Manufacturing Company. In religious matters he is identified with the Catholic church, and is an active member of the Ancient Order of United Workmen. On April 16, 1890, he married Johannah Fitzgerald of Cairo. Four children have been born to this union: Edna, Richard, Geraldine and Thomas. Mr. Ehs takes great interest in the development of his home city, and there are few of its citizens that do more to bring about the general prosperity than he. Full of push and enterprise he makes everything go that he takes hold of, and as such is a valuable member of his home community.

HENRY G. SANKS, of Shawneetown, Ill., clerk of the court of Gallatin county, is a native of Indiana, having been born near Lawrenceburg in Dearborn county, May 7, 1851. His grandfather, Joshua Sanks, was in early life a farmer near Baltimore, Md. From there he removed to Virginia and later to Indiana, locating near Lawrenceburg, where he lived to the age of eighty-nine years. He was married three times and reared a large family of children. George D. Sanks, the father of Henry G., was born near Winchester, Va., Sept. 2, 1813. After his parents removed to Indiana he became interested in flatboating on the Ohio and Mississippi rivers and followed that occupation for a number of years. About 1849 he was married to Mary Evans, a native of Dearborn county, and they went to housekeeping at Aurora, in that county, where he engaged in the manufacture of brick. Mary Evans was a daughter of Samuel Evans, who was born in the city of Philadelphia, Pa., Feb. 7, 1781, and removed to Dearborn county, Ind., in 1807, where he lived the rest of his life. His father was born in Wales, but came to

America some time between 1720 and 1750. They were both ship carpenters and the subject of this sketch now has in his possession a try-square that formerly belonged to one of them. In 1853 George D. Sanks took his family and their effects aboard a flatboat and floated down the river to Shawneetown. Nine miles west of the town he purchased a farm and followed agricultural pursuits the remainder of his life. His wife died in 1873 and he afterward married Nancy J. Leighliter, who is now also deceased. By his first wife his children were Henry G., the subject of this sketch; Tamson V., Sarah E., and Martha E., all deceased. By his second wife he had four children: Susannah V., now Mrs. Turner, of Danville, Ill.; David R. and George D., who now live on the old home place; and Mary, now Mrs. Riley, of Bowling Green, Ky. He died in 1894. Henry G. Sanks was educated in the common schools and lived with his parents until his marriage, when he engaged in farming near Ridgway for one year, after which he removed to Shawneetown, but after living there awhile returned to the farm and lived there until 1883. He then removed to Ridgway and lived there until 1890, when he was elected sheriff of Gallatin county and again took up his residence in Shawneetown. After serving four years as sheriff he was elected county treasurer and held that office for four years. He was then appointed deputy clerk and continued in that position until 1902, when he was elected clerk, which office he now holds. Mr. Sanks probably inherited his love for political affairs from his father, who was active in politics the greater part of his life. He is now chairman of the Democratic central committee of Gallatin county, and as a political organizer has few equals in Southern Illinois. He is a good mixer and his genial disposition wins friends for him even among his political opponents. In a knowledge of county affairs he is well qualified to transact any of the official business of any office, his long connection with the different offices he has held rendering him thoroughly familiar with the business. His wife was Miss Mary E. Lawler, a native of Gallatin county and a niece of Gen. M. K. Lawler. Of their five children three are living, George D., Margaret E. and Mary E., all at home with their parents. He is a member of the Catholic church and is in every way one of the representative men of his county.

ABNER F. DAVENPORT, of Equality, Ill., treasurer of Gallatin county, was born in the neighborhood where he now lives March 2, 1844. His grandfather, William Davenport, was one of the pioneers of the county, coming from Tennessee in 1825. At that time Randall W. Davenport, the father of Abner, was ten years of age, having been born in Knox county, Tenn., in 1815. In 1843 he married Sarah Flanders, a native of New York, and began farming near his father's home, where he lived until his death in 1852. He was a Democrat and took an active part in the political affairs of his day. They had four children: Abner F., Deborah, now Mrs. Purcell, of Equality; Sarah A., deceased, and George, who now lives at Eldorado in Saline county, Ill. Abner F. Davenport obtained a good practical education in the public schools and remained at home until his mother's death in 1877, when he married Miss Juliett Clifton, a native of Gallatin county, and from that time until 1884 followed the vocation of a farmer in the vicinity of Equality. He then embarked in the general merchandizing business at Equality and continued in that line until 1899, when he became connected with the bank of Equality. In 1901 he was elected treasurer of the county, which office he still holds. He is also school treasurer of Equality township, and is cashier of the First National bank of Equality. In fraternal and church circles Mr. Davenport is a prominent figure about Equality, being a member of the Independent Order of Odd Fellows and a deacon in the Presbyterian church. Of the ten children born to Mr. and Mrs. Davenport six are still living. May is the wife of a Mr. Farmer of Texas; Mattie, William, George, Robert and Charles all live at home with their parents.

HENRY C. STRICKLAND, postmaster at Equality, Ill., was born near Shawneetown, in the same county where he now lives, April 16, 1852. His father, John D. Strickland, was a native of Montgomery county, Ohio, but came to Gallatin county, Ill., in early manhood. He was a hatter by trade, an expert bookkeeper, and for some time followed flatboating between Shawneetown and New Orleans. He married Armilla Dobbs, of Gallatin county, and they had six children. Those living are Henry C., Virgil, now in Louisville, Ky., and Millard F., a farmer five miles west of Shawneetown. The father died in 1860 and the mother in 1882. Henry C. Strickland obtained his elementary education in the common schools, after which he attended the Southern Illinois Normal at Carbondale. During his minority he worked upon a farm, but upon arriving at the age of twenty-one he engaged in the farm implement business. When he was twenty-six he commenced teaching and followed that occupation about twenty years, being the principal of the Equality schools three years of that time. He then embarked in the merchandizing business at Equality and continued in that line for about six years, when he was appointed postmaster by the late President McKinley, and is now serving his fifth year in that position. Mr. Strickland is a member of the Masonic fraternity, is now senior warden of his lodge and has filled other offices. In politics he is one of the active Republicans of Equality, and is always ready to do his part toward winning a victory. He has been twice married. His first wife was Ida, daughter of Moses and Elizabeth Kanada, by whom he had two children, both now deceased. She died in 1888 and he was married to Ella, daughter of E. H. and Druzilla McCaleb. One child was born to this marriage, but it, too, is dead. Mrs. Strickland is a member of the Methodist Episcopal church and takes an interest in promoting its good works.

J. W. HALES, dealer in general merchandise, Equality, Ill., was born two miles north of that town, July 5, 1840. He is a son of James and Matilda (Willis) Hales, the former a native of North Carolina and the latter of Tennessee. James Hales came to Illinois about the year 1830, married shortly afterward, and followed farming in the vicinity of Equality until his death, which occurred when the subject of this sketch was about five years old. After the death of his father, his mother bound him out to George W. Flanders, with whom he remained until he was nineteen years of age. His mother married a second time, her second husband being Leonard Haney. She died in Equality, the mother of four children, of whom the subject is the only survivor. J. W. Hales received such an education as the district schools of his day afforded, and after leaving Mr. Flanders worked in a tobacco establishment at Equality until 1861. He was one of the first to answer the call for troops in that year and enlisted as a private in Company B, First Illinois cavalry. After about six months with this organization he was transferred to Company E, Fourteenth Illinois cavalry, in which he served until the close of the war, rising to the rank of sergeant. His regiment was with Sherman in the march to the sea; was at the siege of Knoxville; the surrender of Cumberland Gap; and in numerous minor engagements. While engaged in a skirmish at Sunshine Church, near Hillsboro, Ga., Mr. Hales was captured and confined for four months in the famous Andersonville prison. In an attempt to escape he was severely hurt, but recovered and was exchanged. From that time to the end of the war he was with his command in all the principal engagements in which the regiment took part. He was discharged at Pulaski, Tenn., in July, 1865, returned to Equality, and for the following three years was a carder and spinner in the Equality woolen mills. He then clerked in a dry goods store for five years, and on Nov. 6, 1875, opened a store of his own, in which line of business he has ever since continued, in addition to which he looks after the management of his farms. Mr. Hales is a Republican in his political affiliations and takes an active interest in promoting the success of his party. He is a prominent member of the Grand Army of the Republic and with his family belongs to the Methodist Episcopal church. He was married on April 15, 1874, to Miss Blanche E. Reed, a native of Tennessee, and they have two children: James E., who lives in Equality, and Hallie I., now Mrs. Burtie.

J. P. SIDDALL, tinner and dealer in hardware, Equality, Ill., is a grandson of William Siddall, a native of England, who came to Equality in his early manhood. Having learned the tinners' trade in his native land, he opened the first tin-shop and hardware store in Equality. The business he established has been in the family for three generations. Some time after coming to America he married Martha Maltby, and to this union there were born five children: John M., now in Texas; William, in Iowa; Elizabeth, now a Mrs. Hine, living in Florida; Joseph and Parmenas, deceased. Both parents lived to be very old. Parmenas Siddall, after obtaining a common school education, learned the trade with his father, and upon the latter's death succeeded to the business, which he conducted through life. He married Johanna A. Probasco, a native of New York, whose acquaintance he formed while she was on a visit to friends in Equality. They had three children, all living. Florence is now a Mrs. Friend, living in Missouri; Etta is a Mrs. McDonald, of Texas; and the son is the subject of this sketch. Parmenas Siddall was an active Democrat in his day, and both himself and wife were devout Presbyterians. He gave the lot upon which the Presbyterian church of Equality stands, and always took an active part in church work. He died in 1885 and his wife in 1889. J. P. Siddall was born Aug. 20, 1869. He grew to manhood in Equality, received a good practical education in the public schools of the town, and after leaving school became associated with his father in business. Since the death of his father he has continued the business, which was founded by his grandfather three-quarters of a century ago. Mr. Siddall takes an active part in political affairs and is now local committeeman of the county central committee. He has served three terms as assessor, one term as village treasurer, and two terms on the school board. He is a member and trustee of the Odd Fellows' Lodge, No. 19; a member of Lodge No. 581, Daughters of Rebekah, and of Lodge No. 381, Court of Honor. In Odd Fellowship he has been through the chairs and is now grand representative. He was married June 10, 1896, to Miss Emma, daughter of Mr. and Mrs. William F. Yost, of Equality, and they have two children, Halton and Kelly, both at home. The family occupy one of the coziest homes in Equality and are members of the Presbyterian church, in which Mr. Siddall is a deacon and trustee.

MARSHALL E. LAMBERT, city attorney of Shawneetown, Ill., is a native of Union county, Ky. His grandfather, David Lambert, was a Virginian, but came with his brother to Kentucky at an early date, locating near Skaggs' Mill, a short distance from Bowling Green, in Warren county. There he married, reared a family of children, and passed the remainder of his life as a farmer. There John M. Lambert, the father of the subject of this sketch, was born Oct. 9, 1836. When he was about twelve years of age he went with his brother Josiah to Henderson county, where he found employment as a farm hand. For ten years he worked for John S. McCormick, and was then employed by other farmers until 1864, when he went to Union county, Ky., as manager of the David R. Burbank estate, and remained in that position for three years.

In 1866 he was married to Elizabeth Ann, daughter of John and Caroline Sprague, and went to housekeeping on a farm directly opposite Shawneetown. The Sprague family was one of the oldest in Union county, and had its beginning there in John Sprague, a millwright of Pittsburg, Pa., who married Margaret Fleming of that city and came down the river in a flatboat to Union county, where he entered government land and passed the remainder of his life. Their son, John Sprague, married Caroline McKinney and they had three children: Elizabeth, who became Mrs. Lambert; Ellen, who married a man by the name of McKinney, and John. In 1884 John Lambert removed with his family to Shawneetown, and there died in 1901. In 1891 he, in connection with his son Marshall, engaged in general merchandizing at Blackburn, Ky., just across the river from Shawneetown, and they conducted this business until 1896, when he retired from active pursuits. His first wife died in 1875 and he was married in 1876 to Lavinia Waggener Jones, widow of Nat Jones, who is still living at the old home in Shawneetown. Marshall E. Lambert was born Jan. 17, 1873, and is the only one of five children born to John M. and Elizabeth Lambert now living. After attending the public schools of Shawneetown and private school at Louisville, Ky., he entered the law department of the University of Michigan in 1896 and graduated in 1899. Upon leaving college he formed a partnership for the practice of law with C. N. Hollerich of East St. Louis, and practiced there until 1900, when he returned to Shawneetown and opened an office there. In addition to his law practice he assumed the management of his father's business, which consisted of large landed interests, and upon the latter's death became the sole heir to the large estate, as no children were born to his father's second marriage. Mr. Lambert, like his father before him, takes a great interest in politics, and is regarded as one of the coming men of his section of the state. In 1901 he was elected city attorney of Shawneetown, which position he still holds. This selection was a tribute to both his ability and his personal popularity. He belongs to the Knights of Pythias, and is always a welcome visitor at the meetings of his lodge, because of his genial disposition and general good-fellowship. On May 15, 1901, he was united in marriage to Miss Katherine I., daughter of Judge James Marshall, of Spokane, Wash., and they have two children: Elizabeth Sprague and William Payne.

DAVID M. KINSALL, of Shawneetown, Ill., ex-judge of Gallatin county, and one of the leading members of the Southern Illinois bar, is of English descent, the first of the name in this country having come from England some years prior to the Revolutionary war and settled in North Carolina. Later he removed to Tennessee, where he reared a large family of children, among whom was John Kinsall, the grandfather of the subject of this sketch. John Kinsall was born in Tennessee about 1791, was reared on a farm, received such an education as the schools of that day afforded and at the age of eighteen years began life on his own account as a wood chopper at Werd's salt works. After working at this for some time he, in company with two friends, bought a barge load of salt and started south with it. The barge struck a snag and sank, the three young salt traders barely escaping with their lives. This unfortunate termination of his first business venture left him considerably in debt, but with courage characteristic of the early pioneers he returned to the salt works and by strenuous efforts and rigid economy succeeded in clearing up his indebtedness. Soon after this he was married to Miss Elizabeth, daughter of John Hancock, of Virginia, a representative of one of the oldest and most prominent families of the Old Dominion, and removed with his young wife to White county, Ill., the region at that time being on the frontier. For two years he lived upon a rented farm in White county, at the end of which time he rented another farm near Shawneetown, and lived there until he entered government land a short distance east of Omaha, where he passed the remainder of his life, he and his wife both dying in 1854, within six months of each other. He took a keen interest in political affairs in his day, his house frequently being the place of holding the election, and he was one of the first commissioners of Gallatin county. Both he and his wife were earnest church workers. He fought in the war with the Creek Indians, and at the beginning of the war of 1812 he enlisted as a private under General Jackson. At the historic battle of New Orleans he received a bullet which he carried to the day of his death. John and Elizabeth Kinsall were the parents of seven children, viz.: Hiram, William, Benjamin, Thomas,

David, Moses and Jane. Moses lives on the old home farm, Jane is the widow of Sterling Edwards, and now lives in Omaha, and all the others are deceased. Thomas Kinsall, the fourth son, was born in 1827, in Gallatin county, and passed his whole life in that part of the state. From the subscription schools of that day he acquired a meager education, which he supplemented by self-study and reading, becoming one of the leading citizens of the community in which he lived. In 1850 he was married to Malinda E. Harrell, and soon afterward settled in the southwest part of White county, where he followed farming for two years, and then removed to Bear Creek township, in Gallatin county, where he lived the remainder of his active life. Upon retiring from the active conduct of the farm he removed to Omaha, where he lived until his death in 1889. His wife, who was born in 1829, died in 1876. They were both members of the Cumberland Presbyterian church, and in politics he was always a consistent Democrat. Their children are all living. David M. is the subject of this sketch; Alvin H. is a banker at Eldorado, Ill.; John H. is a farmer in Clinton county of the same state; Samuel S. is a merchant and farmer in Colorado, and Jennie is the wife of B. L. Rodgers of Harrisburg, Ill. David M. Kinsall was born near Omaha, May 6, 1851, and has always lived in Gallatin county. After attending the public schools until he was eighteen years old he became a teacher, and for four terms taught in the common schools. In 1872 he attended the Fairfield high school for five months, and from that time until 1875 worked at different times as deputy assessor of Gallatin county. While thus employed he devoted his spare time to the study of law. In 1874 he attended the law department of the Indiana State university at Bloomington for the entire school year, and then, after teaching one term, entered the office of Hon. R. W. Townshend and read for one year. In 1878 he was admitted to the bar and commenced practice in the office of Mr. Townshend, who was at that time a member of Congress. In April, 1879, he was elected city attorney of Shawneetown for a term of two years and in September of the same year was appointed master in chancery for Gallatin county. This appointment was for two years, and in November, 1880, he was elected state's attorney for the county and was re-elected in 1884, without opposition, holding the office for eight years and making an enviable record as a public official. In 1890 he was elected to the office of county judge, was re-elected at the close of his first term, making eight years that he discharged the duties of this position. Since his retirement from the judgeship he has devoted all his time to the practice of his profession and in looking after his large landed interests. His clientage is one of the largest in Southern Illinois, embracing all classes of law, in which Judge Kinsall is thoroughly versed. In politics he is one of the strong Democrats of his section of the state, and stands high in the councils of his party. He was married on Nov. 27, 1883, to Miss Edith, daughter of A. K. and Cassandra J. Lowe, of Shawneetown, and to this union there has been born one daughter, Edna, who is at home with her parents.

ALBERT G. RICHESON, proprietor of the Pioneer Store, one of the leading mercantile establishments of Shawneetown, Ill., is a native of Gallatin county. He can trace his ancestry on both sides back to old Virginia families, some of whom played important parts in establishing the independence of the United States. John Richeson, his grandfather, was a farmer in Amherst county, Va., and married Nancy A. Dickinson, whose father, David Dickinson, was a commissary for the Virginia troops during the Revolutionary war. One of his sons was John D. Richeson, who was born in Amherst county, May 16, 1810. At the age of sixteen years he started out for himself. Making his way to Charlestown he hired out to some flatboatmen named Mays for $8 a month. That was on the first day of March, 1826. His first trip was down the Kanawha and Ohio rivers to Cincinnati, then a town of less than ten thousand inhabitants. He continued flatboating until the fall of 1832, when he returned to Virginia and for the next four years followed trading in live stock and slaves and looking after a farm. He was then engaged in contracting on some public work at Louisville for about a year. In 1837 he came to Shawneetown, where he secured contracts for paving the levee in front of the town, and for grading the Shawneetown & Alton railroad to Equality, a distance of eleven miles. Being favorably impressed with the future prospects of Shawneetown he engaged in the general merchandizing business in 1838, and conducted it on both a wholesale and retail basis until his death in 1893, a period of more than fifty years. In 1839 he was married to Mrs. Judith M. Carroll, née Williamson, the widow of James Carroll, and to this marriage there were born three children: Albert G., Mary, wife of Judge McBane, and Eleanora, who married Judge J. D. Turner and died in 1900. Both parents were active workers in the Presbyterian church. Albert G. Richeson received his education in the public schools and at Notre Dame university, South Bend, Ind. Upon leaving college he engaged for about a year in conducting a saw and grist mill at Equality. He was then for a time in the stock trading business; was next in partnership with Henry Richeson in operating a saw mill at Cypress in Johnson county; after which he embarked in the hardware business at Shawneetown and continued in that line until 1887. For the next three years he farmed and traded in stock, and in 1890 formed a partnership with his father, under the name of the J. D. Richeson Co., for general merchandizing. Upon the death of his father he succeeded to the business and is now the sole proprietor of one of the oldest and best known mercantile establishments in Gallatin county. In addition to his mercantile interests Mr. Richeson owns about 1,500 acres of land and is extensively connected with the saw mill business about Shawneetown. He is a member of the Independent Order of Odd Fellows and the Knights of Honor. On April 15, 1875, he was married to Miss Mattie L., daughter of Andrew and Mary McCallen, of Shawneetown. Her father was at one time the law partner of Abraham Lincoln, and Mrs. Richeson has in her possession a great many keepsakes in the way of letters, etc., that have passed between her father and Mr. Lincoln. Mr. and Mrs. Richeson have had four children: May, Judith and Johnnie are deceased, and Helen is a student in school.

EDGAR MILLS, proprietor of the Mills Hotel and postmaster, Ridgway, Ill., was born at Shawneetown in the same county, Aug. 3, 1843. His father, whose name was also Edgar, was a native of New Jersey, of English descent, and came to Shawneetown about 1840, and there engaged in mercantile pursuits, in which he continued until his death in 1846. He married Miss Sarah Ridgway, a native of White county, Ill., and a daughter of John and Mary (Grant) Ridgway. To this union there were born two sons: Edgar and Walter. The latter died at Memphis in 1863, while serving in the Union army. After the death of the father the mother in 1852 married Silas Hemingway, and by this marriage had one daughter, Harriet, now a resident of Chicago. The mother died in 1863 and Mr. Hemingway in 1854. Edgar Mills was educated in the Shawneetown public schools and the Spencerian business college of Cincinnati. In 1855 he began life as a clerk in the store of John & George A. Ridgway, and remained with them until 1861, when he enlisted as a private in Company B, Eighteenth Illinois infantry, commanded by Col. M. K. Lawler. The regiment was first ordered to Cairo, where it was assigned to the command of Gen. John A. McClernand, but was later attached to the Army of the Tennessee. Mr. Mills took part in the first battle of Fort Donelson, was at the battle of Shiloh, and in a number of skirmishes. After seven months of service he returned to Shawneetown, his brother taking his place. From the time he left the army until 1865 he was engaged as a clerk in a store in Shawneetown. He then married Miss Zue E. Hunter, daughter of Matthew Hunter, a native of Pennsylvania. By this marriage he had one child, now deceased. His wife died in 1866, and Mr. Mills went to Evansville, Ind., and remained there until 1871, when he returned to Shawneetown and became a member of the firm of Waggener & Mills. In addition to their store at Shawneetown the firm established one at Ridgway, and when the partnership was dissolved some four years later the latter establishment fell to Mr. Mills. He continued in the mercantile line until 1884. In 1880 he was appointed postmaster of Ridgway by President Hayes. He continued to serve under the administration of Garfield and Arthur and during Cleveland's first term, up to Jan. 15, 1886. On June 10, 1889, he was again appointed postmaster under President Harrison, and in 1897 was appointed by President McKinley, having held the position ever since. Mr. Mills is one of the leading Republicans of Gallatin county, and is one of the two members of that party that have been elected to county office. In 1876 he was elected a member of the board of county commissioners and was re-elected in 1879. For fourteen years he has served as justice of the peace of Ridgway township; was twice elected mayor of Shawneetown; and served two terms on the board of aldermen of that city. Since 1876 he has been nearly half of the time chairman of the Republican county central committee, and has always been active in behalf of his party. After the death of his first wife, already mentioned, he married her younger sister, Eva, in 1872, and they had four children, two of whom are living. Ridgway is a merchant in the town of the same name, and Ella is the wife of Professor Blackard, superintendent of the public schools of Gallatin county. The second Mrs. Mills died in 1884, and in 1886 he was married to Sophronia Crawford, a daughter of John and Mary Kanada. No children have been born to this union. Mr. Mills has been proprietor of the hotel that bears his name since 1895, and in that time he has made it one of the popular hostelries of Southern Illinois. He and his wife are both members of the Presbyterian church.

JOHN T. HOGAN, a prominent grain dealer and vice-president of the Exchange bank, of Omaha, Ill., was born near Dover, Stewart county, Tenn., Jan. 7, 1850. His grandfather, John Hogan, was a native of Virginia and of Irish parentage. On his return from the battle of New Orleans at the close of the war of 1812 he settled in Tennessee, married Sarah, daughter of Noah McGregory, who served with Washington during the Revolutionary war. To this marriage were born six children. Edmund Hogan, father of the subject of this sketch, was born in Stewart county, Oct. 2, 1818. He married Alabama Owens, daughter of Major James Owens, a veteran of the war of 1812 and native of Virginia. After his marriage he followed farming in Tennessee until 1861, when he removed to White county, Ill., where his wife's parents had gone the preceding year. He bought a farm there and lived there until his death at the age of sixty-five years. His wife died at the age of forty-four. They were both members of the Cumberland Presbyterian church, and he was a Democrat in his political views. Their children were John T., the subject of this sketch; Thomas B., now living in Kansas; Bettie, now Mrs. Stevens, living in Missouri; James R., of Omaha; Charles F., who was captain of a company in the First California regiment in the Philippines and now living in that state; George, in Missouri; Waite, deceased; A. P. and Malinda, twins, both dead. John T. Hogan was educated in the public schools and lived at home until twenty-two years of age, having charge of his father's affairs for some time on account of the latter's ill health. At the age of twenty-two he went to Nevada and California and remained there about three years, then returning to Illinois for a short time. In 1877 he again went to Nevada, where he followed farming and mining until 1880, when he came back to White county, married Martha C., daughter of D. W. and Jane (Riley) Galloway, and located on a farm near Roland. His wife died in 1884 and in 1887 he came to Omaha and engaged in the milling and grain business. Since 1893 he has devoted his attention to the grain business alone. By his first marriage he has two children, Claudia and Harry, both living in Omaha, where the former is a teacher in the public school. In 1890 he was married to Mahala C. Kinsall, a native of Gallatin county, and they have two children, Althea and Harold, both at home. Mr. Hogan has been a prominent figure in Omaha business circles ever since coming to the town. In addition to his grain business he oversees his large farm; was one of the organizers of the Exchange bank, of which he is now vice-president; served six years as supervisor; was president of the board of school trustees for nine years, and is one of the active Democrats of Omaha. He is a prominent member of the Masonic fraternity, being a member of Lodge No. 723, and of Royal Arch Chapter, No. 165. In the lodge he has filled all the offices and is a representative to the Grand Lodge. In Lodge No. 472, Independent Order of Odd Fellows, he has also passed through the chairs and is a representative to the Grand Lodge. He and his wife both belong to the Cumberland Presbyterian church, in which he has been an elder for many years.

JOSEPH DEVOUS, of the firm of Devous & Rice, millers and grain dealers, Ridgway, Ill., is of French descent. In 1814, his grandfather, Isadore Devous, left his native province of Alsace-Lorraine and with his wife and two sons, Jacob and Isadore, came to America. For about a year the family lived at New Orleans, where Jacob died. They then removed to New Albany, Ind., where the grandfather followed the business of contractor and builder for many years, dying at the age of ninety-nine. Isadore Devous, the father of the subject of this sketch, was about two years old when his parents came to America. He remained at home until he was thirteen years of age, when he started in to learn the trade of engineer. After serving his apprenticeship he was for two years an engineer on the *Alva Adams*, a steamboat running between Louisville and New Orleans. He then left the river and for about two years was engaged in peddling goods through the country, then a popular occupation, and one in which there was considerable profit. His next venture was to establish a general store in Brown county, Ohio, which he conducted successfully for four years, when he came down the river to Gallatin county, and engaged in farming near Ridgway. Most of the land that he bought at from 50 cents to $10 an acre is still in the possession of his heirs, and is now worth about $100 an acre. He was a member of the Catholic church, and took an active interest in promoting its worthy charities. While living in Brown county, Ohio, he was married to Catherine Bartell, a native of France, who came with her parents to this country in her childhood. To this union there were born fifteen children, eight of whom are still living. John is in Oklahoma; Joseph is the subject of this sketch; Sebastian, Louis and Charles live on the old home place; Leonia is Mrs. Hish, of Ridgway; Kate married a man named Mossman and lives in White county, Ill.; and Mary is the wife of a Mr. White, of Mount Vernon, Ind. The father of these children lived to the age of eighty-seven years and eight months, and the mother died in her eighty-third year. Joseph Devous was born in Brown county, Ohio, Nov. 12, 1845. Up to the age of eleven years he attended St. Martin's academy there, which constituted his entire schooling. He then worked on the farm until he was twenty-six, when he engaged in farming for himself near his father's place. After five years in this occupation he embarked in the grain business. In 1889 he purchased an interest in the firm of Trusty & McDaniel, proprietors of the Ridgway flour mills, of which Mr. Devous is now the manager. The product of these mills, which is placed on the market under the names of Lily, Snow Bouquet and Red Rose flour, is known all over Southern Illinois, and even in other states. This firm also conducts the elevator at Ridgway and buys most of the grain from the farmers of the surrounding country. Mr. Devous is a Democrat in his political views but is not an active politician. In his religious belief he clings to the faith of his father and belongs to St. Joseph's Catholic church. Of this church he was one of the founders and for twenty-five years he has been at the head of the board of trustees. Besides his interest in the firm of Devous & Rice he owns 500 acres of fine land, several pieces of town property, mining stocks and other investments. In 1872 Mr. Devous was married to Miss Anna Aman, a native of Posey county, Ind., and they had two children: Catherine, now a Mrs. Cirkelbach, of Ridgway, and Mary, wife of John Hansborough of Enfield, Ill. Mrs. Devous died on July 17, 1900, and Mr. Devous was subsequently married to Miss Emma Smith, of East St. Louis. Mrs. Devous is now one of the leading milliners of Ridgway.

DENT REID, dealer in general merchandise, Ridgway, Ill., was born near Saline Mines, in the county where he now lives, Sept. 14, 1860. He is a son of the Rev. Robert and Elizabeth (Campbell) Reid, both natives of Scotland, who came to America on the same ship, and were married some time after their arrival in this country. (See sketch of Rev. Robert Reid, elsewhere in this work.) Dent Reid is the fifth in a family of twelve children. He received a good common school education and up to the time he was twenty-five years of age lived at home with his parents. On Feb. 18, 1885, he was married to Miss Laura Dossett, who was born near Cave in Rock, in Hardin county, where her parents, I. F. and Minerva Dossett, were old settlers. Before his marriage Mr. Reid had been engaged in farming, and he continued to follow that occupation afterward until 1890, when he opened a store at Saline Mines. The venture proved a successful one, and in 1894 he removed to Ridgway, where he enlarged his stock and soon became one of the successful merchants of the place. In his political affiliations Mr. Reid has followed in the footsteps of his honored father, who at one time was one of the only eight Republicans in Gallatin county. His success in business is largely due to that persevering disposition so characteristic of the Scotch people, which he possesses to a marked degree, and to his rugged honesty. He is a member of Ridgway Lodge, No. 816, Free and Accepted Masons, and with his family belongs to the Cumberland Presbyterian church, in which he holds the office of elder. Mr. and Mrs. Reid's children are Robert, Ila D. and Wiley, all at home with their parents.

ROBERT J. BRUCE, a well known citizen of Omaha, Ill., now deputy sheriff of Gallatin county, was born near Norris City, White county, Ill., Jan. 25, 1836. His grandparents, Robert and Sallie (Bantam) Bruce, were natives of Tennessee, were married in that state, came to Gallatin county about 1820, removed soon afterward to White county and there passed the remainder of their lives. Robert Bruce was a cooper by trade, but after settling in White county he followed farming the rest of his life. He was an ardent Democrat in his political views, and both himself and wife were members of the Methodist Episcopal church. He died at the age of seventy-six years and she at the age of seventy-eight. Their three children are all deceased. William M. Bruce, one of the sons of this couple, was born in Tennessee, Nov. 12, 1812. He came to Illinois with his parents and lived with them until his marriage to Sallie Millspaugh, a native of Hamilton county, Ill., after which he lived until 1848 on a farm near Norris City. He then removed to Gallatin county, bought a farm near Omaha, where he and his wife both died some years later. They both lived to a good old age, the father being seventy-six at the time of his death and the mother eighty. Of their six children five are still living. Robert J. is the subject of this sketch; Benjamin F. lives at Ridgway; Margaret J. is now a Mrs. Shaw, of Omaha; Isaac T. is deceased; Solomon S. lives at Omaha; and Sallie is a Mrs. Rollman, of Evansville, Ind. In his day William M. Bruce was a man of prominence in the community where he lived. Soon after his removal to Gallatin county he was elected justice of the peace, an office which he held altogether for twenty-six years. He was active in politics, being one of the leading Democrats of the county, and was eight years judge of the county court. He and his wife were both consistent members of the Methodist Episcopal church. Robert J. Bruce acquired his education in the public schools and lived with his parents until the commencement of the Civil war. On Aug. 15, 1862, he enlisted as a private in Company H, One Hundred and Twentieth Illinois volunteer infantry, and was mustered in at Camp Butler. The regiment was on guard duty at Memphis until April 1, 1863, when it was ordered to Vicksburg and took part in the siege and surrender of that place. After the fall of Vicksburg Mr. Bruce fought with his company at Ripley, Guntown, East Point, Miss., and in numerous minor engagements, being mustered out as second sergeant, Aug. 22, 1865. After the war he returned home and took up the occupations of farming and teaching school. On April 5, 1866, he was married to Miss Hulda C. Campbell, who was born July 10, 1841, in White county, and they located on a farm near Omaha, where they lived until 1898, when he removed to another farm nearer the town, and the following year took up his residence in Omaha, living a retired life with the exception of directing the management of his farm. In 1880 Mr. Bruce was elected sheriff of the county, was re-elected two years later and held the office for four years in all. He was for three years marshal of Omaha, has held other minor offices, and for the last twelve years has been deputy sheriff. Few Democrats in the county are more active in behalf of their party, and in campaigns he is always consulted by the party leaders as to how to win a victory. Mr. Bruce is a member of the Cumberland Presbyterian church and belongs to Lodge No. 423, Free and Accepted Masons, in which he holds the office of tiler. His wife died on Sept. 1, 1902, leaving six children: Oscar F., John T., Otis T., Sarah M., Tillis and Eslie. All are living in Omaha. Sarah married a Mr. Lamb.

REV. ROBERT M. DAVIS, pastor of the Cumberland Presbyterian church of Omaha, Ill., is, in point of service, one of the oldest ministers of the gospel in the United States. He comes of that sturdy Scotch-Irish stock, a mere mention of which suggests courage, perseverance and rugged honesty. About the beginning of the Revolutionary war a Robert Davis, a native of the Emerald Isle, came to America and served under Washington in the struggle for independence. After the war he married a Miss McElroy, a native of North Carolina, settled in Tennessee, where he followed farming all his life, reared a large family, and lived to a good old age. One of his sons, William Davis, was born in North Carolina in 1780, grew to manhood in Tennessee, there married Polly Sebastin, also born in North Carolina, and in 1814 came with his family to Gallatin county, Ill. About a year later they went to White county, where he entered 160 acres of land not far from where Norris City now is, and there lived until 1832. They then returned to Gallatin county, locating on a farm about four miles north of Omaha. In 1834 the family removed to a farm where Omaha now stands, where he died in 1838. The children of William and Polly Davis were Isaac S., Sarah, Margaret, Priscilla, Nancy, Elizabeth, Polly, Robert M., William P., Samuel and Cordelia. Sarah married a Dr. Pearce; Elizabeth married a man named Williams; Polly married a Mr. Riley; William P. lives in Omaha; Cordelia is now a Mrs. Hungate, of McLeansboro, Ill. These with the subject of this sketch constitute the living members of the family, the others all being deceased. In 1824 William Davis entered the ministry of the Cumberland Presbyterian church and continued in the work in connection with his agricultural pursuits until his death on Aug. 25,

1838. The mother removed to White county and lived there until 1860, after which she made her home with her son Robert until her death in 1873. Robert M. Davis was born May 5, 1824, while his parents were living near Norris City. The death of his father left him at the age of fourteen years to not only fight his own way through the world, but to assist his widowed mother in the support of her large family. Under such circumstances his opportunities to attend school were very much restricted, indeed, but with a filial love and fortitude seldom equaled he took up his cross, toiling in the fields by day and in his books by night, the one to secure the physical comforts of life for himself and those dear to him, and the other in quest of knowledge. In October, 1839, Mr. Davis became a member of the Cumberland Presbyterian church during the progress of a camp meeting at Village church, near Omaha. Soon after making a profession of religion he decided to enter the ministry and began studying to that end, farming and teaching in the meantime to support himself and his mother. On Sept. 29, 1843, his candidacy was announced to the church; he was licensed to preach on Sept. 28, 1844, and on March 31, 1849, was ordained to the whole work of the church, his ordination taking place at Hopewell, now Enfield, church in White county. From then until 1852 he preached at various places, assisting in revivals, etc., preparatory to the organization of a church at Omaha. His first effort in this direction was to found a Sunday school in 1850, with John Kinsall as superintendent. On Christmas day, 1852, the church was organized by Mr. Davis, assisted by Revs. John Crawford and Benjamin Bruce. It was first known as "Palestine" church, and since its organization has received into membership about 800 people. The fiftieth anniversary was celebrated with appropriate ceremonies on Dec. 28, 1902, the sermon on that occasion being delivered by H. Clay Yates, D.D. During that entire half century the church had been under the pastoral charge of Mr. Davis and had enjoyed one unbroken era of peace and prosperity. His labors were not confined to this one congregation, however. In 1851 he took charge of the Village church and was its pastor for twenty-six years; has been pastor of Union Ridge church since 1855; organized Oak Grove church in 1860; the church at New Haven in 1868; the church at Hazel Ridge in 1870; supplied the church at Norris City for several years; reorganized the church at McLeansboro in 1876; was pastor there for eight years and built a new house of worship. Through all this long period of labor in the vineyard of the Master he has always been in favor of all the general enterprises of the church, the liberal endowment of the denominational colleges, and has been generous in his contributions to Lincoln college and Milliken university, as well as other colleges. In 1872 Mr. Davis engaged in the merchandizing business as the head of the firm of R. M. Davis & Sons, an establishment that now occupies the best business block in Omaha. But he never permitted his personal interests in this house to interfere with his ministerial duties. Politically he is a Democrat, firm in his convictions, but always considerate for the opinions of others. He holds a dimit as a Master Mason, formerly being a member of Lodge No. 2, of Equality, Ill. At the same time he united with the church Miss Mary, frequently called Polly Sharp, also became a member. She was a daughter of William and Lavina (Mason) Sharp, natives of South Carolina, who came to White county about 1827. Mr. Davis and Miss Sharp were married on Feb. 27, 1844, and moved to his farm, where Omaha is now situated, and remained there ever since. For nearly fifty years they lived together, happy in the companionship of each other. He has said that her noble assistance in his church work was one of the potent sources of his success as a minister. Her death occurred Dec. 13, 1893, and was the greatest bereavement of his life. Of their children, William I., who died a few years ago at Oxford, Miss., was a graduate of Lincoln university, an educator of far more than ordinary ability, and president of Cumberland Presbyterian Female college of Oxford at the time of his death. Millage M. and Samuel M. are members of the firm of R. M. Davis & Sons, of Omaha, and Jennie is the wife of H. P. Blackard, living in the old home with her father. Her husband is one of the leading Masons of Illinois. Mr. Davis is now more than fourscore years of age, and over three-fourths of his long life has been spent in the active work of the ministry. He has spoken words of cheer from the pulpit, christened prattling babes, united fond hearts in the bonds of holy wedlock, and performed the last sad rites over the departed. He is now in good health, preaching at Palestine and Union Ridge churches as the regular installed pastor of each church, having served each one for fifty years or more without intermission. Through his ministrations many have been brought to Christianity, and now in his declining years he can enjoy the happy reflections consequent upon a well spent life, ready for the call of the Master whom he has served so well to enter upon the life eternal.

GEORGE WASHINGTON COMBS, M.D., the oldest physician of Ridgway, Ill., was born about a mile and a half south of that place Feb. 23, 1838. His grandfather, Andrew Combs, was born in Pennsylvania, of German parentage, married in his native state, and at a very early date removed with his family and two brothers to Kentucky. His children were Jesse, Thomas, Priscilla, David and Jonathan. Jesse was a soldier in the war of 1812 and fought at the battle of New Orleans. Both parents died while the children were still young. Jonathan, the youngest of the family, was born in Muhlenberg county, Ky., Feb. 22, 1806. He learned the trade of blacksmith before he was twenty years of age and in 1826 went to Mount Vernon, Ind. After a short stay there he removed to Gallatin county, Ill., where he found employment as blacksmith for the salt works, remaining in that position for about three years. While working at the salt works he was married, and about 1830 he located about a mile and a half south of Ridgway and opened a shop of his own. This was the first blacksmith shop in that neighborhood and for nearly forty years he conducted it, building up a good trade. Soon after the war he went to New Market, where he remained about a year, then he occupied a place near Inman for a similar length of time. In 1871, while on a visit to the subject of this sketch, he was taken suddenly ill and died. His widow continued to live on the old home place until her death. He died in his sixty-sixth year, and she died at the age of sixty-four. Her maiden name was Isavilla Dolan, a daughter of Patrick Dolan, a native of Ireland, and she was born in either Virginia or Tennessee. Jonathan Combs and his wife had eleven children, viz.: Milton, Mary Jane, William, George W., Trenton, Martha, John, Thomas W., Calista E., Alice and Samuel. William lives at Dexter, Mo.; Dr. Combs is at Ridgway; Thomas and Samuel also live at Ridgway; and Calista, now Mrs. F. Drone, lives near Ridgway; Alice is a Mrs. Moore, of California, and the others are deceased. Dr. Combs completed the course of study in the common schools and while still a young man took up the occupation of a teacher, which he followed for about seven years, reading medicine in the meantime. In 1858 he went into the office of Dr. Samuel Garry, near Ridgway, where he remained as a student until the death of his preceptor, when he went to Equality and continued his studies in the office of Dr. Lando Campbell. He then attended the Cincinnati College of Medicine and Surgery for one term in 1866, after which he studied and practiced with Dr. Secord of New Market until 1868, when he practiced in New Market and Ridgway until 1878 and then returned to the college and graduated from that institution in 1879. After receiving his degree he located at Ridgway, where he has ever since practiced his profession, and has won the distinction of being the oldest physician in the county. Besides his professional work Dr. Combs looks after the management of about 300 acres of land. For about three years he was special examiner, and in the course of his long professional career has visited nearly every home within a large radius from Ridgway. He is a Republican in politics, is a member of the Free and Accepted Masons, Lodge No. 816, and for over thirty years has been a member of the Cumberland Presbyterian church, in which he has for a long time held the office of elder. On April 28, 1868, Dr. Combs was married to Miss Hannah, daughter of John F. and Eliza (Glass) Hemphill, of Pope county, and the following are the children born to this union: John M., Mary Jane, Milton H., Fuller, Eliza, Agnes, Anna, Samuel, Ella and George. Fuller is a teacher of Latin and Greek at Helena, Mont.; Agnes is a Mrs. Campbell, residing at Toledo, Ill.; Anna is a Mrs. Gahm at Thompsonville, Ill.; Samuel lives in Gallatin county; Ella and George are at home with their parents, and the others are deceased.

FRANCIS A. GREGG, a farmer and stock dealer of Omaha, Ill., is of Irish ancestry. His grandfather, Hugh Gregg, was born in Ireland and in boyhood started with his parents to America. On the voyage both parents died and upon his arrival in this country, an orphan boy in a strange land, he was compelled to find a home with strangers. He grew to manhood in South Carolina, married there and followed the occupation of a farmer all his life. One of his sons, Francis Gregg, was born in that state, May 28, 1791. Upon arriving at manhood's estate he married Nancy Riley and in 1832 removed to Gallatin county, Ill., settling near Texas City in White county. Of the fourteen children born to Francis and Nancy Gregg but two are now living, the subject of this sketch and his brother John, both residents of Omaha. Their mother died while Francis was still in his boyhood and their father married a Mrs. Sarah Riley, also a native of South Carolina. To this second marriage there were born three children, all now deceased. The father and his second wife both lived to be seventy-five years of age. He was a prosperous farmer, an extensive dealer in live stock, a Democrat in politics, and both himself and wife belonged to the old side Presbyterian church. Francis A. Gregg was born in Newberry county, S. C., April 3, 1829, received his education in the old fashioned subscription schools and grew to manhood on his father's farm. On Feb. 11, 1851, he was married to Nancy Caroline Eubanks, a native of White county, Ill., and commenced farming for himself not far from where his father lived. Some years later he removed to Hamilton county, where he lived for several years, then spent two years in Williamson county, at the end of which time he returned to Gallatin county. In 1876 he removed to his present residence in the edge of the town of Omaha, where he has ever since carried on the business of farming and dealing in stock. Of the seven children born to him and his wife, Franklin K. and Elizabeth Ann are deceased; William E., John L., James, Emma and Eleanora all live in Omaha. Emma married a Mr. Humphries and Eleanora a Mr. Wilson. Mr. Gregg takes an interest in political matters and is one of the stanch Democrats of his township. His wife and daughters belong to the Presbyterian church.

HARVEY P. BLACKARD, proprietor of the Omaha Flour mills, Omaha, Ill., is of Scotch-Irish extraction. (See sketch of Felix G. Blackard for account of ancestry.) His grandfather, Thomas Blackard, was one of five brothers who came from Tennessee to Illinois some time in the decade between 1820 and 1830, where he entered government land near the line between White and Gallatin counties, and there followed farming the remainder of his life. His son Alfred married Polly A., daughter of Jesse and Polly (McGehee) Pierce, and to this union there were born two sons and three daughters. The daughters, Mollie, Sarah and Emma, are all deceased, and the two sons, Alexander H. and the subject of this sketch, both live in Omaha. About 1877 Alfred Blackard removed with his family to Texas, where he died soon after his arrival. The mother returned to Illinois and located on a farm in Gallatin county, where she lived a few years, after which she removed to Omaha, and there she died in 1892. H. P. Blackard attended the district schools in his boyhood and remained at home until the death of his mother, being employed during that time in various occupations. In 1882 he engaged in the grocery business in Omaha and followed that for about two years; was then in the tin and hardware business for a similar length of time; was appointed postmaster at Omaha under Cleveland's first administration, but resigned at the end of two years to become associated with the mercantile firm of R. M. Davis & Sons. In 1893 he purchased the flour mills, which he still conducts, making the well known brands of family flour—Jersey Cream, Kitchen Queen, and Old Times. Mr. Blackard is one of the brightest Masons in Southern Illinois. He is now serving as worshipful master of Omaha Lodge, No. 723, for the fourteenth term, which has made him a representative to the Grand Lodge at Chicago for that number of times, and is a member of Saline Chapter, No. 165, Royal Arch Masons, of Harrisburg. Politically he is a Prohibitionist. In 1892 he was united in marriage to Miss Jennie V., daughter of Rev. Robert M. and Polly (Sharp) Davis, and to this union there have been born five children, three of whom, Leroy, Reece L. and Mansford W., are still living. Mr. and Mrs. Blackard are both members of the Cumberland Presbyterian church, in which he is also a ruling elder.

CAPT. JOHN M. BOWLING, farmer and stock dealer, living four miles northeast of Equality, Ill., was born in Boyd county, Ky., March 4, 1830. His grandfather, William Bowling, was a native of the eastern shore of Maryland, and was of French descent. He married Elizabeth Roman, a native of Virginia, of Scotch extraction, and after his marriage lived in Virginia, where he followed mercantile pursuits all his life. He had two sons, John and James, both of whom were small when their father died. Their mother married again, her second husband being David Hogan, and after their marriage they removed to Kentucky, where John Bowling grew to manhood. Beginning in early life he learned the trade of gunsmith, working at that occupation in connection with farming until 1842, when he started with his family to Missouri, but died before reaching his destination. The widow returned to Kentucky and lived there until her death in 1868. They had six children, viz.: William, James, Elizabeth, John M., Jasper and Mary. The three eldest are dead; Jasper lives near Eldorado, Ill., and Mary is the wife of a Mr. Willis, of Greenup county, Ky. Captain Bowling attended the subscription schools in his boyhood, after which he took a course in Duff's Mercantile college at Pittsburg, Pa., and then attended Washington college, beginning teaching when he was seventeen years of age to get funds to pay for his education. In 1855 he came to Gallatin county, Ill., where for several years he taught in the public schools. In 1858 he removed to the place where he now lives, beginning with ten acres, but now has 554 acres, all under cultivation except about 100 acres. On Aug. 14, 1861, he enlisted in Company E, Third Illinois volunteer cavalry. The regiment was mustered in at Camp Butler and soon afterward was sent to Missouri on scout duty. After the battle of Pea Ridge, Ark., it returned to St. Louis, where it was assigned to provost duty. Mr. Bowling was promoted to second lieutenant on March 2, 1862, and in January, 1863, was sent into Illinois to pick up deserters. When he got to his old home he raised a company, of which he was elected captain, but on account of some irregularity the regiment was not mustered into service and he returned to his old command, with the rank of first lieutenant, to which he had been promoted March 4, 1863. Rejoining his regiment in front of Vicksburg he participated in the siege and surrender of that place, afterward taking part in all the engagements in which his command played a part, among which may be specially mentioned Pea Ridge, Cache River and Cotton Plant, Ark.; Arkansas Post, Grand Gulf, Port Gibson, Magnolia Hill, Jackson, Miss.; Big Black River, second battle of Jackson, and Nashville, Tenn. The regiment was mustered out in 1864, but he, being a veteran, was assigned to duty at Camp Butler, looking after conscripts and substitutes, where he remained until May 23, 1865, before receiving his discharge. Captain Bowling still carries a gold watch that was presented to him by his friends at Camp Butler. After the war he returned to his farm, where he has ever since lived, giving his attention to his agricultural interests and dealing extensively in stock. He is one of the solid Republicans of Gallatin county, and with his family belongs to the Methodist Episcopal church. Captain Bowling has been twice married. His first wife, to whom he was married in 1857, was Miss Mary Ransbottom, a native of Connecticut. Their children were: William H., now living near his father; Flora, now Mrs. Riley, of Ridgway; Julia Ann, a teacher in Chicago; John E., deceased, and Maggie, now Mrs. Donahue, living near Equality. The mother of these children died March 25, 1879, and in February, 1881, he was married to Miranda, daughter of Riley and Mary Ann Bain, one of the old families of Gallatin county. To this marriage there have been born four children: Anna M., John M., Florence B. and Benjamin H., all at home with their parents.

REV. H. C. GREGG, a well known Adventist minister of Eldorado, Ill., is a descendant of one of the oldest families in that section of the state. He is a great-grandson of Hugh Gregg, who came from Ireland in the Colonial days and settled in South Carolina. (See sketch of F. A. Gregg.) His son Francis married Nancy Riley, a native of North Carolina, and in 1832 came to Illinois, traveling by wagon through unbroken forests part of the way. They were the first settlers in the vicinity of the present town of Texas City in Saline county, where he took up government land and followed farming the remainder of his life. He and his wife both lived to be more than threescore and ten years of age. Of their twelve children, Francis and John, now living in Omaha, Ill., are the only survivors. One of the sons, William R. Gregg, was born in 1821, married Elizabeth A. Cork, a native of Equality, Ill., and this couple were the parents of the subject of this sketch. They began their married life near Elba, in Gallatin county, and lived in that neighborhood until the death of William R. Gregg in 1859. Of their six children three are living, viz.: W. T., living near Eldorado; Mary E., now Mrs. Yost of Eldorado, and H. C., the subject. After the death of the father of these children Mrs. Gregg married Alexander G. Trousdale, and since his death has made her home with her children. To her second marriage there were born three children. Only one, John C., of Omaha, is now living. Rev. H. C. Gregg was born in Gallatin county, Sept. 8, 1856. He received a good education in the common schools and the colleges at McLeansboro and Carmi. When eighteen years of age he commenced teaching and followed that occupation for fourteen years. In 1882 he was elected county superintendent of schools and served four years. Mr. Gregg has been somewhat active in political matters, and in 1888 was elected on the Democratic ticket to the legislature, serving one term. On Sept. 14, 1890, he was united in marriage to Miss Eva A. Hopkins, daughter of Dr. N. E. Hopkins, of Mt. Carmel, and in 1894 moved upon his present farm two miles northwest of Elba.

There he has 230 acres, all under cultivation with the exception of forty acres of timber land. He has his farm well improved, devotes much of his time to stock raising, and is one of the prosperous and influential citizens of the community where he lives. In 1899 he took up the work of the ministry in the Adventist church, and now has two congregations under his charge, Union Chapel and Bethel. He was one of the founders of the former church, which stands upon part of his land, and was one of the largest contributors toward building it. Mr. and Mrs. Gregg have the following children: Eleanora H., Hugh C., Raymond R. and Paul Jennings, all at home with their parents.

WILLIAM INMAN, of Ridgway, Ill., one of the best known farmers in Gallatin county, was born in Lawrence county, Tenn., March 30, 1832. He is a son of William and Polly A. (Ware) Inman, both natives of Tennessee. His father was a wheelwright, who did a good business as chairmaker for many years, picking up the trade himself without serving an apprenticeship. In 1847 he removed with his family to Gallatin county, coming by water, and located not far from Ridgway. About eighteen months later he removed to Union county, Ky., where he died about the year 1850. Soon after his death his widow returned to Illinois and died in Gallatin county at the age of sixty-three years. They had twelve children, only two of whom are now living. Thomas and Bartley, the two oldest sons, enlisted for the Mexican war, but saw no active service. William Inman, the son, began working on a farm when a small boy, working for some time for $5 a month. He came to Illinois about six months after his parents, and though but fifteen years of age rented a farm on shares and gave his money to his father and mother. After the death of his father he continued to live with his mother and provided for her and for his younger brothers and sisters. On Sept. 1, 1862, he enlisted in Company E, 131st Illinois infantry. His regiment was with Sherman in the first attack on Vicksburg; was at Arkansas Post; then in the siege of Vicksburg, at the close of which it numbered only 222 men, and was consolidated with the Twenty-ninth Illinois. Mr. Inman was discharged at

Cairo in December, 1864, returned to Ridgway, and became an extensive farmer. Since 1901 he has been a resident of the town of Ridgway. The town of Inman was named for him. On Jan. 19, 1858, Mr. Inman was married to Miss Mary Johnson, a native of West Virginia. Of their children four died young; the others are James, Sarah, William, Mary, Jessie, Susan, Jennie L. and Thomas. The mother of these children died in January, 1887, and in December of the same year he was married to Mrs. Ellen Cox, widow of Isaac Cox and daughter of Medford and Malinda Shockley, of Monroe county, Ky. Two children, Marshall and Albert, were born to the second marriage, but both died in childhood. Mrs. Inman had one daughter by her first marriage, now Mrs. Daniel Desper. Mr. Inman is a member of the Methodist Episcopal church, and belongs to the Grand Army of the Republic post at Ridgway.

EDWARD RICE, grain dealer and miller of Ridgway, Ill., is a native of White county, that state, having been born on a farm near Enfield. When he was twelve years of age his parents removed to Sacramento, in the same county, where he completed the course in the common schools, after which he attended commercial college at Evansville, Ind., where he completed his education. When he was eighteen he commenced clerking in a store at Sacramento, which position he held for seven years. He then went to Enfield as a bookkeeper for two years, at the end of which time he was engaged as bookkeeper by a wholesale house at Omaha, Neb. After two years with this concern he returned to White county, and obtained a situation as bookkeeper at Roland, but about a year later went to Omaha, Ill., as a partner of Thomas Martin in the grain business. This partnership lasted for seven years, or until 1886, when Mr. Rice sold out his interests in Omaha and removed to Ridgway as bookkeeper for W. A. Peopples. Six years later he again engaged in the grain business and has continued in that line ever since. In 1894 he built one of the nicest residences in the town, occupying one entire block. Mr. Rice has been married twice. His first wife, to whom he was married in 1872, was Miss Grace J. Mount. Of their children, Grace E. and Clarence M. are deceased;

the others are Estella F., D. R., Mabel C., Laura E. and Edward H. His first wife died in 1888 and in 1889 he was married to Mrs. Laura Porter, widow of Capt. D. M. Porter and a sister to his first wife. Mr. Rice is a Republican in his political affiliations, is a prominent member of the Masonic lodge at Ridgway and a trustee in the Methodist Episcopal church.

WILLIAM J. SANDERS, farmer and stock raiser, living two miles southwest of Cottonwood, Ill., was born Feb. 11, 1850, on the exact spot where his house now stands. His great-grandfather was a native of England, who came to this country before the Revolutionary war and settled in North Carolina, where he reared a large family. He and his son, James, the grandfather of the subject of this sketch, both served in the war of 1812. James Sanders married in North Carolina and soon afterward removed to Tennessee, where he followed farming and stock raising until 1821, when he brought his family to Gallatin county, Ill., and entered government land, not far from the site of the present town of Cottonwood, upon which he lived until his death at the age of eighty-four years. One of his sons was Eli Sanders, who was born on Christmas day in 1810. He came with his parents to Illinois and continued to live with them until 1836, when he married Nancy J. McGill, a native of Tennessee, and they began their married life on the farm where William J. Sanders now lives. Eli Sanders was the first to enter land having a black soil. He became a very successful farmer and at one time was one of the largest land owners in the vicinity of Cottonwood. Then he made a venture in merchandizing that proved disastrous, bringing him to the verge of bankruptcy. He died on Oct. 29, 1884, his wife having passed to her last rest on Sept. 2, 1876. During their lives they were active in church work and were known far and wide for their charity and hospitality. They had twelve children. Those living are Mary Ann, widow of David Rogers; Margaret J., now Mrs. Hale of Cottonwood; Juda, now Mrs. Millspaugh; Frank N. and William J. William J. Sanders received his education in the public schools and lived at home until he was thirty-two years old. He was married at the age of twenty-two to Miss Ann, daughter of Miro and Jemima Harrington, and a native of Gallatin county. They commenced housekeeping on the old home place, where they have lived ever since. Mr. Sanders is one of the foremost farmers in his neighborhood, and takes an active interest in public affairs. He makes a specialty of Poland-

China hogs and Jersey and Hereford cattle. His farm consists of 200 acres, all under cultivation and well improved, the new improvements having been made by him to take the place of the old buildings erected by his father some years before. He and his wife are both members of the Cumberland Presbyterian church, in which he has been an elder for twenty-five years. Their children are Stella, now Mrs. Holland, living in the neighborhood; Claudie, married and living on the home place; Vernon and Cyrus, who are still at home.

FRANK N. SANDERS, a well-to-do and popular farmer, living near Cottonwood, Ill., was born in the vicinity where he now resides Feb. 15, 1850. He received his education in the common schools, married Jemima McGhee, daughter of D. W. and Polly McGhee, who were natives of Tennessee. At the time of his marriage Mr. Sanders was only about twenty years of age. They began their married life on the old home place, but three years later he bought a sixty-acre tract where he now lives, only about six or seven acres being under cultivation, built a hewed log house, and removed to his new home. Since then he has prospered by his industry, owning at the present time about 140 acres, all of which is under cultivation, and has a modern house, together with other good improvements on his farm. He carries on a general farming business and devotes considerable time and attention to stock raising. Mr. Sanders is one of the leading Democrats in his locality and has held some of the minor offices in the township. For several generations his ancestors have been affiliated with the Democratic party. The following named children have been born to Mr. and Mrs. Sanders: Lowry A., deceased; William S., a teacher, and lives at home with his parents; Hezekiah, a teacher in White county; Evolia J., deceased; Carrie B., now Mrs. Holland, living near Cottonwood; Lillie R., wife of a Mr. McDonald, of Arkansas; Ratie May, now Mrs. Clark, living in Missouri; Lulu, Annie, Roscoe and Luther are at home. Ever since they were fifteen years of age Mr. Sanders and his wife have been members of the Cumberland Presbyterian church and interested in promoting its good works.

HENRY M. BEAN, a prominent farmer living near Ridgway, Ill., was born on a farm adjoining that town, March 13, 1850, his parents being Henry and Margaret (Hise) Bean. (For account of ancestry see sketch of James M. Bean.) Henry M. Bean received all the schooling he ever got before he was ten years of age. Since then he has by his own efforts managed to secure as good an education as that of the average man. He grew to manhood on the place where he was born, the old house still standing, but not being occupied. On March 13, 1870, he was married to Miss Jemima Kimbrough, a native of Gallatin county and a daughter of Calvin and Nancy Kimbrough, both natives of Tennessee. Mr. and Mrs. Bean began their married life on the old home place and lived there until 1902, when he built a modern, up-to-date home near the old one but inside the corporate limits of the town of Ridgway. Mr. Bean was supervisor for two years, and was for a long time a member of the school board. His farm at the present time consists of over 300 acres of fine land, all under cultivation, which he manages and oversees, making a specialty of Hereford cattle and Poland-China hogs. He is regarded as one of the best and most progressive farmers in the county, and consequently is one of the most prosperous. In addition to his farming interests he has for twenty years been one of the leading threshermen of Southern Illinois. He and his wife are both members of the Cumberland Presbyterian church. Their children are: George L., living near Ridgway; Laura, now Mrs. Fulkerson, of Beechwood, Ill.; Charles, Marshall H. and Stella, at home with their parents.

JONATHAN DILLARD, a farmer living near Ridgway, Ill., is a descendant of one of the first settlers in that section of the state. About the time of the Revolutionary war Elisha Dillard, the grandfather of Jonathan, came from Ireland and settled in Tennessee, where he followed farming for many years. His son, Olsten Dillard, served in the war of 1812 and fought at the battle of New Orleans, where he was severely wounded, carrying the ball to his grave. He married Eva Crumb, a native of Germany, and in 1817 came to Gallatin county, Ill., where he entered a tract of government land. The following year his family joined him, coming with the Houstons, Eddys, Hutchinsons and others. Olsten Dillard built a log cabin and cleared part of his land. In 1826 he sold that place and bought another in White Oak township, where he lived until 1842, when he removed with his family to Missouri, and died there some years later. The children of Olsten and Eva Dillard were ten in number, only four of whom are now living. James lives in Shawneetown; Betsey is the widow of Jacob B. Hise and lives at Ridgway; Mary is the widow of Elijah Yates and also lives at Ridgway, and Jonathan is the subject of this sketch. Jonathan Dillard is one of the oldest men in the county. He was born three miles southwest of Shawneetown March 15, 1824, and has lived his whole life in Gallatin county. When he was a small boy his mother died and his father married Anna Crumb, a sister of his first wife. To this marriage there were born several children, all of whom are now dead. Jonathan Dillard never went to school a day in his life, but by associating with educated people he has kept in touch with the doings of the world and is a well informed man. He lived with his parents until he was about sixteen years old, when he started in life for himself, working on farms and for five years was engaged in flatboating to St. Louis. In 1849 he came back to Gallatin county, married Roxana Boutwell, a native of the county, and commenced housekeeping on John Richeson's place. He continued to live on rented land until 1856, when he bought eighty acres, all wild land, where he now lives. This he has added to until he now has a farm of 160 acres, all good land, of which over 100 acres are under cultivation. This development has all been made by the labor of Mr. Dillard himself, who has been noted all his life for his industrious habits. Beginning life in a humble log cabin in the true pioneer style, he has kept up with the march of progress, improving his farm with better buildings as time passed. Mr. Dillard is one of the active Democrats of his neighborhood, notwithstanding his age. For four years he was road supervisor, which is the only office he has ever sought or held. For thirty-two years he has been an active worker in the Presbyterian church, to which his wife also belongs. He has been twice married. After the death of his first wife he was united in marriage to Dicey Ann Harris, a native of Tennessee, who came with her father, Matthew Harris, to Illinois in 1863. To his first marriage there were born eleven children, viz.: Milbrey, Martha E., Celia, Mary, Elisha, Famariah, Albert, Jonathan, Eva, William and Harriet. Milbrey, Eva and William live in Missouri; Elisha and Harriet live near Ridgway; Jonathan is at home, and all the others are deceased. To his second marriage there were born: Viola, Fannie, Eliza, Jemima, Matthew and Aaron. Fannie married a man named Rambler and now lives with her parents; Jemima is in Missouri; Matthew and Aaron are at home, and Viola and Eliza are deceased. Mr. Dillard has passed the fourscore mark in age, and although he has reached that age when many men grow childish he still retains his faculties, remembering with vivid distinctness incidents that occurred three-quarters of a century ago. He is a popular man in his locality for his genial disposition and many sterling qualities, and "Uncle Jonathan Dillard," as he is familiarly called, is a welcome visitor in many homes.

FREDERICK NAAS, a farmer living one and a half miles west of Ridgway, Ill., was born near St. Wendell's in Vanderburg county, Ind., May 10, 1852. He is a son of Frederick and Malinda (Weiss) Naas, both natives of Germany, where the father was born in 1817. When he was about ten years of age, or in 1827, he came with his father, Jacob Naas, to America and settled in Posey county, Ind., where Jacob Naas took up government land and followed farming the rest of his life. His four children, Fred, Christ, Jacob and Sally, are all deceased. Jacob Naas lived to be ninety-two years old, and his wife died at the age of seventy. Frederick Naas, the father of the subject of this sketch, lived with his parents until after his marriage, when he went to farming in Vanderburg county. In 1860 he removed to Gibson county, Ind. When the war broke out he enlisted in the Union army and was killed at the battle of Shiloh. Of their ten children four are now living. Mary is a Mrs. Wormit of Evansville, Ind.; Joseph lives in Poseyville in that state; Peter still lives in Gibson county, and Frederick is the subject of this sketch. After the war Mrs. Naas married again, her second husband being Leonard Cole, and they lived in Gibson county the rest of their lives. Fred. Naas attended the public schools in his boyhood, and at the age of sixteen years started in to learn the blacksmith trade. He worked at this occupation for eight or nine years, at the end of which time he became a farmer in Vanderburg county. In 1884 he bought a farm near Omaha, in Gallatin county, Ill., and lived there until he purchased his present place of 232 acres near Ridgway. Mr. Naas has spent considerable time and money in improving his farm since it came into his possession, and has one of the best dwellings in the neighborhood—a comfortable two-story frame house, with all conveniences usually found in the homes of the most progressive farmers. In 1874 he was married to Barbara Wormit, of Gibson county, and they have the following children: George, Emil, Mary, Fritz, Edward, Barbara, John, William, Katie and Maggie. George is in Evansville; Mary is married and lives near her parents; Maggie is dead, and the others are all at home. The family all belong to the Catholic church.

CAPT. WILLIAM HENRY STILES of Ridgway, Ill., was born at Windsor, Conn., on Oct. 22, 1828. His ancestry dates back to John Stiles, who was born in Bedfordshire, England, Dec. 25, 1595, and who came to America in 1635, settling at Windsor, Conn., where he died on June 4, 1662. John Stiles had a son, John, who was born in 1633 and died at Windsor, Conn., Dec. 8, 1683. He was married to Dorcas, a daughter of Henry Burt, of Springfield, Conn., and they had a son, John, who was born at Windsor on Dec. 10, 1663. This son died at New Haven, Conn., on May 20, 1753. His wife was a Miss Ruth Bancroft, of Westfield, Mass., who died at Windsor in 1714. To this union was born, at Windsor, on July 30, 1697, Isaac Stiles, who was twice married, his second wife being Ester Hooker of Farmington, Conn. She died at North Haven on Jan. 2, 1779. Isaac was a minister and was educated at Yale university, where he graduated with the degree of B.A. in 1722 and A.M. in 1725. The union of the Rev. Isaac Stiles and Ester Hooker was blessed with a son, Ashbel, who was born at North Haven on Aug. 30, 1734, and died at Norwich, Mass., in October, 1810. Ashbel Stiles married his cousin, Hannah Stiles, who died at Norwich in September, 1810. They had a son, Job, who was born on Jan. 12, 1765, and died at Windsor April 15, 1813. He married Mary Drake of Windsor, who died on March 16, 1839. Their son, Hylas, was born at Windsor, June 11, 1793, and married Harriet L. Roberts, of Sandersdale, Mass. To this union was born a son, William Henry, the subject of this sketch. Hylas Stiles removed with his family to Cleveland, O., and later to Lancaster in the same state, where Captain Stiles received his education, numbering among his schoolmates Gen. William T. Sherman and Gen. Phil Sheridan. While still a young man, Captain Stiles moved to Cincinnati, and later to New Market, Gallatin county, Ill., in which county he has since resided, following successfully the occupation of farming. He now lives at Ridgway in that county. Captain Stiles was married at New Boston, Ohio, on Aug. 8, 1847, to Catherine Smith, of Owensville, Ohio, and they had the following children: Harriet Louise, born Oct. 6, 1848; William Andrew, born Jan. 6, 1850; Mary E., born Dec. 7, 1851; Catherine M., born Oct. 10, 1853; Hylas C., born Aug. 27, 1855; Joseph F., born July 27, 1858; John D., born May 26, 1861; Theoba J., born Dec. 11, 1863; George Trafton, born Jan. 6, 1866; Laura E., born Jan. 26, 1868; Edwin L., born Nov. 11, 1870; and Adaline, born May 3, 1874. His wife died on May 27, 1881, and he was again married on Sept. 1, 1884, his second wife being Julia A. Fulks of New Market. To this union was born one child, Clemma L., born June 13, 1885. At the outbreak of the Civil war Captain Stiles enlisted from Gallatin county, on Aug. 12, 1861, and was mustered into the service on Sept. 13, at Camp Butler, Ill., as second lieutenant of Capt. George W. Trafton's company, G, Seventh regiment Illinois volunteer cavalry, Col. William Pitt Kellogg commanding. In the latter part of October, 1861, the regiment was ordered to Birds Point, Mo., and in January, 1862, moved to Cape Girardeau, where it performed scout and guard duty until the following spring. At New Madrid, Mo., the regiment was recruited, forming a part of Hatch's division, Army of the West, and participated in the following engagements: New Madrid, Mo.; Island No. 10, Farmington, siege of Corinth, Iuka, battle of Corinth, Summersville, pursuit of Price, Coffeeville, Miss.; Grierson's raid, Plains store, Port Hudson, La.; Byhalia Road, Miss; Moscow, Campbellsville, Harts Crossroads, Franklin, Brentwood Hills, the routing of Hood's army at Nashville, Tenn., and numerous scouting expeditions and raids. At the close of the war the regiment received its final muster out at Camp Butler. Captain Trafton having been promoted to major, Second Lieutenant Stiles, by petition from the entire company, was promoted to captain and was mustered in with that rank on Nov. 8, 1863. He received honorable discharge at Springfield, Ill., Oct. 15, 1864, his term of service having expired. He was wounded by gunshot in the right thigh and by a piece of shell in the right ankle on Dec. 3, 1863, and was confined to the hospital for one month. He was also injured in the engagement at Colliersville, Tenn., Nov. 3, 1863, causing the loss of hearing in his left ear. He was at all times with his command, participating in all its engagements, and by gallant and meritorious service he achieved a proud record for bravery and proficiency in action. Captain Stiles is a member of and past post commander of R. Loomis Post, No. 583, Department of Illinois, Grand Army of the Republic; also member of the American Protective association. Although past seventy-five years of age, the captain is hale and hearty and active for one of his years.

WILLIAM G. EDWARDS, a farmer living about two and a half miles south of Omaha, Ill., was born on the farm where he now lives, Sept. 8, 1867, his parents being Leonard and Sarah L. (Abney) Edwards, old settlers of Gallatin county. (See sketch of Leonard Edwards elsewhere in this work.) William G. Edwards was educated in the public schools, and about the time he attained his majority was married to Miss Martha Garrett. She died in 1891 and he subsequently married Miss Lida Robb, a native of Indiana. Mr. Edwards owns 192 acres of fine land, all under cultivation except about four acres. He has lived upon his farm practically all his life, and the improvements, which are equal to those of any farm in the neighborhood, were all made by himself. As a farmer and stock raiser few men have a better reputation, or know more about the business. He takes a lively interest in public affairs and is one of the leading Democrats in his township, but has never been a candidate for office. In religious matters he is a consistent member of the Presbyterian church, and carries the tenets of his faith into his daily life. He has three children, Luther, Eval and Hurtis, living at home, and one deceased. Mr. and Mrs. Edwards are both popular in the neighborhood where they reside, their home being noted for its hospitality and good cheer.

JOHN GRUMLEY, one of the best known and most popular farmers in the neighborhood of Ridgway, Ill., was born near Hopkinsville, Ky., Oct. 16, 1853, his parents being John and Mary (Jeffreys) Grumley. The father was killed in 1855 by the falling of a branch from a tree he was chopping down, and some years later the mother married a man named Posey Cisney and removed to Hamilton county, Ill. After a short stay there they returned to Kentucky, where Mr. Cisney died and the mother married a third time, her third husband being John D. Latham. They now live near Elkton, Todd county, Ky. Two children were born to John and Mary Grumley: Melissa, now a Mrs. Kelley, living in Kentucky, and the subject of this sketch. Shortly after his father's death John

Grumley was bound out to a Kentucky family by the name of Muckelwagner, with whom he lived until he was about nine years of age, when he started out to seek his fortune in his own way. He first went to Posey county, Ind., where he worked on a farm until he attained his majority. In 1872 he was married to Parthena Miller, a native of that county. She died in 1874, leaving one child, and he married Mary J. Mills, also a Posey county girl, and lived there until 1876, when he removed to Gallatin county, Ill., and bought eighty acres, three and a half miles northeast of Ridgway, most of which was in an uncultivated state. With an energy and ambition worthy of the highest emulation he went to work, and from the first prospered. He now owns 180 acres, all under cultivation with the exception of about ten acres. As a farmer and stock raiser he is well known throughout the county as one of the most progressive and methodical of men. Mr. Grumley takes some interest in politics and is one of the solid Democrats of his township. He belongs to the Independent Order of Odd Fellows, Lodge No. 843, of Ridgway, and to the Court of Honor. In religious matters he is a member of the regular Baptist church, and for several years he has been one of the directors of the public schools. To his second marriage there have been born the following children: Roseander, now living in Saline county; Lura, now a Mrs. Rister, of Gallatin county, and Amelia, at home.

WILLIAM J. ZIRKELBACH, a farmer and stock raiser near Ridgway, Ill., is a son of Andrew and Katherine (Leutzhuick) Zirkelbach, both natives of Germany, the former of Bavaria and the latter of Prussia. Andrew Zirkelbach was born June 24, 1827, came with his parents to America when he was about ten years of age, settled in Vanderburg county, Ind., where the father carried on farming until his death at the age of seventy-five years. Before coming to this country he followed the trade of baker, but never worked at it after. His wife came with her parents about the same time. They were married in Vanderburg county and lived on the same farm, near St. James, for about thirty-five years. She lived to be eighty-seven years old. Of their children, William J., Andrew, George, Frank and Lena live in Gallatin county, Ill.; Rachel, Mary, Maggie and Peter live in Evansville, Ind.; Barbara, Mena and Mathias are deceased. Andrew Zirkelbach was always somewhat active in political affairs and was one of the prominent Democrats in his neighborhood. His children were all brought up in the Catholic faith, of which church both himself and wife were members. William J. Zirkelbach was born in Vanderburg county, Nov. 14, 1854. He was educated in the parochial and district schools and lived with his parents until his marriage to Anna K. Wencel of Vanderburg county. They continued to live in that county until 1885, when they removed to Gallatin county, locating on a farm, which Mr. Zirkelbach bought, near Ridgway. For sixteen years he lived on this place, one year of that time being engaged in mercantile pursuits in Ridgway. In 1901 he sold the farm and bought his present place, three-fourths of a mile west of Ridgway, where he has a well improved farm of eighty acres, upon which he carries on a general farming business, devoting much of his time to breeding Aberdeen and Polled Angus cattle. Like his father before him, he is a Democrat and a Catholic, and takes an interest in both political and church matters. The children born to William J. and Anna K. Zirkelbach are Andrew, George, Cecilia and Katherine, living in the vicinity of Ridgway; Josie, William M., Eleanora and Rudolph, at home, and one who died in infancy.

LEONARD EDWARDS, farmer and stock dealer, living near Omaha, Ill., was born in the State of Tennessee, Nov. 25, 1836, while his parents, Lorenzo and Eliza (Broughton) Edwards, were visiting relatives and friends there, though they were at the time citizens of Gallatin county, Ill. Charles Edwards, the grandfather of Leonard, came to Southern Illinois at a very early date. There Lorenzo grew to manhood, married and commenced housekeeping in a little log cabin of the primitive type on the forty acres now owned by Mrs. M. C. Daniel. Later a larger cabin of one room was erected, and it is still standing. Lorenzo Edwards died at the age of forty-eight years, and his wife survived until 1898, when she died at the advanced age of nearly ninety. Their seven sons and two daughters all lived to be married and reared families. Charles now lives in Saline county; Jeremiah lives at Omaha; William lives in Calhoun county; Washington died in 1899; Leonard is the subject of this sketch; Milton is in Arkansas; John is a resident of Gallatin county; Jane is the widow of C. R. Williams; and Harriet is the widow of Curtis Rowe. Leonard Edwards grew to manhood in Gallatin county. In 1862 he enlisted as a private in Company B, First Illinois volunteer cavalry, and served about seven and a half months in Missouri, when he was mustered out as first sergeant of the company. After being discharged from the army he married Miss Sarah L. Abney, and to this union there were born the following children: M. H., now living in Hamilton county, Ill.; William J., a farmer near Omaha (see sketch); Josie, wife of a Mr. Lawson, of Gallatin county; James, living in the same county; and Annie, wife of Archibald Yinn, of Hot Springs, Ark. After the death of the mother of these children, Mr. Edwards married Mrs. Jane Foster, widow of John Foster. She had five children by her first husband, viz.: Sarah, wife of W. W. McReynolds; Alpha, wife of Noah Van Bibber; Charles, William and George. Mr. Edwards is one of the active Democrats of his township, and with his family belongs to the Cumberland Presbyterian church.

RICHARD M. HOLLAND, a well known farmer of Gallatin county, Ill., living near the town of Omaha, was born Oct. 13, 1841, near Bowling Green, Warren county, Ky., his parents being Hezekiah and Sarah (Poole) Holland. Hezekiah Holland served in the Mexican war and in 1849 came with his family to Gallatin county, located about a mile and a half southwest of Cottonwood, where he built a log cabin twenty by twenty-four feet, on the place where Bennett Murphy now lives, and died there in 1853. After his death his widow married James Brockett and lived to be sixty years old. The children of Hezekiah and Sarah Holland were Thomas, Richard M., Shandy, Lambert P., James, George, Andrew, John, Sarah, Zachary and Josephus. Thomas lives in Norris City; Richard is the subject of this sketch; Shandy lives in Asbury township; Lambert lives at Omaha, and the others are deceased. Five of these brothers—Thomas, Zachary, John, Lambert and Shandy—enlisted at the beginning of the Civil war and served until the close, taking part in numerous engagements. At the age of eighteen years Richard M. Holland began working for the neighboring farmers at $13 a month. He then rented land on shares for two years. In 1862 he was married to Miss Tempy Sanders, and on October 9th of that year removed to the place where he still lives. His wife died July 20, 1868, leaving two children: Sidora J., wife of Lewis Murphy, and Parnesa A., who died in 1870. On July 21, 1872, he was married to Miss Martha J. Hargrove, and to this union there were born four children: Annie B., Alonzo, and two who died in infancy. After the death of his second wife, he was married a third time, his last wife being Miss Sarah A. Pruitt, to whom he was married on Oct. 10, 1878. To this marriage there has been born one son, Lee A. Mr. Holland has been successful in his farm life. Beginning with forty acres, on which stood a log cabin, he has gradually added to his farm until he is today one of the prosperous men of the community in which he lives. He is a stanch Democrat in his political views, and in 1891 assessed the property of his township. He is a member of the Cumberland Presbyterian church, and takes an interest in church work.

JOHN C. ANDERSON, a farmer and stock dealer, living near Omaha, Ill., is a descendant of one of the oldest families in that portion of the Lower Ohio Valley. His grandfather, Solomon Anderson, was born in South Carolina, Feb. 8, 1806, his parents being James and Polly Anderson. On May 5, 1830, Solomon Anderson was married to Margaret Williams of Kentucky, she being at the time of her marriage but fifteen years of age, and soon afterward settled in Posey county, Ind., on the site of the village of old Springfield. There he followed the occupations of farming and shoemaking, and achieved quite a reputation as a hunter and trapper. The children of Solomon and Margaret Anderson were William N., Urbane, Asa C., Nancy, Martha, Margaret, Mary E., John and Elias. William N. was born Sept. 2, 1831, and died Dec. 26, 1857. He married Mary A. Rusher, daughter of Jerry Rusher, who came from North Carolina in pioneer days and settled in Posey county. This couple were the parents of John C. Anderson, the subject of this sketch, who was born in White county, Ill., Dec. 20, 1854. When he was but three weeks old his parents removed to Posey county, and there he grew to manhood on his father's farm. At the age of twenty-one years he started out for himself. On Sept. 6, 1877, he was married to Miss Hannah Downen and in October came to Gallatin county, locating on the farm where he now lives, only thirty acres of which was at that time under cultivation. For two and a half years he lived in a log cabin, when he built a better house, and by his own industry he has cleared 125 acres of land, leaving only about twelve or thirteen acres of his farm that is not now under cultivation. Mr. Anderson buys and ships a great deal of live stock, most of which is shipped from Omaha. He has followed this business in addition to his farming interests for about fourteen years, and has been very successful as a stock dealer. He is a member of the Ancient Order of United Workmen and in politics is independent, voting for the man rather than for the candidate of any particular party. He and his wife have the following children: William L., Bertha, Stella M., Julia H., Mary A., Dora and Audrey.

THOMAS H. GLASSCOCK, a farmer living near Omaha, Ill., was born in that county, March 26, 1845, on the site of the present village of Cottonwood, and has passed his whole life within two miles of his birthplace. His father, John J. Glasscock, was born in Virginia, but left that state in boyhood, removing with his parents first to Ohio and then to Gallatin county, Ill., being about nineteen years old when the family settled on the ground where William Wilson now lives. Both the grandfathers of Thomas H. Glasscock fought in the Black Hawk war and lived to be very old men. John J. Glasscock married Elizabeth Newman, and to this marriage were born the following children: Thomas H.; Jane, widow of James Bailey; Patsey, and John. In 1862 the father of these children enlisted as a private in Company D, Twenty-ninth Illinois volunteer infantry, and took part in all the battles and skirmishes in which his command participated, serving until the close of the war. He and his wife were both members of the Methodist Episcopal church. Thomas H. Glasscock acquired his education in the old-fashioned log schoolhouse, with slab benches, puncheon floor, huge fireplace and only one window. Even to attend this school he was compelled to walk a mile and a half. His first teacher was a Mr. Dalton. In 1865 he was married to Harriet Bryant, and to this union were born two children, James L. and John W. The former is deceased and the latter now lives near his father. Mrs. Glasscock died in 1869, and he subsequently married Miss Arminda Gwaltney. They have had three children: Clarence (deceased), Elma and Henry. Mr. Glasscock owns 140 acres of fine land, all in a high state of cultivation and well improved. Politically he is a Republican, one of the kind who is always true to his convictions, though he has many personal friends of the opposite political faith. He is a member and one of the trustees of the Cumberland Presbyterian church, in which he has held the office of deacon the greater part of the time since 1863.

AMARIAH GWALTNEY, a well known farmer and stock raiser, living near Omaha, Ill., was born Sept. 24, 1848, near Stewartsville, Posey county, Ind. His grandfather, John Gwaltney, was a native of England, but was banished from that country for picking up an apple under a tree that belonged to one of the nobility. In the course of time he settled in Posey county, where he became a well-to-do farmer. One of his sons, Amariah, was born Feb. 9, 1804, married Sarah Reeder July 24, 1828, and became one of the largest land-owners in the neighborhood where he lived. At the time of his death, July 7, 1848, he left his widow 600 acres, upon which she lived until her death, Oct. 17, 1867. Their children were John, Eliza, Elizabeth, Jeremiah, Anna, Emaline, Fanny, Marinda, Simon, Josephus, Adijah, Arminda and Amariah. Amariah, the youngest of the family and the subject of this sketch, received a good education in his youth by attending the common schools and the Fort Branch academy. After his father's death he continued to live with his mother the remainder of her life. When she died he attended school for three winters, working on the farm in the summer time, and then commenced teaching. For three years he taught in the common schools. In the spring of 1872 he came to Gallatin county, and on August 22 of that year was married to Miss Mary E., daughter of Solomon Anderson. Soon after his marriage Mr. Gwaltney located in Ridgway township, where he bought eighty acres adjoining his present farm. Part of the tract was improved and a log cabin stood on the place. Here he and his wife lived for two years, when he sold out and bought the farm now occupied by J. B. Hale. Twelve years later he traded that farm for the one he now owns. When he took possession of this farm the improvements amounted to almost nothing, but by his industry and good management he has now one of the best improved farms in the county. Mr. Gwaltney is a Democrat in his political affiliations, takes an active interest in public affairs, and for two years served as justice of the peace. He and his wife both belong to the Primitive Baptist church. They have one daughter, Elsie, now the wife of Benjamin Kinsall.

REV. ROBERT REID, a retired Presbyterian minister, living at Saline Mines, Ill., is a native of Scotland, having been born at Paisley, Nov. 6, 1822. His father, whose name was also Robert, was born in 1799. In early life he was for a time engaged in the manufacture of shawls for which Paisley is noted all over the world, but the greater part of his life he followed the occupation of mining. He married Ann Wiley and in 1839 they left Scotland for America. They first settled in Nova Scotia, where they lived until 1842, when they came to the United States. They lived in Pennsylvania until 1850, then removed to Maryland, where the father died and the widow came with her family soon afterward to Gallatin county, Ill. Of their ten children Anna and the subject of this sketch, both living at Saline Mines, are the only survivors. Rev. Robert Reid received the greater part of his schooling in the common schools of his native land. At the age of twenty-eight he married Elizabeth Campbell, a native of Scotland, who came over on the same ship with him in 1839, being at that time but eight years of age, and afterward removing to Maryland about the same time he did. They began their wedded life at Minersville, Pa., where he was employed in the mines. Later they removed to Maryland, and in 1854 to Gallatin county. Mr. Reid took charge of the mines for the Saline Coal Company, and settled at Saline Mines, in which locality he has ever since lived. He continued as superintendent of the mines until 1859, when he engaged in mercantile pursuits. This business he carried on for about fifteen years, though he was also interested in mining operations most of the time, either in connection with the Saline Coal Company or the Martha Iron and Furnace Company, of Gallatin and Hardin counties. He is still associated with the Saline Coal Company. In addition to his interests in the mines he owns about 160 acres of land near Saline Mines, which for years he has managed. In 1856 he took up the work of the ministry, having been an elder in the Presbyterian church for some time previously, and since 1884 he has devoted most of his time to the church, preaching at Equality, Harrisburg, Saline Mines and for other churches. Mr. Reid is a Republican in politics, and in his earlier years took an active interest in public affairs. He has served as justice of the peace and has been identified with many movements for the upbuilding of the community in which he lives. He and his wife had the following children: Agnes, now Mrs. Hamilton, of Victor, Col.; Wiley, living at Carbondale, Ill.; Walter, who lives at Danville in the same state; George, deceased; Dent (see sketch); Thomas, now in Oklahoma; Bessie, at home; May (deceased); Millie, now Mrs. Wiederhold, of Gallatin county; Clara, at home; William (deceased); Robert (deceased). The mother of these children died in January, 1894. In the spring of 1904 Mr. Reid met with an accident that disabled him to such an extent that he has been compelled to forego the active work of the ministry, though he still preaches at times. He has a large circle of acquaintances, with all of whom he is popular, and who esteem him for his many good qualities of both mind and heart.

JOSIAH McCUE, a farmer living five miles southwest of Shawneetown, Ill., was born near Saline Mines, in the same county, Oct. 2, 1859. His grandfather, John McCue, was a native of Ireland, a collier by occupation, who came to the United States in his early manhood, located in Marion county, O., where he married and continued to reside until 1844, when he came to Gallatin county and located near Saline Mines. There he was employed in the mines until his death. He and his wife had four children, none of whom are now living. One of the sons, John Y. McCue, was born in Marion county in 1838, and was six years of age when his parents came to Illinois. His mother died when he was twelve years of age, and for the next three years he made his home with an uncle, after which he went to work in the mines and continued in that occupation for about four years. Toward the close of the Civil war he enlisted in the Union army, but never got any further than Shawneetown, where he was when the news came that Lee had surrendered and the war was over. When he was about nineteen years old he was married to Nancy Marble, a native of Tennessee, and from that time until his death followed farming in the neighborhood of Saline Mines. They had four children: John W. (deceased); Josiah, the subject of this sketch; Sarah, a Mrs. Oxford, of Hardin county; and Mary A., now Mrs. Hill, also living in Hardin county. The mother of these children died in 1867, and the father married Martha Kendrick. To this union there were born three children: Y. Y., in St. Louis; Rachel Robinson, at home; and Mattie (deceased). Josiah McCue received his education in the common schools, and at the age of twenty years began farming on his own account on his father's farm. In 1886 he bought a place of 157 acres, where he now lives. This he has added to until he now owns 275 acres, all under cultivation and well improved. Mr. McCue, like his father before him, takes some interest in politics, and has been elected on the Democratic ticket to some of the township offices. He belongs to the Farmers' Social and Economic Union. In 1881 he was married to Elizabeth Shaffer, a native of Evansville, Ind., and their children are: Joseph A., Clara, George, Katie, Bessie, Raymond, Rachel, Frankie and John. Joseph is in St. Louis, Clara married a Mr. White and lives in the neighborhood, and the others are at home.

JOHN W. HARRINGTON, a farmer living near Omaha, Ill., was born Feb. 4, 1859, on the farm adjoining the one on which he now lives. His father, Miro Harrington, was a native of Long Island, N. Y., where he was born in 1813. When he was a boy his parents removed to Ohio, locating near Gallipolis, where he grew to manhood and married Jemima Irion in the year 1840. For a number of years he followed boating to New Orleans and in 1857 he removed to Illinois, lived one year in Hardin county, and then came to Gallatin county. He bought 140 acres in what is now Ridgway township, the tract of land now being occupied by his daughter, Mrs. William Rogers. At the time he bought it there was a log cabin on the place and about forty acres cleared. He died on that farm in 1881, aged sixty-seven years. His wife survived until 1897, when she died at the age of seventy-five. They are buried side by side in Union Ridge cemetery, in White county. She was a member of the Methodist Episcopal church for many years prior to her death. Their children were Amanda, Henry I., Hezekiah, Romelia, Ann, John W., Orlenia, Albina, Alice, Rosetta, Sarepta and Vienna. Amanda is the wife of a Mr. Holt; Henry lives in Ridgway; Hezekiah is in Kansas City, Mo.; Romelia is the widow of William Rogers and lives on the old home place; Ann is the wife of W. J. Sanders; John W. is the subject of this sketch, and the others are deceased. John W. Harrington obtained a good practical education in the public schools, and at the age of twenty-one rented the old home place and began life on his own account. He now owns 200 acres, 160 of which is under cultivation, and is regarded as one of the foremost farmers of the community. Mr. Harrington is a Republican in his political views, and, although firm in his convictions, he has a large number of Democratic friends who value his friendship because of his many good qualities. He has been twice married, first in 1880 to Miss Mary E., daughter of James T. Ramsey of Indiana, and to this union there were born two sons, Leroy and Lawrence. His first wife died in 1884, and in 1887 he was married to Cordelia Rogers, by whom he has three children: Clarence, Vera, and Henry. Mr. Harrington belongs to the Court of Honor, and is always interested in any and every movement for the betterment of the neighborhood where he has passed his whole life.

WILLIAM R. McKERNAN, a prominent lawyer of Shawneetown, Ill., is of Irish extraction, his great-grandparents coming from County Cavan, Ireland, and settling in what is now West Virginia. They had a family of twelve sons and as these sons grew to manhood they scattered to different parts of the country. Three of them, Peter, Charles, and Reuben, went to Kentucky, and subsequently settled in Gallatin county. Here Reuben McKernan (the original Irish spelling of the name was McKiernan) engaged in farming for the remainder of his life. He was born in Ireland, and coming to the New World in early life the privilege of attending school was practically denied him, yet he developed into a man of strong character and fixed convictions, a leader among his neighbors and highly respected by all who knew him. He married a Miss Addison of Gallatin county and they had a family of four children, only one of whom is now living. Henry, Elizabeth, and Julia are all dead and Charles is living in Kansas. Elizabeth married a man named Calvert. Henry McKernan, the eldest son, was born in 1829, and passed his whole life in Gallatin county, where he followed the occupation of a farmer. He was a man of fair education. On Nov. 28, 1852, he was married to Miss Lydia, daughter of Thomas Spivey, an old resident of Gallatin county. To this marriage were born the following children: Maria, deceased; William R., the subject of this sketch; Mollie, living in Louisville, Ky.; and Charles Henry, a farmer living near Equality, in Gallatin county. The father of these children died in February, 1864, and the mother died in 1871. William R. McKernan, the eldest son of Henry and Lydia (Spivey) McKernan, was born May 27, 1856. He was therefore but eight years old when his father died, and only fifteen when his mother passed to her final resting place. Consequently, the responsibilities of a man were thrust upon him early in life. The care of a younger sister and baby brother was thrown upon him and his elder sister, who was his senior by a little more than a year, but with true Irish spirit they accepted the responsibility, and with heroic sacrifice they kept the little family together. William worked for the neighboring farmers for twenty-five cents a day, taking his pay in provisions, while his sister spun and wove the cloth, from which she made the clothing for the orphaned children, the wool being the product of ten head of sheep that had been left by the parents. Under these conditions attendance at school was out of the question. But the boy made up his mind to secure an education. With such assistance as his sister could give him he studied of evenings and at odd times until he was twenty years of age, when, with not more than six months altogether in school, he secured a teacher's certificate and commenced teaching. He taught for two years, saving all the money he could, and then attended the Illinois academy at Enfield for a year. Again he entered the schoolroom as a teacher for a year, after which he went to Ewing college for a year. From that time until 1888 he taught continuously in the school at Waltonborough, studying law in the meantime, as opportunity offered, under the directions of Judge E. D. Youngblood, of Shawneetown. In 1887 he was admitted to the bar and in 1888 was nominated by the Democracy of Gallatin county for the office of state's attorney, and at the ensuing election was victorious by a decisive majority. In 1892, at the close of his first term, he was re-elected, serving two terms of four years each. In 1891 he was appointed master in chancery for Gallatin county, and served with signal ability for four years. Mr. McKernan is a splendid example of a self-made man, a worthy son of an honored sire, whose family were among the pioneers of the Lower Ohio Valley. The young man who reads this sketch of his life may find in it an inspiration to make a mark in the world. In fraternal circles Mr. McKernan is a prominent figure, belonging to the time-honored Masonic fraternity, the Independent Order of Odd Fellows, and the Knights of Pythias. He has been twice married. In June, 1892, he was married to Miss Margaret Smith, of Indianapolis, Ind., but she died without issue in October, 1893. In 1901 he was married to Miss Grace Phile, daughter of William Phile, an old resident of Shawneetown. Mr. and Mrs. McKernan are both members of the Presbyterian church and take an interest in its good works.

F. E. CALLICOTT.

FRANK E. CALLICOTT, one of the largest land owners in Gallatin county, Ill., living three miles west of Shawneetown, is a descendant of one of the oldest families in America. His ancestry can be traced back to an Englishman of that name, who came to this country and settled in Virginia, long before the Revolution. He had three sons, John, Beverly, and Harrison, all of whom fought in the Revolution, John being a captain in Washington's command and present at the surrender of Lord Cornwallis. Beverly Callicott was born in 1752. He married and reared a family of eight children, viz.: John, Beverly, William, Samuel, Jordan, Dicey, Nancy, and Polly. Samuel, the fourth child, was born in Virginia in 1797. He married a Miss Anderson, whose father was a major under General Marion, and in 1829 came with his wife and family to Gallatin county, settling in the Pond settlement about eight miles north of Shawneetown, where they passed the remainder of their lives and are buried in the Callicott cemetery. Their children were Aggie, Claiborne, John, Polly Ann, Harrison, Talitha, Wade, and Washington. In those pioneer days he was a noted hunter, was twice married but no children were born to the second marriage. John A. Callicott, the third of the family, was born in Smith county, Tenn., March 31, 1824. He received his education in the old fashioned subscription schools and about the time he reached his majority went to Shawneetown and served

J. A. CALLICOTT.

an apprenticeship with Orvil Poole and Jobe Smith at harness-making. At the breaking out of the Mexican war he enlisted in Capt. M. K. Lawler's company of dragoons and served through the entire war. After being mustered out he returned to his trade of harness-making, which he followed for several years, then becoming interested in transporting grain by flatboat on the Ohio and Mississippi rivers. The last trip he made to New Orleans was just at the beginning of the Civil war, and he lost his load of corn which he had taken down the river. Upon his return home he, with John Eddy and others, raised a company of volunteers, of which he was elected captain and Eddy first lieutenant, and which was mustered in as Company C, Twenty-ninth Illinois infantry. The regiment was attached to McClernand's division of Grant's army and fought at forts Henry and Donelson, Pittsburg Landing, Corinth, around Vicksburg, and toward the close of the war assisted in the reduction of Spanish Fort and Fort Blakely, after which it was sent to Texas, where it was mustered out in November, 1865. At Fort Donelson, Captain Callicott was wounded five times and sent home to recover. He rejoined his regiment in time to take part in the fight at Pittsburg Landing, and remained under Grant until the latter was assigned to the command of the Army of the Potomac. Captain Callicott was soon promoted to major, then to lieutenant-colonel, and during the last three years of service was in command of the regiment. After being discharged he returned to Shawneetown, where he engaged in the saddlery business until 1875, when he again took up flatboating and followed that occupation for about four years. He then turned his attention to agricultural pursuits until his death, which occurred on April 3, 1898, when he and his brother Washington fell victims to the great flood that did so much damage about Shawneetown, twenty-six lives being lost. He was buried on his farm in what is known as the Kanady graveyard. In 1850 he was married to Miss Sarah, daughter of John Ellis, whose father, William Ellis, was with Jackson in the war of 1812, and settled in Gallatin county about 1815. He entered a large tract of land and was the first county surveyor. His children were William, Abner, John, Caleb, Benjamin, James and Nancy. All married and reared large families, so that at the present time a large number of his descendants are living in Southern Illinois. The sons, like the father, took a deep interest in public affairs, and the family played an important part in shaping the early destinies of the county. The widow and one son, William, lived to be over 100 years old. John

E. H. CALLICOTT.

Ellis, the father of Mrs. Callicott, married Letitia McCool, daughter of Abraham McCool, who was an officer under General Marion in the Revolution. After the death of William Ellis his widow married a man named Hogan, after whom the Hogan graveyard near Bowlesville was named, and where William Ellis and a number of his descendants are buried. After the death of Abraham McCool in North Carolina, his son, also named Abraham, with his mother and her children came to Gallatin county. Two of his sons, William and Marion, were killed while serving in the Union army during the war, one at Fort Donelson and the other at Guntown. To the marriage of John A. Callicott and Sarah Ellis was born one son, Frank E., the subject of this sketch. His mother died in 1854, when he was only about one year old, and his father in 1856 married Eliza Hamilton, but no children were born to this union. The second wife died in 1860, and in 1865 he married Hester Kanady. To this marriage there were born four children: Rebecca, now Mrs. McGhee, living five miles west of Shawneetown; Mary (deceased); William B. (deceased), and one who died in infancy. The mother of these children died in 1872. For many years John A. Callicott was prominently identified with the civic life of Gallatin county. He was one of the first four men to vote the Republican ticket in that county in 1856, and for nearly half a century afterward took an interest in political affairs. After the war he served two terms as mayor of Shawneetown and held other offices, in all of which he made a creditable record. He belonged to the Independent Order of Odd Fellows, more for the good that he could do others than for the benefits he might receive. Frank E. Callicott was born April 18, 1853, in the house now occupied by Mrs. Frank Eddy in Shawneetown. His early education was acquired in the public schools of his native town, and he still cherishes very highly a number of books awarded him by his teachers as prizes for good conduct, the highest scholarship, and regular attendance. Afterward he graduated from Miami university at Oxford, O., with the class of 1873, standing at the head of his class, and receiving the degrees of Bachelor and Master of Arts. He then took up the work of teaching and was for four years the principal of the Shawneetown schools. During that time he studied law, and in 1878 was admitted to the bar. He never practiced his profession, however, as he had become interested in farming operations in 1876, and from the time of his admission until 1893 was in partnership with his father. In 1877 he also engaged in the harness and implement trade, and while in this business had the distinction of introducing into Gallatin county some of the modern farm implements, among which might be named the twine binder, the disc harrow, the corn planter, the traction engine and the drilled well. In 1900 he sold out this business and the following year removed to the place where he now lives, and where he owns about 2,500 acres of land, most of which is under cultivation. To oversee this large farm requires most of his time and attention. All of this property has been accumulated by his own industry and business sagacity, and he is regarded as one of the most successful men in the county in whatever he undertakes. During the war he was with his father's regiment for a while each year, thus becoming acquainted with military movements, an experience he still vividly remembers. He is a member of the Independent Order of Odd Fellows and the Knights of Pythias, and as a Republican takes an active part in political affairs, though he has never held any office, either by election or appointment, although well qualified for almost any position. In his younger days he was a member of the Illinois National Guard as a member of Captain Nolen's company, and participated in their drills, encampments and sham battles. In his youth he took great delight in athletic sports and excelled in running, jumping, sparring, baseball and cycling, but in later years his time has all been taken up with his business affairs, though he still enjoys athletics as a spectator. He has never married.

MARSHALL WISEHEART, of Shawneetown, Ill., county judge of Gallatin county, was born in that county, June 25, 1865. The family is of German origin, though the Wisehearts of Gallatin county are of Pennsylvania ancestry. The first of the name to come to Illinois was John Wiseheart, a native of Pennsylvania, who came West in the twenties, entered a tract of land in Gallatin county, and there passed the remainder of his life as a farmer. He married before leaving Pennsylvania and reared a family of seven children, only one of whom is now living. Richard was a minister of the Christian or Campbellite church; John followed farming and merchandizing; William, the only survivor of the family, is now a farmer of Gallatin county; Samuel was a merchant; Ellen married William

Bird; Hannah married Alvin DeWitt; and Mary was the wife of James Rice. William Wiseheart was born in Gallatin county, Ill., Jan. 7, 1832, and has always lived in the county. He received a common school education and upon reaching manhood adopted the occupation of farming, which he has followed all his life. He married Sarah, daughter of Henry Gill, an old resident of the county, and to this union there have been born the following children: Laura, widow of William Mattingly; Albert, a farmer of Gallatin county; Anna, wife of James Purcell, of Equality, Ill.; Marshall, the subject of this sketch; and Lucy, wife of William Powell, of Gallatin county. Marshall Wiseheart, familiarly known as "Marsh," has always lived in Gallatin county. As a boy he worked on his father's farm, attending the district schools during the winter months. At the age of nineteen years he commenced teaching and followed that occupation for three years, when he was appointed to a position as deputy in the circuit clerk's office at Shawneetown. Later he went into the sheriff's office as deputy, remaining in the two positions until 1892. While thus employed he spent his spare time in the study of law, and in May, 1892, he passed the examination before the state supreme court and was admitted to the bar. He then commenced the practice of his profession at Gallatin and continued in it until August, 1894, when he was appointed postmaster at Shawneetown and held the office for a little over four years, retiring in September, 1898. In November of that year he was elected treasurer of Gallatin county on the Democratic ticket, and served a full term of four years. In 1902 he received the nomination of his party for county judge, and at the election in November was chosen by a handsome majority to administer the affairs of that office for a term of four years. He is now serving in that position. Judge Wiseheart is prominent in fraternal circles, being a member of the Independent Order of Odd Fellows, the Knights of Pythias, the Court of Honor, and the Loyal Americans. He was married on April 4, 1894, to Miss Fannie Boyd, a daughter of John R. Boyd, an old and honored resident of Gallatin county, who at the time of his death in 1896 was a member of the Illinois State board of equalization from the Twenty-fourth Congressional district. Mr. and Mrs. Wiseheart have four sons, viz.: Malcolm, William, Raymond and Marshall Clarence.

CHARLES CARROLL, a well known merchant of Shawneetown, Ill., and the only surviving child of James and Judith M. (Williamson) Carroll, was born at Lynchburg, Va., Feb. 25, 1833. About 1824 three brothers, Patrick, John, and James Carroll, came to America and located at Richmond, Va., where they established themselves in the mercantile business. There Patrick died and some five years later the other two brothers removed to Lynchburg. In 1828 James was married to Judith M. Williamson, of an old Virginia family, and in 1834 removed to St. Louis, Mo. In 1836 he went to St. Charles, Mo., and died there in the fall of that year. He and his wife had two sons, John, who died in infancy, and Charles. After the death of her husband Mrs. Carroll went to Louisville, Ky., and in 1837 removed with her son, then some four years old, to Shawneetown. There she was married in 1839 to John D. Richeson, by whom she had one son and two daughters. Elenora married Judge J. D. Turner and died in 1899. Albert G. is now a merchant in Shawneetown, and Mary is the wife of Judge McBane of the same place. The mother of Charles Carroll died on Sept. 6, 1856. As Charles Carroll grew up he attended the schools of Shawneetown, where he received his primary education. In 1846 he entered Cumberland college at Princeton, Ky., and studied in that institution for three years. Returning to Shawneetown in 1849 he entered the law office of Albert G. Caldwell as a student, and continued to study law until 1852. He then went into the wholesale and retail dry goods business in partnership with his step-father, under the firm name of Richeson & Carroll. This partnership was dissolved in 1868, and since that time Mr. Carroll has been engaged in conducting a general store at Shawneetown. For a number of years he was also a large operator in grain and tobacco, and was interested in river navigation. In connection with Thomas S. Ridgway and Charles A. Beecher he was one of the projectors of the Illinois & Southeastern railway (now a part of the Baltimore & Ohio Southwestern), and supervised its construction from Shawneetown to Beardstown, Ill., a distance of two hundred and twenty miles. Mr. Carroll is president of the Gallatin county agricultural board, and under his management very successful fairs have been held for several years past. He takes a lively interest in all political affairs, but has never been a seeker for public office. Notwithstanding this he was nominated by the Democratic party for the office of state treasurer in 1874, but he was defeated along with the rest of his ticket by the usual Republican majority. In 1856 he was married to Miss Elizabeth K., eldest daughter of the late Henry Eddy, who was for many years regarded as the leading lawyer of Shawneetown. To this marriage there have been born the following children: Charles Jr., now mayor of Shawneetown; Mary Eddy, wife of E. R. Sisson, a lawyer at Storm Lake, Ia.; Judith Mimms, wife of William Ridgway, a lumber dealer in Chicago; and Bessie, wife of William R. Higgins, formerly a grain dealer of Chicago, but now in the real estate business at Spencer, Ia.

WILL A. HOWELL, of Shawneetown, Ill., master in chancery of Gallatin county, is a representative member of one of the oldest families in America. The Howells of Kentucky and Southern Illinois are of Irish extraction and can trace their ancestry back to one of three brothers who came from the Emerald Isle with Capt. John Smith's colony and settled at Jamestown, Va., in 1607. Much of the early history of the family is veiled in obscurity, but it is known that some of the descendants settled in Kentucky at a very early date, where they played an important part in wresting the "Dark and Bloody Ground" from the possession of the Indians. Some of the family finally located at Cynthiana, where Chester Howell, the immediate ancestor of that branch of the family now living in Shawneetown and vicinity, was born. He had three sons: Squire, James D., and one whose name has been lost. Squire Howell had two sons and two daughters: Thomas, Chester, Susan and Anna. James D. Howell, who was the grandfather of the subject of this sketch, was born at Cynthiana, Jan. 27, 1809. He received his education in the schools of that period, the course of study being confined to the simplest rudiments of an English education. During his boyhood he engaged in hauling freight from Cynthiana to Cincinnati, but upon arriving at man's estate he removed to near Lexington, where he became a farmer. In 1840 he removed to Trimble county, Ky., where he lived for about twelve years, when he went to Union county, and there passed the remainder of his life, dying Aug. 23, 1894, at the advanced age of eighty-five years. On Sept. 6, 1831, he was married to Miss Millicent, daughter of Alexander Breckenridge, living near Lexington. She was a member of the celebrated family of that name, and a first cousin to Gen. John C. Breckenridge. She died June 26, 1876. Her mother's maiden name was Wickliffe, a sister to George and Robert Wickliffe, who were among the Kentucky pioneers. James D. and Millicent Howell were the parents of the following children: William A., who died young; Ann Martha, born Feb. 2, 1834, married Lemuel Holt, Nov. 26, 1857, and is now living a widow in Union county, Ky.; James Elmore, born April 27, 1830, and died Sept. 28, 1837; John Lloyd, father of the subject of this sketch; Nancy J., born Nov. 18, 1839, and died Feb. 21, 1886; Warren, born March 31, 1841, married Anna Harth, and now lives at Caseyville, Ky.; Harriet Matilda, born Nov. 23, 1842, and died Dec. 27, 1842; Harrison, born Nov. 22, 1844, now lives in Union county, Ky.; Walker T., born April 17, 1846, married Carrie Haskins in 1883, and now lives in Colorado; George W., born April 2, 1848, and died Aug. 21, 1893; Elizabeth Morris, born April 2, 1849, and died in 1885; Susan Howe, born Sept. 5, 1851, died July 19, 1871; Thomas Henry, born in November, 1864, married Fannie Wall, and now lives in Morganfield, Ky. John Lloyd Howell, the fourth child of this family was born at Lexington, Nov. 18, 1837. After such an education as the common schools of that day afforded he turned his attention to farming, and at the beginning of the Civil war was living near Hannibal, Mo. He returned home to Kentucky and enlisted in Company G, First Kentucky Confederate cavalry, which afterward became part of the famous "Orphan Brigade." After the war he located in Union county, Ky., and there followed farming and conducting a sawmill until 1885, when he became a pilot on the river, in which occupation he continued the rest of his active life. On April 25, 1867, he was united in marriage to Miss Mary L. Givens, of Trimble county, and she is now living in Shawneetown. To this marriage there were born four children: Nannie, widow of W. S. Callicott, and who for the last fourteen years has been a teacher in the Shawneetown public schools; Harry H., now a merchant in Shawneetown; Will A., the subject of this sketch; and Ray L., now the wife of C. L. Patterson, a postoffice inspector, living at Las Vegas, New Mexico. Will A. Howell was born in Union county, Ky., Jan. 24, 1877. His parents removed to Shawneetown when he was about two years old, and here he grew to manhood, receiving his education in the public schools. In 1894 he was appointed deputy clerk of Gallatin county and filled that position for three years, at the end of which time he embarked in the real estate, abstract and loan business, in which line he has continued ever since with the exception of about four months. In April, 1899, he was elected city clerk of Shawneetown, and was re-elected in 1901, holding the office for four years. In October, 1903, he was appointed master in chancery for Gallatin county for a term of two years, and is now discharging the duties of that position. Mr. Howell is prominent in the fraternal societies of Shawneetown, being a member of the Masonic fraternity, the Knights of Pythias, the Modern Woodmen of America, and the Fraternal Army of Loyal Americans. On New Year's day, 1900, he was married to Miss Cleora L. Hite, of Peru, Ind., and to this union there has been born one son, Edward Hite, born Jan. 28, 1901.

JOHN WILLIAM BOWLING, M.D., one of the leading physicians of Shawneetown, Ill., was born near Catlettsburg, Boyd county, Ky., Jan. 21, 1862. His father, Jasper Bowling, was also a native of Boyd county, and of Irish and English parentage. He was born Oct. 17, 1833, and grew to manhood near Catlettsburg, where he obtained a common school education, afterward graduating from the Cincinnati business college. For several years he was deputy clerk of Boyd county. During the war he was provost marshal, stationed at Catlettsburg, and for some time immediately after the war he served as deputy internal revenue collector. He was also interested in farming operations. In the fall of 1868 he removed with his family to Gallatin county, Ill., making the trip by river, and upon locating there taught school for about three years, after which he bought a good farm in North Fork township, where he still lives. He continued to teach during the winter months for about twelve years, served for several years as justice of the peace, and also as township treasurer. He was married in 1861 to Miss Pauline Crow, a native of Northeastern Kentucky. She died in the spring of 1885, the mother of seven children, viz.: Dr. John W., the subject of this sketch; Eudora, who died in 1877 at the age of twelve years; Philip S., died in 1896 at the age of twenty-five; Abraham L., a farmer in Gallatin county; Edwin, a school teacher in the same county; Addie, wife of Louis McLain, of Halliday, Ark.; and Hattie, at home. Some time after the death of the mother of these children Mr. Bowling was married to Miss Jane Stinson, of Saline county, Ill., and one daughter, Helen, has been born to this second marriage. Dr. John W. Bowling was about seven years of age when his parents came to Gallatin county. After a preliminary education in the district schools he spent one year at the Southern Illinois college, located at Carmi, and one year at Ewing college in Franklin county. He then taught for three years, studying medicine in the meantime as opportunity presented. He then took three courses of medical lectures, one year at Evansville, Ind., and two years in the College of Physicians and Surgeons, of Keokuk, Ia., from which he was graduated with the class of 1887. Returning to Illinois he commenced the practice of his profession at Omaha, in Gallatin county, and soon built up a lucrative business. In the winter of 1901-2 he took a post-graduate course in the Post-Graduate school of Chicago, and in the latter year removed to Shawneetown, where he has ever since been engaged in general practice. In recent years he has devoted considerable attention to general surgery, in which he has performed some noteworthy operations. Dr. Bowling is a member of the American, the Illinois State, the Southern Illinois, and the Ohio Valley Medical associations, and the Medical society of Gallatin county. He is surgeon for both the Louisville & Nashville and the Baltimore & Ohio Southwestern railways; was county physician for eight years; is examiner for all the reputable old line insurance companies doing business in Southern Illinois; and is a member of the pension examining board of Shawneetown. In politics he has always been a stalwart Republican; was a member of the county central committee from the time he attained his majority until his removal to Shawneetown; served for ten years as secretary of the committee, and has several times been called upon to serve as a delegate to state conventions. He is a member of the Masonic fraternity and the Modern Woodmen, in both of which he is popular because of his many sterling qualities. In 1885 he was united in marriage to Miss Eliza Davis, a native of Posey county, Ind., and to this union there have been born three children: Albert Leslie, Emory Emmons and Ethel Gail.

GEORGE L. HOUSTON, of Shawneetown, Ill., state's attorney for Gallatin county, was born in that county June 8, 1870. His parents, Samuel and Nannie (Adams) Houston, were both natives of the county and there passed their whole lives. Samuel Houston received a common school education, and upon arriving at manhood became a farmer, which occupation he followed through life. When the Civil war broke out he enlisted in Company L, Sixth Illinois cavalry, and served until the close of hostilities. The exposure incident to army life affected his eyesight, and soon after the war be became totally blind. His general health was also impaired and he died on Dec. 24, 1874, his wife having died in the first week of the same month. They left three children: George L., the subject of this sketch; Alexander, who died in 1883; and Walter, now a farmer in Gallatin county. George L. Houston was only about four years old when his parents died, and he was taken into the family of his father's brother, William Houston. About a year later his uncle died, and he then found a home with Martin Doherty, living about ten miles from Shawneetown, where he remained until he was about twenty years of age. Up to the time he was sixteen years old his opportunities to attend school were very much restricted by circumstances, and being without parents, or other intimate relatives to direct his course, his knowledge of books was quite limited. But, beginning when he was seventeen, he applied himself assiduously to his studies in the district schools for three seasons, and when he was twenty secured a teacher's certificate. After teaching a six months' term he attended the Hayward college at Fairfield, Ill., for a ten weeks' term, and then worked on a farm the remainder of the season until the school year opened. He taught another term, the following winter, and then attended a short term at the Southern Illinois college at Enfield, after which he again found work as a farm hand. In the spring of 1892, after teaching another term in the country schools, he went to Shawneetown, and in the following September was appointed to a position as deputy in the office of the county clerk. Mr. Houston filled this position very creditably for six years. During the first three years of that time he devoted his leisure hours to the study of law and in February, 1895, was admitted to the bar. Although engaged in the clerk's office he commenced the practice of his profession in a limited way and soon won the respect of both bench and bar by his earnestness and dignified bearing in the courts. In the spring of 1895 he was elected city attorney of Shawneetown, and was twice re-elected, serving six years in all. In 1900 he was nominated by the Democracy of Gallatin county for the office of state's attorney, and was elected to the position in November of that year. His record during his four years' term was so satisfactory that when the Democratic convention met in the spring of 1904 he was nominated for a re-election. Mr. Houston owes his success entirely to his own energy and determination to succeed. Left an orphan at a tender age he has fought the battle of life up to the present time against odds that would have discouraged one with less courage. Yet he never faltered, believing in the old adage that "Where there is a will there is a way," and his career is proof that such is the case. He was married on July 6, 1901, to Miss Mabel, daughter of George Grater, an old resident of Gallatin county.

ANGUS M. L. McBANE, a retired lawyer and merchant of Shawneetown, Ill., and ex-judge of Gallatin county, is justly entitled to be classed as one of the foremost citizens of the city. The McBane family is of Scotch origin, the grandfather of Judge McBane coming from Scotland in the early part of the nineteenth century and settling at Cannonsburg, Pa., where he reared a family of children. One of his sons, Dr. A. M. L. McBane, was born at Cannonsburg in 1808. He received a fine literary education, which was supplemented by a complete course in the science of medicine. After graduating from medical college he traveled extensively through Europe, and upon returning to America located at Louisville, where he soon won eminence as a physician. In 1836 he went to Parkersburg, W. Va., and practiced there until 1842, when, in company with his brother William, he came to Illinois. The two brothers bought 1,600 acres of land where Metropolis City now stands, and 600 acres on the opposite side of the Ohio river in Kentucky. Here Dr. McBane passed the remainder of his life, in the practice of his profession and in looking after his large landed and commercial interests. His death occurred July 3, 1860. In 1836, while living in Louisville, he was married to Miss Ellen Willard of that city, though a native of New York. She was of English and French extraction, her father, Rev. Joseph Willard, having been an Episcopal minister at Newark, N. J., as early as 1806. Later he came West and died at Marietta, Ohio. He was a descendant of Maj. Simon Willard, who was somewhat famous in the early history of Boston. Dr. McBane and his wife had five children, viz.: Angus M. L., the subject of this sketch; Joseph, a graduate of the New Orleans Medical college, died on shipboard while crossing the Atlantic and was buried at sea; Ellen, deceased; Marietta, widow of William Ward, living in Chicago, the mother of three children, one son, Frank, being a traveling man and secretary of the Standard club; and William A., who was a real estate and insurance man of Metropolis City at the time of his death in 1903. Angus M. L. McBane was born at Parkersburg, W. Va., Sept. 8, 1837. He was but five years of age when his parents came to Illinois. Ever since that time he has resided in that state and has been identified with the growth and development of Massac and Gallatin counties. He obtained his early education in the schools of Metropolis City, one of his teachers being Robert G. Ingersoll, who afterward achieved a world-wide reputation as an exponent of Agnosticism. Although nominally a student at this time young McBane was really an assistant teacher, Mr. Ingersoll devoting most of his time to Latin and history, leaving the greater part of his other school work to McBane. Later Judge McBane graduated from Princeton college of New York, after which he returned home, took up the study of law under Hon. C. G. Simons and W. H. Green, and in 1860 graduated from the law department of the Kentucky State university, at Louisville. He began practice at Metropolis City, but scarcely established himself when the Civil war broke out. His desire was to enter the service of his country, but the recent death of his father made it necessary for him to remain at home to look after the large estate and to care for the family. However, he organized two companies, one in White county, Ill., and the other at Ford's Ferry, Ky., both of which were mustered into the army as part of the Forty-eighth Illinois infantry, of which he was made adjutant, but for reasons already stated he was compelled to resign the position. He accompanied Grant's forces from Paducah to Pittsburg Landing, and in the capacity of expressman for Grant's army was present at the historic battle of Shiloh. In 1864 he removed to Shawneetown, where he was elected county judge the following year and held the position for four years. In addition to his large law practice Judge McBane became interested in the mercantile affairs of Shawneetown. For several years he conducted one of the largest general stores there and was a large buyer of grain. In 1877 he practically retired from both professional and commercial life, and since then has devoted his time to the management of his large and varied investments. He was married in 1862 to Miss Mary, daughter of John D. Richeson, whose sketch appears elsewhere in this work. They have no children. Judge McBane is a member and past dictator in the Knights of Honor; has been president of the Business Men's association ever since it was organized in 1890; was once a candidate for state senator, and is always active in promoting the general welfare of the community in which he lives. His wife is a member of the Methodist Episcopal church.

LUCIEN WINSLOW GORDON, M.D., who for almost a quarter of a century has practiced his profession at Equality, Ill., can trace his ancestry back to Archibald Gordon, a native of Scotland, who was the leader of a powerful clan during the Stuart uprising about the middle of the eighteenth century, and was compelled in consequence to leave his native land to save his life. For a time he lived in France, but just before the beginning of the French and Indian war he came to America, settling either in South Carolina or Northern Georgia. He lived to a good old age, his death occurring about the time of the beginning of the Revolutionary war. His three sons, John, William, and Robert, all served under General Greene in the Revolution, the first named attaining the rank of colonel. This John Gordon was the great-grandfather of Doctor Gordon, who is the subject of this sketch. He was born in Scotland, accompanied his parents to France and afterward to America. As a reward for his services during the Revolution he received the customary grant of land, located in what is now either Portage or Trumbull county, O., where he passed the remainder of his life. He married Susanna Bacon, a member of the old Virginia family of that name, and they had four sons: James, Robert, Archibald and Jonathan. (The names of the last two are not certain.) Robert Gordon, the second son, was born at Warren, Trumbull county, Ohio, about the year 1794, and passed his whole life in that vicinity. At one time he was, one of the most prominent men in that section. He followed the vocation of making brick and erecting brick buildings, and did an extensive business. He was still in his minority when the war of 1812 broke out, but he enlisted as a "powder-monkey" in Commodore Perry's fleet, and served in the famous battle on Lake Erie. After the war he married Janet Porter, and they were the parents of the following children: Thomas Winslow, Isabella M., Anan Irwin, Robert Porter, George Washington, Maria, Alta, Zina, Etta C., William Wallace, and Samuel Quimby. Thomas died in 1901, aged eighty-two; Isabella now lives at Ravenna, O., as the widow of John Wheatly; Anan lives at Cameron, Mo.; Robert died at Beaver Falls, Pa., where some of his descendants still live; George Washington was the father of the subject of this sketch; Maria married John Gottschell and died soon afterward; Alta also became the wife of John Gottschell and died at Waterloo, Ill.; Zina died single; Etta C., lives at Warren, O., as the widow of Walter Nichols; William Wallace served in the Second Iowa infantry during the Civil war and died at Trenton, Mo.; and Samuel is now living at Ravenna, O. George W. Gordon was born at Warren, Sept. 23, 1830. He was educated in the high school of his native town and about 1856 graduated from the Cincinnati College of Medicine and Surgery. In 1852 he was united in marriage to Miss Sabine M. Tweed, of Ripley, O. Her father, John Tweed, was an ensign at the battle of Lake Erie, and his father was settled on a Revolutionary land grant in Brown county, O., in the Virginia Reserve. Soon after graduating from the medical college Dr. G. W. Gordon was elected demonstrator of anatomy in the institution and held that position until the death of his wife in 1859, when he removed to Little Rock, Ark. Here he soon established a lucrative practice, but in 1861, on account of his pronounced opposition to secession, he again returned to the North, and at St. Louis enlisted in Foster's Independent Ohio cavalry. He was at once elected lieutenant and was later commissioned captain in Birge's Second Missouri sharpshooters. He was next commissioned assistant surgeon of the Eighteenth Indiana infantry by Gov. Oliver P. Morton, and subsequently rose to the position of surgeon with the rank of major. In July, 1864, he was discharged for disability, came to Gallatin county, Ill., where he owned some land, and took up his residence there. As soon as he had sufficiently regained his health he resumed the practice of medicine, locating at Equality, and continued in that occupation until his death, Aug. 6, 1892. In November, 1864, he was married to Laura M. Campbell, widow of Lieut. Josiah Campbell. She was a daughter of Rev. Z. S. Clifford, who was chaplain of the Twenty-ninth Illinois infantry and a Lincoln elector in 1864. He was a native of New Hampshire and a cousin of Daniel Webster. Mrs. Laura Gordon died in 1888, and Major Gordon afterward married Flora R. Dively of Equality, who is still living. To the first marriage there were born two sons, John Robert and Lucien Winslow, the former of whom died in infancy and the latter is the subject of this sketch. To the second marriage five children were born, viz.: Laura, now the wife of Harry Huntsman, of Stamps, Ark.; George Ravenscroft, living at Acme, La.; Louise, wife of M. R. Moore, of Equality; and two who died in infancy unnamed. No children were born to the third marriage. Dr. Lucien W. Gordon was born at New Hope, O., Aug. 9, 1858, and was but seven years of age when his father located at Equality. He received his education in the public schools, the Enfield college and the Southern Illinois Normal university at Carbondale. In 1877 he entered the Miami Medical college of Cincinnati, and graduated with the class of 1880. On June 26, of that year, he opened an office for the practice of medicine in Equality, and has followed up his profession there ever since. As a physician he is both successful and popular, enjoying the respect of his brother practitioners and the confidence of his patients. He is a member of the Masonic fraternity, and both himself and wife belong to the Methodist Episcopal church. On Oct. 26, 1880, he married Miss Mollie Alexander Lewis, of Ripley, O., and they have one son, Frank Henderson, born Dec. 26, 1882, and graduated from the Cincinnati College of Pharmacy in 1902. Mrs. Gordon is the granddaughter of Capt. Enoch Lewis, who fought under Harrison at the battle of Tippecanoe. Her grandmother was Hannah Potts, of the old Quaker family that founded Pottsville, Pa.

JACOB BARGER, a prominent citizen and member of the board of aldermen of Shawneetown, Ill., is a descendant of one of the early settlers of Gallatin county. The Barger family originally came from Germany. The first of the name to come to America was George Barger, who settled in Pennsylvania prior to the Revolutionary war. Later he removed to Kentucky and became one of the pioneers of Breckenridge county. His son Jacob was born in Pennsylvania in 1784. After receiving a limited education there he went to Breckenridge county, Ky., where he learned the carpenter's trade and worked at it for a number of years there. In 1815 he removed to Illinois, locating at Shawneetown on the first day of May of that year. There he entered three hundred acres of land, though for several years he continued to work at his trade before he settled down to farming. He was prominent in local affairs and was for some time trustee of Shawneetown. He died in 1847. In 1809, while still living in Kentucky he was married to Miss Elizabeth Seaton. She was a native of Kentucky, was born in 1787, and was a half-sister of Gen. John A. McClernand, who won distinction in the Union army during the Civil war. She died in 1860. The seven children born to this couple are all dead. One of the sons, Joseph B. Barger, was born in Breckenridge county, Feb. 2, 1814, and was little more than one year old when his parents came to Shawneetown. As he grew up he attended the schools of the town and began life as clerk in a store. Subsequently he engaged to some extent in flatboating on the Ohio and Mississippi rivers. In 1847 he was appointed postmaster of Shawneetown by President Polk and served until 1850, when he was elected sheriff of the county, holding the office for a term of two years. From 1854 to 1856 he was bookkeeper in the State bank of Illinois, and in the latter year was elected county clerk. This office he continued to hold by repeated re-elections for twenty-six consecutive years. When he retired from the office his fellow-citizens presented him with a fine gold-headed cane in token of their appreciation of his efficient services, his uniform courtesy to every resident of the county, and his fidelity to his duty. Upon retiring from his long and honorable career as a public official he lived a quiet life until his death, which occurred Oct. 19, 1900. In March, 1834, he was married to Miss Louisa M. Carter, who, like himself, was a native of Kentucky and about the same age. She died in 1861. They had seven children, viz.: Elizabeth, Richard, Harrison O., George, Jacob, Josephine, and one who died in infancy. Of these children Jacob is the only one now living. He was educated in the Shawneetown public schools and at the age of seventeen years went into the office of county clerk as a deputy. He served four years under James R. Loomis; four years under Joseph F. Nolen; was then two years with Mr. Nolen in the sheriff's office, and two years with S. M. Smith in the treasurer's office. Mr. Barger then removed with his family to the old homestead which his grandfather had entered, and which has ever since been in possession of the family, and there lived for about ten years, when he returned to Shawneetown. He still manages the farm of 204 acres, making frequent trips to it during the spring and summer seasons. Mr. Barger is a member of Lodge No. 838, Independent Order of Odd Fellows, and No. 638, Knights of Pythias, and has gone through the chairs in both orders. For the past eight years he has been one of the aldermen of the city and may properly be called a man of affairs. Politically he is a Democrat, and comes from old Kentucky Democratic stock. He has been twice married.

His first wife was Miss James Ella Parks, a daughter of James S. and Adeline (Goodwin) Parks, of Shawneetown, though natives of Tennessee. To this marriage there were born two children: Louise, now deceased, and James S. Mrs. Barger died in 1896, and in January, 1898, he married his second wife, Miss Anna Lawler, a daughter of Thomas B. and Sally Lawler, and a niece of Gen. M. K. Lawler. No children have been born to this union.

CHAS. W. TURNER.

JAMES B. TURNER (deceased), late a resident of Equality, Ill., was born at Oswego, N. Y., Nov. 27, 1837. While still in his early boyhood his parents, Charles W. and Sally (Spencer) Turner, removed to Kenosha, Wis., where the mother died a few years later and James went to St. Louis to live with an elder brother, Dr. Carlos Turner. When he was about sixteen or seventeen years old he went to New Orleans on a flatboat and spent some months in visiting different places in the South. He then located at Elizabethtown, Ill., where he became interested in the study of law. After a preliminary course of reading he entered the law department of the Indiana State university at Bloomington in 1857. Two years later he completed his legal education and began practice in Shawneetown. Shortly after locating there he formed the acquaintance of Miss Eleanora, daughter of John D. Richeson, a prominent merchant of that city and about a year later they were married. He continued to practice in Shawneetown for ten or twelve years, when he removed to Mount Vernon, Ill. After four years there he went to Ewing, in Franklin county, and took charge of a large general store, a woolen mill and a flour mill. Here he organized the Farmers' bank and was president of it for some time. After a residence of sixteen years at Ewing he located at Equality, where he practiced law until his death in 1893. While living at Shawneetown he filled the position of city judge for one term. Judge Turner and his wife had the following children: One who died unnamed in infancy; John D. R., who now lives in Springfield, Mo.; Spencer and Judith Mimms, both deceased; James B., Charles W., and Jesse M., all now living at Equality; Minnie T.; Mary, who died in infancy; Albert R., also deceased, and Eugene Ambrose, now living at Niagara Falls, N. Y. The mother of these children died in 1899. Charles W. Turner, the sixth child of the family, was born at Shawneetown, Dec. 13, 1869. While living at Ewing he attended the college there, after which he attended the Southern Illinois Normal school at Carbondale, and took a course in the Bryant & Stratton business college at St. Louis. After the death of his father, in 1893, he took charge, with his brother, John D. R., of the large mercantile establishment at Equality, and the farming interests of the estate. Upon the death of his mother, six years later, he was appointed executor of the estate. In 1900 he went to Grand Rapids and assumed the management of an aunt's business matters during the last years of her life. In the fall of 1903 he returned to Equality, where now resides. Mr. Turner has been successful as a business man. Just before going to Grand Rapids he built the Turner business block and opera house in Equality, which building he still owns. This marked his public spirit and enterprising disposition and shows that he is one of the progressive men of his town. He is a member of the Independent Order of Odd Fellows, the Modern Woodmen of America, and the Court of Honor, and both himself and wife belong to the Presbyterian church. Politically he is a Democrat, with Prohibition sympathies, though he never "dabbles" in politics. On Dec. 26, 1900, he was united in marriage to Miss Pet, daughter of George W. Moore, an old resident and prominent grain dealer of Equality. Mrs. Turner was born near Equality, Sept. 26, 1877.

GEORGE W. MOORE, a grain and seed dealer of Equality, Ill., is of Scotch extraction, his ancestors belonging to the same family as Sir John Moore, the celebrated British general who was killed at the battle of Corunna, Jan. 16, 1809. George Moore, the father of the subject of this sketch, was born at the little village of Montgomery, Hamilton county, O., in 1799. While still in his boyhood he had the misfortune to lose his father by death, and he became the chief support of his widowed mother. Consequently his opportunities to acquire an education were very much restricted, yet by his own efforts he mastered the intricacies of the profession of civil engineer and surveyor, and followed that occupation for several years upon arriving at manhood's estate. In 1845 he removed to Lawrenceburg, Ind., and in 1852 to Gallatin county, Ill., where he bought a farm three miles east of Equality. Here he passed the remainder of his life in farming and surveying. He died in 1863. His wife was a Miss Mary Ann Cross, a native of Kentucky, who survived him until 1884. They had six children, viz.: Ludwell G., who died in 1853; Dr. Thomas H., who died in Hopkins county, Ky., at the age of forty-four years; James and William, twins, now living in Gallatin county; Jennie, widow of C. C. Smith, of Equality; and George W., the subject of this sketch. George W. Moore was born Sept. 4, 1846, while his parents were living at Lawrenceburg. He was therefore but six years old when the family removed to Illinois. He grew to manhood in Gallatin county, received his education in the public schools there, and has lived all his life in the vicinity of Equality. Upon arriving at his majority he became a farmer and followed that occupation until 1884. In 1886 he engaged in the grain and seed business, in which he has continued ever since. Mr. Moore has always taken an active interest in local public affairs, and he has served several terms as mayor of Equality. In 1870 he was married to Miss Martha, daughter of Owen Riley, an old citizen of Gallatin county, and to this union there have been born three children, two sons and a daughter: Marshall R. and Harry, the two boys, are partners in the drug business at Equality, and Pet is the wife of Charles W. Turner, a sketch of whose family appears elsewhere in this work.

WINFIELD SCOTT PHILLIPS, lawyer and bank president, of Ridgway, Ill., is a native of Tennessee and a descendant of one of the old pioneer families of that state. Several generations have lived in Tennessee, though the family came originally from Virginia. Richard Newton Phillips, the grandfather of the subject of this sketch, was a man of considerable influence in his county. He was a large land owner and at the breaking out of the war possessed eight slaves. Notwithstanding this he was a pronounced opponent of secession and cheerfully gave his negroes their freedom. He died about 1878 or 1879. He married a Miss Margaret Poole and they had a family of six children: William, Samuel Poole, James B., John Milton, Sarah, and Eliza Word. The last named is the only survivor of the family and now lives at Shelbyville, Tenn. John Milton was a captain in one of the Union Tennessee regiments during the war, and afterward held the position of deputy internal revenue collector for some time. Subsequently he removed to Macon, Ga., and after living there awhile started for California. The last heard of him was when he was near Salt Lake City, and it is supposed that he met his death by foul play. James B. Phillips, the third son, was born in Rutherford county, Tenn., in 1819. He was given a good common school education and upon reaching manhood became a farmer, which occupation he followed through life, though he was a natural mechanic and did a great deal of work in the construction of cotton gins and wool carding machines. While still a young man he removed to Bedford county, Tenn. In politics he was a Whig, and during the life of the American party affiliated with that organization. When the war broke out he organized an independent company, and for about two years was engaged in drilling newly enlisted troops. In December, 1863, he removed with his family to Golconda, Ill., making the trip by way of the Cumberland and Ohio rivers on the *Argonaut*. He bought a farm six miles west of Golconda and lived there until 1884, when he removed to Creal Springs, in Williamson county, and farmed there until his death in November, 1897. He was twice married. His first wife was Miss Agnes Caroline Wise, a native of Monroe county, Miss., and a distant relative of Gov. John S. Wise, of Virginia. To this marriage there were born the following children: Radford Reedy, now living at Puxico, Mo.; Virginia, wife of James A. Adams, of Southeastern Texas; Clay and Epiminondas, both of whom died in infancy; Tennessee Belle and Campbell, also died young; Alice, wife of John F. Glass, of Marion, Ill.; Winfield Scott, the subject of this sketch; William Monroe, now living at Chanute, Kan.; and Melissa Ellen, wife of Robert M. Morrison, of Ridgway. The mother of these children died in January, 1864, and the father married Margaret Zerinda Crawford, of Pope county, Ill. To this union there were born five children, viz.: Eugene B., now at Morrell, Ark.; Ida, died at the age of sixteen years; Horace Poole, died in childhood; Ethel, wife of Oscar Williams, of Marion, Ill.; and Irenæus, who died in infancy. The mother is still living and makes her home with her daughter Ethel. Winfield Scott Phillips was born at Normandy, Bedford county, Tenn., Jan. 20, 1854, and was about nine years old when his parents removed to Illinois. His mother died on his tenth birthday, and he went to live with an uncle, Samuel P. Phillips, in Pope county. Here he remained until his father remarried, when he returned to the parental roof. In the public schools he secured a good practical education, one of his teachers being James A. Rose, afterward secretary of state, of Illinois. When he was about twenty years of age he began teaching and taught for six successive terms in Pope and Gallatin counties. While thus engaged he devoted his spare time to the study of law under Thomas H. Clark, of Golconda, and finished his studies with D. M. Kinsall, of Shawneetown. On July 8, 1880, he was admitted to the bar and at once opened an office in Ridgway, where he has continued in practice ever since. Mr. Phillips is prominently identified with the financial interests of Gallatin county, being president of the Gallatin County State bank, and the Exchange bank at Omaha. He is one of the active Republicans of the county, and in 1902 was the candidate for county judge. Although the Democratic majority for the state ticket that year was 620 in the county, Mr. Phillips was defeated by only 217. By appointment of Governor Yates he is one of the trustees of the Southern Illinois Normal school at Carbondale, and he is also a trustee of the James Milliken university at Decatur. He is a member of the Masonic fraternity and the Independent Order of Odd Fellows, and both himself and wife belong to the Cumberland Presbyterian church, in which he holds the office of elder. On May 11, 1879, he was united in marriage to Miss Luella, daughter of Braxton Carter Parter, an old resident of the State of Illinois. To this union there have been born the following children: Sarah Agnes, wife of Otis C. Moore, of Ridgway, who was one of the Jefferson Guards during the St. Louis exposition; William Braxton, cashier of the Exchange bank of Omaha; Anna Alice and Clyde Winfield, at home.

HARMON PINNELL BOZARTH, attorney at law and insurance underwriter, of Omaha, Ill., can trace the origin of his family in America to a French soldier of that name who came over with La Fayette and fought in the Revolution. After the war he received a grant of land in Virginia from the new government, and passed the remainder of his life in the country whose freedom he had helped to establish. He reared a large family of children, and one of his sons, Elihu Bozarth, crossed the mountains and located in Central Kentucky. There he entered a tract of land, became a well-to-do farmer and reared a family of children. Israel Bozarth, a son of Elihu, was born in Kentucky, received a common school education

there, and in 1815 came to Illinois, locating near the present village of
Equality, in Gallatin county. He entered government land, cleared a
farm and lived there for several years, after which he removed to Miller
county, Mo., and died there. His wife was a Miss Wilson, also a native
of Kentucky and a very successful physician. She had a large practice in Gallatin county and continued to practice after removing to
Missouri. She died at the advanced age of eighty-seven years, the
mother of eight children: Bryant, Tilford, Stephen, Jonathan, Finis,
Franklin, Mary and Nicinda, all now dead with the possible exception
of Stephen and Mary, who, if living at all, reside somewhere in Missouri. Franklin P. Bozarth, the youngest son of the family, was
born while they lived near Equality, and passed his whole life in Gallatin county. He received a limited education, entered land from the
government, and became a farmer. At the age of thirty years he was
stricken with total blindness, but notwithstanding this discouraging
handicap he continued to manage his farm and between that time and
the age of forty-seven he had cleared 200 acres and accumulated considerable personal property. It was his greatest satisfaction at that age
to know that he had not become a burden to his friends because of his
misfortune, and that he did not owe a dollar in the world. He died
in 1866, as he had lived, out of debt and with a large number of
friends. About 1848 he was married to Lucretia, the daughter of
Wiley Pinnell, an old settler of Saline county, Ill. Wiley Pinnell was
born in Kentucky, his father having been a French soldier who fought
under La Fayette. While still a young man he was married to Elizabeth Easley and located in Saline county, where they reared a family
of children, viz.: Lucretia, Willis, William A., Gilbert, Greene, Juda,
Harmon, Carlin, Nancy, Ambrose and Wesley. During the Mexican
war Wiley Pinnell held the rank of captain in the American army, and
at the commencement of the Civil war, although sixty-six years of age
offered his services to his country, passed a physical examination, was
appointed sergeant and served for two and a half years. At the second
battle of Atlanta he was overcome by the heat, was sent home to recover, but died a few months later. He was one of the few men in
that great contest that came of a family three generations of which
were on the firing line. Besides his own enlistment he had four sons,
Willis, Gilbert, Ambrose and Carlin, and two grandsons, John W.
Bozarth and Carroll Pinnell, in the Union army. Truly, a remarkable
military record! Franklin P. Bozarth and his wife had a large family
of children, only four of whom are now living; John W. is a farmer
in Missouri; Harmon P. is the subject of this sketch; Lucy is the

wife of William M. Davis, of East St. Louis, and Alice is the wife of R. M. Edwards, of Gallatin county. Harmon P. Bozarth was born on a farm near where he now lives, Feb. 2, 1852. As he grew up he worked on a farm during the summer months and attended the district schools in the winter time. He made good use of his time in school and at the age of thirteen could boast that he had "gone through" Ray's third book in arithmetic, which in that day was the height of mathematical ambition of the average school boy. Much of his early education was obtained by self-study. Frequently he could be seen taking a book to the field with him, in order that he might snatch a few moments study while his team was resting. At the age of seventeen he commenced teaching and for seventeen years taught in the common schools of Pope county. In 1872 he attended one term at Ewing college in Franklin county; spent one term in the Enfield high school the following year, and in 1875 attended the Southern Illinois Normal school at Carbondale. In 1881 a change was made in the county superintendent law, which left a year unprovided for and he was appointed by the board of education of Gallatin county to fill the interim. This was done by a board of the opposite political faith to Mr. Bozarth, several members of the board expressing their belief that he was the best and most progressive teacher in the county. Mr. Bozarth continued to teach until 1886, having in the meantime taken up the study of law. In 1886 he retired to the farm, engaged in agricultural pursuits and in pursuing his legal studies until 1892, when he was admitted to the bar. It has been a maxim of Mr. Bozarth's life to do thoroughly whatever he undertakes. The judges who examined him for admission said afterward that he was one of the best informed men in the basic principles of law that they had ever examined. He at once began the practice of his profession at Omaha, in which he still continues. In addition to his law practice he has a large fire insurance business, and he has always taken an interest in public affairs. In 1890 he was the census enumerator for Omaha, and for two terms held the office of justice of the peace. At the beginning of the Spanish-American war he raised a company, of which he was commissioned captain, but the war closed before it could be mustered into service. Mr. Bozarth owns a fine fruit farm in White county, a fine residence and other property in Omaha. He is a member of the Masonic fraternity, the Independent Order of Odd Fellows, the Court of Honor, the Loyal Americans, and belongs to the Methodist church. Mrs. Bozarth is a Presbyterian. He was married on April 9, 1874, to

Miss Sarah M. Wolfe, the youngest daughter of Dr. A. A. Wolfe, of Hamilton county, and today they have the following children: John A., a freight conductor, living at El Paso, Texas; Charles Edwin, at home; William Franklin, who enlisted May 31, 1901, in Company A, Twenty-eighth United States infantry, was mustered at Vancouver barracks in the State of Washington, sailed for the Philippines in November, served there a little over two years, being present at the capture of General Melvar, was made corporal for bravery in action, and was the youngest noncommissioned officer in the regiment. He is now at home. The others are Fred D., Minnie May, Pearl, Lillian and George, all at home.

JAMES M. BEAN, a well known farmer of Gallatin county, Ill., living near the town of Ridgway, is a descendant of one of the pioneer settlers of that locality. His grandfather, Jonathan Bean, was born in the State of Tennessee, but in the spring of 1832 came with his family to Gallatin county, where he bought land and followed farming the remainder of his life, living to an advanced age. He married Catherine Skeef, a native of Tennessee, and they were the parents of the following children: William, Henry, John, James, Nancy, and Elizabeth, all now deceased. Henry Bean, the second of the family, was born in Tennessee in 1809, and was therefore twenty-three years of age when his parents removed to Illinois. He became a farmer and at the time of his death in 1852 was the largest land owner in Gallatin county. His wife was a Miss Margaret Hise, a native of Tennessee, and a daughter of Jacob Hise, who removed from South Carolina to Tennessee and later to Illinois, where he died at the age of 103 years and six months. His wife, who was of German extraction, lived to be 101 years and six months old. Henry and Margaret Bean were the parents of ten children, viz.: Jacob, Turana, James M., Catherine, Jane, Jasper, Elizabeth, George, Margaret, and Henry. James M. is the subject of this sketch; Jasper died in the army during the war; Margaret is the wife of George Dillard, of Gallatin county; Henry lives in Ridgway; and the others are deceased. James M. Bean was born near Ridgway, April 10, 1832, and has passed his whole life in Gallatin county. He received a good common school education and upon reaching manhood became a farmer, in which occupation he has ever since continued, being regarded as one of the progressive farmers of the county. On Aug. 13, 1862, he enlisted as a private in Company K, One Hundred and Thirty-first Illinois infantry, and served with that command until Nov. 15, 1863, when he was transferred to Company C, Twenty-ninth Illinois infantry, where he remained until the close of the war. He was in the siege of Vicksburg, the engagement at Arkansas Post, and in numerous minor skirmishes. After the war he returned home and again took up the duties of farm life, in which he has continued ever since. Mr. Bean has been a member of the Cumberland Presbyterian church ever since he was fifteen years of age, and his entire life has been consistent with the teachings of his religious faith. He was married in 1854 to Miss Mary, daughter of James Glass, an old resident of Gallatin county. She died on July 15, 1893, the mother of nine children, viz.: Monroe, now living in Gallatin county; Nazarene, wife of Elijah Nelson, of Kansas; Jerome, a resident of Ridgway; Josephine, wife of Harvey Hemphill, of Enfield, Ill.; Sherman, living in Gallatin county; Fastina Ellen, wife of Jacob Willis, of Ridgway; Logan Grant and Belle, deceased, and Susan Catherine, wife of William Hatfield, of Ridgway.

ROBERT MONROE RUDOLPH, a prominent grain dealer and president of the town board of Omaha, Ill., is of German lineage. The origin of the family in this country is traced back to one Peter Rudolph, who came from the Fatherland just before the Revolutionary war and settled in North Carolina. When the contest for independence was commenced he cast in his lot with the patriots and was murdered by some of his Tory neighbors. About the year 1800 one of his descendants, Joseph Rudolph, left North Carolina and located near Clarksville, Tenn. There he followed farming until 1823, when he removed with his family to Illinois and settled in White county, where he continued to farm until his death about 1855. He was considered a man of more than average intelligence and was an influential citizen in his community. Before leaving North Carolina he was married to Miss Rachel Lowe, to which union eleven children were born; Peter, David, Margaret, Elizabeth, John, Phœbe, Jane, Andrew, Robert, Frederick and Sarah. All are now deceased. Frederick Lowe Rudolph, the tenth child of the family, was born at Clarksville in 1821, and was therefore but two years old when his parents located on a farm in White county, a few miles northeast of Carmi. There he grew to manhood, received a good common school education and passed his entire life on a farm a few miles from his father's old homestead, dying in 1889. Farming and stock raising was his occupation and he was looked upon as a model farmer and good business man. At the commencement of the Civil war he enlisted in Company K, Eighty-seventh Illinois infantry, and was elected captain of the company, but the serious illness of his wife compelled him to resign his commission. He was married about 1844 to Elizabeth Graham, a native of White county, and they had the following children: Sarepta, George, Robert, Ella, one who died in infancy, Daniel, Benjamin, Harlan, Thompson and Jacob. Sarepta, George and Harlan are deceased; Robert is the subject of this sketch; Ella is the wife of Horace Cleveland and lives at Ridgway, Ill.; Daniel lives on a farm in White county; Thompson is postmaster at Thomaston, Ga., and Jacob is a merchant and grain dealer at Crossville, Ill. The parents died within a week of each other in 1899. Robert M. Rudolph, the oldest living child of Frederick L. and Elizabeth Rudolph, was born in White county, Sept. 4, 1849, and there grew to manhood, receiving a good common school education in the public schools. Upon arriving at his majority he became a farmer and followed that occupation for about ten years, after which he was for five years engaged in the manufacture of brick and tile at Crossville. In 1885 he removed to Gallatin county, where he engaged in farming and dealing in grain at Omaha until 1889, since which time he has given all his attention to the grain business. While living in White county he was elected to various local offices, and for some time has held the position of president of the Omaha town board. For ten years he taught school during the winter months. Mr. Rudolph is a member of the Free and Accepted Masons and the Independent Order of Odd Fellows, and both himself and wife belong to the Methodist Episcopal church. He was married in 1870 to Miss Anna Dickens, a native of White county, Ill., and to this union there have been born ten children. Charles Dickens died at the age of seventeen years; Frederick L. and Harold L. both live at Crossville; Amy is the wife of Otis Bruce, of Gallatin county; Nellie is the wife of Thomas Bruce, of Harrisburg, Ill.; Mark is at Los Angeles, Cal.; Robert M., Jr., Jessie, Laura and Hubert are at home.

DR. JUDSON E. STRONG, an eminent homeopathic physician of Cairo, Ill., is a native of Ohio, having been born in the city of Cleveland Nov. 27, 1854. He is a son of A. C. and Harriet M. (Pelton) Strong, both natives of the Buckeye state. On the paternal side Dr. Strong is of Scotch descent, the first of the family in America being John Strong, who came from Scotland in Colonial days. Charles E. Strong, a cousin of Dr. Strong's father, served as mayor of Cleveland some time in the later seventies. Thomas J. Strong, the grandfather of the doctor, was a native of Connecticut, but came to Ohio, settled near Cleveland, and there followed farming all his life. A. C.

Strong was a Republican in his day, and with his wife belonged to the Baptist church. Both are now deceased. They had two children, Edgar C., who died at the age of twelve years, and Judson E. Dr. Strong received a high school education in his native city, after which he attended the Western Reserve college at Hudson, Ohio. In 1878 he went into the office of Dr. George F. Turrell and commenced the study of medicine, and in 1880 graduated from the Cleveland Homeopathic Medical college. He began practice at Clinton, Mich., but soon removed to Hillsdale, in that state, and remained there until January, 1883, when he came to Cairo, where he has built up a lucrative practice. He is a member of the Independent Order of Odd Fellows, and in political matters is a Republican. Dr. Strong has been twice married. In June, 1879, he was married to Miss Emma E. Healy, an adopted daughter of Daniel Fish, of Hudson, Mich., and to this marriage there were born two children: Mabel, Mrs. G. F. Yeagley, of Chicago, and Florence E., an expert stenographer in that city. Mrs. Strong died in March, 1882, and on March 9, 1887, he was married at Olney, Ill., to Miss Julia, daughter of Richard and Harriet Nall, of Olney, Ill., her father being a Methodist minister. To this second marriage there have been born the following children: Eugene, Alice, Margaret, and Julia, all at home with their parents.

WILLIAM C. CLARKE, M.D., physician and surgeon of Cairo, Ill., was born at Momence in that state, July 28, 1865, being the third in a family of five children born to Dr. M. O. and Martha (Williams) Clarke, the former a native of New York and the latter of Kentucky. Dr. M. O. Clarke was eminent in the profession and before leaving New York was for several years in partnership with the celebrated Dr. Lester Sprague. Dr. W. C. Clarke spent four years at St. Viateur's college at Bourbonnais, Ill.; two years at Grand Prairie seminary, at Onarga, and in 1894 graduated with high standing from Rush Medical college of Chicago. After one year's hospital service in Chicago he located at Cairo, where he rapidly built up a magnificent practice. As a surgeon he is recognized as being one of the best in Southern Illinois, being a student under the celebrated surgeon, Dr. A. J. Oschner, of Chicago. He has doubtless inherited his father's ability and being a close student of everything pertaining to his profession he has kept fully abreast of the progress of the science of medicine. Doctor Clarke is a member of the American, the Illinois State, and the Southern Illinois Medical associations, and the medical society of Alexander county. In 1898 he was united in marriage to Miss Jessie Lincoln, of Momence, Ill., and to this union there have been born two children, Martha and William C. Jr. Politically he is a Republican.

FELIX GRUNDY BLACKARD, a retired farmer, living near the town of Omaha, Gallatin county, Ill., is a descendant of Scotch-Irish stock. A little while before the commencement of the Revolutionary war two brothers left Scotland for America, having previously left Ireland to escape political persecution. Upon their arrival in this country they located in South Carolina, where they were married and where the descendants of one of them are still to be found. The other brother removed to Virginia and subsequently to Tennessee, where a large number of his descendants still reside. Some time in the twenties five of these descendants, brothers, named William, Spivey, Jabe, Thomas and Joshua, came to Illinois and located near where the boundary line between White and Gallatin counties now runs. There each of them entered government land and followed farming. Several of their descendants still live in that section. William Blackard, one of the above named brothers, was born about the year 1800. Consequently he was still a young man when he came to Illinois. With the exception of a few years in Lebanon, Ill., all his life after coming to the state was passed in White or Gallatin county. His death occurred about 1874. In his day he was one of the leading citizens of his locality and was generally respected by his acquaintances. He was twice married, first to Miss Jemima Trousdale, one of an old Illinois family, and to this union were born the following children: Felix G., the subject of this sketch; Margaret, widow of James Armstrong and now living at Omaha; Thomas and Sarah, who died in childhood; Alexander, who died in early manhood; Abner McCord, now of Mt. Carmel, Ill., and Alfred Benton, who died at Garden City, Kan. The second marriage was to Miss Teresa Armstrong, of Gallatin county, and to this marriage were born the following children: Three that died in infancy; Margie Ann, also deceased; Josephine, widow of Edwin Foster, of Herrin, Ill.; Franklin L., living in Tennessee; Mary, widow of Thomas Coats, living in Missouri, and Nancy, deceased. The first wife died about 1843, and the second died at Herrin in 1903. Felix Grundy Blackard, the eldest child by the first wife, was born in White county, Sept. 16, 1830. He received such an education as the common schools of that day afforded, and by reading and self-study he has added to that until he is one of the well informed men of his section. Upon reaching manhood he became a farmer, which occupation he followed all through his active life. In his earlier years he was noted for his talent for music and taught singing schools over a large part of Southern Illinois, being the first teacher of music to introduce the "round note system" in that part of the country. Mr. Blackard has been twice married. His first wife was Miss Sarah Gott, of Gallatin county. Her children were Sarah Catherine and Martha, who died in childhood; and Solon Douglas, who died in 1881. The second marriage was to Mrs. Harriet A. Oliver, *née* Pearce, a daughter of James Pearce of White county. Ten children have been born to this second marriage. Herman Madden lives at Omaha; Mamie Ann married Edward Moore and died in 1889; William J. is superintendent of the Gallatin county schools; John C. is in Omaha; Nellie and Edwin died in childhood; May is at home; Ethel died in infancy; Alma married Charles C. Green and died in January, 1904, and Lou is at home, a teacher in the public schools.

JAMES CYRIL SULLIVAN, M.D., a well known physician of Cairo, Ill., was born at Weston on the Humber, York county, Ontario, Dec. 17, 1844, his parents being John L. and Hannah (Warren) Sullivan. In 1867-68 he took his first course of medical lectures in college at St. Louis. In 1871 he entered the University of Louisville and received the degree of M.D. from that institution on February 29th, of the following year. Since that time he has been in continuous practice at Cairo, where he has built up a lucrative business and has accumulated considerable property. Doctor Sullivan belongs to the American, State, District and County Medical associations, in the work of which he takes an active part, having read papers on some phase of medical practice before meetings of all. At the present time he is a member of the Illinois State board of health. In addition to his profession he is deeply interested in astronomy, and in 1892 published a text book on the subject called "Celestial Physics."

On Sept. 11, 1883, Doctor Sullivan was married to Miss Hannah, daughter of Patrick and Ellen Smith, old residents of Cairo, and to this union there has been born one son, James Albert. He was born Nov. 7, 1884, graduated from the Cairo high school, and is now a student in the College of Physicians and Surgeons of St. Louis. Politically Doctor Sullivan is a Republican. In religious matters he has followed in the footsteps of his parents, who were Catholics, though his mother's people belonged to the Episcopal church. He also belongs to the Catholic Knights of America.

ALPHEUS ALONZO BONDURANT, M.D., one of the leading physicians of Cairo, Ill., and a specialist in diseases of the eye and ear, is of French descent, his great-grandfather, Benjamin Bondurant, coming from that country to America before the Revolutionary war. He first located in Virginia, where he engaged in mercantile pursuits, but later removed to Tennessee. One of his sons, Robert Alfred, married in Tennessee and went to Kentucky after reaching middle life, where he passed the remainder of his days. His son, John S., was born in Tennessee, not far from Dresden, married Julia Edmiston, a native of that state, went with his father to Kentucky and there followed farming all his life. In his lifetime he was an ardent Democrat, a prominent member of the Masonic fraternity, and with his wife belonged to the Baptist church. She is still living in Fulton county, Ky. Dr. Bondurant is the second of nine children born to John S. and Julia Bondurant, five of whom are still living. He was born in Fulton county, Ky., and acquired his education in the common schools and the Fulton high school. In 1872 he went into the office of Dr. Charles W. Miles, at Jordan, Ky., and commenced the study of medicine. During the years 1873-74 he attended the medical department of the university of Louisville, and in 1875 graduated from the Bellevue Hospital Medical college of New York. He located at Charleston, Mo., and practiced there until 1892, when he came to Cairo, having first taken a special course in the New York Eye and Ear infirmary, of which class of diseases he makes a specialty, though he has a large general practice. Dr. Bondurant is a member of the American and the Illinois State Medical associations; the Medical society of Alexander county, and was one of the charter members of the Southeast Missouri Medical association, of which he served as president the first year of its existence. In addition to his professional interests he is a member of the McKnight-Keaton Grocery Company. He is a Democrat in his political views, though not an active politician; is a Knight Templar Mason, and with his family belongs to the Baptist church. On Sept. 8, 1875, he was married to Miss Mary J. Boker, of Charleston. The children born to this marriage are: Levie, wife of C. L. Keaton, Jr.; Eunice, now secretary of the McKnight-Keaton company; Earl, wife of J. W. Bradford, of Union county, Tenn.; Flint, attending the Northwestern university; Vela, Alonzo, David S., and Iona, at home; and one who died in infancy. Levie and Eunice are graduates of Stephens Female college, Columbia, Mo. Dr. Bondurant and his family live in one of the handsomest residences in Cairo, and are identified with the social life of the city. As a physician he enjoys the confidence of his patrons and the respect of the profession, and as a man he stands high in the community as a progressive, patriotic and law abiding citizen.

REV. JAMES GILLEN. It is a pleasure to the biographer to head this sketch with the name of the priest who is in every sense worthy of the distinction afforded by honorable mention among the notable citizens of Cairo. Both of the flourishing Catholic churches there have been fortunate in having him for their pastor, as he was first located at St. Patrick's parish, and is at present the rector of St. Joseph's. Among the people of the community in general, as well as the parishioners, he is justly considered as a gentleman of large resources and unquestioned ability. To his efforts may be attributed the success which has come to the church in recent years, and he is at present engaged in erecting a parochial school which when completed will be a magnificent edifice, one of the most modern and up-to-date structures of its kind in the State of Illinois. This fine Gothic school building is conveniently situated near the church and residence, and will for many years to come be a credit to the educational advantages of the city. Rev. Father Gillen was born in Heisterberg, Feb. 23, 1861. His parents, John and Frances (Gross) Gillen, natives of Germany, emigrated to America in 1875 and settled near Toledo, O., where they still make their home. The subject of this sketch received the rudiments of his education in the parochial schools of his native place, and afterward entered St. Joseph's college at Cleveland, O., where he remained five years. His literary training was subsequently continued at Teutopolis, Ill., where he improved his excellent educational advantages to their fullest extent. On the completion of his studies at Teutopolis he took a philosophical course of two years at Montreal, Canada, and afterward went to Europe, commencing the study of theology at the North American college at Rome, where he graduated with high honors after a brilliant career of four years. Upon his return to the United States, he was ordained to the priesthood at St. Francis., Wis., May 9, 1886, and on the 14th of the following month accepted the pastorate of St. Joseph's church at Lebanon. It was at this place that Father Gillen's executive ability so largely displayed itself, where, with about sixty-five families, he erected a beautiful church at a cost of $15,000. Fresh labors were thrust upon the young and zealous priest when he was transferred to Waterloo. After gaining the esteem and love of the entire community there, he was sent to Prairie du Rocher, where the people were for two years favored and encouraged by his presence and example. Three years ago he became stationed in the city of Cairo, the past year of which has been spent as pastor of St. Joseph's parish. This parish is among the largest and best in the diocese of Belleville, and is constantly increasing in importance and in the number of its communicants. Besides the 250 pupils on its school roll, there is also located in the parish St. Mary's infirmary, to which all classes of citizens are hastened for the relief of their bodily ailments, and which is unanimously acknowledged to be an institution of which Catholics and non-Catholics are equally proud. Father Gillen is a very popular priest, a man of education and great energy, and to his untiring efforts is to be credited the fact that his congregation enjoys a steady numerical growth. He has devoted himself persistently to the task of raising the money necessary for the erection of the new $15,000 school, and his efforts have been rewarded with success. Although he speaks and is master of seven languages, personally he is one of the most modest and unassuming of men. He is of a kindly, pleasant address and sociable disposition. He is not only a priest among priests, but a man among men. As a public speaker, he is earnest, ready, and fascinating because of the ever present touch of human kindness in his tone and manner. He has labored not for his own temporal advancement, but for the highest spiritual welfare of his parishioners, and it is not strange, therefore, that he is esteemed by each one as a personal friend.

McKNIGHT-KEATON GROCERY COMPANY, of Cairo, Ill., wholesale dealers in groceries, fruits and produce, was organized and incorporated on Aug. 1, 1901, with a capital stock of $35,000. The company occupies a building 50 x 175 feet, four stories in height, that was erected especially for its accommodation, at the corner of Fourth and Ohio streets. Four salesmen are employed on the road, the trade extending to Southeastern Missouri, Northeastern Arkansas, Southern Illinois, and Western Kentucky and Tennessee. The officers of the company are C. L. Keaton, president and treasurer; W. A. McKnight, vice-president; E. Bondurant, secretary. Though one of the youngest mercantile establishments of Cairo it is one of the most up-to-date concerns of its kind in the Lower Ohio valley. By modern methods of advertising it has come prominently into notice, with the result that its trade is constantly on the increase, and new territory is being added to its already large field.

Clarence L. Keaton, president of the company, was born at Bloomfield, Mo., March 27, 1874, his parents being C. L. and Sallie E. Keaton, natives of Carroll county, Tenn. His father is an attorney, now located at Dexter, Mo. After a common school education in the schools of Bloomfield Mr. Keaton came to Cairo in 1891, and for about ten years was employed by the New York store as a clerk and traveling salesman. When the McKnight-Keaton company was organized he was elected president and treasurer and has held these offices ever since. He is a member of the Knights of Pythias, the Commercial Travelers' organization and the Baptist church, to which his wife also belongs, and in politics is a Democrat. He was married on Dec. 27, 1899, to Miss Levie Bondurant (see sketch of Dr. A. A. Bondurant), and to this union there have been born two children, Fern Bondurant and Clarence Alonzo.

W. A. McKnight, vice-president, was born Jan. 2, 1865, at Porterfield, Tenn., where his father, A. G. McKnight, is a prominent stock raiser. After attending Burritt college, Spencer, Tenn., he engaged in the retail grocery business in connection with Hodge, Smith & Co., of Murfreesboro, with whom he remained for eight years. He then went to Waxahachie, Tex., and traveled for a wholesale grocery house there for two years, after which he was with F. Smith & Son, of St. Louis, until 1901, when he became one of the organizers of the company of which he is now vice-president. Mr. McKnight is a Democrat, a member of Ascalon Lodge, No. 51, Knights of Pythias, of Cairo, and belongs to the Royal Arcanum at Murfreesboro, Tenn On Dec. 19, 1900, he was united in marriage to Miss Edna Tucker, of Tucker, Ark., and they have one son, W. A., Jr., now in his fourth year. Mr. and Mrs. McKnight belong to the Presbyterian church, and are prominent in the social life of Cairo.

NEW YORK STORE MERCANTILE COMPANY, of Cairo, Ill., was first started in 1862, under the firm name of C. O. Patier & Co. In 1883 it was incorporated as the New York Store Company, and in 1891 was reincorporated under its present name, with a capital stock of $30,000. The officers at the present time are Charles E. Hessian, president; Charles O. Patier, vice-president; John B. Greaney, secretary and treasurer. The company handles all kinds of merchandise; occupies a building at the corner of Commercial avenue and Nineteenth street 100 x 125 feet, two stories high; one on the opposite side of the street 125 x 160 feet; covers territory in Tennessee, Arkansas, Missouri, Kentucky and Illinois, and keeps four men constantly on the road as salesmen.

Charles E. Hessian, president of the company, was born at Mound City, Ill., Jan. 24, 1865, his parents being Timothy and Winifred Hessian, natives of Ireland. Timothy Hessian was a railroad man, and both himself and wife are now deceased. Of their seven children but two are now living: the subject of this sketch and Katherine, now a Mrs. Curran, of St. Louis. Charles E. Hessian came to Cairo in 1866, and entered the employ of the New York store as a cash boy Oct. 18, 1881. After two years in this capacity he was promoted to a clerkship, and in 1888 became a stockholder in the company. In June, 1891, he was made secretary; was elected vice-president in January, 1896, and since January, 1902, has been president of the company. Mr. Hessian and the business have thus grown up together, and with the growth of the company he has assumed new responsibilities, yet has never been found wanting in any of the essentials of the successful merchant and manager of a large business enterprise. The Cairo *Bulletin* recently said of him: "No man in the city occupies a more enviable position in the business and social circles than does he, and no man in the city is more worthy of the general esteem and confidence in which he is held by our people." Upon the death of Captain Patier, the founder of the business, Mr. Hessian was made one of the executors of the estate, an office he filled with signal ability and fidelity. He was married in April, 1892, to Miss Cecilia, daughter of James and Mary Greaney, of Cairo, and to this marriage there have been born the following children: William, died in infancy; Edwin Patier; Harold; Clarence, died at the age of three and a half years; Ralph; LeRoy, and Rose Mary. Mr. Hessian is a member of the Benevolent and Protective Order of Elks, and is a Democrat in his political affiliations. He and his family occupy a handsome residence on Twenty-first street, and he and his wife belong to the Catholic church.

JOHN H. ROBINSON, of Cairo, Ill., prominent in real estate circles and now city judge, was born in Chillicothe, O., May 31, 1833, his parents being John J. and Katie (Hutt) Robinson, both natives of Virginia. His grandfather, Thomas Robinson, came from Scotland when he was a young man, located in Virginia, and there passed his whole life. John J. Robinson learned the trade of baker, and after going to Chillicothe served for years as justice of the peace. In 1875 he removed to Springfield, Mo., where he died, a Republican in his political faith and a member of the Methodist Episcopal church. On the maternal side Judge Robinson is of English descent. His grandfather, Girard Hutt, came from England in the Colonial days and settled on the banks of the Potomac in Westmoreland county, Va. During the Revolutionary war he was driven from his home by Lord Cornwallis, who used his residence as headquarters. He had a brother who was a member of the British Parliament. His son, John Hutt, the father of Judge Robinson's mother, was born Sept. 5, 1763. He enlisted in the American army at the age of fifteen years and served under General Nelson until the close of the war, being present at the siege and surrender of Yorktown. In a number of engagements he fought under Washington, was promoted to sergeant when only seventeen, and in 1781 was discharged as captain. In 1794 he was given a license to preach by Francis Asbury, the first bishop of the Methodist church to come to America. In 1801 he removed to Chillicothe, and there passed the remainder of his life. Katie Hutt Robinson died at Springfield, Mo., in 1898, at the advanced age of eighty-nine years. For years she had been a devoted member of the Methodist Episcopal church. She was the mother of eleven children, six of whom are still living. Judge John H. Robinson received a common school education and learned the trade of cigar maker. For several years he worked at this occupation in Chillicothe and Zanesville, O., and New Orleans, La. In May, 1858, he came to Cairo, and after working at his trade there for a while he was appointed deputy sheriff. When the war broke out he left the sheriff's office, raised a company, of which he was made captain, and which was mustered in in 1862 as Company C, 130th Illinois infantry. He served as captain through the entire war, though during the last nine months he commanded the regiment, owing to the disability of the colonel. The regiment was at Port Gibson, Champion Hills, Black River, the siege of Vicksburg, and was with General Banks on the Red river expedition. After the war he returned to Cairo and was appointed chief of police. Later he held the position of superintendent of the land and levees of the city for nine years, part of which time he also served as justice of the peace. He next engaged in the cigar business for a time, but in 1882 was elected county judge, which office he held for twelve years. In 1896 he was elected to his present office of city judge, and since 1893 has been United States commissioner. Judge Robinson is one of the active Democrats of Cairo, is a member of the Grand Army of the Republic and the Independent Order of Odd Fellows, and is one of the best known men in the city. On March 17, 1853, he was united in marriage to Miss Clara M. Brunner, a native of Somerset, O., and a daughter of Jacob and Julia (Trout) Brunner, the former a native of Pennsylvania and the latter of Maryland. To this marriage there were born two daughters: Kate B. was twice married and died leaving six children, and Florence N. died at the age of twenty-five years.

JEFFERSON B. WARNER, manager for the house of John A. Haynes, wholesale and retail grocer and dealer in steamboat supplies, Cairo, Ill., is a descendant of the Pilgrims who came to America from England early in the seventeenth century. His grandfather, L. J. Warner, was a Vermont farmer, and his father, Carleton Henry Warner, was born in the Green Mountain State. He married Aurora A. Batchelder in that state and in the early sixties went to Tama City, Iowa, where he worked for some time at his trade of blacksmith. Subsequently he went to Quincy, Ill., and from there to Cairo in 1882. Three years later he removed to Alton, Ill., where he still lives. He and his wife are members of the Methodist Episcopal church; he belongs to the Ancient Order of United Workmen, and in politics is always independent. Jefferson is the third child in a family of five, three sons and two daughters, all married and living at the present time. He was born at Tama City, Oct. 7, 1864, and was the first white male child born in that city. His early education was obtained in the common schools of Quincy while the family were living there, and at the age of fifteen years began his business career as a clerk in a cigar store. In November, 1882, he came with his parents to Cairo. The following year he entered the employ of Barclay Bros., wholesale druggists, as a bookkeeper, and remained with this firm until 1890. He was then employed for two years as assistant cashier in the East St. Louis freight office of the Mobile & Ohio railroad, and with the Newport News, now a part of the Illinois Central railroad system, at Memphis, Tenn. In July, 1892, he came back to Cairo, where he became associated with Capt. G. D. Williamson, the then proprietor of the leading boat store of the city, with which he is still connected. (See sketch of C. C. Haynes.) Mr. Warner is a Democrat in his political convictions, though he can hardly be called an active party worker. On Oct. 10, 1893, he was married to Miss Clara Bryant, daughter of the late Frank Bryant, an old-time lumber dealer of Cairo, and to this union there have been born two sons: Kenneth B., aged ten and J. Howard, aged six years. Mr. and Mrs. Warner are members of the Methodist Episcopal church, in which he is one of the trustees.

CLAUDE WINTER, mayor of Cairo, Ill., and member of the firm of Winter Bros., grocers and proprietors of the cold storage plant, was born in that city, May 30, 1858, his parents being Henry and Margaret Winter. His father was born in England, but came in early manhood with several of his brothers to America. He was a tinner by trade and soon after arriving in this country located at Cincinnati, where he worked for a short time, after which he went to Cannelton, then came to Cairo and embarked in the tin and stove business. Later he was engaged in conducting a hotel. He was successful in his business ventures, but toward the close of his life met with financial reverses of a serious nature. He was largely instrumental in giving to Cairo a good fire department, being one of the old volunteer firemen. Both himself and wife were members of the Episcopal church. Their children were William, Josephine, Belle, Alfred E., Claude, Gus., Jessie, Jennie, Albert and Flora. Claude and Gus are twins, Jennie and Albert are deceased, and all those living reside in Cairo. The mother of these children died in 1902. Claude Winter attended the Cairo public schools until he was sixteen years of age, when he began his business life as clerk in the hotel. Later he was in the employ of John McNulty for about ten years in the hardware store, when he and his brothers William and Gus embarked in the grocery business. They started in a small building, but now occupy one of the most modern buildings in the city, as well as one of the largest. The upper floor contains a large public hall. Gus withdrew from the firm after some time and the business is now conducted by Claude and William. Their ice manufacturing and cold storage establishment is one of the best equipped in the lower Ohio valley, and each year shows an increased volume of business in these lines. Mr. Winter is a Democrat and takes a keen interest in public affairs. He served two terms as alderman, where his record was so satisfactory that the people of Cairo called him to a higher position, and in 1903 he was elected mayor. He is a member of the Independent Order of Odd Fellows, the Knights of Pythias, the K. and K. C., and the Alexander club. He was married in 1880 to Hannah, daughter of William Gerrin, of Cairo. She died in 1901, the mother of the following children: Claude, Jr., Ethel, Josephine, one who died in infancy, William and Margaret. All received good educations, Claude spending two years at Culver Military academy.

WILLIAM R. HALLIDAY, one of the leading contractors of Cairo, Ill., and proprietor of a large brick manufacturing plant, was born at Portland, Ky., now a part of the city of Louisville, June 30, 1859, his parents being Samuel B. and Elizabeth Halliday. The Hallidays are of Scotch descent, the first of the family in this country coming from Scotland at a very early date. Samuel B. Halliday removed with his family to Cairo about the time of the commencement of the Civil war, and engaged in the real estate business. He soon became prominent in the commercial life of the city as cashier of the City National bank, and was at one time a member of the firm of Halliday Bros. He died in September, 1868, and his wife in 1880. Both were members of the Episcopal church. Their children are Ada, wife of John Aisthorpe; William R., the subject of this sketch; Edwin C., president of the Cairo Hardware Company; Horace H., a prominent business man, of Cairo. William R. Halliday was educated in the common schools and the Southern Ohio university, which institution he attended in 1878-79, but did not graduate. After leaving school he was in the employ of the American Express Company for about a year; was then with Halliday Bros. for a short time, after which he built a corn meal and feed mill, which he conducted for about four years under the name of W. R. Halliday & Co. He next formed a partnership with H. H. Halliday for dealing in grain, hay and builders' supplies. About 1889 he commenced the manufacture of brick and soon afterward became interested in the business of contracting for the construction of buildings, etc. His brick works have an annual capacity of about 20,000,000 brick, and during the busy season he employs about 125 men. In 1901 he again became associated with H. H. Halliday in the organization of the H. H. Halliday Sand and Gravel Company, which dredges and washes the sand from the Ohio river, thus guaranteeing a clean sand, the resulting gravel being used for concrete work. The company is equipped with the steam dredge *Virginia* and a number of barges, the daily output being from twenty to twenty-five cars. Shipments have been made to various parts of the country, and contractors of heavy stone work, fine cement work, etc., have pronounced the sand far superior to that taken from gravel pits or natural sand-bars. Mr. Halliday still gives much of his attention to his contracting business, and quite a number of buildings in the city owe their existence to his skill as a builder. He is a member of the Knights of Pythias and the Benevolent and Protective Order of Elks, and is a Democrat in his political opinions. On Sept. 21, 1882, William R. Halliday and Miss Frances A. Rexford, of Centralia, Ill., were married, and to this union there have been born two children. Julia is the wife of Otis W. Severns, of Centralia, and Norman is connected with the State bank of Parma, Idaho. Mr. and Mrs. Halliday live in a fine residence which he built at the corner of Twenty-eighth and Elm streets in 1890.

C. C. HAYNES, one of the managers of the John A. Haynes steamboat supply store, Cairo, Ill., was born in Livingston county, Ky., May 11, 1852. His parents, E. P. and Elizabeth (Lake) Haynes, were both born in Kentucky, the father of English and the mother of Scotch-Irish descent. E. P. Haynes began his business life at Smithland, Ky., as proprietor of a wharfboat and steamboat supply store. In 1860 he came to Cairo, where he formed a partnership with Capt. G. D. Williamson, in the same line of business, and the Williamson & Haynes Co. was organized. Some ten or twelve years later Mr. Haynes sold out his interest and returned to Smithland, where he died June 17, 1904. Captain Williamson continued to conduct the business in Cairo until 1895, when he sold out to John A. Haynes, who conducted it until his death, Feb. 25, 1904. Since then the business has been managed by C. C. Haynes and J. B. Warner. (See sketch of Mr. Warner elsewhere.) E. P. Haynes' wife died in July, 1886. Both were members of the Methodist Episcopal church. In his early life he was a Whig, but in later years became a Democrat. They had twelve children, six of whom grew to maturity and four are still living, viz.: Mrs. Addie Dunn, of Smithland; Mrs. G. F. Phillips, of Paducah, Ky.; H. L. Haynes, of Austin, Tex., and the subject of this sketch. John A. Haynes lived in Cairo nearly all his life, and was connected with the business from the time of leaving school until his death. He left one daughter, Miss Anna Lake Haynes, who is the owner of the store, and who resides with an aunt in Kentucky. C. C. Haynes received his education in the common schools, and has been engaged in mercantile pursuits most of his life since. For two years and a half he was in business in Oklahoma, and after returning to the Ohio valley was with Fowler, Crumbaugh & Co. of Paducah for several years. He then became associated with his brother, and upon the latter's death became one of the managers of the business, as already stated. In September, 1904, he was married to Miss Lou Phillips of Paducah, and now resides in Cairo.

CHRISTOPHER L. SMITH, of Cairo, Ill., superintendent of the Cairo, Memphis & Southern Railroad and Transportation Company, which is a branch of the Chicago Mill and Lumber Company, was born at Kingston, Jamaica, Sept. 10, 1870. He is a son of Christopher and Emily Smith, both natives of England, and who were married in that country. The father was a government contractor, who, some time in the sixties, was called to the West Indies in connection with his business. He died there in 1875, leaving three children: George, Christopher L. and Adeline. George afterward died, Christopher is the subject of this sketch and Adeline is the wife of T. G. Medinger of New York city. The mother still lives in Jamaica. Christopher L. Smith attended the collegiate school of Jamaica and finished his education in grammar school No. 55 of New York city. In 1887 he entered the employ of the American News Company of New York, and was with that concern for about eight years, at the end of which time he came to Cairo, where he entered the employ of the Three States Lumber Company. In 1899 he left that company to accept a position with the Chicago Mill and Lumber Company and shortly afterward was made superintendent of the Cairo, Memphis & Southern Railroad and Transportation Company, a very important adjunct to the Chicago Mill and Lumber Company in the handling of logs and lumber from down-river points, and both being branches of the Paepcke-Leicht Lumber Company of Chicago. The parent company, with its various branch concerns at Cairo and elsewhere, is one of the greatest corporations in the country, and is perhaps the largest manufacturer of boxes in the world. It operates four large plants, two of which are in Chicago, where the general offices of the company are located. The outside branches are the Cairo companies and the Marked Tree Lumber Company, of Marked Tree, Ark. The Chicago Mill and Lumber Company, at Cairo, occupies a tract of some sixty acres of ground, has a saw mill with a daily capacity of 85,000 feet of lumber, a box factory 280 x 320 feet, equipped with the most approved machinery, with a capacity of seven carloads of box shooks per day; a large veneer works, which turns out a vast amount of material for the manufacture of egg cases, fruit boxes, etc.; and eight large dry kilns, each 140 feet long, for drying the product. The fan used in these dry kilns requires an engine of 225 horse power to operate it, while the power to the entire plant is supplied by two immense Corliss engines of 600 and 800 horse power, respectively. A large warehouse is also a part of the plant, where 3,000,000 feet of veneering is constantly carried, and storage provided for 250 carloads of box shooks. Everything in connection with the place is of the most modern and labor saving character. Recently a refuse burner twenty-eight feet in diameter and 140 feet high was erected as a means of disposing of the waste and keeping the works in a sightly and sanitary condition. The Cairo, Memphis & Southern Railroad and Transportation Company, the other Cairo branch, occupies 800 feet of river front above the Cairo bridge. It operates over 117 miles of standard gauge railroad and covers nearly 500 miles of river traffic, extending as far as Greenville, Miss. The railroad equipment consists in part of four locomotives of modern build and over 100 cars. On the rivers the company operates a line of towboats, steamers and barges, notably among them being the steamer *Herman Paepcke,* and three large derrick boats. The general offices of the company are located in the *Tribune* building in Chicago. Mr. Smith, although a comparatively young man, has all that portion of the business so thoroughly under his control that no friction is allowed to interfere with obtaining the best possible results. In politics he is a Republican; in religion a member of the Lutheran church; in fraternal matters a member of the Benevolent and Protective Order of Elks, and in the community one of the representative citizens.

WILLIAM H. SUTHERLAND, president of the Cairo Milling Company, Cairo, Ill., was born at St. Joseph, Mich., July 8, 1858. His parents, J. H. and Martha Sutherland, were both natives of Michigan, and passed their whole lives in that state. J. H. Sutherland was a merchant, and died when the subject of this sketch was only about four years old. From that time until he was fifteen he lived with an uncle, attending the common schools during the fall and winter months. When he was fifteen he secured employment as a helper in a flour mill, attending school for two years longer. At the age of twenty-one he came into possession of some property and invested it in a mill, but the venture proved unsuccessful. He then left St. Joseph and went to Athens, Tenn., as head miller for a large concern there, but a year later returned to his old home town and became head miller in the same mill where he served his apprenticeship. After three years he went to Independence, Ia., to accept the position of general manager with the Independence Milling Company. He remained with this company two years, at the end of which time he entered the employ of the Bemis Bag Company as a traveling salesman. In 1892 he formed a partnership with John Schultz, of Beardstown, Ill., and they purchased and rebuilt the mill at Astoria, about fifteen miles north of Beardstown, and Mr. Sutherland conducted this mill successfully for about eight years. In 1900 the partnership between him and Mr. Schultz was dissolved, when he came to Cairo and organized the company of which he is the president. The capital stock of the company is $40,000, and the other officers are J. G. Hollman, vice-president, and William Calgan, secretary and treasurer. The company does a merchant milling business, the mills having a capacity of 500 barrels of flour daily, the trade covering the whole Southern states and extending into several of the Northern states. They also do a large business as dealers in grain. Mr. Sutherland is a Republican politically, but he is first of all a miller of more than exceptional ability, and devotes but little time to politics, although he is interested in public questions. He is a member of the Benevolent and Protective Order of Elks, and he and his family belong to the Presbyterian church. In 1882 he was married to Miss Ida Kingsley, of St. Joseph, Mich., and they have four daughters, all living at home and attending school.

E. L. TADLOCK, one of the leading farmers of Gallatin county, Ill., was born near Batter Rock, Hardin county, of that state, March 18, 1848. His parents, Michael and Sarah (Baer) Tadlock, were both natives of that county, where the father was a farmer and passed his whole life. They had three children. Isaac and Nancy are both deceased, the subject of this sketch being the only surviving member of his family. Michael Tadlock died while the subject was still a small boy, and his widow married William A. Scroggins. E. L. Tadlock continued to live with his mother and stepfather until his marriage to Miss E. J. Benson, a native of Saline county, and rented a farm near Shawneetown, where he lived for four or five years, when he bought ninety acres where he now lives, six miles west of Shawneetown. Since then he has prospered and now owns 400 acres of land, most of which is in a high state of cultivation and well improved. For the last ten years Mr. Tadlock has been conducting a general store on his place in connection with his agricultural pursuits. His success in life is due mainly to his energy and foresight, and he is regarded as one of the best business men in his locality. Mr. and Mrs. Tadlock have had the following children born to them: Laura E., Charles, Mamie, Kate, Maud, Edgar, William C., Clarence and Lewis. Charles and Lewis are deceased and the others are all married and live near their parents. Mrs. Tadlock is a member of the Baptist church.

P. T. LANGAN, manufacturer of sash, doors, blinds, and builders' supplies, and dealer in all kinds of rough and dressed lumber, Cairo, Ill., was born in the city of Louisville, Ky., but came in his boyhood to Cairo. He began in the lumber business when he was still quite young, and has learned it in every detail. His immense business is the outgrowth of his thorough knowledge of every phase of the lumber trade, and his long experience has placed him at the front of the lumber dealers of the Lower Ohio Valley. His factory is located on Commercial avenue, extending from Tenth to Twelfth streets, where he uses about 3,000,000 feet of rough lumber annually in the production of his wares. Two traveling salesmen are constantly employed in calling upon the hardware trade and builders of Kentucky, Missouri, Tennessee and Arkansas, as well as a large portion of Illinois, his trade extending to both the wholesale and retail fields. Mr. Langan organized this business in 1891, and since that time the history of the concern has been one unbroken line of successful business operations. It is such men as he that build up a city, and few men in the city of Cairo have done more to advertise her name abroad in commercial circles. Politically he is a Democrat, and in church matters he is a Catholic. While true to his political principles, and a consistent practitioner of the tenets of his religious faith, he is first of all one of Cairo's most energetic and successful business men. Mr. Langan is married and has an interesting family of five children.

EDWARD C. ALLEN, proprietor of the Hotel Illinois, at Cairo, is of Scotch-Irish descent, his grandfather coming from Scotland early in the nineteenth century and locating in Pennsylvania. At the time he came to this country he was already married, his wife having been a Miss Martha Drake, a descendant of Sir Francis Drake, who was one of the first to circumnavigate the earth. Joseph G. Allen, the father of Edward C., was born at Allegheny City, Pa., in the year 1814, and lived there until 1858, when he went to Lockland, Ohio, where he engaged in the manufacture of paper. His paper mill was burned by the guerrilla forces under General Morgan in the famous raid of 1863, after which he received a contract from the United States government, through the influence of President Lincoln, for making coffins for the dead soldiers. To carry out this contract to better advantage he located at Kingston Springs, Tenn., where he made coffins for eighty-one thousand of the nation's gallant dead. Joseph G. Allen and Abraham Lincoln were warm friends and corresponded with each other on the most intimate terms. The subject of this sketch has in his possession a number of old letters that his father received from the martyred president. Mr. Allen had a dream during the war, in which he saw the termination of the great conflict. This dream he related to Mr. Lincoln, who was so impressed with it that he secured a special act of Congress providing for the printing and distribution of a million copies of it. After the war Joseph Allen returned to Ohio, located in Grant county, and there followed the lumber business until his death in 1882. He married a Miss Mary E. Morris, who is still living in Northern Indiana, aged eighty-one years. She is of Scotch-Irish extraction. Of their eleven children, six of whom are living, Edward C. Allen, who is the eighth child of the family, was born July

20, 1861, while his parents were living at Middletown, Ohio. He received a good practical education in the public schools, after which he became associated with his father in the lumber business in Indiana before railroads were built in that section of the state, when they located in Marion, in Grant county. Upon the death of his father he settled up the estate and went to Tennessee, where he was for over nine years connected with the great lumber concern of L. Laughran, of Philadelphia, as superintendent, his eldest brother being general manager. In 1893 Mr. Allen returned to Indiana and engaged in business for a short time., then returned to Tennessee for a few months, and in 1894 came to Cairo. Here he was associated with the Chicago Mill and Lumber Company as manager, and in that capacity had charge of the erection of most of the buildings now constituting their immense plant, which is the largest in the world of its kind. In the spring of 1902 he bought the Hotel Illinois, but went to Texas and remained there until in 1904, when he returned to Cairo to assume the management of the house, which he has made one of the most popular hostelries in the city. The Illinois is centrally located and fully equipped with all those little conveniences that go to make hotel life enjoyable, such as long distance telephones, a telephone in each room, a fine cuisine, everything scrupulously clean, and, above all, a genial proprietor to "welcome the coming and speed the parting guest." In fraternal circles Mr. Allen is one of the best known men in Cairo, being a member of the Free and Accepted Masons; the Knights of Pythias; the Benevolent and Protective Order of Elks; the Modern Woodmen; the Royal Arcanum, and the Concatenated Order of Hoo Hoo, a society composed of lumbermen. In his political views he is a Republican, as might be expected of one whose father enjoyed the personal friendship of the first Republican president. He has also adopted the religious faith of his parents, as both himself and wife are members of the Presbyterian church. Mr. Allen was married in 1883 to Willabelle, daughter of William and Elizabeth Reeves, of Ohio. Her father was a shoe dealer, who later removed to Marion, Ind., where he passed the closing years of his life. Three children have been born to Mr. and Mrs. Allen: Harry E., H. Davis, and Marybelle. The two sons are living, but the daughter died on Nov. 24, 1901, aged thirteen years.

CHARLES LANCASTER, president of the Lancaster & Rice Company, dealers in sewer pipe, roofing and building paper, sash, doors, paints and picture frames, Cairo, Ill., was born in St. Clair county, of that state, Aug. 21, 1836. His grandfather, Mahlon Lancaster, came from England in early life and settled in Virginia. Charles is a son of Levi and Elizabeth Lancaster, both natives of Virginia, who came in 1801, soon after their marriage, to St. Clair county. There they lived a typical pioneer life, the father frequently killing deer upon his farm. They continued to live on the farm until in middle life, when the father engaged in mercantile pursuits in Illinois and Minnesota for the rest of his days. He died in Minnesota in 1859, the mother having died in 1841. They were members of the Baptist church. Charles Lancaster is the fifth of a family of nine children, two sons and seven daughters. He received a common school education and began his business career in connection with his father in the general merchandise business. From 1862 to 1865 he was employed by the government in making repairs on the vessels belonging to the Mississippi squadron, and during that time was stationed at Cairo. After the war was over he embarked in the lumber business at Cairo, which was at that time already beginning to be recognized as a great lumber market, and continued in that line until 1881. In that year he and Newton Rice organized and incorporated the Lancaster & Rice Company, with a capital stock of $50,000. Four years later they erected a large warehouse and a mill 75 x 100 feet, which they fully equipped with modern machinery, etc., and were soon on the high road to commercial success. Mr. Rice died in 1889, and in January, 1901, the main buildings of the company were destroyed by fire at a loss of some $20,000. Prior to that time the concern did a large wholesale business, but since the fire has limited its trade to the retail demand, operating two stores in the city of Cairo. Mr. Lancaster is a Republican politically and takes great interest in public affairs, particularly those of local interest. For seventeen years he has held the office of alderman. This long incumbency in an office that has for its object the passing of legislation affecting the local affairs of the people of Cairo tells the story of his popularity, and shows in what

esteem he is held by his fellow-townsmen. He is a member of the Knights of Honor, and with his family belongs to the Presbyterian church. By his close application to business, and his intelligent and well directed investments he owns considerable property in the city. In 1866 he was united in marriage to Miss Sarah E. Hodge, who was born near Louisville, Ky., and to this marriage there have been born eight children, five of whom are still living, viz.: Minnie E., manager of one of the stores of the Lancaster & Rice Company; Pearl, wife of George B. Osgood, of Chicago; Mabel, a teacher in Michigan; Geraldine, wife of Wilber B. Thistlewood, of Cairo; and Beatrice, at home with her parents.

ALEXANDER S. FRASER, contractor of brick work and manufacturer of concrete building blocks, Cairo, Ill., is a native of that city and one of its representative men. His grandfather, Peter Fraser, came from Scotland in his early manhood and located at Niles, Mich., where he passed the balance of his life. Alexander Fraser, the father of the subject of this sketch, was born at Niles, married Elizabeth Morris, a native of Madison, Ind., and settled in Cairo in 1852. There he conducted a steamboat repair shop until his death. He was somewhat active in politics as a Democrat, was a charter member of the Cairo Odd Fellows' lodge, a Knight of Pythias, and with his wife belonged to the Episcopal church. He died in 1883, but his widow is still living in Cairo. Their children were George, Niles Llewellyn, William P., Charles and Alexander. George and Charles are deceased; Niles Llewellyn married Herman C. Schuh and is also deceased; and the other two sons live in Cairo. Alexander S. Fraser was born June 3, 1869. After attending the common schools of his native city he entered the Glendale institute at Kirkwood, Mo., at the age of fourteen years, and graduated in 1889. He was then in Colorado for about two years in charge of a force of men for a roofing company, after which he went from one city to another in the capacity of a journeyman bricklayer, working awhile in each. In 1896 he returned to Cairo and commenced contracting on his own account. Since then some of the best buildings in the city have been erected under his supervision, notably among them the buildings of the Cairo Brewing Company, and the Andrew Lohr Bottling works. In connection with his business as a contractor he is also interested in dredging sand from the Mississippi river, taking out about 500 car loads annually, most of which is used by himself in the manufacture of concrete building blocks, in which he is building up a good trade. Mr. Fraser is one of the active Democrats of Cairo. He is the alderman from the Third ward; chairman of the police, jail and fire committee; was the designer of the Sycamore street subway, an important street improvement, and in 1904 was one of the Democratic candidates for presidential elector, representing the Twenty-fifth district on the Parker and Davis ticket. He is a member of Melrose Park Lodge, No. 530, Knights of Pythias, of Chicago; Cairo Lodge, No. 237, Free and Accepted Masons, and is a charter member of Cairo Lodge of the Fraternal Order of Eagles. In 1900 he was married to Miss Tillie Blattau, daughter of Louis and Margaret Blattau, of Cairo, and one child has been born to this union. This son, William L., died in infancy. Mr. Fraser was baptized in the Episcopal church and his wife is a member of the Catholic church.

ARTHUR STEPHEN MAGNER, assistant engineer of the water works, Cairo, Ill., is a son of Michael and Abby Magner, old residents of that city. He was born in Cairo, Nov. 7, 1870, was educated in the common schools there, and has passed his whole life in his native town, except when temporarily absent in connection with his railroad service. While still in his teens he went into the Singer Manufacturing Company's plant at Cairo, and there learned the business of stationary engineer under Harry Wilson, one of the best engineers in the city. After this young Magner worked for some time for the Illinois Central Railroad Company on bridge work, his service with this company extending from 1889 to 1894. He was next employed in a similar capacity by the Big Four Railroad Company for a few months, when he was appointed to his present position. Mr. Magner is a Democrat in his political convictions, and for almost a decade has been called upon to serve as judge of election of the Seventh precinct in every campaign. He is a member of the Ancient Order of Hibernians, the Fraternal Order of Eagles, and is the captain of the Anchor Fire Company. On Nov. 26, 1901, he was united in marriage to Miss Ellen, daughter of Conrad Shaughan. Mrs. Magner was born in Ireland, but came to Cairo while still in her girlhood. They have had one child, Edward Michael, who died at the age of nine months and seven days. Mr. and Mrs. Magner are both members of the Catholic church and take an interest in its many worthy charities.

WILLIAM SCHATZ, a well known contractor and builder of Cairo, Ill., was born in Germany, April 5, 1850. When he was about six years of age his parents, Will'am and Sophia (Huncy) Schatz, left the Fatherland and came to America, locating at Cape Girardeau, Mo., where they still live retired from the active cares of this busy world. They reared a family of several children, only three of whom are now living. The father served as a soldier in the Union army during the Civil war, and is an unswerving Republican in his political affiliations. William Schatz, the subject of this sketch, lived with his father until he was about eighteen years of age, when he learned the carpenters' trade. In 1872 he came to Cairo and worked as journeyman until 1879, when he commenced contracting for himself. His practical knowledge of all branches of the building business, in connection with his untiring industry, soon won for him a place among the foremost contractors of the city. Some of the best business blocks and the finest residences were built by him, and in every instance his patrons have been satisfied with his promptness in executing his contracts and his honest workmanship. Mr. Schatz is a member of the Independent Order of Odd Fellows and the Ancient Order of United Workmen. In religious matters he has adopted the faith of his parents, both himself and wife belonging to the Lutheran church, but in politics he has elected to do his own thinking, and belongs to the Democratic party. On April 22, 1878, he was united in marriage to Miss Hannah, daughter of Henry Vellmer, a farmer and merchant of Scott county, Mo. To this marriage there have been born the following children: Henry, who died at the age of nine years; Fred, associated with his father; Edward, a carpenter at Cairo; Clara, wife of W. L. Russell, one of Cairo's leading dentists. Mr. Schatz owns his own home, one of the best appointed in the city, and is also the owner of other real estate.

FRED D. NELLIS, wholesale and retail coal dealer, Cairo, Ill., was born in that city July 2, 1876. He is a son of Captain Charles and Anna (Kaha) Nellis, the former a native of Ohio, the latter of Germany. During the Civil war Capt. Charles Nellis was a pilot on one of the Federal gunboats. After the war he located in Cairo, coming to the city in 1866, and he became the owner of the dry docks as well as acquiring an interest in several steamboats. Sometime in the eighties he was elected to the legislature from the Twenty-fifth district and was subsequently elected city treasurer. He was one of the active Republicans in the city and county; was a Knight Templar Mason and in his day was one of the best known men about Cairo. His wife was a member of the Lutheran church. Their children were: W. O., captain and engineer on the Western rivers; Etta, now the wife of William Steele, of Corry, Pa.; C. F., pilot and captain of transfer steamers; Anna, deceased; Fred D., the subject of this sketch; DeWitt C., a resident of Cairo; Juanita, widow of Van B. Miller and a resident of Denver, Col. Fred D. Nellis finished his education in the Cairo schools and at the age of eighteen went to steamboating with Capt. J. F. Beatty, of Paducah, Ky., following this occupation until in 1898, when he formed a partnership with D. F. McCarthy for dealing in coal. This partnership lasted until 1901, when Mr. Nellis bought out his partner and since that time has conducted his business alone. He conducts a wholesale business extending over Illinois, Missouri and Kentucky, and has the satisfaction of seeing his trade constantly growing larger. In addition to his immense coal trade, he manages a farm of 100 acres, and during the summer he is interested in contracting in various ways. Politically Mr. Nellis is a Republican and takes an active interest in scoring victories for his party. In April, 1903, he was elected alderman from the Fifth ward. That office he still holds and is also a member of the Republican county central committee. He is a member of the Free and Accepted Masons, the Modern Woodmen, the Fraternal Order of Eagles, the Commercial club of Cairo, which is composed of the business men of the city, the Knights of the Mystic Krew of Comus, and the Ohio Valley Improvement association, in all of which he is very popular because of his genial disposition. On Oct. 4, 1903, Mr. Nellis and Miss Sarah Blanche Langsdon were united in marriage. She is the youngest daughter of Sarah Elizabeth and Dayton Langsdon and was born in Warren county, Ind.; her mother deceased and father living retired at Cairo.

ED. P. FITZGERALD, wholesale dealer and distributing agent for Pabst's Milwaukee beer for the territory adjacent to Cairo, Ill., was born in that city Oct. 19, 1870. His parents, Patrick and Catherine Fitzgerald, were both born in Ireland. The father was born in County Limerick in the year 1840, came to America when he was sixteen years of age and located in Cairo in 1860. The mother was born in County Armagh. She came to America in childhood, was married to Patrick Fitzgerald in Cairo in 1861, and still lives in that city. Patrick Fitzgerald died on May 14, 1896. During his life he was a prominent and highly esteemed citizen, a very industrious man, and from the first took great interest in public affairs. During the war he was in the hotel and restaurant business and was a member of the Cairo city council. He was afterward engaged in the livery business and still later in contracting until his death. As a contractor he built part of the levees around Cairo, and took great interest in securing the construction of these levees. He also graded a great many of the streets of the city and constructed about twenty miles of the Mobile & Ohio railroad north of Cairo. By his industry and good management he accumulated considerable property and died respected by all who knew him. He and his wife were members of the Catholic church. Of their children Daniel, Margaret, and James are deceased; Mamie lives in Cairo as the widow of Frank P. Walsh; and Edward and Frank constitute the firm of Fitzgerald Bros., dealers in sand, lime, cement, plaster, brick, etc., and contractors for street filling, and earthwork for railroads, levees, etc. All the children attended college. Ed. P. Fitzgerald, after attending the common schools of Cairo, entered the Christian Brothers' college of St. Louis in 1885, and graduated from the commercial department of St. Vincent's college in 1889. Upon leaving college he returned to Cairo, where he was manager for his father until the latter's death, when he and his brother formed the firm of Fitzgerald Bros. In 1903 Ed. P. Fitzgerald took the wholesale agency for the Pabst Milwaukee beer for a territory extending over Southern Illinois, and parts of Kentucky, Missouri and Arkansas. His business for the year 1904 amounted to over $25,000. He personally travels over the territory and is familiarly known as "Eddie Pabst." Mr. Fitzgerald is a member of the Benevolent and Protective Order of Elks, the Fraternal Order of Eagles, and the Knights of the Mystic Krew of Comus. Like his father, he is an enthusiastic Democrat and always takes an interest in local politics. He is very popular among "the boys." His genial disposition and merry nature win friends for him wherever he goes, and his many sterling qualities hold these friends to him for all time.

CAPT. FRED BENNETT, steamboat owner and general contractor, of Cairo, Ill., was born in Clermont county, O., April 22, 1863. His parents, Peter and Elizabeth Bennett, were both born in Germany, but some time in the forties came to America and located at New Richmond, O., where the father followed farming until his death in July, 1903. His widow is still living. They had three sons and two daughters, all living. Both parents were members of the Catholic church, to which the mother still belongs. Captain Bennett received a common school education and began his business career as an employe of the J. M. Blair Brick Company, with which he was employed from 1881 to 1887. He was then with the Huntington & St. Louis Towboat Company for about ten years, at the end of which time he embarked in business for himself. He is the owner of the steamer *Carrie V.*, also a steam derrick boat and several barges, and covers both the Ohio and Mississippi rivers in a general logging business amounting to about 6,000,000 feet a year, the logs being towed to Cairo and Mound City from the lower river chiefly. Captain Bennett is a Republican in his political creed, although his father was a life-long Democrat. In fraternal circles he is well known as a member of the Knights of Pythias and the Benevolent and Protective Order of Elks. In August, 1897, he was married to Miss Jennie L., daughter of William D. and Rachel C. Gaskins, of Nine Mile, O., her father being one of the best known farmers in Clermont county. Mr. and Mrs. Bennett have had two children: Ruth, born Nov. 22, 1898, and Velma, born Sept. 7, 1901, and died in the second year of her age.

JOHN B. WALTERS, farmer and justice of the peace, living about six miles west of Shawneetown, Ill., was born in that county, Sept. 25, 1846, on the farm now owned by A. Meyer, in Bowlesville township. His grandfather, Hiram Walters, was a Virginian, who went to Tennessee when he was a young man and located near Sparta. There he married and had one son, John T., who was the father of the subject of this sketch. Hiram Walters' wife died soon after the birth of this son, and the widowed husband returned to Virginia, carrying the infant all the way on a pillow. There he made his home with a sister until 1834, when he came with his son to Gallatin county, entered government land in Bowlesville township, and followed farming there until his death. After coming to Illinois he was married to a Mrs. Kinsall, but no children were born to this second marriage. John T. Walters was born at Sparta, Tenn., in 1820, and was therefore about fourteen years old when his father brought him to Gallatin county. A year or two later he began life on his own account as a farm hand, and continued in this occupation until he married Eliza Brown, a native of South Carolina, and commenced farming on part of the old home place. There they both lived until death overtook them, with the exception of a short time they lived in Shawneetown. He was prominently identified with the affairs of the county, served as constable, sheriff, and county commissioner, as well as school treasurer and other minor officers. He was for many years regarded as one of the leading Democrats of the county, and was a member of the Independent Order of Odd Fellows. Generous to a fault, he went security for his friends, and in the latter part of life was made almost bankrupt from this cause. He and his wife had three children: Hiram, living at Equality, Ill.; John B., the subject; and William, residing at Shawneetown. John T. Walters died at the age of sixty-two and his wife lived to be seventy-four years of age. John B. Walters was educated in the common schools and at Notre Dame university, South Bend, Ind. He married Nannie, daughter of James M. and Rebecca Wathen, of Gallatin county, and commenced life on his own account as a farmer near where he now lives. In 1878 he bought his present place of 100 acres, forty of which were under cultivation. Since then he has added by purchase another fifty acres, and nearly all of his farm is now under cultivation and well stocked and improved. Mr. Walters has been for years one of the Democratic wheel-horses of Gallatin county. With the exception of about eighteen months he has served as justice of the peace for the last twenty-six years. Of the children born to him and his wife Bertha, Mattie and one who died in infancy are deceased; Estella and Lydia are married and live in Gallatin county; John T., Edith, Hiram, William I., Rebecca, and James are at home. Mrs. Walters died on Nov. 23, 1900.

JAMES MITCHELL, a farmer of Gallatin county, Ill., living five miles southwest of Shawneetown, is a native of Ireland, having been born on Dec. 20, 1838, in County Londonderry. His father, John Mitchell, was a farmer, but died when James was about eleven years of age, and from that time the son was thrown upon his own resources. In 1855 he came to America and made his way directly to Cincinnati, where he had uncles. These relatives found him a place in a machine shop, where he served his apprenticeship, becoming an expert machinist. He was working at his trade when the Civil war broke out, but left the bench to enlist in Company B, Sixth Ohio infantry, and was mustered into service at Camp Dennison. The regiment was first assigned to duty in Western Virginia, but was soon transferred to the Department of the Tennessee and took part in the engagements at Pittsburg Landing, Stone River, Chickamauga, and a number of minor engagements and skirmishes. At Stone River Mr. Mitchell was wounded in the shoulder, and at the battle of Chickamauga his left leg was shattered and he was left on the field. In his helpless condition he was captured and held a prisoner for ten days, when he was exchanged and sent to the hospital. Altogether he served for three years and three months, being mustered out at Camp Dennison, June 1, 1864. After the war he returned to work at his trade in Cincinnati and remained there until 1868, when he came to Gallatin county, as engineer and machinist for the Bowlesville Coal Company, and remained in the employ of that corporation for seventeen years. In 1885 he gave up his position with the mining company and began farming. In 1901 he bought the place of 100 acres where he now lives, and where he has been successful as a farmer and stock raiser on a modest scale. Mr. Mitchell was married in 1864, to Miss Minnie Heitzelman, a native of Germany, and to this union have been born twelve children, seven of whom are yet living. Mary Ann, William, Robert, and Rena are all married and live in Gallatin county, and Minnie, Jennie and James are at home. Mr. Mitchell is an unswerving Democrat in his political views, and with his family belongs to the Cumberland Presbyterian church.

JOSEPH LOGSDON, a farmer, living five miles southwest of Shawneetown, Ill., is of German extraction, and a descendant of one of the first settlers in that section of the Lower Ohio Valley. His great-grandfather came from Germany some time prior to the Revolutionary war, settled in Maryland, and there passed the remainder of his life. He married there and reared a family of children, one of whom, a son named Joseph, served with Braddock in the French and Indian war, and afterward fought in the Revolution. This Joseph Logsdon married Susan Durban, whose father owned the ground upon which a part of the city of Baltimore now stands, and who leased it for a period of ninety-nine years. The leases have long since expired and the tenants remain in possession, though the land rightfully belongs to the Durban heirs. Soon after his marriage Joseph Logsdon packed his worldly goods upon horses, and with his wife made his way to Virginia, then to Kentucky, next to Indiana, and finally to Southern Illinois, settling in what is now Gallatin county. The region was at that time the extreme frontier, and troubles with the Indians were of no uncommon occurrence. After a short stay in his new location he and his wife were compelled to seek the protection of old Fort Massac, in what is now Massac county, and there he passed the rest of his days. Most of his life was spent on the frontier and he had frequent brushes with the Indians. While living in Kentucky he was attacked by two Indians, one of whom shot him from his horse, but the ball glanced and saved his life. In the hand to hand fight which followed he killed one of the Indians with his knife, and wounded the other so badly that he committed suicide afterward. He was known as "Big Joe" or "Bulger Joe" Logsdon, the latter name having been given to him while he was with Braddock. Although a man of great physical strength he was not quarrelsome, and few of the pioneers had more friends. During the latter part of his life he took great interest in encouraging immigration to Southern Illinois. He and his wife had the following children: Thomas, Polly, Prudy, Peggie, Susan and Joseph. Thomas married in Ripley county, Ind., while the family were living there, and his descendants still live in that state. Polly married Isaac Williams, and Prudy married James Meyer, both of Ripley county. Peggie married a man named Cox, after the family came to Illinois, and died at Shawneetown. Susan died young and Joseph was the father of the subject of this sketch. He was born near Covington, Ky., Aug. 19, 1795. After the death of his father at Fort Massac he returned with his mother and one sister to Gallatin county, and bought a farm near Shawneetown, where his mother died some years later. On Dec. 16, 1829, he was married to Matilda Thompson, who was born Aug. 13, 1802, and they commenced their married life on the farm above mentioned. He no doubt inherited some of his father's liking for a military life, for he served in the Black Hawk war. In the cholera epidemic of 1832 he, his mother and his sister Peggie all fell victims to the dread disease. His widow afterward married Richard Tarlton, a native of Gallatin county, and lived until 1837. Joseph and Matilda Logsdon had four children: Eliza married a man by the name of Rogers and is deceased; Peggy lives north of Shawneetown; Joseph is the subject of this sketch, and Thomas died in Oregon from the effects of a kick from a horse. Joseph Logsdon, the third to bear that name, was born about a mile southwest of Shawneetown, Oct. 22, 1825. In his boyhood he attended the old subscription schools for six months, which constituted his entire schooling. After the death of his mother he went to Indiana, where he lived with relatives for four years, at the end of which time he returned to Gallatin county. For some time he was employed as a farm hand, after which he followed the river for a while, making nine trips to New Orleans. In 1850 he made the trip overland to California. Leaving Fort Leavenworth on May 22, he reached Hangtown, Cal., on August 22d, which was then the quickest trip on record. After working in the mines and in Sacramento for about eighteen months he returned to Illinois in 1852, and took up the occupation of a farmer, which he has followed ever since. In 1859 he bought 185 acres where he now lives, and the following year built the house he occupies. He now owns 435 acres, all under cultivation but about forty acres, and is one of the successful farmers of the county. In 1853 he was married to Mary A. Rogers, who was born Feb. 10, 1835, and died Jan. 23, 1892, leaving no children. On April 23, 1896, he was married to Mrs. Ann

Lacey, widow of George Lacey. Mr. Logsdon is an ardent Democrat; has been an Odd Fellow since 1866; and he and his wife belong to the Cumberland Presbyterian church in which he has been either deacon or elder for the last twenty-eight years.

JOSEPH ROBINETT, a farmer living near Spark's Hill, Hardin county, Ill., was born Feb. 8, 1841, on the farm now owned and occupied by J. B. Hetherington, ten miles southwest of Shawneetown. He is a son of Joseph and Clara (Nighswonger) Robinett, the former a native of Kentucky and the latter of Ohio. Joseph Robinett, the father, was born in 1790, came to Illinois in 1818, fought in the Black Hawk war, and at the time of his death in 1853 was one of the largest land owners in that section of the state. He owned land in Gallatin, Hardin and Saline counties, and was an extensive dealer in live stock, the market for which in those days was New Orleans. He was twice married. His first wife was Rachel Tatman, by whom he had five children, all now deceased. After her death he was married to Clara Nighswonger, and of the eight children born to this union three are living. Blueford lives in Shawneetown; Rachel Jane lives with her brother Joseph, who is the subject of this sketch. The mother lived to be eighty-six years of age. Joseph Robinett attended the subscription and district public schools in his boyhood, and remained with his parents until about twenty-two years of age, when he enlisted as a private in Company I, One Hundred and Eighteenth Illinois volunteer infantry, commanded by Col. John G. Fonda, and was mustered in at Camp Butler. The regiment was first sent to Memphis, where Mr. Robinett was taken sick and was assigned to hospital duty. He continued in this capacity for over two and a half years, and was then discharged. Before going into the service he had bought the farm of two hundred and eighty acres where he now lives. In 1867 he was married to Angie Thomson, a native of Saline county, and with the exception of eight months spent in Eldorado they have lived on this farm. Mr. Robinett has about two hundred and thirty-five acres under cultivation, devotes a great deal of attention to stock raising, and has one of the finest orchards in Southern Illinois. In political matters he is a Republican, but is not an active politician.

He and his family belong to the Presbyterian church. Two children have been born to Mr. and Mrs. Robinett: William Allen, deceased, and Mrs. Laura Zinn, a widow, now living with her parents. She has four children: Gertie, Jacob, Gretchen and Angie.

JOHN HART CRENSHAW, the son of William Crenshaw and Elizabeth Hart, the daughter of John Hart of New Jersey, one of the signers of the Declaration of Independence, was born in the southern part of North Carolina on Nov. 19, 1797. His parents moved to New Madrid, Mo., in 1808, and in the earthquake of 1811 their home was ruined. They then removed to Gallatin county, Ill., and settled on Eagle Creek, not far from the salt wells called the "Half Moon." His father died soon after coming to Gallatin county, leaving his mother and seven children. John, being among the oldest children, went to the salt works and began drawing water for the company who were making salt. He continued in this business until after he married Miss Sina Taylor in 1817. He went to housekeeping in the "Half Moon," and in a few years rented the wells from the state and began to make salt, which industry he followed for many years. He bought a large body of land near Equality, and moved his salt works to his own land, which was heavily timbered. He used the wood in the salt works, and in that way cleared his land. When the production of salt became unprofitable, he turned to farming, which he continued to follow until his death, Dec. 4, 1871. He and his wife were members of the Methodist Episcopal church. His wife died Sept. 14, 1881, at the age of eighty-two years. They had ten children, five of whom lived to maturity, viz.: Mary, widow of John E. Hall; Elizabeth, widow of Gen. M. K. Lawler; William T., deceased; Margaret, who married Charles Lanphier, of Springfield, both now deceased; and Julia, widow of James Foster, a native of Bledsoe county, Tenn. He was born Dec. 14, 1827. On arriving at man's estate he became a dealer in live stock. This business made it necessary for him to make frequent trips to the North, and on one of these occasions he formed the acquaintance of Mrs. Julia A. Morris, *née* Crenshaw, to whom he was united in marriage on April 6, 1858. From that time until the commencement of the Civil war he followed farming on what is now known as the old Crenshaw place. At the beginning of the war he enlisted in the First Illinois cavalry and was made captain of his company. In September, 1861, he was captured at Lexington, Mo., and soon afterward was paroled. He returned home while on parole and never rejoined his command. He continued agricultural pursuits on the farm where his widow still lives until his death on Dec. 16, 1875. They had four children, three of whom died in infancy. Edward, their youngest son, lives on the old home place with his mother. He married Miss Mary Lamb, of St. Louis, and they have seven children.

GEN. M. K. LAWLER.

RAPHAEL E. LAWLER, a farmer, living three and a half miles east of Equality, was born in December, 1858, on the spot where he now lives, though the house in which he was born was destroyed some years ago by fire. His father, Gen. Michael K. Lawler, was born in County Kildare, Ireland, Nov. 16, 1814. When he was about a year old his parents, John and Elizabeth (Kelly) Lawler came to the United States. After about a year in Baltimore, Md., they came to Gallatin county, Ill., making the greater part of the journey by way of the Ohio river in a flatboat. John Lawler was the first Catholic to settle in that part of the state, and was regarded with some curiosity by his neighbors for this reason. He first bought land in what is known as the Pond, or Irish Settlement, which land is still in the possession of his descendants. It was largely through his influence that the first Catholic church was established in that section. The old hewed log house with puncheon seats has long since been replaced by a more modern structure, and many of the Catholics now living in the vicinity are descendants of men who were induced to come there by John Lawler. He and his wife both died comparatively young. Their children were Mary, Margaret, Michael and Thomas, all now deceased. Michael K. Lawler grew to manhood in Gallatin county. On Dec. 20, 1837, he was united in marriage to Miss Elizabeth, daughter of John and Sina Crenshaw, old residents of the county. At the time of the marriage her father was the largest land owner in the county, and gave the young couple the farm where Raphael E. now lives. They commenced their married life in a log cabin of one room, later built a cheap frame house, then one of more modern character—the one that was burned. When the Mexican war broke out M. K. Lawler was bookkeeper for his father-in-law. He gave up his position, organized a company, of which he was elected captain, and was immediately sent to the front. At Cerro Gordo the company distinguished itself, and from that time until the close of the war was in several of the fiercest engagements. After the war Captain Lawler took up the occupation of farming, which he followed until the commencement of the Civil war. Then the old military spirit revived and he organized the Eighteenth Illinois volunteer infantry, afterward known as the "Bloody Eighteenth," of which he was commissioned colonel. The regiment was in many of the hottest engagements of the war, particularly in Tennessee, Alabama and Mississippi. At Fort Donelson Colonel Lawler was severely wounded in the arm, but after a short time rejoined his command and remained in the field until the end. On April 15, 1863, he was made brigadier-general by President Lincoln, and on April 17, 1866, received the rank of brevet major-general from Andrew Johnson. At the close of the war he was appointed commandant of the post at Baton Rouge, and while there bought a cotton plantation, but soon afterward sold it, having been appointed to a position as government storekeeper at San Antonio, Tex., where he remained for two years. He then returned home and lived on his farm until his death, July 26, 1882. Since his death his widow has made her home with the subject of this sketch. The children of Michael and Elizabeth Lawler were Margaret, deceased; Sina, now Mrs. Evans, in Mexico; John C., deceased; Mary, who married a man named Riley and now deceased; Addie, Mrs. Walters, of Equality; Judith, also a Mrs. Walters, now dead; Michael, Elizabeth and William, all three deceased, and Raphael E. The parents were both members of the Catholic church, in which General Lawler took great interest. He was also active in politics and was one of the best known Democrats in Southern Illinois. Raphael E. Lawler attended different colleges in his youth, but left college to assume the management of his father's business, on account of the latter's failing health. On Jan. 10, 1881, he was married to Elizabeth, daughter of Lewis and Elvira Fowler, and a native of Gallatin county. After his marriage he lived with his parents until the death of his father, and since then has had full control of the farm, which he now owns. Like his father, he is a Democrat and a Catholic, now being one of the trustees of the church. The children born to him and his wife are: Margaret A., now Sister M. Veronica, O. S. M., of St. Mary's convent at Enfield, Ill.; Mary E., now Mrs. Luckett, living near Equality; Michael K., Louis F., Raphael E., John C., Lawrence C. and George F., at home; Elizabeth, deceased; Mary R., Paul, and Judith A., at home; Philip, deceased; Anthony, deceased; Mary, at home; Mary N., deceased, and Monica A., deceased.

JAMES O'ROURKE, a farmer of Gallatin county, Ill., living six miles west of Shawneetown, was born in County Limerick, Ireland, Sept. 5, 1849. His father was a peasant farmer, but died when James was only about two months old. He remained on the farm with his mother until 1865, when he came to this country with an uncle, William O'Rourke, who had previously been here, and who is now living in Evansville, Ind., about eighty-six years of age. James found employment as a teamster in Evansville, and continued to work at that occupation until 1872. He then came to Gallatin county, where for several years he worked in the mines. Upon leaving the mines he rented a farm near Bowlesville, and lived there nearly twenty years, when he bought eighty acres of what is known as the "Old Huston Place," where he now resides, and where he carries on a successful farming business. Mr. O'Rourke has the true Irish sentiment, and the love for the Emerald Isle that has been celebrated in song and story by men like Carleton and Tom Moore. He has made two trips to his native land since first coming here, and on the occasion of each visit has come back to his labors refreshed by happy recollections of his old home. In politics he is a steadfast Democrat, and in his religious faith is a member of the Catholic church. On April 23, 1880, he was married to Miss Belle Pettery, daughter of James and Rachel (White) Pettery, of Gallatin county, and to this union have been born the following children: Henry, Kate, James, Willie, George, Mayme, and Charles. Henry, Willie and Charles are deceased and the others are living at home with their parents. Mr. O'Rourke is a fine example of what industry and frugality will accomplish. Coming to this country at the age of sixteen, an orphan and almost penniless, he has, by his energy and good management, become one of the successful farmers of the community in which he lives, while by his genial and generous disposition he has made friends in whatever walk of life his lot has been cast.

ISAAC A. FOSTER, M.D., of New Haven, Ill., is one of the best known and most popular physicians in Gallatin county. His ancestors originally came from England, and the Fosters were among the very first settlers of Southern Illinois. About the beginning of the nineteenth century Asa Foster, the great-grandfather of Doctor Foster, came with his father from Virginia, and located in Pope county, where he married and reared one son. This son, Horace Foster, was born Jan. 8, 1811; married Phoebe Davis, born May 1, 1808, in that part of Pope county which afterward became a part of Hardin county; entered government land near Elizabethtown, and there they passed their lives. They were married on Sept. 29, 1826, and had four children: Asa, Horace, Lyman and Mary Jane. The mother of these children died comparatively young, the father on Dec. 1, 1834, married Mary or Polly Davis, a sister of his first wife, born May 9, 1819, and to this marriage there were born several children, all now deceased. He died about 1847, at the age of thirty-five years. The only one of the children of these two marriages now living is Horace Foster, the second child by the first wife. He was born on the farm near Elizabethtown, Nov. 18, 1829. He was married Dec. 9, 1849, to Miss Elizabeth Ann Hobbs, a native of Missouri. They began their married life on the old homestead on Rock Creek, in Hardin county, near where they now live. They had twelve children, five of whom are deceased. Those living are Thomas J., John W., Isaac A., Hannah E., Julia A., Mary A. and Joseph A. Thomas and John W. live in White county; Harriet married M. L. Tyer, now county judge of Hardin county, and lives near Cave in Rock; Julia is a Mrs. Belt, living on Rock Creek; Mary is a Mrs. Patton, of White county, and Joseph lives at New Haven. The parents are both members of the Christian church. Isaac A. Foster was born Oct. 4, 1862. As a boy he attended the public schools and improved his time so well that at the age of nineteen he became a teacher, which occupation he followed for eight years. In 1888 he was elected surveyor of Hardin county and held the office for three years. While serving as surveyor he completed his course in medicine, and in 1891 graduated from the College of Physicians and Surgeons of St. Louis. After practicing on

Rock Creek for about two years he located at New Haven, where he has built up a lucrative business and stands high in his profession. Doctor Foster is a member of the American Medical association, the Illinois State and the Gallatin County Medical societies. He is prominent in Masonic circles, being Worshipful Master of New Haven Lodge, No. 230; a member of Fairfield Chapter, No. 179, Royal Arch Masons, and deputy grand lecturer for the Grand Lodge of Illinois. He also belongs to New Haven Lodge, No. 7591, Modern Woodmen of America; Shawnee Tribe, No. 193, Improved Order of Red Men, and to Herald District, Court of Honor, No. 873. He and his wife belong to the Order of the Eastern Star, in which he holds the office of Worthy Patron and she is secretary. They are likewise members of Gallatin Camp, Royal Neighbors of America. In politics Doctor Foster is a Democrat and at this time holds the office of township collector. He belongs to the Christian church and his wife is a Methodist. He was married, in 1898, to Miss Belle Chastain, a native of White county, and for five years a teacher in the public schools. They have had the following children: Edward H., Paul J., Alice B., and one who died in infancy.

AMOS L. SIEBMAN, one of the most progressive farmers in the neighborhood of Ridgway, Ill., is of Pennsylvania Dutch ancestry, his parents, William and Rachel (Pisal) Siebman, both being natives of the Keystone state and of German lineage. William Siebman was born about the year 1810, and while still a young man learned the trade of shoemaker, which he followed for several years in Pennsylvania after his marriage. He then went to Cincinnati, O., where he worked at his trade until about 1848, when he came with his family to Gallatin county, Ill., and settled near Equality. There he took up farming for a livelihood, adding carpentering some time later, and worked at these occupations the rest of his life. He died at the age of fifty-five years and his wife at the age of sixty-two. They had eight children, three of whom are still living. Sarah is now Mrs. Fox, of Shawneetown; Amos is the subject of this sketch, and Theodore lives with his brother. Amos L. Siebman was born May 5, 1852, on what is known as the Dan Woods farm near Equality, in the same county where he now lives. As a boy he attended the common schools and spent much of his spare time in study at home, a habit he kept up even after reaching manhood. In 1874 he was married to Miss Philomine Brazier, and began life for himself on the place where he now lives. Mr. Siebman has two farms: one of 280 acres, most of which is under cultivation, and the other of eighty-two acres, part of which lies within the corporate limits of Ridgway. His larger farm was nearly all wild land when it came into his possession, and has been brought to its present improved state by his own industry and good management. Mr. Siebman believes in education, and for eleven years was a member of the school board. Politically he is a Democrat, and in religious matters is a consistent member of the Catholic church. Four children have been born to him and his wife, all of whom are living. Rachel is a Mrs. Luckett, of Ridgway; Emma is a Mrs. Beatty and Mary a Mrs. McCormick, both living in that vicinity, and Walter is at home with his parents.

JAMES A. QUICK, manufacturer of vehicles, agricultural implements, pipe, brass goods, mill supplies, etc., Shawneetown, Ill., is one of the representative business men of that city. He was born at Taunton, Somersetshire, England, Oct. 28, 1831, his parents being James and Emma (Summers) Quick, both natives of Somerset. The father was a farmer and contractor, and lived to be seventy-five years of age. The mother died at the age of eighty. They had thirteen children, six of whom are now living. Eliza is a Mrs. Martin, of Bridgewater, England; James is the subject of this sketch; Charles is at Sacramento, Cal.; Elizabeth married a man named Bufford and lives in England; Stephen and Simeon live at Taunton and Edwin lives at Bristol, England. James A. Quick attended the common schools of his native land, and at the age of nine years started in to serve his apprenticeship at the wheelwrights' trade, at which he worked for seven years, receiving twenty-five cents a week the first year, with an increase of twelve and a half cents a week for each succeeding year during his period of service. He boarded with his parents and walked a mile and a half to and from his work. After learning his trade he received good wages as a journeyman for about two years, when he and his brother Charles set sail for America, and landed at New York on June 18, 1854. Mr. Quick worked one summer in Philadelphia, then the following winter in Cincinnati, after which he went to Cleveland, where he worked until 1860. He then came to Shawneetown, arriving there on October 6th, and has ever since been a resident of the place. For two years he was employed by Mr. McMurchy, whom he succeeded in business. Mr. Quick has been successful in his business, has one of the best equipped and largest machine shops in this part of the country, and owns other property in Shawneetown. His practical training in youth, although a hardship then, has been of great value to him in his undertakings, and he is a splendid example of a self-made man. In politics he is a Republican, and he has served with credit as one of the board of aldermen. He was married in 1861 to Margaret Welsh, a native of Indiana, and they have had four children.

RICHARD J. WISEHART (deceased), who in his day was a well known and influential citizen of Gallatin county, Ill., was born Sept. 11, 1819, in the State of Kentucky, and died on the farm where his widow and one son now live, three and a half miles from Shawneetown. While he was still in his boyhood he came with his parents, John and Elizabeth Wisehart, to Gallatin county, crossing the Ohio on a flatboat, and settled on a farm. There he grew to manhood, receiving his schooling in the old fashioned subscription schools of pioneer times, which he supplemented by a course of reading and home study until he became a well informed man. While he was still of tender age he had the misfortune to lose his father by death and was thus thrown on his own resources at an early period in his life. At the time he was married the first time his entire possessions were a two-year-old colt and one dollar and a half in money. But by a life of industry and sterling honesty he accumulated considerable property, the home farm consisting of 200 acres of fine land. He also did an extensive business in stock raising, and was for many years a minister of the Christian church. His first marriage was to Nancy Parks, and they had four children: Harrison and Emily are living and Rebecca and John Henry are deceased. Emily is the wife of Levi Weaver, of Evansville, Ind. After the death of his first wife he was married on Dec. 15, 1872, to Sarah J. Boswell, a native of Bristol, England, who came with her parents, John and Sarah (Harris) Boswell, to America, while still in her girlhood. Her father was an expert in mineralogy and upon locating in Hardin county, Ill., he opened up some lead mines there. Subsequently he went to Kentucky and opened some coal mines, but later returned to Gallatin county, and opened the Old Saline mines, which are still running. In his day he did perhaps more than any other one man to develop the mineral resources of Southern Illinois. He died at Shawneetown about 1864. Richard and Sarah Wisehart were the parents of two children: Richard, who now lives with his mother on the old homestead, and William S., who died in the twentieth year of his age.

WILLIAM M. SATTERLEY, a farmer and stock raiser, living about five miles from Shawneetown, Ill., is one of those men who begin life at the bottom of the ladder, and who, by industry, good judgment and correct habits, win for themselves places among the successful and reputable citizens of the community in which their lots may be cast. He was born in Monroe county, Mo., March 9, 1860, and there grew to manhood on a farm. Circumstances prevented him from securing a first-class education in school and he commenced life as a farm hand, studying in favorable moments those needful branches of a business education. For several years he continued to work on farms by the month, saving his money in the hope that some day he could own a farm of his own. In 1878 he came to Gallatin county, Ill., where he worked for some time for various farmers. All of his old employers speak of him as a faithful and trustworthy man. In 1880 he was married to Miss Elma James, and in 1883 he located on the farm where he now lives. This farm consists of 160 acres, about one-half under cultivation and the rest in timber. All the improvements on the place have been made by Mr. Satterley since the farm came into his possession. He carries on a general farming business, studies how to secure the best results through the rotation of crops, etc., and devotes considerable time and attention to stock breeding. Politically he is a Democrat, and although he takes a keen interest in all those questions that affect the general welfare and is always ready to discharge his duty as a citizen, he is not what could be called an active politician. Mr. and Mrs. Satterley have had two children, Roy F. and Charles A., but both died in infancy.

MRS. LAURA C. YOUNG.

JAMES W. YOUNG (deceased), who in his day was a well known resident of Gallatin county, Ill., was born in Wilson county, Tenn., Aug. 30, 1843, there grew to manhood, and died on the farm where his widow now lives, Sept. 18, 1901. On Nov. 26, 1890, he married Laura Boyd, a daughter of William J. Boyd, who was born near Maysville, Mason county, Ky., April 30, 1824. In 1846 he came with his parents, John and Leah C. Boyd, to Gallatin county, located at New Haven, where he carried on a tanyard for about seven years, and also did considerable business as a boot and shoe manufacturer. He then removed to a farm in what is known as "Nettle Bottom," about five miles from Shawneetown, where he bought eighty acres of wild land. Subsequently he removed to the farm where Mrs. Laura Young now lives. William J. Boyd was a man of fine appearance, weighing over two hundred pounds. He was a Democrat in politics; was a prominent member of the Masonic fraternity; served several years as justice of the peace, and was a man of affairs generally. On March 24, 1847, he was married to Mrs. Jane Hooker, widow of Hiram Hooker, a daughter of Robert Bradford, and a native of Ireland. The children born to this marriage were Leona, Charles W., Rebecca, Walter and Laura C. Rebecca is the widow of James Rice; Laura C. is the widow of James Young and the others are deceased. The mother of these children died Aug. 9, 1887, aged seventy-two years. During the greater part of her life she was a devoted member of the Presbyterian church. William J. Boyd died on Aug. 4, 1887. At the time of his death he was the owner of several hundred acres of land, besides some city property in Shawneetown, where for several years he was in the livery business. After the marriage of James W. and Laura C. Young they lived on the farm where she now resides, and where he carried on a general farming and stock raising business. Since his death Mrs. Young continues to manage the farm, which consists of 160 acres. She also owns eighty acres in another tract. The children of James W. and Laura C. Young were Charles W., aged twelve years, now living on the old homestead with his mother, and Irene, Susie and Mary Frances, all deceased.

THOMAS B. HICK, M.D., one of the best known physicians of Gallatin county, Ill., was born at New Haven, in that county, Dec. 6, 1841, and is now the oldest native resident of that place. He is the third in a family of five children born to Thomas and Fatima C. (Barger) Hick, the former a native of Yorkshire, England, and the latter of Gallatin county, where her father, Jacob Barger, was one of the early settlers. The other children were John, born in 1838 and died in 1875, a merchant during his lifetime; Mary J., who married George L. Hanna, and died in 1901; Elizabeth J., wife of Mathew Land, born Jan. 13, 1844, and one who died in infancy. Doctor Hick's father came from England in his boyhood with his parents, settling near Golconda in the year 1816. He was bound out to a tobacconist until he was twenty-one years of age, but not liking the arrangement ran away before he completed his term of service. In 1835 he located at New Haven, where he engaged in mercantile pursuits. He took a prominent part in political affairs and in 1845 and again in 1858 was elected to the legislature on the Democratic ticket. He continued in business until 1866, and upon his death his sons succeeded to the store. The mother of Doctor Hick died in 1855. Doctor Hick received his early education in the common schools, after which he took a course in the Eastman Business college, at Poughkeepsie, N. Y. On Dec. 1, 1861, he enlisted as a private in Company G, Seventh Illinois cavalry, joining the regiment at Bird's Point, Mo. He was at the siege of Vicksburg; participated in the battle of Arkansas Post, the military operations about Corinth, and was in a number of minor skirmishes. In 1862 he was promoted to sergeant, and in August of that year was detailed for special duty by order of General Grant. When the postoffice of the Thirteenth army corps was created he was appointed a clerk in that department and remained in that capacity until August, 1864. He was then transferred to the military postoffice at Cairo and served there until he was mustered out on December 19, at Nashville, Tenn. Before the war he had been associated with his father in the store and had spent some time in reading medicine. After being discharged from the army he again took up the study, though he continued in the store with his brother until 1869. During the years 1870-71 he attended the Jefferson Medical college, of Philadelphia, and in 1872 graduated from the Cleveland Medical college. He located at New Haven, where he has been in continuous practice ever since. Although a third of a century has elapsed since Doctor Hick first received his degree of M.D. he has not allowed himself to fall behind in the progress of medical science. In the treatment of diseases he is looked upon as one of the successful physicians of his section of the state, and consequently has a large and lucrative practice. In addition to his professional interests he owns a farm of one hundred and sixty acres, and has accumulated considerable town property. Like his father before him, he is an unswerving Democrat, though the only political position he could ever be prevailed on to accept was the postoffice at New Haven, where he served as postmaster for several years. Doctor Hick is a member of the Ancient Order of United Workmen; Rhodes Post, No. 586, Grand Army of the Republic, of New Haven, and belongs to the Cumberland Presbyterian church.

BLUEFORD ROBINETT, a retired farmer, of Shawneetown, Ill., was born in that county, not far from Ford's Ferry, Jan. 18, 1833. His father, Joseph Robinett, was a native of Bourbon county, Ky., where he was born in 1785. In 1818 he came with his wife and four children to Gallatin county, Ill., making the journey by wagon, entered 280 acres of government land, for which he paid $1.25 an acre. On this land Mr. Robinett built a hewed log house of two rooms, and there passed the remainder of his life as a farmer. This farm is the one where the subject of this sketch was born. Joseph Robinett was twice married. His first wife was a Miss Hughes, by whom he had four children, all born in Kentucky. John was a soldier in the Black Hawk war; Irene married John Potts: Phœbe married Joseph Potts, and Matilda married James Barlow. The second wife was Clarissa Nighswonger, a native of Ohio, who came down the Ohio river with her brother in a flatboat, about 1824, and settled in Gallatin county. To this marriage there were born the following children: James, who died at the age of seventy-eight years; Louisiana, who married Todd Dunn and died at the age of forty; Allen, who died when he was about thirty years old; Cynthia A., who married Jeremiah Potts and died at the age of forty; Blueford, the subject of this sketch; Rachel, now living in Gallatin county as the widow of Henry Rose; Joseph a farmer of Gallatin county, and Alfred, who died when but nine years of age. The mother of these children died at the age of eighty-four years and the father when he was about sixty-six. Blueford Robinett was about nineteen years of age at the time of his father's death and he was called on to take charge of the farm and conduct it for his mother. He continued to live on the farm until 1892, when he removed to Shawneetown. Although in his boyhood he was denied the privilege of attending school as much as most of the boys of the present generation enjoy, he has succeeded in life. At one time he owned over 1,000 acres of land. Much of this has been divided among his children, but he is still the owner of a fine farm of two hundred acres. In politics Mr. Robinett has always been a Democrat, one of the kind who always have the courage of their convictions and ready to defend their principles, but he has never been a seeker for public office. In 1853 he was married to Miss Eliza J. Rose and to this union were born the following children: Charlotte, wife of John C. Brinkley, of Shawneetown; Lucy, wife of J. W. Rogers, a well known farmer of Gallatin county; Cynthia, who died at the age of six years; Minerva, wife of J. B. Hellington, a stock dealer of Harrisburg, Ill., and John, who died at the age of twenty-four years. The mother of these children died a few years ago, and since that time Mr. Robinett has made his home in Shawneetown.

GEORGE P. CASSIDY, M.D. (deceased), late a prominent physician of Shawneetown, Ill., was born on a farm near that city, June 6, 1860, and died at Shawneetown, May 15, 1903. His parents, John A. and Bridget Cassidy, were natives of Ireland. Both are now deceased. Dr. Cassidy received his early education in the public schools. At the age of sixteen years he entered the Notre Dame, Ind., university, and graduated in the class of 1881. The following year he entered the Miami Medical college of Cincinnati, where he continued until he had taken three full courses of lectures, when he traveled south to Cuba and the surrounding islands for about a year. He then re-entered the medical college and graduated with the degree of M.D. in the class of 1885. From that time until his death he practiced his profession in Shawneetown, winning the reputation of being one of the most progressive and successful physicians in the place. After graduating from the Miami college he took a special course in diseases of the eye and ear. In his untimely death the profession lost one of its most brilliant members. He was the founder and first president of the Gallatin County Medical society; was a member of the State Medical society; and also of the Southern Medical society. In all these organizations he was ever to be found working for the advancement of the profession. In his religious views he accepted the faith of his parents and belonged to the Catholic church. On April 18, 1893, Dr. Cassidy and Miss Olive Grattan were united in marriage. She is a native of Saline county, Ill., and a descendant of one of the first families. Three children were born to Dr. and Mrs. Cassidy: Grattan, Claudia, and one who died in infancy.

GEORGE HARRELSON, a retail grocer of Shawneetown, Ill., was born in what is known as the "Pond Settlement," in that county, May 3, 1847. He is the second and only surviving child of George and Mary (Callicott) Harrelson. Rebecca, the eldest, married Henry Young and later died, and Joseph, the youngest, died at the age of twenty years. George Harrelson, the father, was twice married. His first wife was a Miss Fleming, by whom he had four children, only one of whom is now living, viz.: Nancy, wife of Henry Young, of Omaha, Ill. When the subject of this sketch was about eight years of age his parents removed to New Haven, in Gallatin county, and there the father died the same year. The mother afterward married James Smith, who died in 1867. George Harrelson lived with his mother until he was twenty-one years old, when he commenced working by the month for some of the neighboring farmers. After a few years passed in this way he bought out the other heirs to his father's estate and became the owner of the old homestead, consisting of 160 acres of land. He conducted this farm for three years, when he rented it and engaged in other pursuits for about four years, at the end of which time he returned to the farm and lived there until 1887. In that year he located in Shawneetown and embarked in the grocery business, in which he is still engaged. Mr. Harrelson has built up a good patronage by his close attention to business, studying the demands of his trade, and his correct business habits. Politically he is a Republican, though he is not particularly active in political work, and in religious matters he belongs to the Presbyterian church. He has been twice married. His first wife, who died about a year after their marriage, was Mary Williams. His second and present wife was Sarah E. Hill. To this marriage there was born one son, Joseph, who met his death by an accident. One day, during recess at school, a boy named Jesse Barr caught a schoolmate, Harry Docker, and bumped the back of his head against Joseph's right temple, causing an injury that resulted in his death.

FELIX DOWNEN (deceased), late a farmer near Ridgway, Gallatin county, Ill., was born near Mount Vernon, Posey county, Ind., May 28, 1858, and died on the farm now occupied by his widow, Oct. 22, 1900. He was reared to manhood in Posey county, received his education there in the public schools, and upon arriving at man's estate adopted the life of a farmer. On Feb. 13, 1879, he was united in marriage to Miss Kate Allyn, who was born and reared in the same neighborhood, and in September of that year removed to Gallatin county, locating on the farm where he lived the remainder of his life. At the time he took possession of this farm there was but eighty acres, about half of which was cleared. He improved this place and added to it until at the time of his death he was the owner of 200 acres of land, well equipped with improvements, and which is now occupied and owned by his widow and her children. Mr. Downen did a general farming business in his life-time and gave considerable attention to stock raising. He was a member of the Court of Honor, a fraternal organization, and with his wife belonged to the Baptist church. In the ordinary affairs of life he was a consistent practitioner of the tenets of his religious faith, dealing fairly with his fellowmen, sympathizing with the unfortunate and contributing to worthy charities as his means would permit. He and his wife had the following children: Lemuel, born Oct. 6, 1880, now deceased; Ora, born Sept. 15, 1882, now the wife of Charles Foster; Inez, born Nov. 9, 1884, now Mrs. Edward Barnett; Mattie, born Sept. 17, 1886, at home with her mother; Mary, born Sept. 9, 1889, and Hattie Olive, born Aug. 31, 1896.

CALVIN M. BAKER, a farmer near Equality, Gallatin county, Ill., is one of the oldest residents in that section of the state. He was born in Walker county, Ala., Dec. 27, 1824, his parents being William and Phoebe (Collinsworth) Baker. In 1828 William Baker loaded one wagon with his worldly goods and with his wife and children came overland to Shawneetown. He located at the John Crenshaw salt works, where he was employed for about two years. He then entered forty acres of land on Eagle creek, built a log cabin and devoted the rest of his life to agricultural pursuits. He died near Equality in 1841, aged fifty-two years. His wife died some time later at the age of fifty-five. Of their children but three are now living, viz.: Calvin M., the subject of this sketch; Sarah, widow of William Dorsey, and William, who lives in Arkansas. Those dead are Elizabeth, who married Wallace McKenney, and lived to be eighty-seven years old; Preston, who died at the age of twenty-three years; Covington, died at the age of seven years; Henry, died when he was about twenty years old; Phoebe, died in early childhood; James and Felix, who each died when about two years old; and Caroline, who married Thomas Scudmore. When Calvin M. Baker was about seventeen years old he commenced the battle of life by renting a farm, raising a crop in the summer months and working at the Illinois Iron Works in the winter time. He continued in this way for a few years, when on Jan. 10, 1850, he was married to Miss Frances Calvert and for the next four years lived in Hardin county. He then returned to Gallatin county and bought a tract of 120 acres of land, upon which, to use the old familiar expression, "there was not a stick of timber amiss." This place has been his home for fifty years, though he has added to his original farm until he now owns 360 acres. Here he has seen his children grow to maturity, marry and found homes of their own, and here in 1879 he lost his wife by death, after nearly thirty years of happy married life. Their children are Sarah, widow of Wiley Rose, now living at Elizabethtown, Ill.; William, who lives near his father; Phoebe, wife of John Harvey, also living in the neighborhood; Rena, deceased; Mary, wife of Harry Pearson, living near Harrisburg, Ill.; Lucy, wife of Charles Walsen, also living near Harrisburg; Effie, wife of John Brown, living near

Equality. Mr. Baker has been one of the successful farmers and stock raisers of Gallatin county for many years. He is a Democrat and cast his first presidential vote for Lewis Cass in 1848. Since then he has always been a stanch defender of Democratic principles, though he has many warm personal friends among those of the opposite political belief because of his sympathetic nature and genial disposition.

JAMES T. COLBERT, a well-to-do farmer, living near Equality, Gallatin county, Ill., was born in the neighborhood where he now lives, May 3, 1827. His father, James Colbert, was born in Alabama about 1792. When he was a young man he came with his brothers, Henry, Drury, and Hiram, to Illinois, and after working for a while at the salt works entered eighty acres of government land and passed the rest of his life as a farmer. This farm is now in the possession of the subject of this sketch, and it was there that he was born. James Colbert fought in the Black Hawk war and died in 1834. His children were: Allen B., William, Nancy J., Elisha, Hiram, James T., Thomas and Frances. Allen died at the age of thirty-five years; William lived to be seventy-seven; Nancy married Robert Pinson and after his death Johnson Kanady, and died at the age of seventy-five; Elisha died in 1862 while serving in the One Hundred and Twentieth Illinois infantry; Hiram died in 1834; Thomas died in 1890; and Frances is the wife of Calvin Baker. The mother of these children died at the age of seventy-six years. James T. Colbert commenced life on his own account when he was twenty years old, his only capital being an ax, a fiddle, and a determination to succeed. His education had been acquired in the old subscription schools, in a log house with no floor but the ground and split saplings for seats. From the time he was twenty until he was thirty years of age he followed farming during the summer seasons and worked at the Illinois Iron Works in the winter time, devoting all his leisure time to self-study, until today he is one of the best informed men in his locality. He has also prospered in the accumulation of this world's goods. When he was first married in 1847 he went to housekeeping in a log cabin, about a mile from where he now lives. He remained there until 1891, when he removed to his present location, where he has a well improved farm, all the improvements having been made by himself. He now owns eight hundred acres of fine land, five hundred acres of which are under cultivation, and has given something like four hundred acres to his children. As a stock raiser

Mr. Colbert has been quite successful, though the greater part of his attention has been devoted to a general farming business. He takes an interest in public affairs and has served as county commissioner, to which office he was elected on the Democratic ticket, having affiliated with that party ever since he became a voter. Mr. Colbert has been twice married. His first wife was Miss Mary J. Seets, a native of Tennessee, and to this marriage there were born the following children: Lucy A., wife of Jefferson Vinyard, of Hardin county; Allen B., who died at the age of ten years; Frances, wife of Robert Taylor, living near Harrisburg; Sarah, wife of Joseph Vinyard; James, who lives near his father; Mary L., who married Henry Hamp and afterward died; Aaron, who lives in the vicinity; Margaret, widow of Isaac Jennings, who was a farmer in Eagle Creek township; Thomas J.; Isabelle, who married Robert White and died some years ago as his wife; Prudence, wife of George Leadbetter, and John B., who died in 1893. The mother of these children died in 1875 and on Oct. 29, 1879, Mr. Colbert was married to Mrs. Mary A. Frohock, widow of Lucien Frohock, and a daughter of Josiah Hull. Three children have been born to this second marriage, viz.: Virgie, wife of George Blackman, of Eagle Creek township; Virgil, on the farm with his father, and Paul, at home.

THOMAS B. LOGSDON, a retired farmer of Shawneetown, Ill., was born in Ripley county, Ind., Oct. 21, 1841, his parents being Thomas B. and Mary (Muir) Logsdon. When the subject of this sketch was about seventeen years of age he commenced his business career as a farmer, but in 1859 went to Indianapolis, Ind., where he secured a position as clerk in a grocery, and worked there until 1862. He then worked on the railroad for about a year, at the end of which time he came to Shawneetown and engaged in business. A year later he entered the service of the Illinois Central Railroad Company as a sleeping-car conductor, and continued in that capacity for about eighteen months. Then for something over a year he was a night watchman in the railroad yards and in the fall of 1868 again located in Gallatin county. On Jan. 19, 1869, he was united in marriage to Mrs. Margaret Logsdon, widow of Carter Logsdon and daughter of Solomon and Nancy Brown, and went to farming near Bowlesville, four miles west of Shawneetown. In 1891 he removed to Shawneetown, where he now lives retired, though he still owns his farm of three hundred and twenty-seven acres. When he came to Shawneetown in 1891 he went into the store of Jacob Bechtold as a clerk and remained there for four years. Mr. Logsdon is one of the active Democrats of Gallatin county. For two years he was postmaster at Bowlesville, at the end of which time he resigned. From 1870 to 1886 he held the office of justice of the peace; was appointed county commissioner to fill a vacancy caused by the death of Dr. Harmon, and served almost a full term; was then twice elected to the office, serving nearly six years in all; and served as police magistrate for two years. Since 1872 he has been a member of the Independent Order of Odd Fellows, and since 1894 a Knight of Pythias. Mr. Logsdon and his wife both belong to the Cumberland Presbyterian church at Bowlesville, where he was for some time superintendent of the Sunday school. (See sketches of Joseph and James J. Logsdon for extended account of ancestry.)

JOSEPH E. LOGSDON, one of the most prominent farmers and stock raisers of Gallatin county, Ill., living one mile west of Shawneetown, is a native of that county, having been born on a farm about one and a half miles west of Shawneetown, Dec. 11, 1854. His father, Thomas Logsdon, was a son of one of the old pioneer settlers. (See sketches of Joseph and James Logsdon). After such an education as the common schools afforded Joseph E. Logsdon attended Notre Dame university for one year. At the age of twenty-two years he engaged in general farming and stock raising upon the farm owned by his mother until 1899, when he removed to the farm where he now lives. He does an extensive business in raising and feeding stock and is interested in various other enterprises, being generally recognized as one of the leading business men of the county. In 1883 he was united in marriage to Miss Edith Riordan. Two children born to this union are deceased, viz.: Arthur and Edward. Those living are Eugene, Maude, Thomas, Lucy, Isabelle, Horace, Frederick and Bluford. In politics Mr. Logsdon is a Democrat and he takes a lively interest in all questions of public policy. He is in favor of good roads, good schools, good local government, and in fact is one of the most progressive men in his vicinity.

CAPT. LA FAYETTE TWITCHELL, a prominent citizen of Elizabethtown, Ill., at the present time police magistrate, was born on Feb. 26, 1829, in that part of Pope county, Ill., now included in the county of Hardin, his birthplace being on a farm about four and a half miles northwest of Elizabethtown. His father, Moses Twitchell, was born at Bethel, Me., March 6, 1779. In early life he was engaged in rafting lumber from Bethel to Brunswick, and also learned the trade of millwright. He married Lydia Harris in 1810, and in 1812 moved to Pittsburg, Pa., where he engaged in the milling and lumber business. In 1818 he placed all his personal property on a flatboat and with his wife and two children came down the Ohio river to Elizabethtown. He bought eighty acres of land from a Mr. O'Neal, who had built a small grist mill on Big creek, one of the first mills in that part of the state. This mill Mr. Twitchell enlarged and added a saw mill. It afterward became known far and wide as "Twitchell's mill." Moses Twitchell did considerable business in shipping lumber down the river by flatboat, frequently going as far as New Orleans. He also conducted a cooper shop, blacksmith shop and still house. Later he built a saw mill on Three Mile creek but did not operate it for any great length of time. In that early day he held an office that corresponds to the present county commissioner. In the late fifties he had established at his place the first postoffice between Shawneetown and Golconda, known as Twitchell's Mills. He was postmaster until he died in 1832. His wife died in 1836. La Fayette is the youngest of the family, the other children being: Franklin, born in 1812 and died in 1855; Washington, born in 1814 at Pittsburg and died in 1851 in California; Hiram, who died in 1841 near Elizabethtown; Uzial, who died in 1862; and two daughters, both named Cynthia, who died in childhood. La Fayette Twitchell passed his boyhood at his father's mills. In 1837, after the death of his parents, he went to Elizabethtown, where he lived with his brother Franklin, attending the schools there and at Shawneetown. As soon as he was old enough to run on the river he engaged in the occupation of flatboating, his brother Franklin being one of the most noted pilots on the river. In the spring of 1849 in company with James and B. P. McFarland, George

Jackson, William Chipp, John H. Lefler, and Robert Pierson, making seven in all, he started with a six-mule team for California. They left Elizabethtown on April 3, added two more mules to their team at St. Joseph, Mo., and arrived at Weaverville, Cal., on August 24. He remained in California until May, 1852, prospecting and mining, in which he was successful, and then returned by water to New York. From there he made his way back to Elizabethtown, where he engaged in the business of running a saw mill and flatboating until the mill was destroyed by fire in 1854. He and his brother then built a wharf-boat, which they conducted for about a year, when it was wrecked in a storm. Soon after this his brother died. In 1859 Captain Twitchell again caught the gold fever and went overland to Pike's Peak, remaining there for about two years, when he again returned to his home near Elizabethtown. In August, 1862, he helped to raise a company, which was mustered in as Company B, One Hundred and Thirty-first Illinois infantry. He was at first made adjutant of the regiment, and in June, 1863, was commissioned captain of his company. He was in many of the military operations around Vicksburg, fought at Arkansas Post and Milligan's Bend, and was engaged in doing guard and provost duty at Memphis. In November, 1863, he resigned, raised Company I, One Hundred and Thirty-sixth Illinois infantry, for the one hundred days' service, and was made captain of the company. He was discharged in October, 1864, by reason of expiration of service, and from that time until 1870 was engaged in the saw mill business. He then conducted a hotel near Rosiclare for about two years, when he was elected to the office of circuit clerk in 1872 on the Republican ticket and held the office for four years. Subsequently he served six years as master in chancery, and during President Harrison's administration was postmaster at Elizabethtown for four years. He was one of the county commissioners at the time the new court house was built, and took an active part in raising by subscription from the people of the town a sum of $1,200 with which to assist in building the structure. Captain Twitchell has been a member of the Independent Order of Odd Fellows ever since 1853; has passed through the chairs; and has five times represented his lodge in the Grand Lodge. He is one of the charter members of Alex Ragon Post, No. 565, Grand Army of the Republic, at Elizabethtown; has been honored by his comrades by being elected commander of the post, and has been a member of Western Association California Pioneers since 1893. In 1856 he was married to Miss

Angeline, daughter of James and Elizabeth Steele, who came from South Carolina at an early date. Mrs. Twitchell was born near Rosiclare in 1836 and has been a member of the Methodist Episcopal church ever since she was sixteen years of age. Captain and Mrs. Twitchell are the parents of the following children: Robert A., a physician of East St. Louis; La Fayette, an attorney at Denver, Col.; Mollie E., who died in childhood; Benjamin E. and James W., both physicians, practicing together at Belleville, Ill.

BRITTON STACEY, a well known resident of Elizabethtown, Ill., was born near Gainesboro, Jackson county, Tenn., May 1, 1844. When he was about two years old his parents removed to Kentucky and in 1852 to Illinois, locating on a farm about twelve miles north of Elizabethtown. Here the subject of this sketch grew to manhood, working on a farm in summer and attending the public schools during the winter months. On July 4, 1862, he enlisted as a private in Company F, One Hundred and Thirty-first Illinois volunteer infantry, and was mustered in at Metropolis City on September 16th of the same year. He was engaged in the military operations on the Yazoo river, fought at Haines' Bluff, Arkansas Post and the siege of Vicksburg. After the fall of Vicksburg he was taken ill with typhoid fever and sent to the hospital at St. Louis, where he remained for seven months. He then rejoined his command at Paducah, Ky., and soon afterward the regiment was consolidated with the Twenty-ninth infantry at Vicksburg. For the next eleven months he was at Natchez on guard duty, then to New Orleans, Dolphin's Island, at the battle of Spanish Fort and in numerous minor skirmishes. At Spanish Fort he was severely wounded by the explosion of a shell, the left arm being so badly lacerated that it had to be taken off above the elbow. He was discharged on Sept. 16, 1865, just three years after being mustered in, and returned to the farm. On March 22, 1866, he was married to Miss Amy J. Tinsley, who came with her parents to Hardin county when she was about thirteen years of age. After his marriage Mr. Stacey engaged in farming about ten miles northeast of Elizabethtown until 1881, when he moved into town. At one time he owned 220 acres of land.

Mr. Stacey is one of the stalwart Republicans of Hardin county. He was for twelve years a deputy in the sheriff's office, having previously served eight years as constable while living on the farm. He has several times been elected to a place on the town board and served one term as mayor of Elizabethtown. He was one of the charter members of Alexander Ragon Post, Grand Army of the Republic, at Elizabethtown, and has been commander of the post. He also belongs to the Independent Order of Odd Fellows and the Knights of Honor. As a public official he has won the reputation of being a capable and conscientious one, and in his fraternal organizations he has won popularity by his genial disposition and his ready benevolence to those less fortunate than himself.

DAVID ORR, a farmer two and a half miles from Elizabethtown, Ill., was born five miles northwest of that town, May 28, 1848. His father, Joseph Orr, was born near Gallipolis, O., but came to Hardin county, Ill., while he was still a young man. There he married Sarah Williams, a member of one of the old families of the county, settled on the farm where the subject of this sketch was born, and there passed the remainder of his life. He and his wife were the parents of the following children: William, John, James, Joseph, Nancy J., David, and Mary E. William died in infancy; Joseph died in 1873; Nancy J. died in 1858, and Mary E. is now living with her mother on the old homestead. The father of these children died in March, 1852, but the mother, who was born Dec. 17, 1816, is still living and until recently enjoyed good health. When David was twelve years of age he took charge of the farm for his mother and lived with her until 1890, having full control of the three hundred acres constituting the old home farm. On Oct. 16, 1890, he was married to Jane Jackson, a daughter of James N. Jackson, and located on the farm where he now lives. His wife and her father were both born on this farm, which formerly belonged to her grandfather, John Jackson, who was one of the pioneers of Hardin county. It is located on the Ohio river, contains 550 acres and is one of the best farms in the county. Mr. Orr carries on a general farming business, but devotes a great deal of his time to breeding fine stock, especially Shorthorn and Red Polled cattle and Hackney and Percheron horses. Politically he is a Republican but has never been desirous of holding public office. His first wife died on March 5, 1897, leaving two children, Clarissa and David, and on Sept. 6, 1899, he was married to Miss Alice Duley of Kentucky.

JAMES P. FERRILL, a farmer and stock raiser, of Elizabethtown, Ill., was born in that county, Dec. 30, 1847. His father, John H. Ferrill, was born near Chapel Hill, Tenn., April 15, 1823, and lived there until he was about sixteen years of age. About the year 1839 his father, the grandfather of the subject of this sketch, died. Soon after his death the widow, with her two sons, John H. and Charles M., came with one wagon containing all their earthly possessions to Illinois and located near Furnace, in Hardin county. The two boys worked on the farm in the summer time, at the iron works in the winter, cut cordwood, and did various other things to assist their widowed mother. In 1843 John H. Ferrill was united in marriage to Nancy Pillow, a niece of Gideon Pillow, who won distinction as a Confederate general during the Civil war. To this marriage there were born the following children: James P., the subject of this sketch; Martha, who died at the age of two years; John C., now in Los Angeles, Cal.; Anne, who died in childhood; Josie, now living at Elizabethtown, and Nellie, who died as the wife of James B. McFarland. About 1851 John H. Ferrill went to California and remained there for about two years, prospecting and mining, but at the end of that time returned to Hardin county, making the trip by water both ways. From that time until the war he was engaged in steamboat navigation on the Mississippi, the Ohio and Cumberland rivers. He was the owner of the steamers *Winneford, Kate French* and *Governor's Island,* and was doing a good business when the war broke out. In 1861 he enlisted as wagon master in the Twenty-ninth Illinois infantry, but was transferred to the navy by General Grant and made a master pilot, serving in that capacity during the entire conflict. He was the volunteer pilot on board the monitor *Neosho* and in one of the engagements her colors were shot down. Assisted by a German soldier he raised the flag while the fight was still going on and received a medal from Congress for his bravery. After the war he returned to his old occupation and continued in the river traffic until 1878. He was a charter member of the Grand Army post at Elizabethtown. His death occurred on April 17, 1900. His widow is still living, being now about eighty years of age. James P. Ferrill began working with his father on the river just at the commencement of the war and remained associated with him until 1878, both giving up the river at the same time. After that he lived at Metropolis until 1882, when he located on the farm where he now lives. This farm, which is known as the "Colonel Ferrill farm," contains 440 acres. It formerly belonged to Charles M. Ferrill, who raised Company D, of the Twenty-ninth Illinois infantry, and was mustered in as captain. He took part in all the engagements in which his command participated, among them Fort Donelson, Shiloh, the siege of Vicksburg, and the military operations about Corinth. After the war he engaged in mercantile pursuits at Elizabethtown until 1882, when he retired. He was one of the prominent and successful men of the county; a member of the Grand Army of the Republic; the Masonic fraternity, and the Independent Order of Odd Fellows; represented Hardin county in the legislature; served as county commissioner, county judge, and some other local officers, and died in July, 1901. James P. Ferrill and Miss Mary Hayden were united in marriage on June 15, 1872, and to this marriage there have been born the following children: Charles F., a merchant; E. R., engaged on the river; Nellie, wife of Samuel Hosick, of Elizabethtown; James, at home. Those deceased are Rillie, Benjamin and John Henry.

HENRY RITTENHOUSE, a farmer, living near Cave in Rock, Hardin county, Ill., is one of the best known men in his locality. He was born in Switzerland county, Ind., Oct. 14, 1840. When he was about four years old his parents removed to Schuyler county, Ill., where he grew to manhood and received his education in the public schools. On Oct. 7, 1861, just a week before he reached his majority, he enlisted as a private in Company G, Twenty-eighth Illinois volunteer infantry, and was mustered in at Rushville. The regiment was ordered to Kentucky and while there employed in the construction of some earth works Mr. Rittenhouse was seriously ruptured. For some time he remained in the hospital and on Dec. 17, 1861, was discharged from the service on account of his disability. On Sept. 16, 1863, he was married to Miss Charlotte Persinger, who was born and reared in Schuyler county, her parents being Allen and Paulina (Peters) Persinger. About two months after his marriage Mr. Rittenhouse came with his wife to Hardin county, where he rented land until 1875, when he bought forty acres, about half of which was cleared, and lived on that place for five years. He then removed to the place where he now lives. The farm is known as the "Jackson Farm," contains 188 acres, and is one of the best in the neighborhood. Mr. Rittenhouse carries on a general farming business and devotes considerable attention to stock-raising. He is one of the leading Republicans in his part of the county, and was elected on that ticket to the office of county commissioner for a term of three years. The only fraternal organization to claim him as a member is the Grand Army of the Republic, in which he belongs to the post at Cave in Rock. The children born to Mr. and Mrs. Rittenhouse are Rosa, Laura, Peyton, William A., Hattie and Pennington. Rosa died at the age of six months; Laura and Peyton were twins; Peyton died and Laura is the wife of Joseph Riggs living near; William is an attorney and abstractor of titles in Chicago; was educated at the Northern Indiana normal, at Valparaiso, read law with Col. Dick Taylor, and practiced for a while at Shawneetown. In Chicago he was associated with Mr. Deneen, who was elected governor of Illinois in 1904. Hattie and Pennington were twins. The latter died and the former is now the county superintendent of the Hardin county schools. She was educated at the normal school at Carbondale and began teaching at the age of seventeen. Mrs. Rittenhouse is a member of the Methodist Episcopal church. The daughter is a Baptist.

JOHN GILBERT, of Golconda, Ill., president of the Pope County State bank, was born in the town where he now resides, Oct. 13, 1853. His father, whose name was also John, was born in Pennsylvania in 1818. At an early age he was left an orphan and was bound out to an uncle. This uncle procured a position for him with the North American Fur Company, and while in the employ of that concern at the trading post of New Harmony, Ind., he drifted into Pope county buying furs and selling the old Seth Thomas clocks. Upon leaving the fur company he clerked in the general store of Mr. Lowth at Golconda for some time and later bought out his employer. He continued in the mercantile line until 1876, when he went to Evansville to engage in the produce business, pork and tobacco being his specialties. Some time after going to Evansville he became interested in the Evansville & Cairo Packet Company, running mail boats between the two cities, and also in the Evansville & Tennessee Packet Company, which operated a line of boats on the Tennessee river. In 1876 he was made vice-president of the Merchants' National bank, and after that institution went into liquidation, on account of the expiration of its charter, he became vice-president of the Old National bank. In 1899 he was made president of the latter bank and held the office until his death on Aug. 14, 1901. He was a zealous Republican, a member of the Presbyterian church, and was a fine example of a self-made man. He married Camelia Bucklin of Rhode Island, and their children were Harry, who succeeded his father in the steamboat lines; Fannie, who lives at Golconda; John, the subject of this sketch; Minnie; William S., a brick manufacturer of Evansville; and three deceased, viz.: Eliza, Maria, and Augustus. Eliza was the wife of Lewis McCoy. John Gilbert, the subject of this sketch, was reared at Golconda and received his education in the public schools. While still in his youth he went into the banking house of W. P. Sloan & Co., in which his father was a silent partner, and worked his way up to bookkeeper and later to the position of cashier. In 1877 the bank was reorganized under the firm name of Sloan & Gilbert and continued under that name until 1888, when Mr. Gilbert bought the interest of Mr. Sloan. From that time until 1897 the business was continued as the John Gilbert, Jr., Company, when Mr. Gilbert came to his present position as president of the State bank. In addition to his banking interests Mr. Gilbert has developed a number of lead and spar mines in the county, and is now the owner of a spar mine near Hartsville with a vein eight feet in thickness. He is one of the active Republicans of the county; served nine years as chairman of the county executive committee; was elected county commissioner in 1898 and served one term of two years; and has for fourteen years been mayor of Golconda. He belongs to the Knights of Honor and the Independent Order of Odd Fellows, and in the latter order was for many years the treasurer of the lodge. Mr. Gilbert has been twice married. His first wife, to whom he was united on Sept. 21, 1882, was Miss Edmonia Kidd, of Paducah, Ky. Three children were born to this union, viz.: Raymond, now a student at the Northwestern university, Evanston, Ill.; Ethel, attending Ferry Hall seminary at Lake Forest, Ill., and John. The mother of these children died in 1891 and on Jan. 10, 1903, he was married to Miss Lucy Morse.

LOUIS HERBERT, the subject of this sketch, is little prone to boast of his achievements and his modesty makes it difficult to obtain from him sufficient details of his life to form an extended biographical sketch, though no man in the business life of Cairo, Ill., is more worthy of such notice. A detailed account of his successful career would be a good lesson for young men just starting to make their way in the world. Mr. Herbert was born in Germany, Feb. 1, 1840, of parents in comfortable circumstances. He received good schooling, though not a college or university education. His early training, however, gave him a taste for learning and made him a student all his life, the thirst for information still remaining with him, as his accumulation of well read books attests. When seventeen years of age the ambition to seek other parts and fly with his own wings seized him, and was gratified by his parents. He came to America, landing at New Orleans. Although a bright and attractive lad he was handicapped by a lack of knowledge of the English language. He soon obtained a place in a fine restaurant, conducted by a German, where he speedily made a good impression. While he was still working for wages the Civil war came on and materially disturbed his calculations, but after various experiences he reached Cairo in 1863. For a time after coming to the city he continued to work for wages, after which he formed a favorable partnership and started in the restaurant business for himself. At that time there were both ample room and a popular demand for a first-class restaurant in Cairo, and the new undertaking was soon crowned with success. Later he extended the restaurant business, opening in connection with it the best hotel in the city. The tide of travel through Cairo during the last years of the war, and immediately following the return of peace, made Mr. Herbert's hotel and café well known in all parts of the country. As a matter of course, this fame was profitable to him, as it gave him the cream of the trade in his line. As he accumulated money it was wisely invested in Cairo real estate, and the income from such investments was in like manner added to the same line of property. Many years ago he sold his restaurant and hotel business and engaged in the wholesaling of spirituous and malt liquors, in which his trade has been very extensive. Mr. Herbert now ranks among the wealthiest citizens, is one of the largest real estate owners and heaviest taxpayers in Southern Illinois. His property in Cairo is both extensive and valuable, as he has always had an abiding confidence in the future of the city and was not afraid to invest his money there. Subsequent years have demonstrated the soundness of his judgment. He also has a number of valuable farms within easy reach of Cairo, besides owning property in other cities. By industry, close application to business, and an unusual endowment of financial genius or judgment—call it what you like—Mr. Herbert has achieved his success. Through his long and constantly upward career he has never forfeited the good will of his fellow-men through shrewd practices or dishonest methods, but every dollar he has he has earned in a strictly legitimate way.

PETER CALDWELL, superintendent of the Louisville House of Refuge, one of the most important reformatory institutions of the country, was born in Huntingdon, Province of Quebec, Canada, April 23, 1836. He is the son of William and Janette (Elder) Caldwell, both natives of Scotland, who came to Canada in an early day on the same ship. His grandfather, William Caldwell, and his maternal grandfather, George Elder, emigrated to Huntingdon in 1801, when all of that region, now so thickly settled, was a vast wilderness, and there engaged in pioneer farming. Here William Caldwell lived to a patriarchal age, dying on the eighty-second anniversary of his birth. William Caldwell, the father of Peter Caldwell, lived all of his life on a farm in sight of that on which he grew to manhood. A man of fine judgment and high character, he wielded a powerful influence in the community in which he lived. In the French rebellion he saw active service, acquitting himself with credit. For many years he was commissioner of schools for his county and his deep interest in educational matters had much to do with influencing his son to devote himself to the profession which finally carried him into reformatory as well as educational work. He died at the ripe age of fourscore years and four, honored and respected by all who knew him. Peter Caldwell grew to manhood on his father's farm and received his academic education at Huntingdon and Malone, N. Y. In 1859 he entered Middlebury college at Middlebury, Vt., and four years later graduated with the degree of Bachelor of Arts. He had begun teaching at an early age and devoted ten years in all to that work, earning in that way the money which enabled him to complete his education. Immediately after graduation he went to Chicago, where he was first chosen principal and three months later assistant superintendent of the reform school of that city. After serving in this capacity for a year and a half he was called to Louisville, Ky., to take the position of superintendent of the Louisville House of Refuge, which position he has so ably and acceptably filled since 1866. His long experience as a teacher, his tact and ability as a disciplinarian, his thorough appreciation of the responsibilities resting upon him and a conscientious devotion to duty eminently fitted him for the all-important work undertaken by him. Taking charge of the house of refuge immediately after the Civil war and practically at its inception, Peter Caldwell has by his skilful management developed it into a reformatory institution which is the pride of the city and which has no superior among similar institutions in the United States. During all the years of his connection with this institution he has kept in close touch with the noble men and women engaged in reformatory and charitable work in the United States, attending regularly their conventions and co-operating actively in all movements designed to improve the condition of prisons, reformatories and charities. He has made a close study of the conduct and management of such institutions, and the splendid results of his management of the Louisville House of Refuge evidence the fact that he has studied to good purpose. In religious matters he is identified with the Presbyterian church. While he votes with the Democratic party in national issues, he acts independently to the extent of supporting those whom he deems best qualified to fill local offices. In 1866 he was united in marriage to Miss Mary T. Wells, the daughter of Rev. Edward Wells, of Chicago, a native of Canada. They are the parents of seven children: Nettie, the wife of Thomas H. Campbell; Addie, now Mrs. Archibald Campbell; William; Carrie, the wife of John Settle; Hamilton P.; Mary T., and David C. While the work of Peter Caldwell is a grand one that of his noble wife is equally so. More than a third of a century has passed since Peter Caldwell and his bride of a day began life together here. This has been the scene of their honeymoon, as it has been a richly fertile field of labor, abundant in enduring reward and which they would not exchange for great riches. A brief and all insufficient tribute is most certainly due Mrs. Caldwell, who for many years patiently labored with her husband at the outset, with no hope or expectation of other requital than the sense of duty well performed and the grateful and enduring love of its beneficiaries. There has not been an even distribution of either the labor or the reward between her and her husband. While he has largely been a figurehead, hers has been the administering hand. She has borne the brunt of the battle and bears most of the scars. Her midnight vigils for many years with the very ailing ones come back to the memory of her husband from the retrospect, tempered with reverential tenderness and admiration and even were it within his power to reshape the past he would not wish her a single hour of respite, a single pang of anxiety saved, any more than she herself would do. The services she rendered were not those of an hireling, meted out grudgingly, or stinted; on the contrary, she was ever ready, ever willing, ever cheerful in the bestowing of her benefactions both by day and by night.

CAPT. J. G. STUART.

LESTER STUART, one of the leading farmers near Eichorn, Hardin county, Ill., was born on the farm where he now lives, Sept. 5, 1873. He is a son of Capt. J. G. Stuart, who was born on a farm near Hopkinsville, Ky., Oct. 4, 1834, and there grew to manhood. While he was still a young man J. G. Stuart came to Hardin county, bought eighty acres of land, nearly all in timber, a mile and a quarter from Eichorn postoffice, and lived there until the beginning of the Civil war. He enlisted in Company C, Forty-eighth regiment, Illinois volunteer infantry, and was elected first lieutenant of the company. Subsequently he was made captain and was mustered out with that rank after three years and six months of service. During that time he participated in some of the principal battles of the war, as well as numerous minor engagements, and was once slightly wounded. After the war he returned to his farm, married Martha Hobbs and both died on the place that the subject of this sketch now occupies, the father at the age of sixty-six and the mother at the age of forty-eight. Captain Stuart in his day was one of the active Democrats of the county and filled some of the minor offices with credit to himself and to the entire satisfaction of those who elected him. He and his wife had the following children: Prince, deceased; Lester, the subject of this sketch; Stapleton, who still lives on the old farm; Arvilla, now Mrs. Dorner, of Hardin county; and Clyde, at home. Lester Stuart received his education in the public schools and has all his life been a tiller of the soil. The heirs of Captain Stuart own 360 acres of good land, nearly all of which is under cultivation, the farm being one of the best improved in the community. Lester Stuart, like his father before him, is an enthusiastic Democrat, and has filled some of the local offices. He is one of the men who believe in modern methods of farming and is one of the most progressive citizens along all lines in his part of the county.

ALBERT J. RICHARDS, carriage manufacturer and proprietor of the largest livery stables in Louisville, Ky., is a native of Pennsylvania, having been born in the city of Pittsburgh, Feb. 22, 1856, his parents being Adam and Theresa Richards. His mother died while he was still in his infancy, and his father, who was a brass finisher by trade, left Pittsburgh, removed to Dubois county, Ind., where he bought a farm and lived the remainder of his days, his death occurring in 1867. Albert was the youngest of three children, the other two being August and Sophia, the latter now the wife of Louis Lex. The father married again after going to Indiana, his second wife being Maggie Kleinhelter. To this second marriage were born the following children: Henry, Adam, Maggie, wife of John Decamper; Annie, wife of John Bender; and Frank. Albert J. Richards was reared in Dubois county until he was fifteen years of age, acquired there a limited education in the public schools, and at the age of fifteen started in to learn the trade of collar maker. After a year at the business he abandoned it, because it did not agree with him, and apprenticed himself to the Ender Carriage Company, of Louisville, to learn the trade of blacksmith and carriage builder. He remained with the company for nine years, after which he was for three years with the Wheeler Carriage Company, then with other concerns until 1886, when he embarked in the business for himself. Subsequently he added a horseshoeing department and, although other concerns may turn out a larger number of carriages, none have the reputation of producing a better class of work. Everything he handles is of his own manufacture, is of the highest possible standard, and has a wide reputation for its excellence. His factory and shops employ about thirty people, every man a skilled mechanic in his line. Since 1893 Mr. Richards has been the proprietor of the Euclid Livery Stables, the largest in the city, keeping over twenty horses for hire and having boarding capacity for about eighty more. This stable employs nearly twenty men and is one of the best equipped in the Ohio Valley. Mr. Richards deserves great credit for what he has accomplished, owing to the fact that his mother died while he was still in his infancy and his father some ten years later. Left an orphan at the age of eleven years, with a limited education, he experienced many hardships and difficulties during his youth. But he never became discouraged. His ambition and perseverance won every battle and surmounted every obstacle. While working as a journeyman he practiced the most rigid economy until he saved enough to start in business for himself. His start was modest, but his business gradually increased, until in the fall of 1904 he had to add another story to his factory and build a new wood working shop. Such is the reward of energy and honesty. By the exercise of these qualities he has gained the good will and esteem of the trade and the public, which has given him a place among the successful men of his city. His reputation for enterprise is proverbial and the interest he takes in public and municipal affairs marks him as a man of public spirit and progressive notions. He is a member of the Holy Name Catholic church, Louisville Lodge, No. 8, Benevolent and Protective Order of Elks, the Commercial club, and the German Jefferson Benevolent society. In 1888 he married Miss Mary Roth and after her death he was united in marriage to Miss Mary Myer, who has been a helpmate to her husband in every sense of the term, keeping the books of the carriage factory, and in other ways aiding and encouraging her husband in his business undertakings.

REV. THEOPHILUS KELLENAERS, pastor of St. Agnes Catholic church, Uniontown, Ky., was born in Holland, April 24, 1852. After attending the schools of his native land he completed his education at the American college, Louvain, Belgium, and in 1874 came to Kentucky. On Sept. 1, 1875, he came to Union county, where he was for six months an assistant at the Sacred Heart church at St. Vincent. For the next twelve years he was the pastor of the parish of St. Ambrose and of St. Ann's at Morganfield. In March, 1888, he came to Uniontown and assumed the pastorate of St. Agnes' church, one of the finest in Western Kentucky. The corner-stone of the present building was laid in the spring of 1892 and the church was consecrated on Oct. 11, 1893, by Rt. Rev. James Ryan, of Alton, Ky., the bishop of the diocese. St. Agnes has an attendance of about three hundred and fifty families, and from seventy-five to one hundred are baptized each year. Father Kellenaers is fitted by nature for his calling. He has a sympathetic disposition, a kind heart, and a natural love for the spiritual side of mankind. As an instructor he is patient and intelligent, and as an adviser he is well grounded in the tenets of his religion. St. Agnes has prospered under his ministrations and he has the respect and love of his parishioners, as well as the entire confidence of his superiors in the church.

REV. OSCAR PACIFIC ACKERMAN, D.C.L., pastor and founder of St. Philip Neri Roman Catholic church, Louisville, Ky., was born in that city Dec. 12, 1868, a son of Philip and Walburka (Kieffer) Ackerman, both natives of Germany. His father came to the United States in the early fifties and for many years has been permanently identified with the business interests of Louisville, where he still resides. His maternal grandparents, Jacob and Barbara Keiffer, came to America in 1846 and were among the pioneer German families of Louisville, where they lived and died. Father Ackerman's primary education was received in the parochial school of Louisville. He spent one year at St. Xavier's college in that city; five years at St. Meinrad's college in Spencer county, Ind.; was graduated in theology from the University of Innsbruck, Austria, in 1892, and ordained to the priesthood in July of the same year, after which he took a post-graduate course of three years at the Apollinaris Law school in Rome. In 1895 he returned home, and was appointed pastor of St. Lawrence church in Daviess county, Ky., where he remained until 1898, when he came to Louisville. Here he organized his present parish, the corner-stone of the church being laid July 17, 1898, and the church, one of the finest edifices of its kind, was finished and opened April 9, 1899. Its total cost, including site, parish house and school building and furnishings, was over $40,000. Father Ackerman started this church with a congregation of but eight families. Now there are eighty-two and the school has an attendance of seventy-five pupils. Father Ackerman is public spirited, enterprising and greatly beloved by his parishioners and the general public outside of his church.

JAMES WILLIAM CONNOR, one of the leading contractors and builders of Louisville, Ky., was born at LaGrange, Oldham county of that state, in February, 1861. He is a son of John and Lucy (Pince) Connor, natives of Ireland and Kentucky, respectively. His maternal grandfather, James Pince, was a native of Shelby county, Ky., and in his day was one of the most prominent lumbermen in the state. Mr. Connor was reared in the city of Louisville, educated in the public schools there, and began life as a carpenter in the employ of the Louisville, Cincinnati & Lexington Railroad Company. After three years with this corporation he worked as a journeyman until 1888, when he began contracting for himself. His skill as a mechanic and his well known integrity soon placed him among the successful contractors of the city and he has retained his popularity by the prompt execution of all contracts awarded him, and by the strict observance of the terms of the agreement in the erection of buildings. Among the structures erected by him may be mentioned the St. Charles flat building, containing twenty-eight flats and six office suites; the Home Telephone building; the remodeling of the First National bank building; the Kentucky Packing and Provision Company's plant at Floyd and O streets, and a number of business buildings and fine residences in various parts of the city. Mr. Connor started in life with no capital but his brains and energy. He is therefore a self-made man in all the term implies. By his good business management and his indomitable industry he has acquired a competence, and has made a reputation for himself among the progressive men of his city. On all national questions he affiliates with the Republican party, but in local matters he gives his support to the man he considers best fitted for the office, irrespective of party lines. In religious matters he is a member of the Catholic church of St. Charles Borromeo; belongs to the Knights of Columbus and the St. Vincent de Paul societies, and takes an interest in the affairs of his church and kindred organizations. On April 20, 1882, he married Miss Margaret, daughter of William and Eliza Lynagh, of Louisville.

RT. REV. MONS. FRANCIS ZABLER, pastor of St. Martin's Roman Catholic church of Louisville, Ky., was born in Mingolsheim, Baden, Germany, Jan. 14, 1853, educated at Einsiedeln college and was ordained to the priesthood at Salzburg, Sept. 22, 1878. The first charge to which he was assigned was at Bamburg, Bavaria, where he officiated successfully until 1883, when he was appointed assistant pastor of St. Martin's church. So completely satisfactory was his work as assistant that five years later he became pastor of that charge, one of the largest and most influential in the city, in which capacity he is still serving. In 1898 he received the title of Monseigneur from Pope Leo. The present church edifice, which was erected in 1854, has been remodeled in Gothic style at a cost of $40,000 by Father Zabler. In addition to the remodeling of the church building, Father Zabler has erected two fine school buildings, one for the boys at a cost of $22,000 and the other for the girls at a cost of $40,000. This parish, founded by Father Leander Streber, has enjoyed a healthy growth under the able management of Father Zabler, and now numbers 1,000 families, the largest German Catholic parish in the city of Louisville. The schools enjoy the reputation of being among the very best in the city, another proof of the successful work of the present pastor. Nine hundred children are at present receiving instruction in St. Martin's parish schools. For the benefit of the young men of the parish a fine gymnasium, a casino, bowling alleys and billiard parlors have been provided by the progressive pastor. It is impossible to conceive of a more thoroughly equipped organization for successful church work than is that of St. Martin's under the direction of Father Zabler.

SAMUEL JOHNSON HALL, M.D., a prominent physician of Louisville and brigadier-general of the Uniform Rank, Kentucky Brigade, Woodmen of the World, was born in Lyon county, Ky., Dec. 12, 1865. He is of Scotch descent, his grandfather, Delany Hall, a stonemason by occupation, having emigrated to America from Scotland in 1826, locating in Virginia. In 1839 he removed to what is now Lyon county, Ky., where he followed general farming until his death in 1884, aged eighty-three years. His wife, Rachel Thompson, was a native of Virginia. To them were born eight children. They are: Angeline, the wife of Jefferson Cole; Neacy, Mrs. Eleven Oliver, deceased; Alexander Benjamin; Nancy, the wife of John Hall; John E.; Caroline, now Mrs. Thomas Lewis, and James. The maternal grandparents of Samuel J. Hall were Daniel D. and Sallie (Greene) Thorne, the former a native of France and the latter of Ireland. Daniel D. Thorne, a carpenter and millwright by trade, came to the United States when fifteen years old and located in Yellow Creek Forge, Tenn., where he married Miss Sallie Greene. While most of his life was spent in Tennessee and Kentucky, he died at the residence of his daughter at Little Rock, Ark., in 1885, aged eighty-one years, his widow still living at the ripe age of eighty-nine years. The parents of Samuel J. Hall were John E. and Delilah (Thorne) Hall, deceased, natives of Virginia and Tennessee respectively. John E. Hall was born in 1836 and came with his parents to Lyon county, Ky., when three years old, where he spent practically all of his life farming. During the Civil war he served three years as a member of the Fifteenth Kentucky cavalry of the United States army, and was wounded in the knee at the battle of Crab Orchard, Ky. His family consisted of twelve children, as follows: Angeline, the wife of Phinous Gillispie; Samuel J.; Rosa, now Mrs. Frank Trinkle; Daniel D.; Susie, the wife of Floyd Thorp; Joseph; Frank R.; Robert W.; Paul E.; Bion B. (dec.); Sallie, the wife of William Lewis, and Richard H. Samuel J. Hall grew to manhood on his father's farm and his early education was practically received under the tuition of his mother. On attaining to his majority he spent several months in St. Louis and later traveled in the West and Northwest, spending several months in Arizona on a cattle-ranch. On Dec. 25, 1886, he came to Louisville, Ky., and entered the employ of the Ewald Iron Company. In 1892 he began the study of medicine in the Louisville Medical college, from which institution he graduated March 6, 1894. Since that time he has been in the active and successful practice of his profession in Louisville. Among the many organizations of which he is a member are the following: Knights of Pythias; Live Oak Camp, No. 6, Woodmen of the World, of which organization he has been medical examiner for many years, colonel of the Twelfth regiment, Uniform Rank, ten months, and brigadier-general of the Kentucky brigade one year; Knights and Ladies of Security; Modern Maccabees; Independent Order of Red Men and the Delmont club. Doctor Hall is secretary and treasurer of the Live Oak Association, surgeon of the Employers' Liability Insurance Corporation of London, England, and a director in the Kentucky-Arizona Mining, Smelting and Developing Company of Louisville and Phœnix. In politics the Doctor is identified with the Republican party. On May 2, 1889, he was united in marriage to Miss Elmira J., the daughter of George and Mary (Quinlan) Cowley of Louisville. To this marriage four children have been born, as follows: John G., James J., Mary D. and Ethel L.

INDEX, VOLUME II

A
	PAGE
Ackerman, O. P.	406
Allen, E. C.	359
Anderson, J. C.	306
Austin, J. B.	143

B
Baker, C. M.	388
Barger, Jacob	329
Barret, H. P.	52
Barret, J. R.	32
Barret, J. H.	32
Barret, J. H., Jr.	35
Barrett, Strachan	60
Barter, L. E.	119
Bean, H. M.	297
Bean, J. M.	338
Beck, Christopher	251
Becker, G. J.	264
Bennett, Fred	367
Bennett, H. S.	106
Bennett, Z. A.	212
Berry, W. M.	142
Bethel, J. T.	48
Bingham, S. H.	170
Bishop, J. P.	168
Bishop, J. T.	172
Bishop, U. S.	152
Blackard, F. G.	342
Blackard, H. P.	289
Blue, J. S.	138
Boaz, H. C.	45
Bockstege, Frederick	94
Boetticher, Edward	88
Bondurant, A. A.	344
Book, T. B.	59
Bosse, Benjamin	83
Bowling, J. M.	290
Bowling, J. W.	322
Bozarth, H. P.	335
Bradley, B. B.	240
Brashear, Walter	53
Bruce, R. J	282
Bucher, Eberhard	253
Buckman, B. Z.	135
Buckman, J. E	133
Buckman, J. M	134
Buder, E. A	228
Bush, J. W	200
Bush, P. H	206
Butler, W. N	255
Butsch, Alfred	81

C
Caldwell, Peter	401
Callicott, F. E.	314
Cambron, C. Z	130
Cambron, J. M.	141
Carroll, Charles	319
Cassidy, G. P.	385
Caulton, D. E.	132
Champion, W. B	191
Chapman, G. H	122
Charles, A. L.	190
Clark, W. C.	341
Clarke, W. I.	196
Clements, A. W	137
Clements, G. W	125
Clements, S. L	157
Clopton, J. A	211
Coffman, W. C	145
Colbert, J. T.	389
Combs, G. W.	287
Compton, W. H	148
Connor, J. W	407
Cook, F. W.	84
Cook, H. N.	98
Cooley, F. W.	74
Cothron, L. H	199
Covert, C. G.	68
Cowper, R. B	201
Cowper, W. F.	198
Crabb, R. W.	131
Craney, Robert	159
Crenshaw, J. H.	373

INDEX

	PAGE		PAGE
Cruz, J. B.	151	Grassham, C. C.	195
Cunningham, G. A.	77	Grassham, Montgomery	180
		Grassham, R. H.	182
D		Greaney, J. B.	252
Davenport, A. F.	268	Greaney, W. P.	250
Davis, L. B.	214	Green, Reed	222
Davis, R. M.	284	Gregg, F. A.	288
Denby, Charles	100	Gregg, H. C.	292
Devous, Joseph	280	Gregory, C. E.	262
Dewey, E. S.	233	Griggs, J. N.	147
Dewey, W. S.	230	Grumley, John	302
Dillard, Jonathan	297	Gwaltney, Amariah	308
Dixon, Henry	37		
Dorroh, C. C.	184	**H**	
Dorsey, J. L.	30	Hale, Josiah	27
Douglas, S. W.	63	Hales, J. W.	270
Downen, Felix	387	Hall, S. J.	408
Drury, G. L.	139	Halliday, Douglas	243
Dunn, M. C.	47	Halliday, E. W.	248
Dyer, H. R.	167	Halliday, H. E.	241
		Halliday, H. L.	242
E		Halliday, W. R.	353
Edwards, Leonard	304	Harrelson, George	386
Edwards, W. G.	302	Harrington, J. W.	311
Ehs, A. P.	267	Harris, J. W.	148
Emig, Martin, Jr.	98	Harth, J. F.	71
Ensle, J. F.	72	Hastings, Samuel	244
Esslinger, J. A.	76	Haynes, C. C.	354
Evans, S. G.	93	Heeger, E. G.	69
Evans, Thomas	209	Heilman, G. D.	73
		Hemenway, J. A.	114
F		Hendrick, A. G.	197
Farnsworth, R. P.	40	Henson, C. G.	54
Feith, Mrs. M. E.	263	Herbert, Louis	400
Ferrill, J. P.	396	Hercules Buggy Co.	103
Feuchter, Charles	237	Hessian, C. E.	348
Fitzgerald, E. P.	366	Heyns, William	96
Foster, I. A.	377	Hick, T. B.	383
Foster, G. C.	64	Hickman, R. T.	58
Fraser, A. S.	362	Hite, J. W.	158
		Hite, W. P.	160
G		Hodges, John	236
Galligan, J. H.	221	Hogan, J. T.	279
Garnett, B. R.	184	Holland, R. M.	305
Gilbert, John	398	Houston, G. L.	324
Gilbert, M. F.	231	Hovey, A. P.	17
Gilbert, W. B.	224	Howell, Lee	112
Gillen, James	345	Howell, W. A.	320
Glasscock, T. H.	307	Humphrey, B. F.	164
Goad, W. B.	165	Huston, J. H.	99
Gordon, L. W.	327		
Graham, J. T.	177		

INDEX

I
Inman, William 293

J
Jennelle, J. J 219
Jourdan, John 87

K
Karges, A. F 86
Keaton, C. L., Jr. 347
Kellenaers, C. A. J. 126
Kellenaers, Theophilus 405
Kimmel, S. H 39
King, C. L. 55
Kinsall, D. M 274
Kleymeyer & Klute 41
Kluge, William 266
Koepke, Martin 97
Kratz, C. W 65

L
Lambert, M. E 272
Lancaster, Charles 361
Landram, G. W 207
Langan, P. T 358
Lansden, J. M 238
Lasher, O. C. 194
Lawler, R. E 374
Lilly, J. E. 136
Lindle, W. G 162
Little, L. P. 25
Logsden, Joseph 370
Logsdon, J. E 391
Logsdon, T. B 390
Lowery, J. S 188
Lutz, W. M 118

Mc
McBane, A. M. L. 325
McCue, Josiah 310
McCurdy, W. H 104
McFarland, R. C 46
McKeaig, G. W. 172
McKernan, W. R 312
McKnight-Keaton Co 347
McKnight, W. A 347

M
Magner, A. S 363
Markwell, W. S. 156
Marstall, Herman 44
Martin, J. T 149
Mattingly, C. I 123
Mattingly, G. E 123
Mayer, Jacob 95
Menzies, G. V 19
Merritt, R. N 129
Miller, J. A 216
Mills, Edgar 277
Mitchell, James 369
Mitchell, L. P 186
Moore, G. W 332
Morlock, F. A 121
Moss, S. J 187

N
Naas, Frederick 299
Neal, M. R 185
Nellis, F. D 365
New York Store Co 348
Noggle, C. P 174
Noggle, G. W 175
Nunn, J. B 169
Nunn, W. H 166

O
Ogden, H. H 91
Old State Nat'l Bank 76
O'Rourke, James 376
Orr, David 395
Overby, W. H 49

P
Parker, L. P 261
Pendleton, G. H 245
Penn, J. W 193
Phillips, W. S 333
Pierce, J. A 182
Pike, Sylvester 127
Pittman, C. E 82
Powell, J. H 38
Powell, L. W 43
Pride, J. D 178

Q
Quick, J. A 379

R
Ragon Brothers 105
Rankin, J. E 31
Reed, Charles 222
Reed, J. B 246
Reid, Dent 282
Reid, Robert 309
Rennie, J. T 247

INDEX

	PAGE
Rheinlander, John	79
Rice, Edward	294
Richards, A. J.	404
Richeson, A. G.	276
Riggle, E. H.	235
Rittenhouse, Henry	397
Roberts, E. F.	150
Robinett, Blueford	384
Robinett, Joseph	372
Robinson, J. H.	349
Roche, J. S.	215
Roney, J. M.	162
Rosencranz, A. C.	89
Rudd, G. A.	210
Rudolph, R. M.	339

S

Sanks, H. G.	267
Sanders, F. N.	296
Sanders, W. J.	295
Satterley, William	381
Schatz, William	364
Sellers, Elijah	57
Sellers, Elijah, Jr.	61
Siddall, J. P.	271
Siebman, A. L.	378
Sihler, Charles	67
Smith, C. L.	355
Smith, Elmer	258
Soaper, R. H.	36
Sonntag, M. S.	108
Stacey, Britton	394
Stanley, A. O.	28
Steagala, Joseph	260
Stephens, H. T.	259
Stevens, C. R.	193
Stiles, W. H.	300
Strickland, H. C.	269
Strong, J. E.	340
Stuart, Lester	403
Sturgis, S. P.	176
Sullivan, J. C.	343
Sutherland, W. H.	356

T

Tadlock, E. L.	357
Taylor, J. R.	128
Taylor, N. P.	50
Teare, William	124
Thomas, Cyrin	158

	PAGE
Threlkeld, W. T.	205
Towles, W. A.	21
Turner, C. W.	331
Turner, J. B.	331
Twitchell, La Fayette	392
Tyner, J. J.	189

V

Veatch, Abbott	26

W

Walker, J. P.	62
Waller, M. R.	140
Waller, William	153
Walsh, Thomas	116
Walters, J. B.	368
Warner, J. B.	351
Wathen, Ignatius	161
Watson, J. W.	179
Wenger, J. W.	257
West Side Bank	91
Whitehead, John	173
Whitledge, H. E.	132
Willard Library	108
Willis, J. C.	229
Wilson, C. H.	202
Wilson, G. M.	204
Wilson, G. S.	153
Wilson, Harrison	55
Wilson, W. W. W.	51
Winston, J. S.	171
Winston, P. H.	155
Winter, Claude	352
Wisehart, R. J.	380
Wiseheart, Marshall	317
Wolflin, J. C.	146
Wood, E. W.	24
Woodford, B. F.	254
Woolfe, J. T.	181
Worthington, G. N.	70

Y

Yearwood, E. F.	117
Yewell, Martin	24
Young, J. W.	382

Z

Zabler, Francis	408
Zirkelbach, W. J.	303
Zutt, J. C.	92

www.ingramcontent.com/pod-product-compliance
Lightning Source LLC
LaVergne TN
LVHW091527060526
838200LV00036B/519